The Ability to Mourn

The Ability to Mourn
Disillusionment and the Social Origins of Psychoanalysis

Peter Homans

The University of Chicago Press
Chicago and London

Peter Homans is professor of religion and psychological studies in the Divinity School, professor of social sciences in the College, and a member of the Committee on the History of Culture at the University of Chicago. He is the author of *Jung in Context,* also published by the University of Chicago Press.

The University of Chicago Press, Chicago 60637
The University of Chicago Press, Ltd., London
© 1989 by The University of Chicago
All rights reserved. Published 1989
Printed in the United States of America
98 97 96 95 94 93 92 91 90 89   54321

⊗ The paper used in this publication meets the minimum requirements of the American National Standard for Information Sciences— Permanence of Paper for Printed Library Materials, ANSI Z39.48-1984.

Library of Congress Cataloging-in-Publication Data

Homans, Peter.
    The ability to mourn : disillusionment and the social origins of psychoanalysis / Peter Homans.
        p.   cm.
    Bibliography: p.
    Includes index.
    ISBN 0-226-35111-4 (alk. paper)
    1. Psychoanalysis and culture—History. 2. Social change— Psychological aspects—History. 3. Freud, Sigmund, 1856–1939— Psychology. 4. Psychoanalysis—History. I. Title.
BF175.4.C84H66   1989
150.19′5—dc19   89-4656
                                                                CIP

For Celia

Contents

Preface   xi

Introduction   1

PART I **Disillusionment and the Ability to Mourn as a Central Psychological Theme in Freud's Life, Thought, and Social Circumstance, 1906–1914**

1   Framing the Argument: Why "Disillusionment" and Why "The Ability to Mourn"?   15

Literature Review: Freud's Most Creative Phase and Its Relevance for the 1906–1914 Period   20

Mourning, the De-Idealization Experience, and Their Historical Correlates: Disillusionment and Disenchantment   23

2   De-Idealization in Freud's Life and Thought   29

Life: Freud's Struggle with Jung and Abraham's Role in It   30

Thought: "On Narcissism," "The Moses," and the Significance of Rome   41

3   De-Idealization and Freud's Social Circumstance: Movement and Culture   58

Understanding the Psychoanalytic Movement as a Group   59

Politics and Religion as Cultural Forces   68

4   Earlier and Later De-Idealizations: Count Thun and Romain Rolland   82

Count Thun and Freud's Psychology of Politics   82

Romain Rolland and Freud's Psychology of Religion   88

5   Freud's Mother, His Death Anxiety, and the Problem of History   96

Freud's Death Anxiety and the Idea of a Maternal Presence   97

Psychoanalysis, History, and the Study of Freud's Person   100

Freud's Death and Jones's Idealization of Freud   102

PART II **Disillusionment and the Social Origins of Psychoanalysis**

6   Framing the Argument: Why Think Sociologically about Psychoanalysis? 109
        How to Think Sociologically about Psychoanalysis 115
        The Essential Tension: Analytic Access and a Common Culture 122

7   The Sociology of Freud's Self-Analysis and the Psychoanalytic Movement 129
        Sociological Reflections on Freud's Self-Analysis 129
        The Psychoanalytic Movement as a Psychological Culture 139

8   Tracking the Ideal-Type: Disenchantment and Psychological Discovery in the Lives of Three Followers 143
        Carl G. Jung: Psychoanalysis as Hermeneutics 144
        Otto Rank: Psychoanalysis as Art 152
        Ernest Jones: Psychoanalysis as Science 171
        The Dissipation of the Movement and Freud's Turn to the "Cunning of Culture" 191

9   Final Sociological Reflections: Psychoanalysis, Science, and Society 209
        Freud's Metapsychology and the Sociology of Physical Science 211
        1920s London, Object Relations, and the Collapse of the Metapsychology 222
        The Struggle to Mourn in the Sociological Tradition: The Case of Max Weber 231
        Conclusion: The Sociological Mechanism Underlying Psychoanalytic Healing, When It Occurs, in the Analytic Situation 250

PART III **Mourning, Individuation, and the Creation of Meaning In Today's Psychological Society**

10   Framing the Argument with Freud's "Little Discourse" on Mourning and Monuments 261
        Three Contradictions in Freud's Theory of Culture 264
        Mourning, Monuments, and Individuation: A First Approximation 270

11   The Fate of the Ego in "Primitive" and "Civilized" Cultures: First Contradiction 283

12   The Plight of the Modern Ego Cut Off from Its Christian, Communal Past: Second Contradiction   297

13   The Conflict between Religious Absolutism and Curiosity about The Inner World: Third Contradiction   313

14   Toward a Rapprochement with the Past: Mourning, Individuation, and the Creation of Meaning   326

        Epilogue: When the Mourning Is Over: Prospero's Speech at the End of *The Tempest* as a Model of Individuation   344

        Notes   349

        References   369

        Index   379

PROSPERO:
[to Ferdinand, the son of his former enemy
and future husband to his daughter, Miranda,
at the end of the betrothal masque which he
conjured for them by means of his magic]:

Our revels now are ended. These our actors,
As I foretold you, were all spirits, and
Are melted into air, into thin air.
And, like the baseless fabric of this vision,
The cloud-capped towers, the gorgeous palaces,
The solemn temples, the great globe itself,
Yea, all which it inherit, shall dissolve,
And, like this insubstantial pageant faded,
Leave not a rack behind. We are such stuff
As dreams are made on, and our little life
Is rounded with a sleep. Sir, I am vexed.
Bear with my weakness, my old brain is troubled.

FERDINAND AND MIRANDA:
We wish your peace.
          [*Exeunt*]

                    Shakespeare, *The Tempest, IV.1*

Preface

As everyone who writes and reads knows, there is a time-honored rule that a scholar must declare at the outset of a new work that he is possessed in his entirety by two simple but profound sentiments: gratitude to others, without whom he could not, etc., and an equally strong sense of guilt or responsibility for all the many errors of his work, although he does not know what they are. Classically oriented psychoanalysts probably see in this rule a necessary defense against its more primary opposite: the author's unacknowledged wish to name those who, because he was foolish enough to listen to them in the first place, only delayed his progress, and his triumphant claim to the reader's deference for all the many illuminations which are about to be revealed.

I have come to see the intent of this rule and its psychological meaning differently. It is a good rule, partly because of its obvious purpose, but also because it is suggestive of a far more profound issue which—it so happens—is also the most basic of the many basic themes of this book. In its more obvious sense, the rule does little more than keep an author more or less honest while giving him a chance to thank his friends. But it also implies something darker, even sinister, which has to do with a scholar's relationship to his subject, quite apart from his relation to his colleagues. The rule also invites the author and the reader to remember, at least one more time, what both keep on forgetting the rest of the time, namely, that all scholarship is double in nature: it grows from both deep dependence upon the ideas of others, so deep as to amount at times to virtual slavery or seduction, but also from periods of intense aloneness which can approach a kind of mad defiance of everyone's view but one's own. Furthermore, the rule suggests that an author can own and even become tolerant of his own shortcomings, if only for a little while, as they begin to make their unwelcome appearance, something which usually happens a few minutes just before or just after the ink on the final page is dry. That is why prefaces are written last but are made to sound as though they had been jotted down first.

This issue—slavish dependence upon the authority of the past versus defiant repudiation of it—is the central leitmotiv of my book. In it I show how one great man, Freud, broke away from the religious, political, and scientific authorities of his past and, more important, from the communities which supported them and, in so doing, created a wholly new form of thought and life, psychoanalysis. However, in this very act Freud in turn became the authority of the past for all those who chose to follow him, and I describe the ways the best known of these did and did not succeed in their struggles—what place, in other words, each occupied on the continuum between slavish loyalty (the followers) and rebellious defiance (the dissenters). This issue goes well beyond the "academic" question of the origins of psychoanalysis, for even today everyone who reads and takes seriously Freud's works falls under their spell, and the same pattern of response can be observed. In the final portion of this study I propose a psychological point of view which I think breaks the spell, which can reconcile the clash between these opposites.

As such, this book is a continuation of my earlier studies in the psychoanalytic psychology of contemporary culture, but it also takes a decisive step beyond them. Those studies analyzed various forms of contemporary culture psychologically: popular culture, Protestantism, and even certain systems of psychology. Doing so, however, has made me increasingly aware of the limits of the psychoanalytic approach to culture, in particular its lack of any coherent theory of culture and, furthermore, its active antagonism to such a theory. Nor have various "splicing jobs"—attempts to attach psychoanalysis to another discipline such as psychohistory, psychoanalytic sociology, and psychological anthropology—been particularly satisfying because these invariably become territorial battles which end in mutual accusations of reductionism.

So I decided to turn what had been my major approach into a problem. Exploring the origins of the psychoanalytic theory of culture, I thought, would tell me more about its strengths and weaknesses. I set for myself only one "basic rule": I had to include a psychodynamic theory of the individual mind, and to situate it in a social context. This search led me back through and past the so-called cultural texts and into the psychoanalytic movement and Freud's self-analysis, and from there back much further into the origins of the entire psychoanalytic project as a whole in the matrices of Western culture, especially in its religious traditions.

Moreover, I discovered that it was possible to develop out of this essentially genetic approach at least the main outlines and directions of the fresh and much broader theory of contemporary culture I was looking for. My investigations into the origins of psychoanalysis turned into a necessary detour, the only path that would lead to the fuller and richer psychological theory of culture I wanted, although I did not know that when I began. So this book can be read in two different ways: as a sociological study of one of the major intellectual and ideological movements which have come to constitute contemporary life, or as an attempt to rethink and work out better ways to understand the self and its sociocultural "other" within the context of a historically specific set of materials: Freud's life, work, thought, and movement. In both cases the argument has the same cumulative progression: from psychological (part 1) to sociological (part 2) to critical-philosophical (part 3). The introduction explains the entire argument in detail.

A number of persons and institutions made the writing of this book far easier and even more pleasurable than it might otherwise have been, and I wish to thank them for that.

James W. Anderson (formerly of the Department of Psychiatry, Northwestern University, now in private practice), Benjamin Beit-Hallahmi (Department of Psychology, University of Haifa), Bertram Cohler (Department of Behavioral Sciences, the University of Chicago), Malcolm Pines (Adult Department, the Tavistock Centre), Paul Stepansky (editor-in-chief, the Analytic Press), and Ernest Wallwork (Department of Religious Studies, Syracuse University) gave generously of their time and knowledge by reading and commenting at length on earlier drafts and, along with that, offered most welcome support and encouragement.

I owe a special debt of thanks to Dennis Klein for sharing with me his translations of Otto Rank's diaries.

More than a few of the leading ideas advanced in this book first crystallized for me during the weekly staff seminars of the introductory social science course (entitled Self, Culture, and Society) in the College of the University of Chicago. I am grateful to all my fellow teachers there for their stimulating discussions, and especially to Bertram Cohler, Ray Fogelson, Gil Herdt, John MacAloon, and Ralph Nicholas.

The earliest stage of thinking and planning for this book took place while I was a visiting scholar, first at the Tavistock Centre, London, and later at the Chicago Institute for Psychoanalysis. I am grateful to the faculties of these institutions for admitting me to their classrooms and libraries, and especially to Malcolm Pines (Tavistock) and

Saul Siegel (Chicago) for many conversations in which they freely shared their considerable knowledge of psychoanalytic theory and practice.

Without a travel grant from the American Council of Learned Societies, my studies at the Tavistock Centre would not have been possible.

Some parts of this book reached the light of public day elsewhere. Part 1 was published in *Freud: Appraisals and Reappraisals,* vol. 2 (Hillsdale, N.J.: The Analytic Press, 1988, © 1988, by The Analytic Press), and I am grateful to Paul Stepansky, editor-in-chief (and also editor of the series), for permission to reprint the essay, which has been revised for its new context. A portion of part 1 was expanded into a separate article, entitled "Freud's Group and Its Vicissitudes: Understanding the Psychoanalytic Movement as a Group," for *Group Analysis: The Journal of Group Analytic Psychotherapy* (Dec. 1985). A very early sketch of what has become my view of Freud's relation to Jung was presented at the annual (1982) meeting of the American Psychological Association to the symposium "Exploring the Lives of Personality Theorists."

Introduction

The purpose of this book is threefold. First and foremost, it seeks to create a fresh understanding of the origins of psychoanalysis which is deeply social in character, emphasizing cultural values and symbols in the West which go back several centuries. Psychoanalysis arose, I think, as a creative response to the loss of these most meaningful constructions. Second, to establish this point of view I draw upon and integrate to a considerable extent the three major bodies of scholarly literature on the psychoanalytic project as a whole and not just on its origins. And third, having done that, I go on to develop the beginnings of a fresh understanding of the modern ego's relations to the symbols of traditional culture, what I call "the creation of meaning," based upon the recognition that the losses in cultural meaning to which psychoanalysis is a creative response are not reversible. The purpose of this introduction is to explain synoptically the leading ideas of the book's central argument, the sources upon which it is based, and to provide an overview of the contents of its three parts. Because these essays engage diverse studies of substantial size and are also at the same time highly interpretive, such an overview is necessary.

Let us begin with the three major bodies of scholarly literature on psychoanalysis, and move from there to the argument and to the way it unfolds in each part. Excepting from the start clinical articles and books, all the literature on psychoanalysis as a whole breaks down into three sets of materials which are like separate landmasses, where the inhabitants of one rarely visit either of the other two. This isolation is in part due to the sociological fact that the men and women who produce these literatures work in different social loca-tions—the clinic and separate departments in the university, each of which has its own agenda. Still, the problem of isolation goes deeper than this, for today's publishing can overcome any gap in institu-tional life, but not one which involves differing basic assumptions about persons and history.

The first landmass consists of psychobiographical studies of the origins of Freud's discoveries and his creativity, sometimes referred

1

to simply as "the origins of psychoanalysis," written largely by analysts. Their focus is Freud's famous self-analysis. The classic example is Ernst Kris's study of the Freud-Fliess correspondence, which is actually titled "The Origins of Psychoanalysis." These have recently been supplemented by what I call "local historical studies," which usually examine Freud's Vienna and his social context. Schorske's well-known essay "Politics and Patricide" is a good example. These historical studies belong to the first group because they attempt to remain consonant with psychodynamic principles. The second landmass lies close to the first but consists of psychoanalytic studies of society, religion, art, and history and is often referred to as the "application" of psychoanalysis. It also contains scattered attempts to integrate psychoanalytic thought into a theory of society. Since Freud wrote his cultural texts, it has burgeoned into psychoanalytic literary criticism (especially Shakespearean criticism), psychohistory, and psychological anthropology. Erikson's *Young Man Luther* is exemplary, and so is his anthropological work. Jones's paper on *Hamlet* is a good prototype, as are Malinowski's studies. Both analysts and non-analysts practice this "genre," and each group reads the other's works. The third landmass is best described as "the cultural criticism of psychoanalysis." It is devoted to understanding the impact of Freud's thought on contemporary culture, both taken as wholes. Here Freud is drawn into the debate about modernity and the ways in which he contributed to it. By far the best known instances of this genre of psychoanalytic scholarship are Philip Rieff's *Freud: The Mind of the Moralist* and Paul Ricoeur's substantial oeuvre on Freud (for example, "A Philosophical Interpretation of Freud"). Although these two approaches differ completely on what, exactly, Freud's contribution to contemporary culture was, they are similar in the question they ask of it (How did Freud separate modern from traditional culture?), and this distinguishes them entirely from the first two groups of studies (Rieff's answer: Freud created a total break with the past; Ricoeur's answer: Freud's break with the past can become the very means of restoring a creative reunderstanding of the past).

The present study does not belong in any simple way to any of these three bodies of scholarship, but it could not have been written without all of them. Like Rieff and Ricoeur, I think that Freud did indeed create a total break with the (his) Western past, but I also go on to claim, as they do not, that his psychoanalytic theory was a creative response to this break. Furthermore, this is only the beginning. I want to know how this break occurred and how the creative response took place. To find out, it is necessary to make liberal use of the scholarship in the first two groups, which has never interested itself in that of the third group at all. This search can at the outset only be frustrating, since the work of the first two groups is so comfortable with the assumption of a total break. However, as I point out again and again, it is actually driven by critical-cultural issues far more than its practitioners think. Studies of the self-analysis ("the origins of psychoanalysis") are also, implicitly, studies of how this break occurred, and the psychoanalytic theory of culture (the "applications" of psychoanalysis) are also attempts to rethink the entire Western past in the light of Freud's creative response to his sense of its loss. Furthermore, studying the processes involved in Freud's break with the past will also provide clues for understanding other "breaks" as well, in particular, the origins and rise of sociology, which I think followed a similar pattern.

The flaw in all three bodies of literature—including the third, despite its sense of the problem—is that all lack the realization that the origins of psychoanalysis lie deep in the cultural traditions of the West and in its relationship to the religious symbols and values which inform these traditions. There are, in other words, complex "internal relations" between psychoanalysis and the Western cultural and religious traditions. The customary way of speaking about this perception is to refer to the process of secularization, understood cognitively as the decline in the power of religious ideas, or sociologically as the institutional marginalization of religious practices. In such form, the concept of secularization at once says everything and nothing at all. It is, at bottom, a shallow formulation. This observation allows me to introduce the leading theme of my book as a whole, which is, as the title conveys, the process of mourning. The usual understandings of secularization need a richer, psychological dimension which can help explain how and why persons, as individuals, respond to value change and value loss. This dimension is the process of mourning, understood as a complex response to object loss, in which the "objects" that are "lost" are social and cultural objects and not only familial and intrapsychic objects. But this is only half of the picture. Conventional understandings of secularization also need to be supplemented by a sociological frame which speaks of social and cultural objects as symbolic processes which organize and are organized by communities. These symbols in turn organize psychic life. When such symbols become meaningless, when they "die," then the communities they represent undergo fragmentation, and persons in those communities undergo experiences of loss and are confronted by the need to mourn. Freud was ahead of his time in this regard, as he was in so many other ways, when he observed that "mourning is regularly the reaction to the loss of a loved person, or to the loss of some abstraction which has taken the place of one, such as one's country, liberty, an ideal and so on" (1917a, p. 243).

The resources for such a twofold reformulation are actually much closer to hand than one might think. The concept of mourning developed in this book takes the experience of object loss as the central intellectual theme of psychoanalysis as a whole, and so it finds processes similar to mourning in revisionist psychoanalysis, which builds upon this theme. For example, I draw upon Kohut's concept of de-idealization, Winnicott's of disillusionment, and Klein's of pining. But I also consider these in relation to Weber's theory of disenchantment and Durkheim's formulations of social solidarity and of the anomie which follows the breakdown of solidarity. Unlike these authors, however, I think that such social processes have a shared unconscious dimension and that they structure and organize corresponding psychological processes. The many substantial objections to this view from both sides must be worked over and through, which is done as the discussion proceeds.

This fresh perspective allows me to state, this time summarily, the central argument. Against the received views (that psychoanalysis is simply a recent chapter in the history of science, or that it owes its origins to Freud's creative genius, or that it is just another modern ideology), I claim that psychoanalysis arose as the result of a long, historical mourning process begun centuries ago, with roots in the origins of physical science in the seventeenth century and in the theology of the fourteenth. Secularization has been an ever-so-gradual kind of mourning for the lost symbols and the communal wholeness they organize in the West. Second, like so many other cultural achievements in the West—modern literature and modern art both immediately come to mind—psychoanalysis is a creative response to this loss. It seeks to replace what is lost with something new. But mourning is only part of this picture; creativity is the other half. The creation of anything new and valuable, I argue, has its origins in the old and in the particular ways the old is abandoned and then altered. This is why psychoanalysis seems to many like a "secular religion."

This interpretation is based upon an integration of psychological thought and social theory which is not found in either of the two sets of materials upon which it draws. It seems to me possible to use psychology to understand the origins of psychology, provided that one grounds the first psychology in a theory of social reality; otherwise, the effort becomes solipsistic. Still, more than a blend of these two sets of ideas is needed, as I point out in a moment. In order to overcome the exclusiveness which both sets claim, I have constructed what is in effect a double ideal-type, in Max Weber's sense, drawn from psychology and sociology, which I call "the tension between analytic access and a common culture." Analytic access refers to the integrative and depth-psychological probes an individual can make with regard to his inner world. It is by no means limited to psychoanalysis, for it is found in introspective literature, in philosophical reflection, and religious experience as well. A "common culture" refers to "society" or community or to solidarity, in Durkheim's sense. In a common culture, the individual predominately defines himself and is defined by the rules and social representations of society, which he has taken into himself or which have been imprinted upon him. The point, however, lies in the relation between the two, which is a tension: analytic access always exists at the margins of a common culture.

Since this is an ideal-type, it exists in all cultures, but nowhere in pure form. There is a constant tension between the "ideality" and the "reality" of the type. In primitive and traditional cultures, society as a whole dominates the inner world of the individual. In modern societies the individual defines himself more and more by his introspective, individualizing probes and less by the collectivizing, internalized—and largely unconscious—rules of social structure and its shared symbolic processes. Under such conditions persons become freer from the internalizations of culture, but also more vulnerable to the chaos of new forms of experiencing and subjectivity. Still, even this approach does not take us sufficiently far from Freud and Durkheim. Even with it one remains, finally, in the prison of either psychology or sociology, or else just caught between the two. Something entirely fresh is needed. Therefore, I introduce into this construction a third, or mediating, term, the very real phenomenon of "transitional space," intermediate between the self and the social other, drawn from the psychological thought of D. W. Winnicott but elaborated well beyond his formulation of it. I think that here, in this marginal space or area, analytic access and common culture have always intersected to form a genuine reality which exists apart from and is also some part of "psyche" and "culture." It is in this area that the formation of symbols takes place and here creativity also occurs. This space is at once social and psychological.

I am not, however, primarily interested in a general theory of culture (nor would I be capable of constructing one), but rather in

Western culture and in the common cultures of medieval Christianity and Judaism, and principally in the gradual weakening over time of their symbolic structures and of the sense of community and solidarity which these structures have authorized and in the liberation of introspective tendencies which such weakening always inaugurates. This process of weakening/liberation reached greatest intensity in "the origins of psychoanalysis," producing first Freud's self-analysis, then the psychoanalytic movement, and, later still, the psychoanalytic theory of culture, which replaced the Western religious past by way of interpreting it. Clearly, Freud's Jewish identity has to have been an important aspect of the origins of his creative, new theories, and it is also important to show—as I do—that others besides Freud also achieved depth-psychological self-understanding before coming to him, although the prevailing scholarship on their lives and works has obscured this important fact.

These several leading ideas provide, in a small way, the grounding for the contents of this book, and they also dictate its particular form: why it has been necessary to divide it into three relatively independent parts and why each part is in the form of an essay rather than that of the usual scholarly book or monograph (problem statement/hypothesis/literature review/argument/conclusion). The following is an integrative summary which can serve the reader as a map or guide through the discussions.

The three separate parts follow, roughly, the three landmasses of scholarship. A three-part format (each part with its own introduction and so forth) is the only way to recognize and honor the way these bodies of scholarly research on psychoanalysis have different assumptions, make use of different materials, and attempt to accomplish different goals, and also at the same time utilize their richness by not linking them prematurely to each other. Furthermore, each is so compacted that such linking has been—and still is— impossible. Since they have chosen to be separate, it is best to treat them separately.

Part 1 opens by engaging directly and at the outset the most compacted of all three, the psychobiographical studies of Freud's self-analysis and some of the more recent local-historical research. But because the self-analysis has been so overstudied and the literature on it is so cluttered, it cannot be approached head-on. So part 1 next creates a detour around it by deliberately focusing upon the period directly following "the most creative period," that of the relationship with Jung and the formation of the psychoanalytic movement. In contrast to the previous period, this is fresh territory which yields up, nonetheless, the major psychological issues in Freud's life course with rewarding clarity and relative simplicity and prepares the way for reflection backward, into the self-analysis (taken up in detail in part 2).

After introducing the leading ideas of the book as a whole (the experiences of mourning, disillusionment, de-idealization, and their relevance for the social process of disenchantment), the argument moves through the relationship with Jung and on to the movement, the center of the essay as a whole, and from there into Freud's theoretical shift to the theory of narcissism and, with that, to the earliest cultural texts, the first of which was "The Moses of Michelangelo." Studying these events allows me to introduce revisionist perspectives, for I see self-objects and transitional objects in them where others have not, especially in Freud's disillusionment with Jung and in the movement's "group illusion." The final discussion broadens into Freud's cultural surround, especially its politics and religion, and his disillusionment with both of these as well. It is easy to move from the cultural texts to the social context because the texts were really a response to that very context. In his texts Freud emphasized the destructiveness of politics and especially religion, which he had personally experienced. The essay ends with a critique of the psychological-historical approach and the necessity for drawing the data it has produced into a social-cultural framework.

Part 2 is the center of the entire book, into which the unresolved issues raised by part 1 flow, and out of which flow the problems which part 3 attempts to resolve (what I call the "contradictions" in Freud's thought about culture). It begins by setting forth the already-mentioned ideal-type, which holds the essay together as a whole, locates this construction in the history of sociology, and draws into it the process of mourning (breaking with a common culture can produce mourning for it, which can lead to creativity). The discussion uses this framework to examine Freud's self-analysis as an ideal-typical form of introspective experience, and then extends this approach to the social histories of three followers (Jung, Rank, and Jones), arguing that they underwent their own unique forms of analytic access or self-analysis before their association with Freud. These three social histories are essential for my argument because they establish that the analytic access which Freud achieved was not unique to him. Without this information there could be no sociological understanding of the origins of psychoanalysis. With this deeper understanding of the movement's members, I discuss again several features of it established earlier and characterize it as a miniature psychological culture, the integrating frame of which was Freud's metapsychology, his overriding conviction that his psychoanalysis was a pure science like physical science. I also set forth further support for my earlier point that the cultural texts were really an extension of the movement and then analyze in detail the major ones, concluding that the central theme running beneath particular concerns and topics is a profound and mournful sense that the past of Western culture—the common cultures of the West—has been lost.

The remainder of the second essay picks up on the metapsychology, the integrating idea in all of Freud's endeavors, and tests its claims to science in relation to the sociology of physical science. First, I compare my sociology of psychoanalysis with Robert Merton's study of the social origins of science in seventeenth-century England. What links the two together is the presence and then the absence of a religious common culture (Puritanism, Judaism) and a subsequent turn away from attachment to this culture to scientific activities. But there were important differences as well, which Freud in his zeal did not recognize, and these are also discussed. Second, adopting a wholly different strategy, I continue to pursue the scientific status of psychoanalysis by examining the life course of Max Weber, the father of *verstehen* sociology and the creator of such concepts as the ideal-type and disenchantment, who also claimed that his sociology was, like pure science, a value-free science—in other words, this was his "metapsychology." I discover that Weber too underwent a painful and major psychological crisis, as a result of which he turned away from his religious past and subsequently created a wholly fresh perspective on it through his work, just as Freud did. This "Freud-Weber confluence" captures many of the major issues in part 2 and prepares the way for part 3. The essay rounds out the sociological discussion by ending with a brief discussion of the social forces in psychoanalytic healing, in contrast to religious healing.

In an effort to produce a creative, integrative summary, part 3 breaks away from the social origins of psychoanalysis and turns to its contemporary cultural significance. It does this by engaging the third land mass of psychoanalytical scholarship, concerned to assess the impact of Freud's oeuvre as a whole upon current intellectual and social life. Thanks to the labors of part 2, I am in a position to formulate in a fresh and decisive way Freud's contribution to the meaning of modernity and, with the help of recent critical-cultural studies, also to work toward solving the problems which he created for us. This contribution can be formulated by drawing upon the previous, detailed discussion of the basic themes in his cultural texts, and the frame in which I have put both these and his life, the tension between psychological depth and the waning common cultures of his (and our) past. In his cultural texts Freud called for a breaking up of attachments to the common cultures of the past and drove the individualizing, diachronic, and introspecting ego forward, ever into the future. The result was what I have called a "total break" with the past. The purpose of the cultural texts was to announce this break and to interpret the Western past psychologically, thereby proposing a psychological culture in its stead. This is the vision which Freud has given to modern culture, which has in some places accepted all of it and throughout has accepted parts of it.

Like many others, both within and without psychoanalysis, I do not think it is humanly or psychologically possible or desirable for the modern self to exist apart from the appropriation of the cultural worlds of the past. It is certainly possible for the ego to do so, but not the self. But, like some others, again within and without psychoanalysis, I also think that the essence of Freud's introspective and psychological probes should be retained. This means that the culture of the past can no longer be appropriated in the ways it has been by these cultures in their earlier stages of more stable organization. For these several reasons, I call this dilemma the central contradiction in Freud's cultural texts. In order to reconcile this contradiction, I introduce into it a key idea which Freud missed, but which was everywhere present in his life and thought, and which for that reason has appeared from time to time in my own analyses of both. This idea had to wait until part 3 before it could be thematized. The idea is the process of individuation, which is intimately related to the self and only then to the ego.

Individuation refers to the ways the self can remain integrated and psychological while also appropriating meanings from the past in the form of the cultural symbols which infuse it. This formulation owes much to the work of part 1 and part 2, for individuation is, I go on to propose, the fruit of mourning. Somehow, in a way that is not really understood, the experience of loss can stimulate the desire "to become who one is." That in turn can throw into motion a third process, what should be called "the creation of meaning." This action is at once a work of personal growth and a work of culture. In it, the self both appropriates from the past what has been lost and at the same time actually creates for itself in a fresh way these meanings. In modern societies the experience of meaningfulness invariably has two seemingly contradictory dimensions. In other words, the creation of meaning is a paradox which cannot be reduced to either "the past" (a common culture) or to developmental self-understanding (analytic access).

This is the argument, in a nutshell, of part 3. To evolve it, I first break Freud's central contradiction down into its three components and then devote a separate chapter to each one, criticizing and evaluating Freud's thought at each point in the light of what I think is the most relevant discussion of that issue that can be found in contemporary social thought. These three discussions simply cannot follow the pattern of a single discipline, and so I have drawn widely from many possibilities. For Freud's total separation of primitive and civilized (first contradiction), I turn to Lévi-Strauss's far more complex conception of "the savage mind." For Freud's radical splitting of the contemporary ego and its cultural surround, both present and past (second contradiction), I take up Rieff's critical attitude toward psychological man and his psychological culture. And for Freud's cognitive dissociation of religion and science (third contradiction), I explore Blumenberg's philosophical-historical analysis of the origins of science from within, and not over against, Western theological thought, a theory that could not have ever occurred to Freud. Throughout these three discussions I also reflect briefly upon Freud's thought and the new criticisms of it in the light of my own evolving triad of mourning, individuation, and the creation of meaning, although mainly I draw upon both for fresh understandings of these processes. It is possible to do this because Freud's contradictions actually generate the lines of thought and principal issues which a theory of individuation must follow and address: unconscious collective behavior (first contradiction), the interpretation of fantasy (second), and the problem of illusion (third). Finally, in the last chapter I break from both Freud and these eminent social critics to propose new findings which support new ways of thinking about mourning, individuation, and the creation of meaning and their relationship to the three contradictions.

This book was written using the form of the essay rather than that of the research monograph for two reasons: because the three landmasses of scholarship which it addresses are so unrelated and because I nonetheless bring to these strong, integrative ambitions. Such a project requires a vehicle in which some congruence be allowed to exist between the findings and ideas in each body of literature, as these are identified and set forth, and the author's own point of view and goals. This more subjective approach allows me to confront findings and still move the argument along, sometimes quite rapidly, while explaining the reasons for doing so along the way. Second, I think that what is most compelling to the reader, and also more satisfying—at least it has been so for me—is a gradually evolving sense of the whole rather than the exhaustive analysis of parts (although that also has to be done, and is done, to some extent, as well). Above all else, I have tried to create a sense of the whole—first in each essay, but then in the three taken together "as a whole." In this, I hope I have been true to my major intellectual commitments: revisionist psychoanalysis and a social (rather than a purely psychological) theory of culture. Kohut and Winnicott both centered their work on the integrative functions of the self in contrast to the analytic functions of the ego, and the cultural theory I have used emphasizes the integrative functions of culture—culture is always integrating, whether it is individuals into societies or shared symbolic part processes into shared symbolic wholes.

In sum, it has been my good fortune to have been able to write a book which studies the life and works of a great and remarkable man, both of which I admire profoundly, and those of his followers as well, and at the same time to have evolved ideas of my own which, although different from all of theirs, also derive in some sense organically from them.

I Disillusionment and the Ability to Mourn as a Central Psychological Theme in Freud's Life, Thought, and Social Circumstance, 1906–1914

1 Framing the Argument: Why "Disillusionment" and Why "The Ability to Mourn"?

> Mourning is regularly the reaction to the loss of a loved person, or to the loss of some abstraction which has taken the place of one, such as one's country, liberty, an ideal, and so on.
>
> Freud, *Mourning and Melancholia*

> . . . we have undertaken this week a little piece of our collective self-analysis . . . though Freud died in 1939, we have never fully come to terms with his transience and his death. . . . Sigmund Freud remains our lost object, our unreachable genius, whose passing we have perhaps never properly mourned. . . . It is perhaps just because he has been so inadequately truly mourned, and, therefore never given up as a fantasied continuing presence, that so many of us have feelings of a continuing dependency that can both be infantalizing and stultifying. . . .
>
> *Symposium of the International Psychoanalytic Association*
> Haslemere, England, 1976
> (Joseph and Widloecher 1983)

Historical writing on the psychoanalytic movement began by centering upon, and for some time continued to emphasize, the figure of Sigmund Freud in such a way that others were cast as shadows very much in the background, their significance lying chiefly in their relation to the great man—they were *his* acquaintances, *his* followers, *his* critics, and *his* opponents. This understandably deferential approach coalesced in Ernest Jones's definitive study, which appeared in the 1950s (Jones 1953, 1955, 1957). The approach is also understandable when one realizes that much of this history was writ-

ten by men who were themselves, like Jones, part of the psychoanalytic movement, some "part" of Freud in the more intimate sense
either of a friendship or even of the analytic relationship itself.

Since that time, this scholarship has broadened in a number of
ways so as to usher into the light of day a number of what I call
"shadow figures." The concern is now less with issues of Freud's
stature and more with context and with the webs of relationship in
which various men and women found themselves embedded as they
came to associate themselves with psychoanalysis. A major example
of this development was the publication in 1974 of the *Freud-Jung
Letters* (McGuire 1974). That event allowed Carl Gustav Jung to
emerge from the shadows by permitting concrete reflection on the
psychology of his personality and on its relation to his work while at
the same time advancing still further our knowledge of Freud's own
life and thought. Scholars such as Robert Stolorow and George Atwood (1979) and John Gedo (1983) have addressed these issues, and
my own book-length study of the Freud-Jung relationship and its
extraordinary impact upon Jung's work and the cultural situation of
"psychological man" (Homans 1979*b*) also belongs here. Even Erik
Erikson has chosen to write on the subject (1980).

Paradoxically, as the lesser-known figures become more familiar,
Freud's greatness does not diminish. He was once "larger than life";
now only the significance of his stature shifts. As the reader sees with
greater clarity Freud wrestling with circumstances that were both
unique for him as the originator of psychoanalysis and universal for
all those who study his life and work, his greatness persists—but in
new and different ways. To extend this metaphor of shadow and light
to the stage: whereas once the historical spotlight had been on Freud
alone, now smaller circles of light have gradually illuminated others
(Adler, Jung, Abraham, etc.), such that we in the audience are led to
think, yes, they were there all the time, it was just that we could not
see them. But it is only when all the stage lights go up that one sees
that these separate figures are, in fact, a cohesive group each playing a
part to each other and to a wider web of figures, relationships, and
social forces as well.

This essay explores in detail a period in Freud's life which was
populated by many figures who have remained in the shadows and
who have for this reason been badly neglected. Ernest Jones's intense
and persistent idealizations of Freud have virtually institutionalized
a series of perceptions which serve as a deliberate foil for my argument. His observation that Freud's relationship to Wilhelm Fliess
was the only truly extraordinary event in Freud's life has had the

effect of forestalling thought about other possibly extraordinary events, such as the impact of Jung on Freud. Ellenberger (1970) has proposed that Freud underwent a second creative illness during the course of this relationship. Jones's exclusively oedipal interpretations of Freud's relationships and conflicts have made it difficult to introduce the idea of earlier developmental lines into the study of Freud's life, such as the persistence of maternal motifs in his intimate dealings with other men. By using the psychologically weak notion of Freud's "circle" to describe the psychoanalytic movement, Jones has deflected attention from its psychologically intense and often twisted group dynamics. Perhaps most of all, Jones's Freud is a man unmoved by social circumstance, although we now know that German political liberalism, the question of German-Jewish loyalties, and the tension between Viennese Jewishness and Zurich Christianity all deeply affected Freud, his perceptions of others, his ongoing work, and his evolving sense of the historical significance of his ideas.

When these several issues in the study of Freud's life and thought are drawn together and brought to bear on the 1906–14 period, they generate an understanding of those years very different from the one which has come to be taken for granted. Freud was intimately involved with Jung, both personally and intellectually, as some recent analytic studies show, and "the break" profoundly affected his inner world and the ideas he chose to write about at the time, as analytic studies—both older and current—do not show. Psychoanalytic writing on the psychoanalytic movement has noted only its voluntaristic qualities, treating it as a voluntary association or a gesellschaft and has ignored its unconscious group-psychological features. A psychological theory of groups can therefore illumine the Freud-Jung relationship and can explain why the two men feared their separation with such intensity. Furthermore, by understanding the psychoanalytic movement as a group, one achieves a privileged position from which to grasp Freud's relations to the social, political, and cultural forces and ideas which surrounded him, because the group mediated between his personal anxieties and creativity and his ambivalent attitudes toward the culture at large. Indeed, the figures and forces active in this period compelled Freud to initiate what became a serious and systematic struggle to insert his psychoanalysis into the indifferent, even hostile, world of Western cultural values. In this way the so-called cultural texts were born. That is to say, after 1914, Freud began to historicize his ideas, and this effort constitutes, I propose, a second creative phase in his life and thought. Finally, reflection on the 1906–14 period provides invaluable material for the development of a fresh perspective from which one may rethink the origins of psychoanalysis itself, because an unmistakable line of continuity—for the most part entirely ignored by analytic scholars— exists between the self-analysis, the movement, and the cultural texts. Part 2 takes up this problem in detail, although the broad outlines of such reformulation are set forth here.

A single psychological theme unites these many issues, permeating them all, the all-too-human theme of disappointment or mourning or disillusionment, which I will from time to time conceptualize more exactly and psychologically as a specifiable narcissistic issue, the experience of de-idealization. The Freud-Jung relationship began as a narcissistic merger. The breaking up of that merger produced disillusionment and narcissistic rage in both participants. Freud subsequently turned in upon himself, and his writing at this time creatively explored and re-presented this aspect of his inner world. But the psychoanalytic movement, understood as a group, was also characterized by similar processes, such as shared idealizations, identifications, and illusions. The separate "unit selves" of the first psychoanalysts crumbled under the impact of psychoanalytic ideas and practice, and these men reorganized their mental lives by forming a group self. So when group cohesion was badly threatened by Jung's defection and the Great War, Freud responded to the impending sense of separateness with anxiety and weakened self-cohesion. This in turn intensified his lifelong preoccupation with his own death, for he refused to separate the historical future of psychoanalysis from the contents of his own mental life.

Jung's departure and the dynamics of the movement also shaped Freud's relation to culture, understood both as an ideological force impinging upon him and as a suitable object for psychoanalytic reflection. After 1914, Freud mourned his lost hopes for German political liberalism, he renounced portions of his own Jewishness which had in the past provided him with a social identity, and he sought to penetrate, psychoanalytically, the Catholicism which had dominated Western culture and which had authorized the persecution of both Jews and psychoanalysis. Writing "The Moses of Michelangelo"—a paper whose beauty and historical significance have both been woefully neglected—in 1914 in Rome was the first of what became a series of psychoanalytic probes into the psychology of Western cultural and religious experience. These probes have come to be known as the cultural texts. But the composition of this paper was inseparable from the writing of "On Narcissism," from Freud's relation to Jung, and from his "turn" to the psychology of Western religious values. Although religion was an essential ingredient in Freud's inner world, it has not as yet been possible to discuss this, the most unwelcome of all guests in the household of Freud biography. But that discussion does become possible when one understands religion not only as a debate between hostile, conflicting bodies of doctrinal assertions but also a series of diverse patterns of powerful, shared, and unconscious idealizations of esteemed cultural objects.

Although this essay does not dwell upon it, study of the 1906–14 period in this way also opens up an issue fundamental to all studies of Freud's life and thought, that of the relation between psychoanalysis and history. Jones's attempt to wed psychoanalytic and historical approaches was exceptional. Most studies of Freud's life and thought have been either exclusively psychoanalytically biographical or else heavily historical and nonpsychological. Either Freud's inner world is illumined and historical circumstances are viewed simply as a series of stimuli periodically breaking into that world, to be understood after the fashion of "the analytic situation," or else historical events are elaborated with little reference to their subjective-analytic and unconscious significance for Freud the man.

The concept of de-idealization bears upon this methodological issue as much as it does on the contents of the period under scrutiny. Kohut has pointed out (1976) that those who attempt to think psychoanalytically—be they clinicians or psychoanalytic scholars—of necessity immerse themselves in Freud's writings and, again, of necessity, in Freud's very mind and life. So, an invisible psychological bond is formed, composed not only of admiration and grateful idealizations of Freud but also of rebellious repudiations or de-idealizations. And when it happens that one's subject matter is itself Freud's life and thought, further stress is inevitably placed upon that bond. Idealization tends to strengthen the bond, whereas de-idealization has the effect of weakening it.

It is not possible for the psychoanalytic scholar to avoid this dilemma, but it is possible for him to think it through, at least to some extent, by engaging its psychology. All psychoanalytic biography of Freud creates an idealized portrait of him, rendering him "larger than life." However, insofar as this pattern is recognized, there is thrown into motion a natural tendency to return Freud to the realm of the ordinary—that is, a partial de-idealization takes place. And, insofar as that occurs, then Freud's ordinary human motives, subjective intentions, and experienced meanings acquire the capability of coming into view in a fresh and more nuanced way. As this process takes place, Freud gradually becomes a historical figure. As psychological processes are clarified, historical reality begins to emerge.

This unavoidable blend of subject matter and method also shapes the way plausibility or validity occurs, if and when it does. In what follows I do not attempt to establish causality between, for example, Freud's inner experiences and the thematic contents of his work, or between these and the social circumstances which surround him. Instead, I seek to show an affinity or linkage between life, thought, group/movement, cultural forces and issues, and think of these as concentric circles rather than lines of force. To shift the metaphor, the psychology of de-idealization is the thread which stitches together numerous segments of historical occasion, and I call the ensuing patchwork pattern—with sincere apologies to Claude Lévi-Strauss—the "structure" of the 1906–14 period. As the discussion proceeds, I hope this pattern gradually achieves the character of wholeness through my efforts to place historical events in their psychological contexts, and vice-versa, much as Freud sought "meaning" by filling in the gaps and missing links in his patients' lives; except, of course, that in this case the "gaps" and "links" are social and historical as well as developmental.

Literature Review: Freud's Most Creative Phase and Its Relevance for the 1906–1914 Period

A major portion of psychoanalytic scholarship on Freud's life and thought (Jones 1953, 1955, 1957; Kris 1954; and Schur 1972) concurs in the view that the period 1897–1901 was the time in which Freud discovered and set forth those ideas which compose the distinctively psychoanalytic understanding of mental life. While these sources of course vary greatly in their handling of specific materials, they each set forth in their own ways a similar pattern:

(1) Freud thinks intently about a research problem
(2) He enters into relation with another man, and the relationship becomes intense and increasingly conflicted
(3) Freud introspects about this relationship within the context of creating a significant intellectual work
(4) A psychological discovery is made, the work which embodies it is completed, and the relationship with the significant figure is dissolved

The problem was the nature of neurosis, the central figure was Fliess, the relationship was that of a regressive transference neurosis, and introspection led to self-analysis, to the discovery of childhood and the unconscious, and to the writing of *The Interpretation of Dreams.* So, Kris, Jones, and Schur agree that any psychoanalytic study of Freud's life will establish a connection between an introspective struggle and the achievement of a psychological discovery. And, in their characterization of the psychological substrate of Freud's experiences and theoretical advances, they all subscribe to what is in effect Freud's predominantly oedipal point of view.

Since these foundational efforts, a second set of studies has made some rather striking innovations. Whereas the first group proposed conceiving of Freud's creativity in terms of his own understanding of his self-analysis, although more profoundly, the second group asserts that deeper psychological processes, for the most part entirely unknown to Freud, actually shaped his creative discoveries. Erikson's psychohistorical analysis (1964a) broke down Freud's crisis into three components (psychological discovery, innovation in work techniques, and identity formation) and argued that his discoveries resulted from complex shifts in the psychosocial world of his time. Ellenberger's formidable history (1970) employed the notion of a "creative illness." The creative figure invests a special problem with great emotional intensity, undergoes neurotic and even psychotic forms of suffering, but emerges with a grand truth, restored health, and a loyal body of followers. Ellenberger believes that the originative psychoanalysts were only the most recent instances of this universal experience, common also to poets and even shamans.

Kohut (1976) further undercut the first explanations by proposing that Freud's relationship to Fliess was not a regressive transference neurosis at all and that it did not end with insight into the transference. Rather, Freud's creative experience was a "transference of creativity," to be understood on the model of the narcissistic transferences of the narcissistic personality disorders. As the originative figure begins to evolve his new constructions, his self becomes progressively enfeebled and detached from others. To support his threatened inner world, he unconsciously turns to another person, merging, idealizing, and seeking mirroring responses from him. Then, as the creative product emerges, the transference of creativity to the other person gradually dissolves and the demands for merger and the need to idealize diminish.

Ernest Wolf (1971) clarified this line of thinking further by proposing that when Freud's mirror transference to Fliess was interrupted, Freud filled the gap with his creative work, which he then experienced as a self-object. But Wolf's most interesting contribution is that the *form* of the work is shaped by the narcissistic line of development, whereas the work owes its *content* to the line of object love. John Gedo (1968) has pointed to Erikson's observation that a maternal transference characterized the Fliess relationship and has added that Freud's unconscious pregenital identifications with his "two mothers" (Amalia Freud and his nanny) persisted into Freud's perceptions of Fliess.

Probably the most advanced—or "radical," depending on one's point of view—attempt to introduce a narcissistic line of development, and all that it implies, into Freud's most creative period has come from Robert Stolorow and George Atwood (1979). After analyzing Freud's earliest experiences, his dreams and his letters to his wife and to Fliess, they conclude that Freud drastically oversimplified the oedipal mother-son relationship when he characterized it as "altogether the most perfect, the most free of ambivalence of all human relationships" (Freud 1933, p. 133). They think that Freud advanced this theoretical construction in order to mask, from his own self-understanding, a deeper and entirely split-off current of rage toward his mother based on an unconscious sense of loss, separation, and rejection. Again and again, they speak of the strength and persistence of Freud's need for idealization and of the capacity of such idealization to forestall any repetition, in adult awareness, of an infantile sense of betrayal. In sum, Stolorow and Atwood think that this pre-oedipal and maternal "blank" or "gap" in Freud's major relationships (mother, wife, mentors) was responsible for the creation of a psychological theory in which pregenital issues between mother and son were well-nigh eliminated.

I propose to draw upon this reservoir of early and recent psychoanalytic explanation of the most creative period in order to evolve a fresh theoretical perspective on the Freud-Jung relationship and, from there, on the many facets of the 1906–14 period. Only at this time did Freud's accrued body of psychoanalytic ideas leave the confines of his own inner world and his intimate associates, from there to enter the streams of Western thought and symbol which are commonly called "culture." Describing this entrance allows me to trace Freud's evolving psychoanalytic sense of the historical, which was inseparable from his attempts to historicize his analytic ideas. So, while I begin with the above-described established psychoanalytic literature on Freud's life and thought, I quickly move beyond it, in two directions. First, I take as a guiding psychological theme the process of de-idealization. Although the term comes from Kohut, I give it a far broader meaning than he ever did. And second, in order to link Freud's inner world and intimate personal relationships to his movement and to the sweep of Western culture, I draw upon psycho-analytic group psychology and upon historical writings on psycho-analysis, such as those of Dennis Klein (1981), Carl Schorske (1973), and Frank Sulloway (1979). These provide the indispensable histor-ical context for my psychological reflections and make it possible for me to bring the two closer together.

Because it allows the student of psychoanalysis to cross over from person to thought to movement and to culture, the psychological concept of de-idealization also affords some insight into the deepest recesses of Freud's personality and character and into the reasons why so many previous analytic writers have idealized him. Freud's personality of course shaped, and in turn was shaped by, his seminal psychological discoveries during the most creative period. But his character, especially as it evolved after those experiences, continued to be shaped by his emerging sense of the historical import of his work, and his convictions about this also became part of his identity. Freud's readiness to display his own "inner world" (the term is Melanie Klein's) and its conflicting ambitions in his works, his skill in discerning the hidden inner world of others, and his capacity to lift these motives out for all to see, as well as his ability to reduce both, by means of his theories, to their base origins—all were closely linked to what could be called his "style of life" and to what is a key indicator of any style of life, his sense of humor. By means of humor Freud was forever bringing soaring ambitions down to humble earth—his own, those of his friends, his enemies', and, above all, of Western man, who had codified his fondest illusions in many of the great cultural works which Freud interpreted. Freud's capacity to endure in the face of the recurrent disillusionments which his own theories and even history itself inflicted upon him became an essential ingredient of his chosen mode of response to the life circumstances which surrounded him. And these capacities lie at the root of Jones's and other analysts' idealization of him.

Mourning, the De-Idealization Experience, and Their Historical Correlates: Disillusionment and Disenchantment

While it is best to allow the meaning of deidealization to unfold and to accrue specificity in the context of biographical and historical evidence, some preliminary formulation is necessary. The problem of definition is complicated as well as enhanced by the pres-ence of a number of words in ordinary language which convey roughly similar significance—such as disappointment, mourning, pining, disillusionment, longing, deploring, renunciation, and disenchantment. The personal but also universal experience of object loss underlies all these, and many psychoanalytic writers have spoken of it in very different ways. This is hardly surprising, since the experience of object loss (along with, of course, that of object love) is the central conceptual structure of all psychoanalytic thought, from Freud to the present. I have taken the concept from Kohut and then modified it well beyond his usage, in both psychological and sociological directions. My conviction that these two (the psychological and the sociological) belong together distinguishes my approach from the sources upon which it is, at the outset, dependent.

In the most obvious sense de-idealization refers to the pre-oedipal line of development, the figure of the mother more than that of the father, and to issues of unconscious self-esteem, merger, self-cohesion, grandiosity, and the loss of ideals. Kohut has explicated these ideas repeatedly, especially in his *The Analysis of the Self* (1971). I formulate the psychological side of the de-idealization experience specifically and synoptically as follows. It is an inner psychological sequence of states, characteristic of adult life, with a beginning, middle, and end. It is developmentally grounded and can be described both phenomenologically and genetically. It begins with conscious and unconscious idealizations and an enhanced sense of self-esteem, accompanied by feelings of loyalty, merger, and fusion with other objects—persons, ideas, ideals, groups, even a social and intellectual tradition. Since history rarely optimally facilitates psychological development, such mergers are eventually challenged by interpersonal, social, and historical circumstances. As a result, the idealizations lose their firmness and may even crumble, leading to a weakened sense of self, a sense of betrayal, a conviction that an important value has been lost, moments of rage at the object (subsequently perceived as having failed the self in some way or other), and a consequent general sense of inner disorganization and paralysis. The final disposition of the de-idealization experience usually takes one of three directions: (1) it may move toward new knowledge of self, new ideals, and consequent new ideas, or (2) the paralysis can persist, leading to apathy, cynicism, and chronic discontent, or (3) one may disavow the experience entirely and instead attack, often fiercely and rebelliously, the events or persons producing the de-idealization. The first and desired outcome is usually supported by a fresh mandate for introspection, an invitation to self-healing through the building of psychological structure, and the capacity to entertain what could be called "new structures of appreciation" or new values. To some extent, every outcome is a mixture of all three.

It is inevitable that the de-idealization experience resemble certain typical or primary experiences described by other psychoanalytic writers, since the event of object loss is, as I have noted, so central to all psychoanalytic thought. Winnicott's descriptions (1951) of the way transitional objects monitor the infant's loss of omnipotence at the breast and facilitate gradual disillusionment and the eventual formation of a unit self resemble de-idealization, and the psychoanalytic group psychology which I use in chapter 3 to explain the extraordinary energy and rigidity of Freud and his movement is based on Didier Anzieu's (1984) appropriation of Winnicott's theory of illusion—the early analysts unconsciously believed in a group illusion: "We are," they thought, "one." Melanie Klein's emphasis upon the infant's achievement of the depressive position (1940), with its tragic overtones, and her view that mourning permits a transition from the paranoid-schizoid position to the infantile neurosis, also resembles, in all its essentials, the "sadder but wiser" tonalities of de-idealization. The most obvious antecedent of de-idealization is of course Freud's theory of mourning (1917a), grounded as it was in narcissistic issues, and especially his view not only that it is a reaction to the loss of a person but also that it can refer to the loss of "some abstraction" such as one's country, liberty, or an ideal.

My appropriation of the idea of de-idealization differs from these seminal psychoanalytic theories not so much in terms of their nuanced clinical descriptions of object loss—although even here there is some disagreement—as in terms of my broader effort to understand "objects" as ideals, values, and traditions and not only as persons in the family. All such objects (including familial objects) are, I maintain, historically constituted. It could be expected that this emphasis would be entirely lacking from the analysts' understanding of the social location of analysis itself, seen as a phenomenon of modern culture, but this emphasis is also absent from clinical writing as a whole, and Winnicott, Klein, and Kohut are not exceptions. When Winnicott formulated the idea of the transitional object, he did so in part to find a place in the mind for culture which he believed Freud had, so to speak, left empty. But he could find no place in culture for the mind, and so his descriptions of culture remained bereft of any concrete discussion of ideals, values, and traditions and their specific contexts. In a similar fashion one must note that, even in Melanie Klein's discussion (1959) of "our adult world," that world remains the "inner world" of clinical psychoanalysis and not the social world in which the ego is, for better or worse, inextricably embedded.

Although it was Freud who first evolved a depth psychology of mourning, the process of de-idealization used here differs from that understanding in a number of ways. First, de-idealization refers explicitly to prestructural issues. It is an essential component in normal development, and, like melancholia, it includes emptiness in the inner world, as well as a sense of loss in the external environment. Second, de-idealization is progressive in its outcome, leading as it does to new values and new psychological structure, whereas mourning as Freud conceived it was essentially conservative, only consolidating, repairing, and rescuing lost parts of the ego from the wreckage inflicted upon it by the commands of reality. And third, de-idealization involves both horizontal and especially vertical splits in the self such that moments of low self-esteem and narcissistic rage can be experienced both consciously and unconsciously and both with and without distortion. In the case of a vertical split, the fact of injury to self-esteem and the accompanying rage can be experienced without the subject's recognizing the intensity of his or her response, and in my view analytic interpretation can thematize this intensity in such a way as to illumine a subject's total response to a complex historical situation. In the following section I use the idea of de-idealization—not without irony, to be sure, but also with accuracy, I hope—to interpret psychologically the genesis of some of Freud's thinking on narcissism, object loss, and even his thinking about mourning itself.

Because I think that the de-idealization experience always takes place in a historical context, some sort of historical framework must be provided for it here at the outset. The de-idealization experience fits lock-and-key with Max Weber's account of value change in modern Western culture (1904–5), which he described with the ideas of disenchantment and rationalization. With these concepts Weber created a portrait of modern Western man living in a time of general mourning for the lost spontaneity and immediacy which the social formations and symbols of Western religious culture had built up and guaranteed. As these experiences and values eroded, they were replaced by rational, calculative operations in every possible sphere of life.

The world which Weber described was the world in which Freud also lived, worked, and thought—as did his patients and followers. Had Weber had a better grasp of Freud's work, he would certainly have recognized what I now can make explicit, namely, that Freud rationalized the last outpost of charisma and spontaneity in the modern West, the infantile unconscious, by providing scientific rules for its operation. In doing so, however, Freud paid the price of becoming disenchanted with many of the values which he had learned to idealize in his youth—German political liberalism, Jewish faith and tolerance, and a world without war, to mention three. Indeed, it is possible to understand major aspects of Freud's discovery of psychoanalysis as a creative response to disillusionment and disenchantment, for in its farthest reaches analysis is nothing less than the injunction to give up many of the illusions or "enchantments" which traditional culture has praised. The developmental process which analysis describes is, in its most sweeping and general sense, a kind of disenchantment or mourning all its own in which the possible existence of unconscious, infantile objects and wishes is rejected by the reality principle. Then these wishes and objects are subsequently abandoned or "given up" or mourned, as the modified adult mental organization gradually replaces the archaic, infantile one. Such psychoanalytic terms as "optimal disillusionment" and "optimal frustration" readily come to mind. On the other hand, rationalization is a kind of structure building when it is considered psychoanalytically. In the light of this observation it can also be argued—as I do below—that Freud sought to heal Western man's consciousness as well by transforming disenchantment and the loss of ideals into psychological structure. This was a task for which Weber had neither the taste nor the talent, and fate assigned this work of modern culture to Freud.

Furthermore, Freud's theories of culture can also be seen, in their Weberian context, as attempts to respond both critically and constructively—and not just reactively—to a sociohistorical sense of loss. In chapter 3 I describe the specific values and ideals which Freud believed both he and Western man had lost and the ways in which the psychoanalytic theory of culture both documented and overcame such loss. These theories did not evolve in the most creative phase, which was a time of personal isolation, deep introspection, and intensive clinical investigation, for the most part bereft of cultural interpretation. The foundation of these theories was first laid down in the 1906–14 period, the time of Freud's intense involvement with Jung and the formation of the psychoanalytic movement. And so it is with these circumstances that I begin.[1]

In sum, in what follows I deliberately eschew that which clinical psychoanalysis insists upon—sharp and discordant lines of demarcation between theories—and find the "family resemblances" between them more useful than the "narcissism of minor differences" which separate them. So I recognize continuity between Freud's emphasis upon object loss, Winnicott's upon infantile disillusionment, Klein's upon pining and mourning, and Kohut's upon de-idealization, although I take the last as more or less common coin for the others. Likewise, on the historical side I see continuity between disenchantment, disappointment, and disillusionment in the face of lost social ideals, although the last is the more generic. Mourning covers both personal and historical dimensions, for in both cherished objects are lost and then reconstituted on a new plane. But an explication of the complex interplay between conscious and unconscious personal experiences, on the one hand, and the social structures which both contain and produce these experiences, on the other hand, must wait until part 2. Before that can be explored, psychological and historical material must first be covered. Furthermore, in part 2 we will be able to go back to the origins of psychoanalysis and the famous self-analysis, for those are best understood when they are viewed both sociologically and retrospectively from the vantage point of the 1906–14 period. The rationale for such an approach is noted briefly at the close of this essay and in detail in the opening pages of part 2.

2 De-Idealization in Freud's Life and Thought

More than any other psychoanalytic writer, John Gedo (1983) has explored the influence of Jung on Freud's life. Drawing upon self-psychology and his own formulations, Gedo concluded that the relationship was one of merger and idealization and that the most significant event leading to its breakdown was Jung's extraordinarily powerful idealization of Freud and his psychoanalytic theory, for Jung wished to transform psychoanalysis into nothing less than a religious revitalization of modern culture. But unlike Freud, Jung was unable to modify his idealizations and could not tolerate Freud's rejection of them. As Freud gradually withdrew from the relationship, his creativity was stimulated, although Jung exercised no lasting influence upon him. On this point Gedo in effect concurs with Jones (1955) and Schur (1972).

I propose that Freud was deeply involved with Jung and was therefore deeply disturbed by the break and that the relationship was, from Freud's side as well as from Jung's, a very strong de-idealization experience. Evidence for this view lies as much in Jung's social and cultural significance for Freud as it does in their personal psychologies or in their dyadic, interpersonal field. To support my claim, I begin by summarizing briefly Freud's idealization of Jung as it is found in their letters and then turn to the Munich meetings of 1912 and 1913, when the relationship was disintegrating. Lou Andreas-Salomé was present at the second meeting and described in her journal the tensions between the two men. Then I review in greater detail Freud's correspondence with Karl Abraham. These letters reveal, as the letters to Jung do not, Freud's intense bitterness toward and hatred of Jung and his equally intense need for a second, substitutive merger with Abraham. Abraham dutifully met this need and assiduously mirrored Freud, as he gradually gave up or de-idealized Jung, the central figure in his emotional world at this time. This unique combination of loss (of Jung) and gain (of Abraham) stimulated, in a very

significant way, the writing of "On Narcissism" and "The Moses of
Michelangelo" in Rome, as well as "Mourning and Melancholia" a
year later.

After this analysis of Freud's intense relationships to Jung and
Abraham and their intellectual concomitants, I carry forward the
psychological themes of this period into a discussion of the psychoanalytic movement and from there into Freud's turn to culture and
the so-called cultural texts. Throughout these discussions I continue
to accord to Jung a powerful influence denied by analytic biographers
and historians alike. But this emphasis is only initially psychological.
Beyond that stood Jung's fateful historical significance for Freud. It
just so happened that Jung came to symbolize for Freud many of the
cultural (moral, political, and religious) forces with which he was
contending as he sought progressively to insert analytic ideas into
what he regarded as the unforgiving social world which surrounded
him. Neither Freud nor Jung could predict or control this symbolic
process. Freud's psychological attachment to Jung was fatefully reen-
forced by Jung's many other sociological features—such as his
Protestantism, his national identity, his position as a psychiatrist in a
highly regarded mental hospital and his university affiliations.

Life: Freud's Struggle with Jung and Abraham's Role in It

The Freud-Jung relation spanned the years 1906–14, almost
exactly the time of the formation of the psychoanalytic movement,
which began with the appearance of Freud's followers in the early
years of the first decade and was consolidated at the onset of the Great
War. Their correspondence contained four elements: the double merger or idealization and its disintegration; intellectual and theoretical
discussions (the libido theory, the psychoanalytic theory of paranoia,
and the psychoanalytic theory of religion); discussions of organizational issues; and what can be called the "heir theme."

At the outset, Freud idealized Jung intensely, insisted upon conceptual uniformity, and designated Jung as his successor in all
psychoanalytic matters ("crown prince," "son and heir," etc.). As
their discourse progressed, these expectations were gradually frustrated by Jung's independent manner. Then Jung's idealization took a
distressingly florid turn. He proposed to Freud that psychoanalysis be
understood as a fresh source of vitality for Western culture's spiritual
emptiness. Freud rejected this, permanently alienating Jung. But
Freud's decision was based on his conscious, ethical, and scientific

repudiation of the grandiosity underlying Jung's program. Freud had no dynamic psychological understanding either of Jung's need to idealize him or of his own intense wish to be "at one" with Jung. The remainder of the correspondence simply documents the inability of both men to understand the narcissistic issues at work between them and their moralistic attempts to work out these unconscious misunderstandings by focusing on theoretical and organizational issues.

A few critical passages which indicate that Jung had become a self-object for Freud are easy to note. In August 1907, less than a year and a half after they had begun to write each other, Jung was to give a lecture in which he would advance Freud's ideas. Freud's estimate of the occasion (McGuire 1974) boldly united within Jung's own person a strong feminine-maternal element in Freud's personality with an intense preoccupation with the historical destiny of psychoanalysis: "Your lecture in Amsterdam will be a milestone in history and after all it is largely for history that we work. . . . And when you have injected your own personal leaven into the fermenting mass of my ideas in still more generous measure, there will be no further difference between your achievement and mine" (no. 38).[1] Two weeks later, Freud was still thinking about this event, and he decided to place it in the context of an evolving sense of his own personal place in history, which he referred to as "the unknown multitude":

> . . . but now of all times I wish I were with you, taking pleasure in no longer being alone and, if you are in need of encouragement, telling you about my long years of honorable but painful solitude, which began after I cast my first glance into the new world, about the indifference and incomprehension of my closest friends, about the terrifying moments when I myself thought I had gone astray and was wondering how I might still make my misled life useful to my family, about my slowly growing conviction, which fastened itself to the interpretation of dreams as to a rock in a stormy sea, and about the serene certainty which finally took possession of me and bade me wait until a voice from the unknown multitude should answer mine. That voice was yours. . . . (No. 42)

In January-February 1910, roughly midway in the relationship, Jung's crucial idealization took place. Freud had proposed to him that the psychoanalysts associate themselves with a local ethical society. He thought such an affiliation would protect analysis from the authoritarian pressures which he anticipated would eventually come from the state or the church. But Jung had only contempt for such voluntary associations. His reply contained a powerful idealization of Freud and analysis into a form of religioethical revitalization:

> Do you think this Fraternity could have any practical use? . . . If a coalition is to have any ethical signifi-cance it should never be an artificial one but must be nourished by the deep instincts of the race. Some-what like Christian Science, Islam, Buddhism. Religion can be replaced only by religion.
>
> I imagine a far finer and more comprehensive task for psychoanalysis than alliance with an ethical fra-ternity. I think we must give it time to infiltrate into people from many centers, to revivify among intel-lectuals a feeling for symbol and myth, ever so gently to transform Christ back into the soothsaying god of the vine, which he was, and in this way absorb those ecstatic instinctual forces of Christianity for the *one* purpose of making the cult and the sacred myth what they once were. . . . A genuine and proper ethical de-velopment cannot abandon Christianity but must grow up within it. . . . (No. 178)

Freud's disillusioning reply:

> . . . you mustn't regard me as the founder of a religion. My intentions are not so far-reaching. . . . I am not thinking of a substitute for religion; this need must be sublimated. (No. 179)

These exchanges indicate the centrality of a double merger in the Freud-Jung relationship.[2] It is necessary only to note that the merger gradually and painfully broke up. As it deteriorated, each man con-tinued to comment frequently on his own need to reduce his enthusiasm for the other, and each struggled earnestly to understand himself and the other psychoanalytically. Both men utilized Freud's oedipal theory, believing that their conflicts played out the develop-mental clash between father and son. But current pre-oedipal psychologies seem to explain better than does Freud's structural the-ory Jung's incredible overestimation of Freud and psychoanalysis, inflating it "into a religion," and Freud's characteristic "skep-ticism"—that is, his repugnance for all such idealizations, based on his virtually total inability to entertain them imaginatively. If it is recognized that Freud unwittingly made Jung a part of himself, it is also possible to understand his relentless and offensive overbearingness in the face of clear evidence that Jung had no intention of accepting many of the ideas which Freud valued highly and to understand as well Freud's refusal to give Jung up, despite his conscious contempt for Jung's own emerging ideas. Some sort of very primitive unconscious attachment had to be at work. The dynamics of that attachment were not simply infantile-genetic residues, but also social: Jung was "the other" whom Freud's social history had ill-prepared him to understand in a psychological way. The`gradual crumbling of this attachment is conceptualized well as a de-idealization experience. Its social aspect is as important as its developmental roots.

For all its gradualness, this experience came to an abrupt conclusion several months before and after the Munich meeting of 1913. If Freud was in the throes of unconscious disillusionment, one would expect to find strong negative attitudes, some depression and narcissistic rage, and a general sense of inner impoverishment. But one might also expect that this psychological state would gradually undergo reorganization and open out on an acceptance of the loss and the building of psychological structure in the form of creative activity. Still further, the contents of that creativity could well betray the presence of narcissistic issues.

Writing as an historian, Jones portrayed Freud at this time as masterfully in control of all his emotions. Faced with Jung's defection, Freud "very sensibly decided to resign himself to the inevitable, a few mild protests being of no avail; to lessen his expectations; and to withdraw a certain amount of his former personal feeling" (1955, pp. 142–43). Jones's report also contains the essential element of his idealization of Freud: Freud's total mastery of his consciousness through self-knowledge and insight derived from his self-analysis, which Jones called the "only extraordinary" event in Freud's life. Writing as a psychologist, however, Jones also noted that "his [Freud's] daughter tells me it [the break with Jung] was the only time she remembers her father being depressed" (1955, p. 99) and that Freud described himself to Ferenczi as "fuming with rage" while writing "On the History of the Psychoanalytic Movement" in January-February of 1914 (p. 304). Even the always protective Strachey was able to observe, in his editor's note to this paper, that Freud adopted a "far more belligerent tone than in any of his other writings" (Freud 1914c, p. 4).

Jones described the atmosphere of the Munich meeting as simply "disagreeable," and Freud said only that it was "fatiguing and unedifying" (McGuire 1974, p. 550). But Lou Andreas-Salomé, who was not, strictly speaking, part of the psychoanalytic movement, observed this occasion quite differently (Leavy 1964):

> At the congress the Zurich members sat at their own
> table opposite Freud's. . . . One glance at the two of
> them tells which is the more dogmatic, the more in
> love with power. Two years ago, Jung's booming
> laughter gave voice to a kind of robust gaiety and
> exuberant vitality, but now his earnestness is com-
> posed of pure aggression, ambition, and intellectual
> brutality. I have never felt so close to Freud as here;
> not only on account of this break with his "son"
> Jung, whom he had loved and for whom he had prac-
> tically transferred his cause to Zurich, but on ac-
> count of the manner of the break—as though Freud
> had caused it by his narrow-minded obstinacy. Freud
> was the same as ever, but it was only with difficulty
> that he restrained his deep emotion. . . . (Pp. 168–69)

She also noted that "Jung had improperly shortened the time for our paper" (hers and Tausk's). Jones was also critical of Jung: "Jung conducted the meetings in such a fashion that it was felt some gesture of protest should be made" (1955, p. 102).

Andreas-Salomé has also provided important evidence that Freud was intensely preoccupied with the psychological problem of narcissism during the time of Jung's defection. She had achieved a high degree of rapport with Freud; he liked her very much and spoke his thoughts freely to her, and her journal recorded Freud's and her private thoughts. Therefore we can trust her, somewhat in the way an anthropologist trusts a "native informant" to give an empathic report of her subject with a minimum of theoretical explanation. On a Sunday in February 1913, she visited Freud's home and they discussed, as they had before, many things. First Freud spoke of his dislike of pure philosophy and his conviction that "it is really essential to struggle against the need peculiar to thinkers for an ultimate unity in things" in order to protect "the detailed research of positive science." That led the two to think together of the sadness which more and more accompanied their lives and experiences even when fortune was favorable, which Andreas-Salomé referred to as the "diminution of our euphoria." Then she proposed to Freud that the two (longing for unity and diminished euphoria) were connected. Freud concurred. "This striving for unity," he told her, "has its ultimate source in narcissism" (Leavy 1964, p. 104).

This poignant vignette sheds a ray of light on Freud's emotional and intellectual state at the time. A quiet but sad tone runs through Andreas-Salomé's pages. The reference to narcissism, understood as a sort of vision of wholeness which science must—tragically—shatter and such ideas as "longing" and "diminution" suggest a dejected and resigned, if not melancholic, Freud. This Sunday conversation took place only one month after Freud had written to Jung proposing that "we abandon our personal relations entirely" (McGuire 1974, no. 342).

Freud and Jung had in fact discussed these very same issues with each other several years before. In 1909 Jung proposed a vision of wholeness in the form of his then-new interest in mythology: "I have the most marvelous visions," he wrote his mentor, "glimpses of far-reaching inter-connections" (no. 170), to which Freud replied, "Such far-reaching interpretations cannot be stated so succinctly but must be accompanied by ample proof" (no. 201). As Freud struggled emotionally to renounce his merger with Jung in 1913–14, he also continued to renounce the solace and consolation through which a vision of wholeness tempts the positive scientist. Because it was Jung who took such an affirmative attitude toward wholeness, there may be some further sense in which the idea of a "vision of wholeness" also represented to Freud his unconscious psychological unity with Jung. This search for wholeness so haunted Freud that it reappeared at the end of his life in a far more commanding way, as the search for a cherished value, the universal love of all mankind, in his correspondence with another religious figure, Romain Rolland (described in chap. 4).

But the best evidence for Freud's psychological state during the break with Jung comes from his letters to Karl Abraham. These link the break to the creative period which followed it, when Freud abandoned his idealization of Jung. There are five issues in this correspondence, and each is structured by Freud's intense need to polarize Abraham against Jung. They are:

(1) A fresh psychological merger with Abraham, at the time when the merger with Jung was disintegrating
(2) The writing of the paper "On Narcissism," inaugurating a theoretical advance in psychoanalytic thought
(3) A racial or religious issue, for Freud referred to the basis of his attachment to Abraham as one of "racial kinship," which clearly excluded Jung
(4) Rome, a city with multiple conscious and unconscious meanings for Freud, to which he immediately retreated after the Munich

meeting in order to write the paper on narcissism and "The Moses of Michelangelo"

(5) The psychoanalytic movement, in which the relationship between leader and led was modeled upon the relationship between Freud and Jung

I now turn to the interplay between the first two and to the interpersonal aspects of the religious issue. I discuss Rome and Freud's paper on Moses in the next section. Then I take up the psychoanalytic movement and again discuss religion as a cultural rather than an interpersonal issue in chapters 3 and 4.

The relationship really began in 1907, when Abraham asked Freud to refer patients to him. He stated he was moving from Zurich to Berlin and explained that, "as a Jew in Germany and as a foreigner in Switzerland," he could not be promoted (Abraham and Freud 1965, p. 8).[3] Freud's reply minimized the issue of religious prejudice, "for you as a Jew" (p. 9). Five months later, Abraham was set up in Berlin but had become rivalrous with Jung, who was in control of the recently established *Jahrbuch* to which Abraham had submitted a paper. Freud thought that this rivalry was inevitable, but manageable within limits, and warned against dissension: "There are still so few of us" (p. 34). Then he offered Abraham his explanation of his relation to both men, in a passage which has become famous: "Please be tolerant and do not forget that it is really easier for you than it is for Jung to follow my ideas, for in the first place you are completely independent, and then you are closer to my intellectual constitution because of racial kinship [*und dann stehen Sie meiner intellektuellen Konstitution durch Rassenverwandtschaft näher*], while he as a Christian and a pastor's son finds his way to me only against great inner resistances. His association [*Anschluß*] with us is the more valuable for that. I nearly said that it was only by his appearance on the scene that psychoanalysis escaped the danger of becoming a Jewish national affair [*eine Jüdische nationale Angelegenheit*]" (p. 34).

They continued to comment on this religioracial, psychological bond. Abraham replied, "I freely admit that I find it easier to go along with you rather than with Jung. I, too, have always felt this intellectual kinship [*intellectuelle Verwandtschaft*]. After all, our Talmudic way of thinking [*Die talmudische Denkweise*] cannot disappear just like that" (p. 36). Later, referring again to Jung, Freud wrote: "On the whole it is easier for us Jews, as we lack the mystical element" (p. 46). A week later he expressed admiration for Abraham's paper on dementia praecox and added, "May I say that it is consanguineous Jewish traits [*daß es verwandte, jüdische Züge sind*] that attract me to you? We understand each other" (p. 46).

It is well known that Jones and other psychoanalytic biographers have eschewed sustained attention to what Freud himself openly called "racial" or "consanguineous" factors. Their reasons are also well known. Like Freud, Jones dreaded any implication that psychoanalysis was not a science, for that could have only meant the reverse, that it was in reality a religion. Were analysis to be perceived as a religion, its claims to knowledge would be completely discredited. Therefore, Jones and recent analytic writers as well have dealt with "the religious factor" in Freud's life and thought either by suppressing it through the conscious denial of its existence or by unconsciously splitting it off from his life course and isolating it from psychological inquiry. It is better to understand the above remarks of Freud and Abraham about their loyalties to Judaism psychoanalytically and sociologically. And if prestructural issues are investigated, then these references to religion are neither vestigial delusions nor cryptotheological statements, but rather psychological data.

In this case, the key term becomes what I call the "shared psychic formations" of different groups. Race, religion, ethnicity, and the like all refer to the many and various ways in which separate individuals together organize narcissistic processes in relation to sociohistorical givens in order to evolve a shared sense of self-structure. A narcissistic attachment or merger or idealization is, from this point of view, simply the psychoanalytically understood unit of analysis of what is recognized, from a phenomenological point of view, as an ethnic, racial, or religious idea, value, or identity. Such a formulation makes it possible to include race and religion in one's understanding of the vicissitudes of Freud's merger with Abraham, and also with Jung, without becoming distracted by arguments between conflicting systems of beliefs or between ideologically grounded, group-historical loyalties. Such beliefs and loyalties are instead social constructions grounded in unconscious, shared idealizations. The sociological side of this formulation, which in this, its present, form is little more than a hint, is developed in detail in part 2 by means of the concepts of social structure and a common culture (Durkheim, Parsons) and, still further in part 3, with the aid of Lévi-Strauss's theory of primitivity—but both depend upon first setting forth these psychological and historical observations.

By the time of the famous journey to America, Freud had successfully established a firm relationship with both Abraham and Jung, and his correspondence with Abraham turned to issues of theory. Then, from 1909 to 1913, as Jung's defection became increasingly apparent, Freud wrote more and more about Jung to Abraham. This trend reached its climax several months before and after the Munich meeting of September 1913. The emotional tone of Freud's thoughts about Jung was a mix of bitterness, scorn, resignation, revenge, and irony—all typical marks of a de-idealization experience. In March, Freud wrote: "Jung is in America . . . doing more for himself than for psychoanalysis. I have greatly retreated from him and have no more friendly thoughts for him. His bad theories do not compensate me for his disagreeable character. He is following in Adler's wake, without being as consistent as that pernicious creature [*wie dieser letztere Schädling*]" (p. 137). And in June: "Jung is crazy, but I have no desire for a separation and should like to let him wreck himself first" (p. 141).

Jones recorded that Freud went immediately from the Munich meeting of September 1913 to Rome with Minna Bernays for seventeen days (Jones 1955, p. 103). There he continued his correspondence with Abraham. It began with a simple postcard: "The Jew survives it! Cordial greetings and *coraggio, Casimiro!*" (Abraham and Freud 1965, p. 146). These two solitary exclamatory sentences easily yield to psychoanalytic explanation. In the first, "it" refers of course to Jung and the Munich meeting, which so damaged Freud's esteem by calling into question the very existence of the psychoanalytic movement. "The Jew" is Freud, but the article "the" indicates an explicit identification with Jewry and evokes the historic capacity of Jews to persist in the face of persecution by "the compact majority." The second sentence is more obscure, but also richer, psychologically, for it is a well-structured fantasy. As the editors of the Freud-Abraham correspondence explain, *"coraggio, Casimiro"* referred to a private joke between the two men. Abraham had once gone mountain climbing with two guides, supplied with raw meat. When they had reached camp and prepared to cook the meat, it had spoiled, but the first guide urged the second to take courage and eat the bad meat anyway—*"coraggio, Casimiro."* So Freud's fantasy displaced the negative affect of Abraham's anecdote onto his current situation. Now the two guides were Freud and Abraham and the bad meat was Jung and Munich, which they both had to "swallow." But by merging psychologically with each other and becoming "chums" or "buddies," Abraham would give Freud the psychological strength to survive.

Abraham's reply took up what was later to become a central function of the Committee, that of punctually and dutifully mirroring Freud in the face of dissension or attack, and his response to the postcard was psychodynamically exact: "I take it that you are extremely happy in Rome and that you have thrown off the unpleasant memories of Munich" (p. 147). Feeling understood, Freud was able to elaborate further: "In the incomparable beauty of Rome I quickly recovered my spirits and energy," and he added that, "in the free time between museums, churches and trips to the Campagna," he had finished three papers and "the sketch of an article on narcissism" (pp. 147–48). Abraham continued to mirror his teacher: "I must particularly thank you for writing to me at such length from Rome. At the same time, I want to tell you how glad I am that you—and, according to your report, psycho-analysis as well—are so indebted to Rome" (p. 148).

Freud's need for an intensified attachment to Abraham and Abraham's responding acceptance of it continued, however, well beyond the Roman holiday. At the root of this attachment was Freud's renewed need to explore his inner world. The narcissistic injury at the hands of Jung and the rage which accompanied it served as the conscious and unconscious experiential matrix out of which the writing of the paper on narcissism emerged, so it should also be observed that the paper was an attempt at self-healing as well. As this correspondence unfolds, the intimate relationship between these two—Freud's "life" and his "thought"—becomes clearer. This is perhaps the correct place also to note that Freud's relationships to Jung and Abraham at this time appeared to be another instance of his own famous observation about himself: his need to love one person and hate another at the same time. But in addition to oedipal ambivalence, there was also the more primitive process of "splitting the object"—Jung becoming increasingly "bad," Abraham increasingly "good."

Upon returning to Vienna in October 1913, Freud continued to talk about his paper to Abraham: "I came back from Rome feeling fine and with the draft of the paper on narcissism. Here I promptly caught a cold, like all the Viennese, and have not yet been able to take it out of the drawer again" (p. 149). Two weeks later he informed Abraham that Jung's rejection of his theory of sexuality "makes it the more certain that this is the core of psycho-analysis" (p. 151). In February 1914, he told Abraham that he had finished "On the History of the Psychoanalytic Movement" (the reader should recall Freud's letter to Ferenczi saying that he was writing this paper "fuming with rage" [Jones 1955, p. 304]). And then, two weeks after this, two extraordinarily revealing sentiments: "I think of you a great deal, because I am writing the paper on narcissism" (p. 165). Clearly Freud connected his love for Abraham with his emerging ideas about narcissism, but he could not explain how or why. Then, almost a month later, Freud symbolized in a startling, visual, and very bitchy way the tangled interplay in his mind between the idea of narcissism, his loss of Jung, and his fresh merger with Abraham: "Tomorrow I am sending you the 'Narcissism,' which was a difficult birth and bears all the marks of it. . . . Your picture will return tomorrow from the framer's, and will then take the place of Jung's" (p. 167). Hell hath no fury . . . and so forth.

Freud sorted out this seemingly bizarre mélange of forces and figures only slowly, and never completely, throughout the remainder of 1914 and the first half of 1915. In March 1914: "Since finishing the 'Narcissism' I have not been having a good time. A great deal of headache, intestinal trouble, and already a new idea for work . . ." (p. 168). Once again Abraham took up his mirroring function by telling Freud how superior were the concepts of sublimation and the ego-ideal to Jung's idea of "the prospective tendency of the unconscious." Jung had proposed that the unconscious contained a value-constructing, synthesizing function. Abraham's remark evokes Lou Andreas-Salomé's Sunday afternoon visit with Freud in which they discussed the philosophical search for "an ultimate unity in things," which Freud said had its roots in narcissism, and "the diminution of our euphoria" that a scientific approach compels. Once again understood by Abraham, Freud replied with gratitude: "Your acceptance of my 'Narcissism' affected me deeply and binds us still more closely together" (p. 170). Safely attached to Abraham, he could continue to de-idealize Jung, with expressions of bitterness, resignation, and scorn: "Good wishes for the new Jungless era" (p. 174). "I cannot suppress a cheer. So we have got rid of them" (p. 184). "So we are at last rid of them, the brutal, sanctimonious Jung and his disciples [*den brutalen heiligen Jung und seine Nachbeter*]!" (p. 186).

But even at the end of 1914 Freud was still distressed: "I need someone to give me courage. I have little left" (p. 205). In January 1915, he explained: "Physically I am well again and in good spirits, but am not working and have dropped everything on which I had started, including some things that were very promising. I still think it is a long polar night, and that one must wait for the sun to rise again" (p. 209). And then, a month later: "I have finished something new on melancholia" (p. 211). And finally, the creative outburst of 1915: "My work is now taking shape. I have finished five papers" (p. 221).

The sun did rise, as it had before, this time to shine on the famous paper about mourning, which described scientifically so much of what he had undergone experientially, as well as on the foundational metapsychological papers, and also upon what I later call "the protocultural texts," for these two wholly different types of writing were produced side by side, as the following section demonstrates. There were no more references to Jung. Freud had at last rid himself of that "bad object." The agony of disillusionment was over. At least until the next time.[4]

Thought: "On Narcissism," "The Moses," and the Significance of Rome

Since there is evidence for a psychological merger and its interruption in Freud's life at this time, I now suggest that what are today called narcissistic issues made their presence felt in several of his writings composed at the same time. Such an observation only elaborates in an elemental way the most basic precept of the psychoanalytic study of lives, that an inner struggle and a creative advance are somehow unconsciously wedded in a person's life. But to this is now added a developmental line for the most part unknown to the first psychoanalysts. By writing "On Narcissism" (1914b), Freud attempted to engage this line in a more or less scientific way. But "The Moses," as he affectionately referred to his paper "The Moses of Michelangelo" (1914a), with its heavy aesthetic and cultural tones and its anonymous authorship, reads more like a dream. As such, it constitutes a striking symbolic and literary expression of Freud's deepest thoughts and conflicts at the time. I take the two papers together as a kind of diptych, the title of which might easily be, "The Search for the Self in Thought and Symbol," a search activated by the life circumstances just described. Nor was it any accident that, when he finally turned to culture, Freud chose to write about the great and towering figure of Moses which was also housed—this is no accident either—in a Christian church.

The leading ideas in "On Narcissism" and their place in the development of Freud's thought have been well discussed. Bibring's review (1914) continues to be one of the most thorough and accurate theoretical discussions. Ellenberger characterized Freud's paper as "a great metamorphosis." The theory of narcissism, he thinks, "was to be the prelude to a complete re-structuring of the framework of psychoanalytic theory" (1970, pp. 510–11). In addition to providing a useful summary, Jones agrees ("the paper was one of Freud's radical revisions of the structure of the mind" [1955, p. 302]) but goes further: only twice in his life did Freud make fundamental changes in his instinct theory, and "On Narcissism" was the first. Therefore, "One is thus impelled to inquire into the circumstances of its composition and if possible to relate it to Freud's mood and interests at the time" (1955, p. 304).

Freud's first mention of his paper occurred in a letter written in June to Ferenczi: he would complete it on vacation in the summer of 1913 (Jones 1955, p. 304). Actual writing began in Rome in September, and, as we have also seen, the final version was completed in February 1914 along with "On the History of the Psychoanalytic Movement." He was at that time, he had said to Ferenczi, "fuming with rage." From this Jones concluded that "On Narcissism" contained Freud's objective and scientific disagreements with Jung, whereas "On the History of the Psychoanalytic Movement" expressed his polemical side. At this point Jones abandoned his psychobiographical inferences and deferred to clinical-theoretical considerations: the "main stimulus" for the paper was Freud's "reflections on the nature of dementia praecox which Jung's writings had recently stirred" (p. 304). It is possible to build on Jones's psychobiographical hunches without, however, sharing his reluctance to break off from that line of thinking exactly where he does.

Despite their entirely clinical-theoretical orientation, the ideas in Freud's paper are also suggestive of his inner world at the time of its writing. After several introductory allusions to narcissism in the literature on homosexuality, schizophrenia, children, and primitives, in order to set the stage for his "extension of the libido theory" and his "hypothesis of narcissism," Freud launched into the paper's central issue: Why distinguish at all between sexual libido and the nonsexual energy of the ego instincts? Why not instead stipulate psychic energy in general, as Jung had done, which would "save us all the difficulties" of making further differentiations? This question immediately evoked a minitreatise on the nature of scientific thinking and on the importance of introducing speculative constructs which might nevertheless later be abandoned. Like physics, psychoanalysis also breaks wholes down into smaller units. Stimulated by these thoughts, Freud then evolved a chain of distinctions:

> hunger————love
> ego instincts————sexual instincts
> ego libido————object libido
> narcissism————sexual libido
> egoism————object love

After noting bitterly that this was an effort which "I would gladly have been spared," he concluded bluntly: "We may repudiate Jung's assertion."

Just as there was in the most creative period an isomorphism or parallelism between Freud's inner world (self-analysis, conflicts with Fliess) and his creative writing (*The Interpretation of Dreams*), so there is a similar relation between Freud's struggle with Jung (the most important person in his life at the time) and his creative writing. In the case of his personal life, the issue was the breakup of a narcissistic merger and the ensuing problems of separation and individuation; in the case of his theory, the question was that of breaking down Jung's holistic mode of thinking (psychic energy in general) and differentiating it into more fundamentally discrete conceptual entities, suitable for investigative purposes. In the case of both thought and person, then, the issue was that of "making distinctions."

To put the matter in a different way: the interruption of his psychological merger with Jung, brought about by structural-historical circumstances, forced Freud to separate from him. A personal-emotional "unity" of sorts was broken up, and that process can be understood as a kind of "making distinctions" at the level of personal experience. This intrapsychic conflict then became the unconscious, experiential matrix for theoretical work, and portions of it were displaced out of it and into the intellectual activity of arguing for distinctions in psychological theory. By insisting in a theoretical way that the mental apparatus was more differentiated than either he or Jung had previously thought, Freud was able to work over, in the symbolic rhetoric of metapsychology, and to reduce somewhat his unconscious merger with Jung. In such fashion did the "break with Jung" augment Freud's intellectual work. That work was, then, a kind of psychological structure building all its own.

Furthermore, Freud's Sunday conversation with Lou Andreas-Salomé, described above, anticipated this plea for making distinctions. At that time Freud had spoken out against the need of philosophical thinkers to strive for the unity of all things, and he had linked this style of thinking to narcissism. I have also suggested that Jung's view that the libido be understood as psychic energy in general, and that the unconscious contained a prospective tendency, also weighed on Freud's mind during his Sunday conversation.

Two other portions of Freud's paper deserve comment in this regard. In section 2 Freud applied the many distinctions he had just evolved to organic disease, hypochondria, and the erotic life of the sexes. In the course of this discussion he anticipated, in some of its essentials, Kohut's theory of the transference of creativity (1976), albeit in a literary rather than a scientific modality. To illustrate the ego's need to cathect ideal objects despite the threat of maternal object loss, Freud quoted Heine's account of the psychogenesis of creation: "Illness was no doubt the final cause of the whole urge to create. By creating, I could recover; by creating, I became healthy" (Freud 1914b, p. 85). Freud was also able to allude once more to the problem of death, drawing it into narcissistic considerations by identifying the immortality of the ego as "the most touchy point in the narcissistic system."

Perhaps the most creative part of the entire paper, section 3, addressed the developmental vicissitudes of infantile narcissism, the "former megalomania" which in adults is "dampened down." How did this take place? Freud's well-known answer: the building up of the ego-ideal was an effort to preserve lost narcissism—a silent allusion to the idea of mourning, I might add—and was inseparable from the ego's capacity for relations with the social other. Here Freud spoke in a positive way of "public opinion," "the unidentified multitude," and the "common ideal of a family, a clan or a nation." These final points anticipate his later work on group psychology, the psychology of the ego, and the final disposition of the instinct theory. They also anticipate later discussions of the archaic grandiose self and the group self (Kohut) and the disillusionment of infantile omnipotence and the genesis of the transitional object as the capacity for group relations and the acquisition of culture (Winnicott).

Clearly I think that the idea which Freud sought in all this, but which he never quite reached, was therefore the idea of psychological structure as it is understood today. If Freud was in effect attempting to write a theoretical statement about structure building which would complement the inner circumstances in his own life at the time, then the ideal (if one can use that word at all here) outcome would have been an idea which captured the psychological ethos of primitive fusion and separation, such as "internal object" or "transitional object" or "self-object." For the person sensitive to the analytic situation, such ideas can have the further function, in addition to their cognitive significance, of clarifying the turbulent and unruly psychological forces making for unity and separateness—clarifying, that is, the "structure" of such forces in the psychic realm. The point was made by William James when he remarked that "Ideas became true just so far as they help us to get into satisfactory relations with other parts of our experience" (James 1907). Insofar as this is so, I think a symbolic reading of two remarks made by Freud to Abraham is not out of place. When Freud said, "I think of you a great deal because I am writing the paper on narcissism," and later, "Your acceptance of my 'Narcissism' affected me deeply and binds us still more closely together," he expressed conscious gratitude for Abraham's acceptance of the ideas in the paper, but he also announced an unconscious perception of Abraham's empathic mirroring of his enfeebled self-structure. The phrase, "my narcissism," had both denotative and symbolic significance. Writing "On Narcissism" supported the "unbinding" of Freud's merger with Jung and was therefore an attempt at self-understanding and self-healing. The new work took the place of the old object. The relationships between object loss, mourning, and the creation of new meanings are developed in part 3.

But compromise accompanied this creativity as well. Freud was unable to integrate his theories about narcissism into his personal life, an observation which supports further the view that unconscious narcissistic issues were salient at this time. Kohut has called attention to Freud's lack of empathy for the insane and for the narcissistic neuroses, and to his advice that the analyst's attitude toward his patients be modeled after that of the surgeon "who puts aside all his feelings, even his human sympathy" (Kohut 1973*a*, p. 670), an approach Kohut characterizes as experience distant. Freud took a rationalistic, ethical, and finally moralistic stance toward the narcissistic process. This feature of his life and thought is what Philip Rieff had in mind when he proposed that "psychological man" obeys an ethic of detachment (1959). Paul Ricoeur made the same point (1970) with his idea that psychoanalysis is a hermeneutic of suspicion. (Both views are analyzed in detail in part 3). Freud's reluctance to become empathic toward narcissistic processes can be seen in his reproachful theoretical estimate of parental love and in his comments upon two emotionally significant events in Jung's life.

"Parental love," Freud wrote in Rome in 1914, "which is so moving and at bottom so childish, is nothing but the parents' narcissism born again, which, transformed into object-love, unmistakably reveals its former nature" (p. 91). This depreciatory attitude toward narcissism is also found in Freud's impatience with narcissistic attitudes in Jung's life. Early in 1909, when their relationship was still extremely affectionate, Jung indulged himself in a display of parental pleasure by elaborately describing for Freud his four-year-old daughter's exhibitionistic reaction to the birth of a younger brother (no. 126).[5] Freud could only impassively counter with: "Your Agathli is really charming. But surely you recognize the main feature of Little Hans's story" (no. 129). Then, in June 1911, Jung agonized to Freud over the suicide of Johan Honegger, his young patient, friend, and student, of whom he had been enormously fond and to whom he planned to entrust all of his work. He deplored his own lack of experience and knowledge as a therapist and was clearly grieving.[6] But Freud could only reply: "I think we wear out a few good men," and "I don't think you could have saved Honegger" (no. 260). This reproachful attitude toward normal narcissistic sentiments testifies further to Freud's inability to think empathically about Jung's feelings.

Freud's struggle to attend to narcissistic processes in an introspective, experience-near fashion at the time of his break with Jung in 1913–14 set the "inner" stage for the writing of "On Narcissism," a scientific and theoretical effort. A second paper, written at the same time and in the same place, brought that inner stage to life in a literary, artistic, and symbolic way. In "The Moses of Michelangelo," Freud drew upon his unconscious struggle at this time in order to "introduce narcissism" into the nonpsychological realms of Western cultural experience through the interpretation of a supremely valued and idealized cultural object. In addition to giving expression to Freud's inner world in a way very different from that of the first paper, this beautiful, excellent, and badly neglected essay allowed him to engage psychologically for the first time the powerful cultural forces which he felt had begun more and more to surround him and his faltering psychoanalytic movement: his own Jewish identity in the figure of Moses and the Christianity of Jung and of Western culture in the figure of the pontiff whose tomb the statue of Moses adorned. Inseparable from all of this was the significance of Rome itself for Freud and his so-called Rome neurosis, a riddle which has yet to be completely unraveled. In short, writing "The Moses" in Rome was a turning point in Freud's life—as analyst, as leader of the psychoanalytic movement, and as architect of a new, modern, and psychological vision of Western man. It was the first cultural text.

Jones observed that "The Moses" is of special interest to students of Freud's personality. Freud was fascinated with the impact of works of art upon himself, and this statue moved him more deeply than any other work of art with which he was familiar. Freud visited the statue for the first time during what some analytic biographers have called his "triumphant entry" into Rome in 1901, shortly after resolving his transference to Fliess. He continued to study the statue on subsequent trips. In September 1912, he reported from Rome to his wife that he visited the statue of Moses every day, and when he returned to Vienna he continued to research it intensively. At one point Jones sent him photos of the statue which momentarily disconfirmed his evolving interpretation, but he persisted. Then, in September 1913, directly after the Munich meeting, he reported to Jones a decisive advance: "I have visited old Moses again and got confirmed in my application of his position" (Jones 1955, pp. 365–66). Twenty years later he explained to his friend, the Italian psychoanalyst Eduardo Weiss, "My feeling for this piece of work is rather like that towards a love-child. For three lonely September weeks in 1913 I stood every day in the church in front of the statue, studied it, measured it, sketched it, until I captured the understanding for it which I ventured to express in the essay only anonymously. Only much later did I legitimize this non-analytical child" (cited by Jones 1955, p. 367). Were they "lonely" weeks because creative work is always isolating, or because he had just lost Jung? It is a mistake to separate these two issues. Thinking and writing psychologically about his religious past seems to have consoled Freud, much as religion provides the ordinary believer with "consolation."

The understanding which Freud captured is well known. Most existing interpretations of the statue argued that it depicted Moses after he had descended from Mt. Sinai with the tablets of the law under his arm, seeing the Hebrews dancing around the golden calf and preparing to rise up in rage against their defection. Freud reversed this view: the statue depicted Moses restraining an outburst of rage, in a state of subsequent calm, the result of renouncing his rage. So Freud concluded that the statue portrayed "the highest mental achievement that is possible in a man, that of struggling successfully against an inward passion for the sake of a cause to which he has devoted himself" (Freud 1914a, p. 233). Jones connected Freud's writing of "The Moses" to Jung and to the Munich meeting of 1913: "There is no doubt that at the time he was feeling bitterly disappointed at Jung's defection. It cost him an inward struggle to control his emotions . . ." (Jones 1955, p. 366). Jones concluded that Freud had identified himself with Moses (the father) in order to emulate the victory over passion, that the mob was the dissenters (rebellious sons), chiefly Adler and Jung, and that the tablets were the central tenets of psychoanalysis. Jones's interpretation is as allegorical as it is psychoanalytic.

But the thematic content of this scene is only minimally oedipal. Freud was chiefly interested in a man's successful struggle against an inward passion in the face of disappointment and loss. Moses may indeed have been a "primal father" enraged with his sons, but Freud's analysis singles out affront to his values and injury to his esteem as well as oedipal rebellion. The "inward passion" is narcissistic rage. Yet even this view tells only a little, for it is devoted entirely to the scene's manifest content. Furthermore, at the outset Freud himself declared that his essay was an effort of interpretation, and he set himself the task of "divining," so to speak, the meaning of "the Moses" and inferring from that the hidden intentions of the artist. Drawing upon the conventional distinction between form and content, it can be said that the form of this essay is easily as indicative of Freud's mental state at the time as its content. To make this point it is necessary to explain the psychology of interpretation in Freud's paper and the key to that psychology, its implicit theory of movement.

Freud did not approach the statue as a subject entirely separate from an object, like a behavioral psychologist. Instead, his approach was strongly empathic. It is difficult to become empathic toward a statue or a painting because of its static, inanimate appearance. Unlike literary works, which have an aural dimension, the plastic arts are encountered visually, and hearing engages the unconscious far more directly than seeing. However, empathic activity in the presence of plastic forms is facilitated by the imaginative construction of movement. There is an important connection between movement understood as a physical action and movement understood in the psychological sense of "being moved," that is, being stirred or affected. Indeed, Freud in effect confirmed this connection when he placed himself in front of the statue and then used his own unconscious fantasy life to reconstruct a series of dramatic actions. As if to illustrate this very point, he said of one such moment: "I can recollect my own disillusionment when, during my first visits . . . I used to sit down in front of the statue in the expectation that I should now see how it would start up on its raised foot, dash the Tables of the Law to the ground and let fly its wrath" (Freud 1914a, p. 220).

Then, by thinking intently—but not focally, and more in the fashion of free-floating attention—on seemingly insignificant details of the work, such as a particular finger in relation to a strand of "the mighty beard," the position of the head or arms, the angle at which the tablets rested, and so forth, Freud was, he said, able to construct the physical movements which Moses had carried out "before" he decided to remain frozen in his wrath forever. In the midst of this analysis Freud disclosed the key to his entire approach by exclaiming, "In imagination we complete the scene of which this movement . . . is a part" (1914a, p. 224). He then continued by proposing his view of the biblical narrative, already noted. In such fashion was Freud able to make the statue "come alive," that is to say, to move in a physical sense, and then to allow it to move him in an emotional sense. Freud was not simply a subject projecting his intentionality upon an object. Rather, his mental activity at the time was that of merger making. To use E. H. Gombrich's famous distinction, he was "making" rather than "matching" (Gombrich 1961). His was an imaginative achievement which required a psychological merger with a highly esteemed and widely shared cultural object. In this sense, the statue temporarily became for him a self-object.

Further support for this analysis comes from an unlikely source— Rorschach psychology. Suppose one were to conceive of Freud, gazing upon the statue for long periods of time, as a test situation in which the subject (S = Freud) is confronted with a plate (= the statue) in which the examiner (= "we") asks, What might this be? In such a case Freud's own conception of what he was doing ("in imagination we complete the scene"), coupled with his attempt to reconstruct movement, confirms the essentially projective character of his efforts. In the context of the three major variables of the test (Form, Color, Movement) Freud clearly created a strong movement response with associated very good form.

Following Rorschach closely, Samuel Beck has characterized M, as opposed to F and C, as representing "very deep wishes, innermost psychological activity" (Beck 1961, p. 72), a kind of *"feeling oneself into the movement"* (p. 75). The M expresses "something that S is living and that has an engrossing emotional significance for him. S cannot, however, face this fear or the wish consciously" (p. 76). Ernest Schachtel's "experiential" reformulation of Rorschach's psychology heavily emphasizes self-processes or their equivalent. Schachtel states that M differs from perception because in the case of M the subject knows the object "from inside, how the human figure seen in the inkblot moves or holds its posture. It is as if he (the subject) were, for a moment and to some extent, inside the figure seen" (1966, p. 196). Schachtel characterizes such knowing as "the act of kinaesthetic empathy" which is expressive of "the core of the personality" (1966, p. 196). In M and in the construction of movement, "something akin to one's own experience is felt in the other person. . . . It is in this spirit that Goethe once remarked that there exists no crime of which he could not imagine himself capable" (1966, p. 202).

But Freud not only took the statue of Moses as a self-object; he also to some extent dissolved this attachment to it or broke it up. This observation adds psychological depth and nuance to the psychoanalytic truism that Freud identified with Moses many times throughout his life. Freud allowed all his lifelong fantasies, conscious and unconscious, about Moses to collect around Michelangelo's statue. In this, he concretized and brought to summation his identification with the Moses of biblical history and legend. Then, by engaging in the arduous work of interpretation, he was able to bring to consciousness much of this material and thereby rescue the unconscious appeal which the figure of Moses had for him. Put in another way, by detaching himself or separating himself psychologically from the imago of Moses, which he so idealized, Freud also underwent a de-idealization of Moses at this time, as well, through the medium of interpretive action. The biblical Moses and his God, YHWH, both gave in to their passion, whereas the Moses of Michelangelo and the Moses of Freud did not. But Freud's relation to the image of Moses should not be separated from his sense of the Christian tradition, for together these constituted the cultural heritage of his time. Two important points in his paper support this view, his analysis of Michelangelo's motives in relation to the pope whose tomb the statue adorned and his empathic approval of the artist's perceptions.

As I have already noted, Freud opened his paper by declaring it to be primarily an essay in interpretation. By this he meant that only a disclosure of the artist's intention could reveal "what grips us so powerfully." The artist aims "to awaken in us the same emotional attitude, the same mental constellation as that which in him produced the impetus to create . . . until I have accomplished that interpretation I cannot come to know why I have been so powerfully affected" (1914a, p. 212). But even after his own interpretation (Moses struggled successfully against an inward passion, rather than giving in to it), toward the close of the paper, Freud remained dissatisfied. Something was still missing. He continued to wonder *why* the artist created a portrait of Moses so at odds with the biblical one in which Moses did surrender to his passions, did smash the tablets, and did vent his wrath on the unruly Hebrews. The answer was simple. Julius II (the statue of Moses adorned this pope's tomb) was, Freud said, an ambitious and ruthless man. He wanted to unite Italy single-handedly under papal supremacy; "He worked alone, with impatience . . . and used violent means." He was subject to "sudden anger and . . . utter lack of consideration for others." Michelangelo also shared these traits, but Freud noticed that he was also "the more introspective thinker" and that he was able to carve his statue partly as "a reproach against the dead pontiff," partly "as a warning to himself, thus, in self-criticism rising superior to his own nature" (1914a, p. 234).

When the paper is taken as a whole so as to include this last discussion, it becomes clear that Freud was as interested in the inner world of Michelangelo as he was in the psychological portrait of the biblical Moses. It was Michelangelo who had struggled successfully against an inward passion, who was "more introspective," and it was he who had created a Moses more to Freud's liking and had "reproached" a Christian leader. These were psychological activities with which Freud too was struggling inwardly, in relation to Jung—and, one should add, in relation to Abraham as well—when he completed the thinking for this brilliant essay in Rome, only weeks after the disastrous Munich meeting of 1913. The outcome was a partial de-idealization of his own Judaism, symbolized by the Moses legend, and an attempt to work through by working over his idealization of Jung, symbolized by the ambitious, ruthless, and inconsiderate pontiff. As he had remarked to Abraham, he believed that the source of Jung's resistance to his ideas lay in Jung's Christian education. In this essay Freud reproached these two "universal" Western cultural and religious symbols and de-idealized them by creating a psychological interpretation of an artistic work which combined both. In doing so, he also inaugurated the second creative advance of his life's work, the psychoanalytic interpretation of Western cultural experience. Indeed, with "The Moses" the "cultural texts" were officially inaugurated.

This interpretation of the final pages of Freud's essay is further supported by recalling his lifelong ambivalence toward a maternal presence, for the Christianity of the Roman church embodies this presence. Freud alternately envied, hated, and longed for the Roman church's "lie of salvation," with its illusory promise of immortality, a promise which even the city of Rome itself sometimes unconsciously symbolized for him. As is well known, the promise of immortality comes close to the essence of all religions, and Freud at times personalized this promise through what I call his "death anxiety." So, when confronted with an artist and a pontiff, he had powerful conscious reasons for repudiating the latter. The following discussion of Freud's so-called Rome neurosis develops this argument in detail.

A second reason for this view—which unfortunately cannot be discussed in detail—lies in the complex relations between art, science, and religion which Freud envisioned throughout his life. He approved of Goethe's maxim that he who has art and science also has religion. As he repeatedly emphasized, the poets prefigured artistically what psychoanalysis knows scientifically, and both oppose religion. This interplay (between science, art, and religion) is seen with great clarity in Freud's paper on Leonardo, which has all too often been read simply as the first psychobiography (Freud 1910*b*). Such a reading obscures Freud's repeated noting, in the paper, of Leonardo's firm repudiation of religion as well as his enormous admiration for the brilliant artist-scientist. The reason for this particular conviction is not difficult to ascertain. From the psychoanalytic point of view, art and science are two different ways of talking about the same thing: the roots of human imagination in the unconscious of the individuating person. On the other hand, religion is concerned with the social control of individuality by collective forces and with an overvaluation of the conscious will at the expense of unconscious processes, whether these are personal or social. Therefore, throughout his psychoanalytic career Freud associated art with science and juxtaposed both to religion. And so when presented with a concrete, historical instance of this juxtaposition—that of a brilliant artist to a forceful prelate—he would be most likely to identify with the former.[7]

There remains only one further issue in Freud's life and thought at this time which the concept of de-idealization can clarify, his so-called Rome neurosis. Although he overcame this conflict in 1901, the city continued to have special symbolic significance for him throughout his life, and the fact that he wrote "On Narcissism" and worked out his interpretation of the statue of Moses during this, the sixth of his seven visits, belongs psychologically to the original conflict. I think that Freud's activities in Rome in 1913 linked together for the first time two crucial facets of his life and thought, the psychological and the historical. The psychological facet consisted in an unconscious search for a maternal presence and an unconscious dread of its absence, activated in the self-analysis and transferred to Rome. In Rome in 1913 Freud grappled for the first time directly and seriously with the challenge which historical circumstance posed to his psychoanalysis in the form of the Christian culture of the West. At this time he began his attempt to transform his clinical-analytic ideas into social and historical reality.

It is well known that Freud evolved an intense wish-fear for Rome during his self-analysis: "My longing for Rome," he wrote to Fliess, "is deeply neurotic" (Freud 1954, p. 236). One of the fruits of the self-analysis was the capacity to visit Rome, which he called "an overwhelming experience . . . a high-spot in my life" (p. 335), and it was during his visit that he viewed Michelangelo's statue for the first time. There is little evidence about the next three visits—in 1902 with his brother Alexander; in 1907, alone; and in 1910 with Ferenczi—but the remaining three were of great importance.

In the summer of 1912, a time when his personal relationship to Jung had become increasingly strained (they broke off personal relations in January 1913), Freud's physical and psychological well-being was poor. But when he reached Rome in September, he wrote to Jones, "I feel strengthened and relieved by the air and the impressions of this divine town. In fact I have been more happy than healthy in Rome, but my forces are coming back" (Jones 1955, p. 95). To Martha he wrote, "It feels quite natural to be in Rome; I have no sense of being a foreigner here" (p. 96). And he paid his daily visits to the statue of Moses. I have already cited Freud's praises of Rome to Abraham during the 1913 visit (he did not write to Abraham from Rome in 1912), when Jung's defection had become imminent. Other letters from Rome during both visits depicted enhanced psychological well-being—restored self-esteem and the absence of social alienation—and idealization of the city. Rome meant many things to Freud.

Jones guessed that Freud's love of Rome was due simply to his ever-present desire to get away from Vienna for good. He had expressed the wish to his wife that they eventually retire to Rome. But Jones also offered his obligatory oedipal view: Freud's identification with Hannibal (the son) and his wish to triumph over despotic religious authority (the father). Jones connected all this to Freud's analysis of his de-realization on the Acropolis in 1904: an unconscious wish to surpass his father, which also resembled being wrecked by success.

Gedo, however, introduced pregenital issues into the Rome question. He noted Erikson's observation of "strong components of mother transference" which were "not understood by Freud at that time" (1968, p. 294) in the Fliess relationship. Gedo thinks that these components derived from Freud's move from his childhood home in Moravia at age three and that the death of Freud's brother Julius when Freud was only nineteen months old also disrupted "his unusually close relationship to his doting mother" (pp. 294–95). Although Freud had sufficiently decathected his father transference to Fliess at the close of his self-analysis, this unresolved pregenital longing for his mother persisted in the form of travels to the south, and especially to Rome. Because this "prehistoric" level of Freud's psyche was not interpretable, Gedo views the travels as acting out in the service of mastery, analogous to his grandson's famous "fort-da" experience reported in *Beyond the Pleasure Principle*. Rome, Gedo concludes, was also a transitional object serving to reduce the anxiety of separation from his mother. Gedo does not, however, mention Rome in his more recent analyses of Freud's break with Jung (1983).

Stolorow and Atwood have advanced this line of thinking even further by proposing that Freud's periodic reactivation of pregenital, narcissistic issues, established earlier in relation to Fliess, Breuer, Martha, and —earliest of all—with his mother, profoundly colored his relationship with Jung as well. They also propose that the writing of the tripartite metapsychology was a defense against the perception of these forces. Following up on my own conclusion that Freud thought out his merger and de-idealizing vis-à-vis Jung in "On Narcissism" and played it out hermeneutically in "The Moses," it is now possible to see the rich though tangled interplay in Freud's mind at this time between "mother," "merger," "Jung," and "Rome." When in Rome, Freud always recovered, almost instantaneously, his self-regarding tendency or narcissistic balance, which had been lost during the times preceding his visits and which, one must now conclude, lured him to Rome.

On one hand, we see Freud the man gratifying his needs, wishes, and longings in Rome at this time. On the other hand, we also see in Rome the historical embodiment of the culture of the Western world into which he wished to thrust his psychoanalysis. It is very difficult to overemphasize Kohut's observation that, while Freud consciously wished eagerly for this to happen, he unconsciously dreaded it (1976). Consciously, Freud wished for the universalizing of his psychoanalysis, its acceptance by Western, Christian culture, but unconsciously he dreaded abandoning the supportive particularism of the original Jewish-Viennese context in which the historical expansion of psychoanalysis was still embedded. Jung was, to put it bluntly, to do it all for him. But Jung had "defected." Now Freud was faced with what seemed to him an impossible task. Linking Freud's struggle with Jung and the unwelcoming world of Christian, Catholic culture in Rome is the figure of the mother. Psychoanalytic thought has conceptualized this figure in different ways: idealized parental imago or self-object (Kohut), the good-enough mother and the anxiety-reducing transitional object (Winnicott), or the hallucinatory sense of unity with a maternal matrix, to use Erikson's lyrical phrasing. I will speak simply of "a maternal presence."

Freud experienced Rome consciously in three ways. As he explained to Fliess upon returning from his first visit in 1901 (1954): "I contemplated ancient Rome undisturbed. . . . I could have worshipped the . . . remnant of the Temple of Minerva. . . . I found I could not freely enjoy the second Rome; I was disturbed by its meaning, and, being incapable of putting out of my mind my own misery and all the other misery which I know to exist, I found almost intolerable the lie of the salvation of mankind which rears its head so proudly to heaven. I found the third, Italian, Rome hopeful and likeable" (pp. 335–36). But these impressions should be supplemented by the psychoanalytic understanding of Rome's unconscious significance for Freud. Freud was struggling with his own deeper, pre-oedipal longings which had been attached to Jung, and he had engaged these with great intensity while writing "The Moses," with its concluding reproach of the pontiff. How did Rome come to symbolize in Freud's mind a maternal presence, and in what way was that presence conflated with Jung? Clearly ancient Rome (the first Rome) embodies a "good mother" which Freud could revere through the medium of artistic illusion. But Christian Rome (the second Rome) also embodied a far more explicit maternal presence, and it is this which concerns us here.

From the psychological point of view, the ethos of Christian Rome is to be found in the collective presence of its priesthood and in the fact that every priest represents to society a very special relationship between a man and his mother. The conventional oedipal understanding of this cultural fact avers that the priest's celibacy is due to his renunciation of sexual wishes first for his mother and later for other women, and his sublimation of both into religious piety. But, in a more primitive sense, a priest is also a man who never severs as completely as do others the mother tie—that is, he never entirely renounces his merger with his mother, and so she remains "a part of" him and he of her. Both journalists and the mass audience unconsciously understand this psychological fact. As if to underscore this recognition, when the achievement of a priest is the subject of mass-media coverage, he is often shown in the presence of his mother and is so admired. This psychological feature of the priesthood is the source of the Roman church's nurturant pastoral approach to its people and also of its rich symbolic apparatus, for the mass is a ritual which embodies and disguises unconscious mergers between the believer and Christ, the foundational sacred object of the church, as these are mediated by the chief sacerdotal figure, the priest.[8]

Since Freud was reluctant to engage consciously his own deeper, pre-oedipal attachments to maternal images, he would have had to experience the ethos of Christian Rome unconsciously as a temporary reassurance that such a bond might exist, if not in himself, then at least "in the world." On the other hand, Freud was sufficiently analytic in his thinking about himself, others, and life as to be suspicious of such a promise. Hence "the lie of salvation" and his repudiation of its narcissistic root (the lie rears its head "proudly" to heaven). So he reaffirmed his low estimate of Christian Rome, the universal symbol of maternal gratification, when he identified with "the more introspective" Michelangelo, who reproached the pontiff. In such fashion did Freud experience his ambivalence about unconscious wishes to merge pleasurably with a maternal presence which Rome embodied.

The link between Freud, Rome, and Jung is easy to establish and lies in the maternal features of Jung's personality and thought. Jung's theoretical-psychological preoccupation with the feminine and maternal portions of a man's mind—what he called a man's "anima"—is well known. This interest was expressive of his capacity to tolerate maternal-feminine components within his own person and is also found in his romantic appeal to creative, beautiful, and narcissistic young women who idealized him and with whom he formed psychological mergers (Homans 1979b). In this sense Jung could be unconsciously perceived to be like Rome, as the locus of a maternal presence.

Freud's subjective sense of who should accompany him to what he called "this divine town" further supports the view that he perceived Rome in this way. He usually felt the need of a feminine presence, at least during the more important visits. In 1912, also an important year in the crisis with Jung, he was in Rome with Ferenczi and wrote a card to Anna addressed to "my future travelling companion." He had plans, Jones said, to take her to Rome. In the crucial year of 1913, his sister-in-law, Minna, joined him. Much later, in 1923, upon learning of his carcinoma, he immediately took his Anna to Rome (the seventh and last trip).

Further evidence for Freud's fusion of Jung and Rome around the idea of a maternal presence lies in events surrounding a trip to Rome in September 1910. Freud had invited Ferenczi to travel with him. While in Rome with Ferenczi, Freud wrote a letter to Jung which reveals in an unexpectedly clear way the complex lines of relation between Freud, Jung, Rome, and nurturance:

> The trip has been very rich and has supplied several wish-fulfillments that my inner economy has long been in need of. Sicily is the most beautiful part of Italy and has preserved unique fragments of the Greek past, infantile reminiscences that make it possible to infer the nuclear complex. . . . My travelling companion is a dear fellow, but dreamy in a disturbing kind of way, and his attitude towards me is infantile. He never stops admiring me, which I don't

like, and is probably sharply critical of me in his unconscious when I am taking it easy. He has been too
passive and receptive, letting everything be done for
him like a woman, and I really haven't got enough
homosexuality in me to accept him as one. These
trips arouse a great longing for a real woman. (No.
212)

This frank letter may have had the purpose of reassuring Jung that he
(Freud) would not erotize their relationship; it may also have been a
momentary expression of Freud's wish for what he unconsciously
perceived to be the supportive, maternal presence of Jung.

Eager to accentuate the differences between Freud and Jung, analytic biography has failed to note that Jung, too, had a "Rome
neurosis." But he never overcame his. It would seem that Freud may
have invited Jung to join him in Rome, and that Jung had declined. As
he explained in September, 1910 (McGuire 1974): "Sicily is too far.
Furthermore, I have secret obligations to my unconscious . . . as regards Rome and the south. . . . Rome in particular is not yet
permitted to me, but it draws nearer and I even look forward to it at
odd moments" (no. 206). Many years later, while dictating his psychological autobiography (Jung 1961), Jung reminisced about the
significance of Rome for him at the time of his break with Freud. At
the close of his chapter "Travels," which recounted trips to North
Africa, India, and America, Jung remembered that in 1913, while on a
ship sailing past Rome, "I stood at the railing. Out there lay Rome,
the still smoky and fiery hearth from which ancient cultures had
spread. . . . There classical antiquity still lived in all its splendor and
ruthlessness." Then he mused in a prophetic vein about why people
visit Rome, and ended his chapter on a highly personal note: "If you
are affected to the depths of your being at every step by the spirit that
broods there . . . then it becomes another matter entirely. Even in
Pompeii unforseen vistas opened, unexpected things become conscious . . . which were beyond my powers to handle. In my old age—
in 1949—I wished to repair this omission, but was stricken with a
faint while I was buying tickets. After that, the plans for a trip to
Rome were once and for all laid aside" (1961, p. 288).

Just as they had shared many ideas together, and had shared psychologically parts of each other with each other, each man becoming
"a part of" the other for a while, so Freud and Jung also shared a
special relationship to Rome. For each, Rome was a powerful symbol
of historical and cultural forces, difficult to reckon with because of its
unconscious significance.

3   De-Idealization and Freud's Social Circumstance: Movement and Culture

It is the time-honored habit of psychoanalysis to prefer the individual over all large social formations: first the intrapsychical, then the interpsychical, and only after that groups and cultural forces, say the analysts. The intense and exclusive preoccupation with the transference and with the evolving introspective skills of the analysand are primary for the analytic situation, and these are the model for all subsequent "applications." When analysts turn to culture, they follow Freud and write about art, which evokes experiences of singularity and inner depth, rather than about groups, politics, and religion, which embody experiences of sameness and likeness. They prefer the unique to the typical.

So, most analytic studies of Freud's life and thought have centered upon his Beethoven-like individuality, his stature as a "great man" or a "monumental self," impervious to social conditions. Consequently, the psychoanalytic movement has come to be viewed as a mere voluntary association concerned only with instrumental, organizational issues. While these many idealizations of Freud's person have made it possible to understand his tremendous capacity to resist cultural forces, they have also deflected attention from the ways in which these very same forces may in fact have made an indelible mark upon him and his stance toward them.

But psychoanalysis also insists that the individual is social from his or her beginnings. The primacy and persistence of such key terms as identification, internalization, and introjection attest to this. The evolving mental apparatus is forever intertwined with "the other," be that the mother of the infantile dyad, the father of the childhood triad, or the social others of latency and adolescence. Object relations theory and self-psychology assert that the social actuality of the other is very early. So they also emphasize the developmental vicissitudes of socially shared unconscious psychic formations and processes. The British school has always been interested in groups, and Kohut could not separate his own interest in Freud's personality and the psychology of the self from the idea of a group self.

The second emphasis makes it possible to show that the Freud-Jung relationship belonged to a far wider context. Jung's significance for Freud was also sociological and cultural. Jung was attached to bourgeois European society in a way that Freud was not, and he identified with the regnant ideals of European Christian humanism in a way that Freud could not. And Freud knew this. That knowledge caused him consciously to wish for, and unconsciously to dread, the expansion of analysis beyond his Jewish-Viennese "circle." This so-called circle, the psychoanalytic movement, absorbed much of Freud's dread by mediating between his immediate attachments or mergers (e.g., with Jung and Abraham) and the surrounding sea of cultural and civilizational forces. Analysis became the raft he built to keep from being swept away by that sea. Therefore, any exploration of the cultural forces in Freud's life must begin with the movement, and the Freud-Jung relationship was the sociopsychological axis on which the movement turned during the 1906–14 period. The following analysis of the movement and its role in Freud's turn to culture is discussed again and built upon in part 2, where explicitly sociological considerations are introduced. For that to be done, psychological forces and issues should first be identified and clarified.

Understanding the Psychoanalytic Movement as a Group

When the men who became the first analysts were first moved by psychoanalytic ideas and came together to discuss the powerful forces of the unconscious with their admired teacher, disturbing introspective probes, multiple transferences, and other regressive phenomena were the inevitable result. While this fact is taken for granted by candidates and senior analysts alike in today's institutes, it was far more problematic for the first followers of Freud, who were denied the psychologically efficacious support of sociological institutionalization. In this case, it was inevitable that a group would be constructed which would "carry," so to speak, the surplus of unconscious intrapsychic and interpsychic conflict. It is simply not realistic to imagine that Freud's first followers were able to retain their premovement mental organization as moderately cohesive selves (Kohut) or as unit selves (Winnicott), although there can be no doubt that self-analysis and the brief analyses which some underwent helped a great deal. Rather, they would have had to undergo varying degrees of regression, which led to the unconscious sharing of psychical activities and to subsequent symbolic re-presentations of these activities within the frame of a group as a whole. Therefore, while the movement was certainly a professional society, it was also a group in the psychoanalytic sense, and the Freud-Jung relationship needs to be seen in the light of its group context. So I speak of the two together, as group/movement.

Kohut has speculated that, in the case of a group, "group processes are largely activated by narcissistic motives" (1976, p. 840). So understood, a group is composed of shared idealizations and mergers, such that the leader embodies the idealized parent imago and monitors the unintegrated portions of the archaic grandiose self of each member. A messianic leader superintends the shared ego-ideal; a charismatic leader, shared archaic grandiosity. Making use of Winnicott's thought, Didier Anzieu has evolved an elaborate empirical theory of groups which resembles Kohut's speculations (1984). Central to it is the concept of the group illusion: individual members share the unconscious conviction that they are fused together, that "we are one." This unconscious conviction supports the conscious, technical or rational problem-solving tasks which each member undertakes with a strong sense of individual separateness. Anzieu thinks that the phenomenon of a group illusion is modeled after the transitional object and that it functions in the deepest psychological sense to provide members with an unconscious sense of contact with the pregenital mother. Any threat to the solidarity and permanence of the group illusion appears as separation or "fragmentation" anxiety. Such anxiety takes many forms, a principal one being fantasies of breaking apart, or of being torn apart, sometimes even by wild animals.

Both Kohut and Anzieu emphasize the self-cohering effects of unconscious attachment to a group and, conversely, the self-fragmentation which follows upon separation from a group. Stolorow and Lachmann have observed (1980), clinically, that self-fragmentation is often linked to experiences of depersonalization, hypochondria, and death anxiety. It is therefore possible that an unconscious sense of impending separation from a group and from the maternal presence which it embodies can be experienced consciously as death anxiety. This formulation provides a clue to the social context of Freud's lifelong preoccupation with his own death and illumines further his relationships to the group/movement.

When it is understood as a group as well as a voluntary association, the psychoanalytic movement can be broken down into four stages

during the period 1906–14: the inception, consolidation, fragmentation, and reconstitution of its group illusion. The figure of Jung
occupied a central place in each stage. Taken together, the four stages
portray different patterns of three interwoven themes in Freud's self-
experience: group cohesion, maternal presence, and death anxiety.
As the fortunes of group cohesion waxed, they were experienced
consciously by Freud as enhanced esteem and self-cohesion, as joy in
being alive, and as a sense of unconscious contact with a maternal
presence; as they waned, they were experienced consciously as self-
enfeeblement and death anxiety and unconsciously as the loss of
contact with a maternal presence.

As in all important matters pertaining to Freud's life, Jones set the
tone for the prevailing view of the inception of the psychoanalytic
movement. Freud, he said, sought "a wider organization than a local
society" (1955, p. 67) in order to bring analysts together "in a closer
bond" (p. 69). Freud wanted "a broader basis for the work than could
be provided by Viennese Jewry" (p. 69). Internally, there were also
what must be called "terrible tensions." For example, early on Freud
stressed "the virulent hostility" everywhere, and on one occasion,
"dramatically throwing back his coat," he said that "my enemies
would be willing to see me starve; they would tear my very coat off
my back" (pp. 69–70). Ferenczi's behavior at the 1910 meeting was
appallingly dictatorial. Jones also reported that the Vienna Society
was "torn by jealousies and dissensions" (p. 86). As late as 1912 there
had been "a very ugly scene" between Stekel and Tausk, and Freud
referred to Tausk as a "wild beast" (p. 136).

In the face of such intense and unmanageable feelings, Freud's
proposal for a formal organizational structure and even for transferring that to Zurich made good group-psychological sense. But the
inception of the movement had a third source. Freud fused his sense
of self-esteem as an individual human being with the validity and
historical future of his psychoanalysis and invested both of these in
Jung. His idealizations of Jung were therefore not only interpsychic
but also transgenerational, a process which involves not only the
bureaucratic transfer of administrative authority but also the trans-
mission of a life essence, upon the death of the first party, to the
second. Freud made this quite clear in his historical paper (1914c).
"What I had in mind was to organize the psychoanalytic movement,
to transfer its centre to Zürich and to give it a chief [Oberhaupt] who
would look after its future career. . . . I was no longer young. . . . I
knew only too well the pitfalls that lay in wait for anyone who became engaged in analysis and hoped that many of them might be

avoided if an authority [*Autorität*] could be set up who would be prepared to instruct and admonish. . . . I felt the need of transferring this authority to a younger man who would then as a matter of course take my place after my death" (pp. 42–43). Writing to Binswanger as late as March 1911, Freud could say, "When the empire I founded is orphaned, no one but Jung must inherit the whole thing" (Binswanger 1957, p. 31). Freud's strongest idealizations of Jung occurred in that segment of their correspondence in which Jung's role as mitigator of Freud's isolation by means of extending the boundaries of Freud's self were inseparable from his role as the future leader of the psychoanalytic movement. Sometimes Freud even condensed psychological merger and group/movement into the same sentence. For example, in May 1908, he wrote to Jung: "These last few days I have been wondering how we might establish closer scientific ties between Zürich and Vienna, so as not to lose sight of each other between now and the next Congress" (no. 92). Designations such as "crown prince," "son and heir," and "Moses and Joshua" must be understood not simply to represent Freud's psychological merger with Jung; they also expressed the transgenerational wish that Jung carry Freud's own person and thought beyond the mortality of his life course. To the surface of organizational issues, valid in their own right, Freud attached deeper historical and symbolic significance.

Further evidence for this point of view comes, surprisingly, from Jones himself. Despite the regularity of his oedipal and as such "orthodox" psychological observations of Freud's life—and perhaps, on the very basis of these—his insights often open up, paradoxically, issues of self, a point I develop in part 2. Reflecting on the dreams Freud shared with Jung and Ferenczi during their American trip in 1909—dreams which Jung believed disclosed Freud's care and anxiety about the future of his children and of psychoanalysis—Jones observed: "These two ideas must have been closely associated, since there is much reason to suppose that in his unconscious his work in psychoanalysis ultimately represented some product of his body, i.e., a child. We [the Committee] were trustees for that child" (1957, p. 44).

It is possible to enhance this view with more genetic information than was available to Jones. Of the child struggling with issues of merger and idealization, Kohut has remarked that "the expected control over the mother and her ministrations is closer to the concept a grownup has of himself and of the control he expects over his own body and mind" (1966, p. 430). The reverse is also true: in moments of frustration and lapses of empathy, the mother may make a similar sort of demand of the child. Since narcissistic issues were present in Freud's relation to Jung—and Abraham—it seems likely that Freud's wish to control the fate of his psychoanalysis and the thinking and actions of those to whom he entrusted it were at moments as unconsciously primitive and intense as issues of control sometimes are between mother and child. Anzieu's observation that the group illusion provides members of the group with an unconscious shared transitional object and a shared sense of unconscious contact with a maternal presence lends additional support to this interpretation.

Two universal features of groups, jokes and stereotypes—both indicative of unconscious group processes—are also relevant here. As Freud was the first to note, jokes of course signify the disguised gratification of libidinal pleasure. But jokes also symbolize a shared unconscious matrix and a sharp sense of "us and them." When they are about the group's work, jokes enhance the cohesion of a group by shoring up its boundaries and consolidating its identifications. Periodically throughout his narrative, Jones mentions jokes specifically about analysis which the first analysts enjoyed telling to each other (1955, pp. 59; 163; 1957, p. 88). Freud's taste in jokes and his sense of humor consistently displayed a preference for wry, bitter, skeptical, tragic, and ironic themes, and these lay at the heart of his sense of life. His sensitivity to human grandiosity and to its inevitable disillusionments and his capacity to bridge the tensions between the two through humor constituted his style of life. I note one especially telling instance of Freud's use of humor to support his experiences of de-idealization at the close of this section.

Like jokes, stereotypes are also diagnostic for the presence of unconscious group processes. By means of the activity of typification, one person classifies another according to that person's likeness to a type.[1] In this fashion "the other" loses his personal uniqueness as he is gradually assigned symbolic, displaced significance. Jew and Christian, Viennese and Swiss, leader and dissenter, dissenter and follower—these were some of the more obvious stereotypes in the early years of the psychoanalytic movement. In the case of Jung, the stereotype of dissenter was paramount. Jung was in a personal and immediate sense just one man who disagreed with just one other man, Freud. But Jung was also "a dissenter," the heir to a string of typifications. Freud likened Adler to Fliess (McGuire 1974): "It is getting really bad with Adler . . . in me he awakens the memory of Fliess" (no. 223). Jung was terrified that Freud might come to think of him as another Adler (no. 320) and, alas, Freud did. Then Abraham came to view Jung as another Adler (Abraham and Freud 1965, p. 121), and finally Jones was able to exploit Jung's symbolic standing by likening Rank's deviations directly to those of Jung (Jones 1957, pp. 70, 77). Gradually Jung was given first stereotypical and then finally virtual archetypal significance in the movement: he became the "arch" dissenter. Such unconscious stereotyping simply does not take place in voluntary associations, in what Jones regularly referred to as a "circle." Although he had direct, personal access to this process, Jones continued to perceive only its surface, voluntary aspects. Therefore, it is correct to characterize his insistent use of the word "circle" as an instance of disavowal. The progressive assigning of badness to an individual, so that he comes to embody or encode symbolically the badness of a group as a whole, is of course an instance of what Melanie Klein described as projective identification.

One could reasonably infer from these group-psychological observations that others in the movement also wished to "dissent"— which is to say, have their own thoughts and realize their own creativity apart from Freud—but that they were afraid to. Beyond those of group psychology, however, there were even more powerful cultural forces which, by opposing the revolutionary understandings of human consciousness, reason, and will that psychoanalysis entertained, drove the first analysts into the defensive position of "group psychology." The "fragility of the enterprise" and the more sweeping forces which brought that about are taken up in the next section.

It is now possible to propose an explanation of Jung's symbolic significance for Freud within the context of the group/movement. Freud was the openly acknowledged leader and Jung the openly acknowledged next leader or heir. This arrangement assured the members of the group that psychoanalytic ideas, which they idealized, would not perish, nor would those portions of their own mental lives which were attached to many of these ideas. As long as Jung continued to carry out the life-historical task which Freud had assigned to him, group cohesion grew. Then Jung's theoretical innovations, his organizational laxities, and his increasingly distressing psychological alienation from Freud became more and more obvious. When the two men began to break up, the group illusion and the historical continuity into the future which it promised were threatened. Their shared existence called into question, members of the group experienced what Anzieu has called "fragmentation anxiety" or "breaking apart anxiety." Freud became profoundly apprehensive: his analytical "child" might not live, depriving him of the consolation for which he longed. His self-esteem diminished as these thoughts made him more anxious about his own mortality, and they took the new form of what I have called "death anxiety."

Because Freud's anxiety about the future of his analytical child was activated by Jung's defection, that anxiety cannot be separated from the creation of the famous Committee, which reintegrated the movement immediately after Jung's departure. Just before Jung left, several analysts sensed the need for a new and more flexible mechanism for mirroring Freud's fluctuating esteem and future creativity. In point of fact, that mechanism was already virtually in place and needed only to be mobilized. A tacit or unconscious contract was drawn up: Freud would give fresh psychoanalytic ideas and analytically toned support to the members of the Committee and to those parts of the world which saw fit to be interested; in return, the members would mirror Freud, assiduously withhold criticism and independence, and continue to work for the expansion of analysis along a nationalistic, colonial pattern. Freud confirmed all this when he wrote to Ferenczi in July 1913: "Let us carry on our work in calm self-confidence. That assurance that the children will be provided for, which for a Jewish father is a matter of life and death, I expected to get from Jung; I am glad now that you and our friends will give me this" (E. L. Freud, 1964, p. 302). As the editor of this letter explains, the word "children" did not refer to Freud's own children but to "the future of the psychoanalytic movement, the product of his mind." Freud expressed these feelings even more frankly to Jones: "I daresay it would make living and dying easier for me if I knew of such an association existing to watch over my creation" (Jones 1955, p. 153).

The formation of the Committee enhanced Freud's self-esteem, reduced his death anxiety, and made him feel that life was again worth living, in a very literal sense. Jones noted that while the Committee was important to Freud scientifically and administratively, its significance was "above all" personal. "The ever-hopeful Freud," he said, responded to the idea of the committee "with joy." To Abraham, Freud wrote, "You cannot know what happiness [the Committee] gives me." And in two letters to Eitingon, quoted by Jones (1955), he disclosed the linkage between his fear that he would die, his "child" (psychoanalysis), and the support of the Committee: "The secret of this Committee is that it has taken from me my most burdensome care for the future, so that I can calmly follow my path to the end. . . . The care that weighs me down about the future I can best convey to you genetically. It comes from the time when psychoanalysis depended on me alone, and when I was so uneasy about what the human rabble would make out of it when I was no longer alive. In 1912, when we saw an example of these possibilities, the Committee was formed. . . . Since then I have felt more light-hearted and care-free about how long my life will last" (p. 154).

The contents of the shared "secret" was simple: anyone who wished to depart from "the fundamental tenets of psychoanalytical theory" would discuss his plan with the others before declaring himself publicly. In referring to the secret of the Committee, Freud meant only its conscious meaning for him. But the idea of secrecy had far more profound psychological significance. Jones proposed a "secret council," and Freud insisted that it had to be "strictly secret," and he offered to keep "the utmost secrecy." With his customary disregard for narcissistic issues, Jones brushed aside any deeper significance to this idea of a secret society: "The whole idea of such a group had of course its prehistory in my mind: stories of Charlemagne's paladins from boyhood, and many secret societies from literature." And Freud did the same: "I know there is a boyish and perhaps romantic element too in this conception, but perhaps it could be adapted to meet the necessities of reality" (Jones 1955, pp. 152–154). For Jones and Freud the purpose of such secrecy was simply to facilitate the administrative advancement of the psychoanalytic movement. But what was its depth-psychological purpose?

The answer to this question lies, I think, in the psychology of persecution. Winnicott has proposed that the psychological essence of democracy, in contrast to that of authoritarian regimes, is the secret ballot, for it protects the individual from physical persecution and at the same time psychologically prevents the true self from becoming twisted into a false self by the forces of a conformist and totalitarian social milieu (Winnicott 1950). In this sense, secrecy authorizes and supports inner or psychological space and the capacity to construct transitional objects, thereby enhancing the potential to remain a unit self. The committee worked with the equivalent of a secret ballot. Consequently, each member's potential for persecutory behavior was reduced, thereby reassuring the others, and no member of the Committee needed to fear that he would be persecuted, as Jung had been.

The Committee became a smoothly functioning group within the more loosely organized movement, a kind of shared unit self (all members identifying in the ego), into which Freud merged himself as the leader (playing the part of the ego-ideal). In this way the Committee virtually took the place of Jung's previous psychological significance for Freud, somewhat after the fashion of a replaceable part. As a result of these cathectic shifts in Freud's immediate personal surroundings, his transference of creativity, begun with Fliess, repeated with Jung, and reactivated further in Rome when he took Michelangelo's statue as self-object, was once again allowed to flower. I have already referred to Freud's subsequent production of the metapsychological papers and the turn to culture and the creation of the protocultural texts. An equally interesting hypothesis, which cannot be pursued here, is that Freud's experiences with the Committee served as the genetic stimulus for the writing of *Group Psychology and the Analysis of the Ego,* a paper often cited today, along with "On Narcissism," as an anticipation of ideas found in self psychology and in psychoanalytic group theory. The Committee was not as ideological a group as were the church and the army, described in his essay, for it permitted dissent.[2]

The prominence of de-idealization in Freud's life and thought at this time suggests that it describes a very profound, perhaps even essential feature of his personality and character. Freud coupled his capacity to express openly many of his idealizations and a reluctant readiness to alter them and to undergo disappointment or disillusionment with a related capacity to tolerate and support the destruction and loss of his ideals without undergoing permanent isolation or cynicism. He repeatedly unified these two through the imaginative use of humor. This trait earned for him the applause of his followers, and this trait accounts for such epithets as "heroic" and "Herculean."

This feature of Freud's style of life is nowhere better seen than in the closing sentence of his polemical essay, "On the History of the Psychoanalytic Movement," written at the same time as "On Narcissism" and "The Moses." The object of his wrath was of course Jung, to whom he had entrusted his life's work and, in some more subtle sense, a part of his inner life itself, and who had failed him. So Freud wrote (1914c): "In conclusion, I can only express a wish that fortune may grant an agreeable upward journey to all those who have found their stay in the underworld of psychoanalysis too uncomfortable for their taste. The rest of us, I hope, will be permitted without hindrance to carry through to their conclusion our labors in the depths" (p. 66). Freud's sentences first fused religious myths of the resurrection; then he inserted Jung into this scenario, Jung's presence being felt all the more strongly by virtue of his recent absence; finally, Freud wittily demythologized—that is to say, disillusioned— what he had come to perceive to be his enemy's lofty unconscious religious aspirations and even parodied, for still further effect (a mock de-idealization), his own theory of wish fulfillment. The master at his best, I dare say. But admiration should not mask the origins of this artful conceit in its author's bitter disappointment at having been abandoned by someone he had loved.

Politics and Religion as Cultural Forces

The psychological dimension of disillusionment was also prominent in Freud's encounter with the broader and more sweeping social circumstances which at first dwarfed his little movement. From the commonsense point of view, nothing is as impersonal, permanent, and nonpsychological as culture. From the psychological point of view, however, even culture is constructed, and discerning the constructed character of culture was a task which forced itself upon Freud with increasing urgency at the end of the 1906–14 period. Two cultural forces which bore in upon Freud with heightened intensity at this time were politics and religion. At first both inspired his hopes, but then each provoked intense disappointment. Freud's response to these forces tells us something about the motivation to write the so-called cultural texts of the 1920s and 1930s. In all this the *"odium Jungium"* and the psychoanalytic group/movement continued to have their own special places.

Politics and religion were more often than not mixed in Freud's life. Both were powerful social forces, composed of conscious ideals and unconscious desires, with which Freud had to contend in order to make his new ideas acceptable. As a youth, he had placed high hopes in German liberalism; as a young adult, he felt it failed him entirely. Earlier in his life, Jewish communal life served Freud as a source of self-esteem and social identity; later, he came to see it more as a social context from which he gradually had to detach himself. Christianity on the other hand had powerful but entirely negative significance. Earlier, Freud had perceived it simply as an inspiration for politically toned anti-Semitism; later, it became for him a normative pattern of thought and experience which, because it contradicted the perceptions of psychoanalysis, had to be addressed more and more directly.

Despite Freud's unambiguous references to "the cause," to "my politics," and of course to "the movement"—all terms he himself chose—Jones attempted systematically to disassociate Freud and the group/movement from both politics and religion. His was what can be called the "ur-anxiety" of all the first and most of the subsequent analysts, the dread-laden thought that psychoanalysis might come to be perceived by the surrounding culture "as a religion." But Jones's efforts were only the culmination of a long tradition of Freud biography which has sought to distinguish sharply between Freud as German, Viennese, and scientific and Freud as Jewish and therefore religious (Miller 1981).[3] David Bakan (1958), Marthe Robert (1976), and John Murray Cuddihy (1974) reversed this pattern, although none took a historical approach. These three works are discussed in more detail in part 2 in conjunction with the social origins of the self-analysis. Quite recently, however, Dennis Klein (1981) has written a strictly historical study of the influence of politics and religion on Freud's life before 1902, arguing convincingly that both profoundly affected him during the most creative period. Klein's study is an invaluable source for understanding the social circumstances in 1906–14, for the forces at play during this time are transformations of those of the most creative period. Klein's theory also lends itself to psychological reflection.

Throughout Freud's youth and up to the 1880s (he was twenty-four in 1880), German political liberalism had successfully advocated the values of human freedom and social rationality. So German Jews had the opportunity to assimilate: "In government, the press, and the arts, Jews embraced German culture and German political ideals" (Klein 1981, p. 6). During his years of secondary education, Freud sought this worldly acceptance and came to understand himself more as German than as Jew. Although Freud took courses at the gymnasium on the Hebrew Bible from Samuel Hammerschlag, he evolved an entirely ethical and humanistic understanding of religion. Totally skeptical of religious authority and scripture, he was "Godless, but ethical—and German" (p. 42). Both politics and religion supported an assimilationist identity or social self-concept and humanitarian and universalistic ideals.

But after 1880, the Austrian state gradually took a distinctly anti-Semitic turn. Being an East European Jew was singled out as a special form of disgrace. Opposition to Jews increased and spread into the major sectors of public life. It culminated in the papacy's insistence (but against the wishes of the emperor) in 1897 upon the election of Karl Lüger, who had campaigned for mayor of Vienna on a platform of anti-Semitism. The disintegration of German political liberalism forced Freud to abandon his assimilationist hopes and to seek a new basis for social self-respect and social identity. By the mid-1880s Freud was deeply disappointed and disillusioned by liberalism. He "mourned the escalation of anti-Semitism in a deeply personal way" (Klein 1981, p. 59). So bitter was he that, throughout the 1880s, he "had a low estimation of non-Jews and expressed the desire to remain separate from, indeed above, them" (p. 62). His disappointment led him to search out other Jews as a source of emotional support, pride, energy, courage, and self-defense.

Klein thinks that these shifts motivated Freud's scientific collaboration with Breuer in a way that has not yet been understood: Breuer "was the most important single influence in shaping Freud's growing pride in his Jewish heritage as well as his sense of Jewish unity" (p. 58). Freud sought advice from Breuer on personal and Jewish matters and depended upon him "like a son." In this regard Breuer served as a new edition of Freud's earlier relationships with his father and Samuel Hammerschlag. Fliess too belonged to this complementary series. Klein thinks that Freud wrote the metapsychology in "The Project," as well as *The Interpretation of Dreams*, in order to discover "a uniform structure of the psyche" which would characterize all people and thereby make sense out of "the chaos and divisiveness of his social environment" (p. 71). Finally, Freud's gradual turn to Jewish friends and to the sense of belonging and Jewish self-identity that these associations conferred upon him provided the energy which initially fueled the psychoanalytic movement, giving it the character of what I have referred to as group/movement.

Although he rightly eschews psychological ideas, Klein cannot avoid making generous use of such words as "disappointment," "disillusionment," and "identification" to describe Freud's responses to his political and religious surroundings. Drawing upon Klein's descriptions and my own delineation of experiences of de-idealization in Freud's life, I now propose the following abbreviated interpretation of Freud's most creative period in preparation for understanding the events of the period under discussion (the self-analysis is discussed again in much greater detail in part 2). The self-analysis did not take place in "splendid isolation." There was, it seems, a movement before "the movement," a group before "the group." It was composed of Freud's identifications, idealizations, and mergers with Hammerschlag, Breuer, Fliess, and other men and was rooted in their shared sense of Jewishness. In the midst of this movement-before-the-movement psychoanalysis was "discovered." But as we also know, Freud also progressively de-idealized his father, Fliess, and Breuer. Therefore, the "origins" of psychoanalysis did not lie, as Freud feared, and as Jung and Bakan, among others, have implied, in a Jewish national affair, nor did psychoanalysis spring from the pure, ratiocinative efforts of Freud's mind, as Freud and Jones said and as most analysts continue to believe. Rather, something more complex occurred. As Freud gradually de-idealized the Jewish men to whom he had attached himself, he broke up his identifications and mergers with them and the community of heritage which they embodied to some degree. As Freud detached himself from these friends, a psychological vacuum was formed, and Freud filled this vacuum with his creative intellectual and scientific constructions. So the origin of psychoanalysis was related to "Jewishness" after the fashion of a key to its wax impression or a statue to a plaster cast of the statue— psychoanalysis emerged as the negative image, so to speak, of its Jewish surroundings.

While the concept of de-idealization is the right one to explain the psychology of the most creative period, it cannot account for its historical aspect. For this, one must go to sociology and in particular to the idea of an "internal relation" between two social forces: the Jewish community to which Freud was loyal and physical science. These forces represented the ideal and the real, or material, in history. Freud drew upon both and then resolved the tension between both by creating a "third term," psychoanalytic psychology. In so doing he created a new and unique historical reality. I take the phrase "internal relation" from Max Weber, who used it to characterize noncausal connections between the Protestant ethic and the spirit of capitalism (Weber 1904–5). These connections were hidden from the awareness of the actors in history (the early Protestants), who nonetheless creatively produced a new human relation to the material world (capitalism) under the pressure of a religious ethic.

Freud repeated his de-idealization of a Jewish context in a second social setting, when he joined the B'nai B'rith in 1897. There, religious and scientific issues continued to play themselves out in his mind. He immediately presented the germ of his theory of dreams to men he called his "brothers." During the next several years he spoke on other closely related psychological subjects, sometimes before publishing them. But only much later, in 1926, did he explain to the lodge why he joined them when he did. His insights into the unconscious, he said, had made him feel outlawed and shunned, and so he longed for "a circle of excellent men with high ideals." Then he disclosed an even deeper, more emotional reason (E. L. Freud 1964): "Whenever I have experienced feelings of national exaltation, I have tried to suppress them as disastrous and unfair, frightened by the warning example of those nations among which we Jews live. But there remained enough to make the attraction of Judaism and the Jews irresistible, many dark emotional powers [*viele dunkle Gefühlsmächte*] all the stronger the less they could be expressed in words [*umso gewaltiger, je weniger sie sich in Worten erfassen liessen*], as well as the clear consciousness of an inner identity [*ebenso wie die klare Bewusstheit der inner Identität*], the familiarity of the same psychological structure [*die Heimlichkeit der gleichen seelishen Konstruktion*]. . . . So I became one of you" (pp. 366–67). Strachey translated "*die Heimlichkeit der gleichen see-*

lischen Konstruktion" as "the safe privacy of a common mental construction" (Freud 1926, p. 274). I think the Sterns's rendition is closer to the mark.

Clearly, Freud acknowledged here his perception of B'nai B'rith as a group self (social locus of "national exaltation"), his fear of collective behavior ("the warning example"), his reluctance to reflect upon it analytically ("dark emotional powers" which could not be "expressed in words"), and his identification with the Jews in the group ("the same psychological structure"). In the late 1890s Freud idealized and merged with this group and allowed it to support him by mirroring his displays of intellectual boldness, thereby greatly enhancing his lowered self-esteem. But, as soon as his work had been published (by 1902), he drastically reduced his contact with the lodge, just as he had withdrawn from Breuer and Fliess, for he no longer needed their support. In attaching himself to and then detaching himself from Jewish friends and later the B'nai B'rith, Freud first idealized and then de-idealized a historical and cultural force. In this instance his transference of creativity took an entire group, rather than a single individual, as its object. But as his letter points out, he never gave up this attachment entirely, either because he thought it unanalyzable or because he simply did not choose to work analytically with this portion of his mental life.

Jones of course saw nothing in all this and only claimed that Freud went to the B'nai B'rith meetings for "relaxation." So Jones discussed the meetings in the course of his chatty, informal summaries of Freud's hobbies and vacations (1953, pp. 329–30). As I have already mentioned, the only word Jones could think of for collective behavior of any sort was a "circle," but he chiefly used this term to describe the men who began to gather around Freud after 1902 and before the Vienna Psychoanalytic Society of 1908 and the "International" of 1910. Klein points out that everyone in this circle of twenty men was a Jew, until Jung and Binswanger visited it in 1907. Jones entered in 1908. Freud's attachment to this group was so strong, Klein adds, that "when non-Jews first entered the movement, he responded with an uncomfortable feeling of 'strangeness' " (1981, p. 93). Freud's remarks to Abraham about their "consanguineous Jewish traits," cited earlier, also belong here.

From 1908 onward, Freud gradually attempted to disregard the particularities of Jewishness as a source of energy, pride, and group cohesion—that is, as a source of "movement." This meant yet another effort at gradual detachment from significant others, which led inevitably to a fresh sense of vulnerability. This new search for a more universal, rational, and less mythic context for support was accompanied by fear and dread of non-Jewish "strangers."

In the light of these developments, Jung's appearance on the scene in 1906 acquires considerable symbolic significance, well beyond interpersonal issues. By this time Freud had repeatedly idealized and subsequently detached himself from or de-idealized several very important men and groups. Jung was not simply a young, promising, enthusiastic—and unknown—psychiatrist; he also represented to Freud very strong attachments to European culture and to its Christian, humanistic heritage. Furthermore, he could claim to embody the clean, almost aseptic, tolerant internationalism which one stereotypically accords to the ever-neutral Swiss. The mutual idealization and group collaboration which followed were therefore drenched in the cultural symbols of the time. Nor did Freud hesitate to subordinate—perhaps a better word is sacrifice—his particularism to Jung's apparent universalism. He saw in Jung the ideal (the word is used deliberately) opportunity for the universalization of his psychoanalysis, beyond the confines of Viennese Jewry. And this is precisely what they discussed in their letters: the extension of psychoanalysis into medicine (the psychoses) and into culture (so both wrote books on religion, the most powerful historical force in Western culture). Psychological accounts of the intensity of Freud's idealization and de-idealization of Jung are enriched when they take into account the fact that Freud's many political and social needs at the time fitted, hand-in-glove, with Jung's social, political, and cultural attributes.

Anzieu (1984) has observed that a group serves to mediate between the inner life of the individual and the wider, culturally grounded world of everyday life. But everyday life is not the neutral and value-free average expectable environment of the reality principle. Everyday life is historically and culturally shaped. As a segment of shared transitional space, the psychoanalytic group/movement gave Freud some much-needed opportunity to keep the value-laden cultural world of politics and religion at some distance. But when Jung failed to fulfill his symbolic function as a path of access into this surrounding and unfriendly cultural world, Freud had to face that world more directly, without a mediating figure. Writing the paper on Moses in Rome allowed him to begin this work, for the statue embodied his own political and religious conflicts. Fascinated by the close juxtaposition of the biblical Moses and a Christian pope, Freud offered analytic observations on both. A sense of disappointment must have surrounded these reflections. Did not the Catholic church symbolize the unity of Western civilization in its ethic of universal love? And had it not artfully condensed this ethic with anti-Semitism? And did not belief in the Moses of legend forestall reflection on the Moses of history? So, writing this paper helped Freud clarify further his personal relationship to the image of Moses. While it is true that Freud identified with Moses from time to time throughout his life, he also at this time wished to free himself from this "imago," for it was the symbolic embodiment of that Jewish community whose particularism he now realized he had to renounce. Disenchanting the image of Moses freed him psychologically for what I have called the group/movement. This may well be the reason why Freud chose to publish his paper anonymously: he simply did not want entirely to break his identification with his Jewish community.

In 1914, as a result of powerful, psychological conflicts with Jung and within the psychoanalytic movement, Freud's thought took two new directions. He centered more directly on the idea of narcissism, and he felt the need to reflect more explicitly and more consciously upon the social forces which surrounded him and upon their political and religious manifestations. Taking the image of Moses as a self-object and making psychological interpretations of Judaism and Catholicism were creative efforts in this direction. This effort prepared him for reflection on culture and religion from the point of view of the psychology of narcissism and on the role of social forces in the organization of the mind. As time went on, Freud came to think of religion as an even greater obstacle to the historical—rather than to the simply clinical—success of his psychoanalysis. This trend reached its first open articulation in 1916 in what I call "the three blows theory" of Western history and culture. In it Freud explicitly defined religion as a narcissistic issue and offered his psychoanalysis of it as a historical solution. By means of this theory Freud also achieved, for the first time, an explicit historical understanding of the place of psychoanalysis in Western culture. In doing so, he in effect distinguished between neurosis as a clinical category and neurosis as a cultural category. So this theory is of great significance for understanding the relations between psychoanalysis and history. In order to understand best that theory, I must first briefly review its precursors.

Freud began his first book on religion, *Totem and Taboo*, in 1909, when his relationship to Jung was at its friendliest, and finished it in 1913, when their bitter separation took place. According to Jones, Freud was more emotionally involved in the writing of this work than in any other, with the single exception of *The Interpretation of Dreams* (Jones 1955, p. 353). He discussed it with Jung many times

(Jung was also working on religion and mythology). Freud feared that his book would permanently alienate Jung, and Jung believed that the publication of his own work on mythology would destroy his relationship to Freud. In this book Freud did not associate narcissism directly with religion. Instead, he linked phases of "men's views of the universe" with the stages of libidinal development. Narcissism characterized the first stage and supported animism and the omnipotence of thoughts. The second stage was that of object choice within the family, and a religious view of the world belonged there. In the third stage, the libidinal organization became psychologically mature or adult, and the view of the world was therefore scientific.

Ideas of omnipotence and animistic thinking received further, important elaboration in "The Uncanny." There Freud spoke of two classes of experience rather than three stages. The first type of uncanny experience consisted of repressed infantile conflict, which today would be identified as structural conflict. The second was the return to consciousness of ideas of omnipotence and primitive beliefs which had been "surmounted" (*überwunden*) and overcome rather than "repressed" (Freud 1919, p. 235), and it was with this second class of experiences that Freud associated religious beliefs or ideas and narcissism. He added that these very primitive activities could be "restricted" or modified by the emergence of the self-observing and self-critical agency of the ego—that is, by the introduction of society into the structure of the mind. Finally, in *Group Psychology and the Analysis of the Ego* (1921), Freud openly linked narcissism, religion, and the social forces of group life. He spoke of a recalcitrant, primitive sector of mental life—the omnipotence of thoughts which corresponded to the second type of uncanny experience—and of its modification by the observing and critical functions of the group. Freud analyzed the Catholic church as one of the two types of groups which illustrated his theory. Although Freud gradually moved to a direct linkage between narcissistic processes, religion, and social formations in these works, none of his discussions addressed a concrete, Western historical situation.

But in "the theory of the three blows" Freud explicitly and deliberately turned to his own immediate historical context, there to associate narcissism with religion and both with the historical clash between scientific and religious ideas and ideals in Western European culture. Written in 1916 and published the following year as "A Difficulty in the Path of Psychoanalysis" (Freud 1917*b*), the theory was also incorporated into lecture 18 of the *Introductory Lectures*. The brevity of this essay should not obscure its significance. It is really a penetrating attempt to formulate a "psychology of knowledge," for its method is very similar to that of the sociology of knowledge. In both, men's ideas are shown to have an infrastructure which escapes conscious recognition. In Freud's essay the infrastructure was developmental rather than societal or economic.

The point of the essay is well known: Copernicus, Darwin, and then Freud himself each delivered in his own way a terrible blow or affront to man's most grandiose and narcissistic illusions: that he was the center of the universe, that he was elevated above and separate from all animal life, and that his conscious self-understanding had direct and truthful correspondence with the reality it perceived. It is necessary to set aside Freud's argument about resistances to psychoanalysis to realize that his paper also uses the idea of narcissism to situate psychoanalysis in the historical sweep of Western culture as that culture continued to be shaped by religious values and institutions. Religiosity was a cultural force which worked against the efforts of psychoanalysis to achieve a rightful place in Western history.

The psychological theory in *Totem and Taboo* was oedipal. Its subject matter was historically remote, and narcissism was linked to the omnipotence of thought and to art, but not to religion (Freud 1912–13, pp. 88–90). In the language of today's human sciences, Freud's approach was synchronic and structural, and he rightly attended carefully to Durkheim's ideas, just as today he would have called upon Lévi-Strauss. But the theory of the three blows is diachronic and historical, and Freud might well have turned to Max Weber's ideas of rationalization and disenchantment for sociological support. Freud built into Darwin's theory of biological evolution a psychological theory of historical development in order to claim that Western science had forced upon Western man and the religious values which supported his consciousness profound disenchantments with his special, privileged, and narcissistically conceived relationship to the order of the world. Freud's acceptance of Darwin's thinking allowed him to claim that Western history consisted in the gradual accrual of ego strength which could fortify the progressive loss of illusions grounded in narcissistic processes.

Most important of all, Freud's theory of the three blows in effect recognized that the origins of psychoanalysis bore an intimate, albeit internal, relation to the religious ideals of the West. This point was made earlier, when I adduced Weber's concept of "internal relation" and gave a historical account of Freud's introspective discoveries during the most creative period. The idea of an internal relation can now be expanded further by calling attention to the likeness between Freud's thinking and Marx's, for Marx also used the ideas of internal relation and contradiction (Marx 1927, p. 81). Just as Marx inverted the Hegelian dialectic, searching out the material-economic base hidden within the superstructures of the religiohistorical category of spirit, Freud sought the unconscious and developmental base or infrastructure to the very same spiritual ideals, and in this sense he too turned them upside down. Freud's word for "material" was of course "libido." In both cases, however, the new psychoanalytic and economic theories bore an internal relation to the old spiritual theory: the new was a precipitate of the old, as a crystal precipitates from a solution. For Freud, astronomy, evolutionary theory, and psychoanalysis all "individuated" out of the matrix of Western religious values and experiences. The theory of the three blows describes, psychologically, the de-idealization of Western religious ideals which science forced upon Western man and which set the stage for the appearance of psychoanalysis. These complex relationships between religion, physical science, and psychoanalysis are reopened and discussed critically at length, sociologically (part 2, chap. 4) and philosophically (part 3, chap. 4).

The present discussion of the theory of the three blows suggests that it be seen as yet one more extension of the psychoanalytic movement and of the thinking begun in Rome with the writing of "The Moses." But Freud refused to grant that paper analytic status. He referred to it as his "nonanalytical child." Presumably, he meant that his interpretation of the statue lacked any classic oedipal shape. Much the same could be said of the theory of the three blows, which is also lacking in structural conflict. One can conclude only that Freud's thinking at this time did nonetheless very much press about the edges of the pre-oedipal line, and one need only note how very resourceful he found these ideas to be.

It is now possible, and necessary, to take up an issue which has continued to haunt the psychoanalytic movement from its beginning—what is sometimes referred to as its sectarian or religious character. Discussing this subject permits still further clarification of the clash between Freud's claims to science for his analysis and its internal or hidden connections to religious ideals, and even makes possible reflection upon the historical and psychological genesis of science itself in the West, as Freud sought to understand that. Allegations that the movement was sectarian or "really religious" have been in the past largely polemical. Now, however, a truly learned and articulate account of this view exists for the first time, in the work of Frank J. Sulloway (1979).

The claim to science was of course essential to Freud's psychoanalysis, but he made this single claim for two different reasons. On one hand, he insisted that his science was grounded in the ideal of objectivity and its correlate, the testing of hypotheses about the unconscious mental life of patients within a community of analyst-investigators modeled after the medical and biological research centers in which he himself had worked earlier in his life. On the other hand, whenever Freud and the first analysts attempted to make themselves understood to the indifferent and suspicious social and cultural world which surrounded them, they also insisted that their work was scientific. Objections to the first were disturbing enough, although they could in principle be met through further research, communication, and reformulation. But objections to the second were simply devastating: if analysis was not scientific at all, then there was only one other thing it could be, and that was religion, that is to say, a drive toward the institutionalization of power and control, devoid of concern with knowledge. So, from the beginning of the movement, Freud fought desperately for the mantle of science. But his reasons for doing so were both methodological or epistemological *and* sociological.

Toward the end of his long, sweeping, and information-laden book, Sulloway builds upon his earlier argument that Freud was consistently loyal to biological and evolutionary modes of thought in order to discuss what he calls the politics of the psychoanalytic movement. He points out that it created and nurtured the myth of Freud as a "pure psychologist," and in doing so denied his commitments to biological and evolutionary modes of thought. Turning to the social characteristics of the movement, Sulloway argues that it was not at all a scientific society but instead had all the marks of a religious sect. Freud led a medical crusade and his followers were zealous, proud, and arrogant. Together they shared a fanatical degree of faith, a special jargon, a sense of moral superiority, and a messianic vision of reality, such that adherents to the group resembled religious converts. Sulloway carefully builds his case from the historically recorded perceptions of men within and without the movement. For example, he cites Hans Sachs's observation (Sachs was a member of the Committee) that "analysis needs something corresponding to the novitiate of the church" (Sulloway 1979, p. 486) and the observation of the music critic Max Graff that in the first meetings "there was an atmosphere of the foundation of a religion in that room. Freud himself was its new prophet. . . . Freud . . . ejected him [Adler] from the official church" (p. 481). Sulloway in effect depicts a group of men bound by a totalistic and absolutist sense of loyalty to a single system of ideas, offering their leader exaggerated reverence and motivated by a zealous sense of mission and hostility toward the surrounding social world. For this reason, he argues, the ideas of the movement served a mythic rather than a rational, scientific purpose.

It is not possible to review Sulloway's elaborate support for this conclusion, nor is that necessary. As historical description, his view is convincing and unexceptionable. The question is not *whether* the movement was sectlike, but *why*. To begin to answer, I return to my own earlier observations of the movement, which include an unconscious group self and a group illusion; projective identification, in which all badness is placed upon an outsider and all goodness upon the leader and loyal insiders; the genesis of such projective identification in the intense, shared idealizations and subsequent de-idealizations undergone by Freud and Jung; and the group/movement's function of mediating between intrapsychic conflict and the indifferent world of social circumstance. In fact, it is even possible to augment Sulloway's view beyond its own evidence and add the parallel to Marxism: an absolute sense of destiny, claims to science, and a relentless depreciation of all other forms of thought and social experience.

But the substance of my answer lies less in the relations of the first analysts to each other and more in the psychoanalytic sociology of their marginal relation to the surrounding culture. In a nutshell, the movement was sectarian because Freud and the first analysts de-idealized with too great rapidity and without sufficient psychological understanding of their attachments to traditional social and cultural values which they possessed before exploring with Freud their own and others' unconscious mental lives. All the early analysts were alienated from their religious traditions and were consequently searching for new forms of cultural experience to heal their alienation. As Sulloway points out, many were deeply neurotic and a surprising number even committed suicide. But it is also true that many were extremely gifted and sensitive to the waning of traditional ideals and values in an era of rapidly shifting social and axiological change. They rightly perceived in Freud's revolutionary theories what I would call "a new mode of consciousness in the West" which was capable of providing them with forms of inner, personal autonomy through the creation of fresh modes of self-knowledge. I can only quote with approval, as do Fred Weinstein and Gerald Platt, Heinz Hartmann's cogent formulation that, when attachments to a common culture break down, the "ego will attempt to fulfill its organizing functions by increased insight into internal processes" (Weinstein and Platt 1969, p. 138). But I think that the concept of de-idealization makes far clearer, psychologically, the relation between the breakdown of an "attachment to a common culture" and the ego's attempt at greater insight than does ego psychology. For, in the case of the first analysts, the self, rather than the ego, was more affected.

This too-rapid de-idealization of a cultural heritage resulted in an impoverishment of the narcissistic sector, for no suitable fresh cultural objects could be easily or quickly found. Socially shared traditional ideals have always bound unconscious developmental processes. The crumbling of these ideals propelled the first analysts to study with Freud, and the analytic process further facilitated inner disorganization. The first analysts became vulnerable. For the most part, they bypassed narcissistic issues in their analytic work, especially as these pertained to unconscious mergers with each other, to wider social formations and especially to the symbols of culture. Tragic as it was, they only very partially mastered the de-idealization process which was forced upon them, and their achievements in the realm of structure building were limited. As their only recourse, they reified their unconscious need for ideals and—here tragedy passed over into irony—attached them to Freud himself and to his new analytic ideas.

The psychology of disillusionment also helps explain why Freud chose to model his analysis on the sciences of his day. His theory of the three blows attests to the conviction that his science partook of the historical process of disenchantment initiated by the thinking of Copernicus and Darwin. Psychoanalysis, Freud thought, simply carried this program to its psychological conclusion in relation to the inner, unconscious world of the individual person. In each case, science de-idealized: the theories of Copernicus and Darwin broke up in people's minds massive idealizations supported by a religious-cultural order, and of course the analytic situation asks that the analysand reexperience and work through primitive identifications. If one understands religion as the intense sharing of unconscious idealizations of cultural objects which have come to acquire the status of heritage, then science provides an experience-distant perspective on this powerful emotional activity. Insofar as the theory of the three blows is Freudian, psychoanalytic science can be said to be the science of ideals and their unconscious vicissitudes. Therefore, Freud rightly sensed an internal, inverse relationship between his work and religiously inspired cultural values, and he chose to critique them with increasing regularity and intensity after 1914 in what have come to be known as the cultural texts.

After 1914, a major portion of Freud's thought gradually took its well-known turn toward metapsychological ego psychology, epitomized in his 1923 effort, *The Ego and the Id*, in which a psychology of the ego and a rigorous, positivistic sense of science were wedded. For some, this was his crowning achievement; for others, ego psychology became the reification of theory at the expense of clinical advance. Reflecting on this alternative from within the structure of the 1906–14 period, we may make a simple but no less important observation. If Jung, who was so central to all that happened to Freud at this time, tried above all else to make a religion out of psychoanalysis; if the charge that analysis was "really a religion" haunted Freud; and if Freud himself deeply feared that this could well-nigh ruin his work; then it would seem likely that he would have had to exert comparable force in the opposite direction—that his ideas would simply "have had to be" scientific, at all costs. If the word "anatomy" in the 1932 title, "The Anatomy of the Mental Personality," captures the fierce rigor which Freud applied to his science, then the metapsychology of 1923 was born in part of Freud's sense of urgency at this time: the metapsychology was a frozen idealization of science as Freud had come to understand science at this time.

Nietzsche said that Christianity was "the Platonism of the people"—it kept depth at a distance, and that was something everyone could agree to do. These reflections on the psychoanalytic movement and its turn to culture suggest that the metapsychology became "the Platonism of the analysts"—it kept them from thinking about deeper self-processes and the linkages between self and culture. The subsequent essay explores the prominence of disillusionment in the lives of Freud's three most famous followers, examines the ideological function of the metapsychology in more detail, and redefines the movement as a "psychological culture" all its own.

4   Earlier and Later De-Idealizations: Count Thun and Romain Rolland

As his movement gained momentum, Freud's propensity to idealize and de-idealize certain men became increasingly enmeshed with the social forces of politics and religion. While this pattern was most intense during the 1906–14 period, it was not absent either before or after it. By reflecting backward once again into the most creative period, it is possible to explore further the way political issues shaped Freud's life and thought with the help of Carl Schorske's well-known historical essay and to bring psychological depth to Schorske's historical observations. Reflecting forward makes it clear that Freud pursued his intense preoccupation with religion right up to his final years, in his correspondence with Romain Rolland. In both cases he worked out his concerns through a special kind of contact with a socially significant man and his ideas. Could de-idealization and its historical correlate, disenchantment, have been a master theme in Freud's life and thought?

Count Thun and Freud's Psychology of Politics

Like the preceding discussion, Carl Schorske's much-admired historical account of the origins of psychoanalysis (1973) also attempts to connect in a decisive way Freud's life and thought to his social circumstances. Schorske calls attention to the sociopolitical and Jewish-Catholic tensions so prominent in several dreams in *The Interpretation of Dreams*, especially the famous dream of Count Thun (Freud called it a "revolutionary dream"), and concludes that Freud's inability to tolerate political tensions—what Schorske calls "the pain of general history"—virtually forced upon him his psychoanalytic discoveries: Freud in effect spared himself this pain by reducing political reality to psychological forces. Like Klein's, Schorske's work gives priority to social circumstance (politics, culture, and religion) in the genesis of Freud's ideas. But it also provides the data for a deeper understanding of the place of disillusionment and disenchantment in Freud's relations to the surrounding culture and his perceptions of it.

The report of the dream about Count Thun and the Rome dreams appear together in the section "Infantile Material as a Source of Dreams" in *The Interpretation of Dreams* (Freud 1900, pp. 208–19). In August of 1898, Freud arrived early at the railroad station in Vienna to take the train for his summer holiday. On the platform he noticed Count Thun, the reactionary Austrian political leader who opposed German nationalism. The count waved the ticket inspector aside "with a curt motion of his hand," without explanation, and entered his carriage. Freud's head swarmed with "all kinds of insolent and revolutionary ideas" because *he* had had to buy a ticket and *he* had had to wait before entering his carriage, and even then the car had no lavatory. He protested to one of the railway officials, saying rudely and sarcastically that they could at least have made a hole in the floor "to meet the possible needs of the passengers." Then late that night on the train Freud awoke with a pressing need to urinate and with the revolutionary, or Count Thun, dream fresh in his mind.

In the first scene of the dream, Freud was attending a student meeting at which Count Thun, or a speaker like him, took a contemptuous attitude toward the Germans. Freud responded with intense resentment. In the second scene he fled this antagonistic political atmosphere by way of one of the university halls and, after a series of minor episodes, found himself again on the station platform. There he joined an elderly gentleman who was apparently blind and took the role of a sick-nurse by handing the man a glass urinal in order to help him urinate.

As usual, the flow of associations and interpretations which followed this dream report was complex and subtle. But Freud drove all of them along toward the third scene and an early memory from the age of seven or eight. He had entered his parents' bedroom while they were there and had "disregarded the rules which modesty lays down and obeyed the calls of nature." His father reprimanded him by saying that he would come to nothing, which was "a frightful blow to my ambition." In the dream, of course, he *had* come to something, for it was he who held the urinal for the blind and infirm father surrogate. In a sweeping, integrative summary, Freud concluded (1900): "And indeed the whole rebellious content of the dream, with its *lèse majesté* [its "high treason"] and its derision of the higher authorities, went back to rebellion against my father . . . the father is the oldest, first, and for children the only authority, and from his autocratic power the other social authorities have developed in the course of the history of human civilization" (p. 217; quoted in Schorske 1973, p. 197). The revolutionary dream, Schorske says, moves from political encounter, through flight into academia, to the conquest of the father, who has replaced Count Thun. "As the father replaces the prime minister on the station platform, patricide replaces politics" (Schorske 1973, p. 197). Freud's idea, that a political struggle is "really" only a displacement of an unconscious developmental struggle, owes its origin to his deeper wish to avoid "the pain of general history," the wish to "make bearable a political world spun out of orbit and beyond control" (p. 203). Schorske's essay also cuts beneath issues of life, thought, and social circumstance in order to show that these are in turn shaped by an even more fundamental problem, the relationship between psychoanalysis and history.

But this explanation of how analytic thinking emerged is deceptive, for it is covertly more psychological than it is historical. Schorske creates for the reader an either/or dilemma between "psychic forces" and "political impulses and political guilt" (1973, p. 196), between psychology and history. As with Freud, so with Schorske; it is all one or all the other: just as Freud reduced politics and history to psychic forces, so Schorske reduces psychoanalysis to history. And like Freud, Schorske also makes use of the concept of defense. Freud said his political struggles disguised or defended against the "real" truth of unconscious developmental conflict. Schorske says that analytic thinking "really" defends against the pain of history by eliminating history from consciousness. In each case, one orientation devours the other.

But Freud's situation, and Schorske's interpretation as well, lends itself to a deeper and more thorough explanation, one which is both psychological and historical. Freud's relationship to Count Thun was not only one of oedipal revenge; it also contained an important element of de-idealization, the mournful giving up of his attachment to the leading ideas of German political liberalism. Earlier in his life Freud had high hopes for this political movement, but by 1898 his inner disillusionment with it lacked only outer confirmation. Coming face-to-face, literally, with the aristocratic and conservative count momentarily reawakened these disappointments. So intense was his de-idealization that it forced upon him an abandonment of political-cultural reality in favor of inner, psychological reality. From this point of view, one comes to experience history as "painful" and "unbearable" only insofar as one cannot identify with or connect with others who possess "the same psychological structure." Finding that he could not "cathect" these others, whom Count Thun symbolized—that is, realizing that he could not belong to or "occupy" the inner world of these others—Freud became isolated and absorbed in his own inner life.

This explanation will appear convincing insofar as one is able to recognize narcissistic issues in the Count Thun episode. In fact, both Freud and Schorske do so, albeit inadvertently. Count Thun's unshakable conviction of his own superiority made him a study in narcissistic grandiosity. Freud hinted at this when he wrote that the count had waved aside the ticket inspector, who had not recognized him and had asked for a ticket, with "a curt motion of his hand." And Schorske elaborated further the count's narcissistic features. The count, he said, was "stalking onto the platform." In his bearing he was a "*Feudalherr* from top to toe"; he was "tall, thin, dressed with exquisite elegance"; "His monacle never left his eye"; he displayed "aristocratic aplomb" as he entered "a luxurious compartment"; and his behavior was "imperious" (Schorske 1973, p. 194). The count's arrogant mien dashed once more Freud's hopes for the ideals of political liberalism, as he was forced to accept the fact that this intolerant, grandiose man had power over him and cared nothing for his values.

Schorske's account also obscures the constructive side of Freud's experience. His disillusionment on the platform reactivated unconscious narcissistic wishes (hence the dream), but he also took the experience as an invitation to be introspective. He spoke of his "pathological ambition" and his "absurd megalomania" in the course of creating his interpretation of his dream. As he had said in *Totem and Taboo* and as he had repeated in "The Uncanny," all modern adults have "surmounted and overcome" these primitive, narcissistic forces. But, apparently, Count Thun and his ilk had not, and history was allowing this "*Feudalherr*" to indulge them. So Freud played out some of his own propensity to narcissistic gratification on the figure of the count in an effort to turn mourning into self-understanding.

According to Jones and Schorske—and Freud himself—psychoanalysis and politics are polar, irreconcilable opposites. In each man's argument there is the equivalent of a "U-tube" relationship in which one column of water (psychoanalysis) gains in volume when the opposite column (politics) decreases. The more politics, the less psychoanalytic thinking; the more appreciative one is of the analytic situation, the less can political activity be entertained. Perhaps without intending to, Schorske has opened up, in the context of empirical and historical evidence, the fundamental issue in all discussions of psychoanalysis and history, politics, social theory, religion, and culture. Clearly the issue is far more comprehensive than can be contained in the label-like cliché of "reductionism." But the Count Thun episode cannot be fully understood apart from this fundamental issue.

Sensibilities derived from the psychology of the self and, in a broader sense, from the sociology of disenchantment create a very different view of "psychoanalysis and history." In this second view, de-idealizing the sympathetic political realm of liberalism led, paradoxically, to more introspective activity, and that in turn led to fresh research into the workings of the unconscious. This sequence of mental events is best described not as a "replacement operation" (parricide replaces politics) but as a partial creating and building up of psychological structure—structure necessary to tolerate the intolerable psychological pressures which dictatorial political figures invariably exert upon all those who choose neither of the easy solutions—to comply or to rebel. Freud's unconscious thoughts during the Count Thun episode might thus be thematized as follows: "I idealized and identified with German political liberalism earlier in my life and shared its principal value, that of universal tolerance; since then this tolerance of my life has been progressively denied to me, and, moreover, I see the forces which led to this denial condensing before my very eyes in the figure of this one man, Count Thun—it is as though *he* has deprived *me* of a highly significant value; but I *can* think about it in my sleep, and then I can think psychoanalytic thoughts about that." In this sense it can be said that Count Thun precipitated an unconscious moment of de-idealization and the ensuing work of creating psychoanalytic thought was a form of structure building.

A further piece of evidence for this point of view comes from direct and commonsense observation of the fate of psychoanalysis in different political contexts. It fares best in advanced, industrialized, and democratic nations and worst in dictatorial political structures, whether fascist or communist. The reason for this does not lie in whether or not the political entity in question permits or restricts the gratification of libidinal cathexes and object love, as the structural theory asserts, for all states—and for that matter, all cultures as well—permits this. Rather, democratic political structures support, more than do dictatorial ones, an ethos of empathic, introspective tolerance of the citizen's unconscious inner world, by means of the secret ballot. This inner world is populated by good and bad internal objects and self-objects which are, as is well known, the fundamental precursors of persecutory anxiety and behavior. So, there is an internal relationship between democratic political structures and empathic, introspective activity, as this is understood psychoanalytically, and the Count Thun episode was, in its deepest aspect, about this relationship.

Sixteen years later, in 1914, the disillusionment so characteristic of the Count Thun episode reasserted itself with great strength and hardened into disgust and a kind of cynicism. Freud was deeply moved by the Great War, but in his mind its effects were indistinguishable from events in the psychoanalytic movement. In his mind, the movement virtually replaced political reality—at least for the time being. Writing to Lou Andreas-Salomé in November 1914 (she was to his mind hopelessly optimistic), Freud lamented (quoted in Pfeiffer 1972):

> I do not doubt that mankind will survive even this war, but I know for certain that for me and my contemporaries the world will never again be a happy place. It is too hideous. And the saddest thing about it is that it is exactly the way we should have expected people to behave from our knowledge of psychoanalysis. Because of this attitude to mankind I have never been able to agree with your blithe optimism. My secret conclusion has always been: since we can only regard the highest present civilization as burdened with an enormous hypocrisy, it follows that we are organically unfitted for it. We have to abdicate, and the Great Unknown, He or It, lurking behind Fate will someday repeat this experiment with another race. (P. 21)

A month later he wrote deploringly to Jones: "What Jung and Adler have left of the movement is being ruined by the strife of nations" (Jones 1955, p. 179). In his mind, the war was simply another defection. Jones captured well Freud's mournful decathexis of political reality by noting that his productivity was still high, as it often was when he was in "low spirits," and that "inner concentration was taking the place of interest in the dismal happenings in the outer world" (p. 177). He was, of course, working on the famous metapsychological papers. The "Schorske thesis" is reopened in part 2 (chap. 7), where the psychological theory of the origins of the self-analysis is discussed again and integrated into a sociological perspective.

Romain Rolland and Freud's Psychology of Religion

Reflecting back from the 1906–14 period to Freud's struggles with sociopolitical reality at the time of the most creative period has shown that the psychological theme of de-idealization was more pervasive, throughout Freud's life and thought, than other writers have realized. Reflecting forward enhances this view even more, at least with regard to one highly significant relationship, Freud's attachment to the eminent French man of letters Romain Rolland. Many of the issues found in the Freud-Jung relationship were duplicated and elaborated with Rolland.

The intensity of Freud's idealization of Rolland has astonished many analytic biographers. The issue which initially attracted Freud to Rolland was the relation of religion to psychoanalysis, and the psychology of narcissism (the "oceanic feeling") was central to that issue. Although Rolland had left the Catholic church early in his life, he continued to embody for Freud the established Western Christian humanistic tradition. Freud's idealization of Rolland forced upon him once again a self-analytic mode which resulted in his discovering the meaning of an event in his life which he had never understood, thereby building psychological structure: his disturbance of memory on the Acropolis in 1904.

In all this Freud largely repeated the pattern already established in relation to Jung: he met a representative of "mainstream" European and Christian culture and idealized him; they exchanged ideas; Freud was then provoked to relate his analytic thinking to these ideas, through creative work; then he explored his own inner life in yet greater depth; and this led to deeper self-understanding. Whereas in the case of Jung, Freud's creativity manifested itself in his exploration of narcissism and his discovery of the historical import of culture for the future of his work, in the case of Rolland Freud created a fresh chapter in his psychology of religion.[1]

Romain Rolland was recognized throughout Europe for his intellectual and artistic achievements and humanitarian views. He wrote plays, novels, and biographies (two on the Indian religious personalities Ramakrishna and Vivekananda), received a Nobel prize, and espoused internationalism and tolerance among all peoples. Freud was so impressed by Rolland that he asked a friend to convey his respects anonymously, and with this gesture their relationship began. To Freud's delight, Rolland replied by lavishing praise on him, saying that he had been following his works since 1900. The published portions of the correspondence which ensued consist of seven personal letters from Freud and the open letter (describing the experience on the Acropolis) and span the years 1923–36. During this time Freud read some of Rolland's works and sent him copies of *Group Psychology and the Analysis of the Ego* and *The Future of an Illusion*. The diverse subjects which these letters discuss should not obscure Freud's overriding concern with the relationship between analytic ideas, religious experiences and ideals, and the problematic place of narcissism and illusion in understanding the latter. Because the discourse with Rolland carries forward the major cultural issues forced on Freud by Jung in 1914, it must be understood as yet another effort on his part to thrust psychoanalytic thought and the psychoanalytic movement into the cultural ethos of his time by attempting to write a psychology of culture.

The opening phase testifies to Freud's need to idealize non-Jewish intellectuals and his related, persistent search for a universal ethic of tolerance, an ideal Klein rightly linked to Freud's preoccupation with his Jewish heritage and identity during the most creative period, which became the initial impetus to the group/movement. Freud announced his fervid idealization of Rolland in a letter of January 1926 (E. L. Freud 1964): "Unforgettable man, to have soared to such heights of humanity through so much hardship and suffering! I revered you as an artist and as an apostle of love for mankind many years before I saw you. I myself have always advocated the love for mankind . . . as indispensable for the preservation of the human species" (p. 364). In May 1926, in a letter for a volume honoring Rolland, Freud spoke of his adulation of Romain's religious ideals: "Your lines are among the most precious things which these days have brought me. . . . When men like you whom I have loved from afar express their friendship for me . . . I enjoy it without questioning whether or not I deserve it, I relish it as a gift" (p. 370).

But this idealization was not without content. Around Rolland's person he allowed to cluster his intense concerns with his own Jewishness, religious hatred, the psychological problem of ideals and illusions, and the place of psychoanalysis in all of this. He had spoken of these forthrightly and unambiguously in his earliest letter, written in 1923:

> That I have been allowed to exchange a greeting with you will remain a happy memory to the end of my days. Because for us your name has been associated with the most precious of beautiful illusions, that of love extended to all mankind. I, of course, belong to a race which in the Middle Ages was held responsible for all epidemics and which today is blamed for the

> disintegration of the Austrian Empire and the Ger-
> man defeat. Such experiences have a sobering effect
> and are not conducive to make one believe in illu-
> sions. A great part of my life's work . . . has been
> spent (trying to) destroy illusions of my own and
> those of mankind. But if this one hope cannot be at
> least partly realized, if in the course of evolution we
> don't learn to divert our instincts from destroying our
> own kind, if we continue to hate one another for
> minor differences and kill each other for petty
> gain . . . what kind of future lies in store for us? . . .
> My writings cannot be what yours are: comfort and
> refreshment for the reader. But if I may believe that
> they have aroused your interest, I shall permit myself
> to send you a small book. (Pp. 341–42)

As this passage also indicates, Freud was equally concerned with his
own personal experiences of political and religious opposition to psychoanalysis, the relationship between psychoanalysis, understood as
the destroyer of illusions, and cultural forces (the book he enclosed
with his letter was *Group Psychology and the Analysis of the Ego*),
his own psychoanalytic explanation of hatred and persecution, and
the problem of what I would call "a good illusion," which Freud
called "this one hope."

These many concerns rapidly devolved onto a very specific issue of
central importance to both men, the famous "oceanic feeling." After
reading *The Future of an Illusion*, Rolland proposed this idea to
Freud. It was an alternative understanding of religion which would
meet all of Freud's criticisms and still qualify as religious. The
oceanic feeling was not associated with institutional religion or its
ethics and doctrines, nor was it to be confused with belief in immortality. It was instead a subjective sensation of being connected to the
eternal or the entire world, and it could be studied empirically. It was
shared by millions of men, although many would describe it differently, depending upon their cultural background, and Rolland
declared that he himself was never without it.

This very abstract description acquires psychological depth from
Jeffrey Masson's careful and informative research on Rolland's
sources, for "oceanic" was first a vivid symbol and then only a simple
adjective (Masson 1980). Rolland coined the phrase while researching
his biography of the nineteenth-century Bengali saint Ramakrishna.
On one occasion, so the account ran, Ramakrishna found himself in a
frenzy. Because he might not have a vision of the Mother of the

Universe, he decided to take his life. But before he could do so, a vision appeared to him, that of an ocean with large luminous waves. It engulfed him for two days and produced a highly satisfactory outcome (Masson 1980): "Round me rolled an ocean of ineffable joy, and in the depths of my being I was conscious of the presence of the Divine Mother" (p. 36). Masson proposed that Ramakrishna's vision was an instance of what Kohut called cosmic narcissism and also that it revealed obsessive concern with states of depersonalization and narcissistic fantasies of world destruction.

It is not necessary to pursue Masson's lengthy analysis or his particular interpretation to realize why Freud replied to Rolland by telling him that the idea of an oceanic feeling "has left me no peace" (E. L. Freud 1964, p. 388). If one recalls the complicated psychology of Freud's break with Jung and the writing of "The Moses" in Rome in 1914, it is possible to realize that Rolland had in effect presented Freud with symbolic evidence of a universal maternal presence in human mental life, which he believed men constructed, reified, merged with, and idealized. Furthermore, although Rolland had consciously rejected his Catholic religion early in his adult life (no doubt one more reason for Freud's admiration for him—Freud too had rejected a religious context for his life and, like Rolland, was seeking a nonreligious equivalent for religious illusions), it is safe to say that the deeper portions of his personality, in which his intellectual life remained rooted, probably maintained unconscious contact with the maternal, nurturant features so evident in all Catholic thought and life. In any case, Rolland was, like Jung, deeply attached to the intellectual and cultural streams of Western, Christian humanism upon which Freud always gazed with ambivalence, envy, suspicion, and longing. Of interest, too—although it cannot be pursued here—is Masson's well-documented observation that Rolland's writings clearly contained noticeable anti-Semitic thoughts (Masson 1980, p. 44). Surely these did not escape Freud.

If the idea of an oceanic feeling left Freud no peace, he quickly regained that peace by writing the opening chapter of *Civilization and Its Discontents*. That chapter is a direct and explicit psychoanalytic response to Rolland's proposal, and one can see from this how important it is to understand the context of this major "cultural text." After respectfully summarizing the key idea, Freud firmly described the pre-oedipal, narcissistic features of the oceanic feeling and emphasized the shadowy and elusive nature of these states—they simply were not analyzable. He confessed that he himself had never entertained such feelings, a conclusion which the preceding psychobiography both denies and supports. Then, in the midst of this short chapter, Freud abandoned discursive reasoning and proposed an extremely significant metaphor to convey his crucial, central psychological idea—the city of Rome. Freud announced (1930) that even the earliest developmental experiences are retained in the unconscious throughout life: "Now let us, by a flight of imagination, suppose that Rome is not a human habitation but a psychical entity with a similarly long and copious past—an entity, that is to say, in which nothing that has once come into existence will have passed away and all the earlier phases of development continue to exist alongside the latest one" (p. 70). Beneath modern Rome and Christian Rome (Rolland's Rome) lay classical Rome (Freud's Rome), analogous to the deepest layer of the unconscious mind. It seems likely that the "long and copious past" is a reference to the narcissistic line of development which finds its origin in an unconscious sense of a maternal presence.

But Freud was far from finished with the oceanic feeling. After having stated his "psychology of religion" in chapter 1, he abandoned metaphor for personalized reflection. He began chapter 2 with a striking instance of de-idealization of the Catholic ideal of universal love and of similar ideals in his own Jewish heritage—the very ideal which had attracted him to Rolland. First he set aside the oceanic feeling in favor of the religion of the common man and reiterated the conclusions of *The Future of an Illusion*. Then he permitted himself a surprisingly frank moment of intensely personal bitterness. "The whole thing" (religious beliefs), he said, "is so patently infantile, so foreign to reality, that to anyone with a friendly attitude to humanity it is painful to think that the great majority of mortals will never be able to rise above this view of life. It is still more humiliating . . ." (1930, p. 74). If religion was so "foreign to reality," why not call it primitive, or stupid? But why "painful" and "humiliating"? Freud attempted to answer this question in his next sentence: "One would like to mix among the ranks of the believers in order to meet these philosophers, who think they can rescue the God of religion by replacing him by an impersonal, shadowy, and abstract principle, and to address them with the warning words: 'Thou shalt not take the name of the Lord thy God in vain!'" (p. 74). But this answer needs explanation.

What was "painful" and "humiliating" was being forced to exist in a culture whose norms for mental life were essentially religious and as such were organized along psychologically primitive lines. The person who is truly "friendly to humanity" was the person who thought psychologically, who could support "this one hope," the good illusion of universal love for all mankind. Freud knew the common man was no philosopher; Rolland was the real philosopher. And so Freud shielded himself from disappointment by momentarily re-identifying with his Jewish past and with its prophets' awesome capacity for sublimation from primitive polytheism to "neutralized" monotheism. It was as if he were thinking to himself as he wrote these lines: "It would be so good to be a complete Jew again, for then I could rise above the primitivity of religious belief; for then there would be given to me what I can now acquire only through self-analysis: the capacity to surmount and overcome my own unconscious developmental primitivity." Freud's ambivalent attitude toward his own Jewishness received his most extreme statement in the very first sentence of *Moses and Monotheism*, in which he broke up—but not entirely—yet another strand of his lifelong identification with Moses: "To deprive a people of the man whom they take pride in as the greatest of their sons is not a thing to be gladly or carelessly undertaken, least of all by someone who is himself one of them" (1939, p. 7).

Freud brought to a close his pattern of idealization and de-idealization which Rolland had stimulated by means of a creative action: writing the famous self-analytic essay about his disturbance of memory on the Acropolis (1936). For obvious reasons the paper has fascinated and puzzled many scholars, mostly analysts. Essays by Schur (1969) and Slochower (1970) are especially suggestive, the first emphasizing maternal themes and imagery, the second Freud's pre-occupation with his own death during his final years. After making only passing reference to Rolland and his appeal in behalf of the oceanic feeling, thereby discounting his symbolic and cultural significance for Freud, both bear down upon the ahistorical intricacies of Freud's psyche. More to the point, neither analyst really answers the paper's most puzzling question: Why did Freud write of such a personal experience, which happened much earlier in life, in an open letter, as a gift, to a man like Rolland?

My argument does not conflict with these analysts' findings, although it does add to them the social-symbolic dimension of Freud's drama with Rolland, of which this paper is the denouement. This denouement consisted of Freud's appealing to Rolland as a representative of Western Christian humanistic culture; offering an experience of his own not unlike—at least psychodynamically—the oceanic one in which Rolland was so highly invested; interpreting his own experience analytically; and then—by offering all this to Rolland, the Christian humanist—attempting once again to insert psychoanalysis into the mainstream of Western culture. For these reasons this paper must be seen as a highly personalized continuation of the psychoanalytic movement and of the theory of the three blows to Western man's narcissism, as well as a fragment of the psychoanalytic theory of culture. Freud's essay replied to Rolland's facile attempt to incorporate psychoanalytic insight into his religious theory of the oceanic experience. Freud saw the matter quite otherwise. Although he never de-idealized Rolland, nonetheless the Rolland episode stimulated a de-idealization in Freud's mind, leading him to further self-analysis and theoretical inquiry. The paper which followed was a disguised reproach.

He began his open letter with a brief and mannered idealization and then quickly announced that his task was analytic. Its subject matter was a feeling of de-realization which he experienced upon arriving at the Acropolis with his brother Alexander in 1904 at the age of forty-eight. He found himself marveling that "all this really *does* exist, just as we learnt at school!" (1936, p. 241). His was an experience of "too good to be true," of "incredulity" (pp. 241–42). To explain it he first wondered whether, as a boy, he in fact had doubted the actual existence of the Acropolis, which would have been a denial of a piece of reality. He quickly discarded this view and replaced it with one which was almost as sociological as it was psychological. As a boy, he had not doubted the existence of the Acropolis, only that he would ever see it. Continuing to reminisce, he recalled that it seemed to him "beyond the realms of possibility that I should travel so far— that I should 'go such a long way' " (p. 246). His longing to travel was, he confessed, a wish to escape from the limitations and poverty of his childhood, a wish fulfillment in the analytic sense. Then, his narcissism intact, he rhapsodized: "When first one catches sight of the sea, crosses the ocean and experiences as realities cities and lands which for so long had been distant, unattainable things of desire— one feels oneself like a hero. . . ." So he might just as well have said to his brother, "We really *have* gone a long way," and then, his grandiosity unfurling still further, bannerlike, he related his achievement to Napoleon's remark during his coronation to *his* brother: "What would *Monsieur Notre Père* have said to this, if he could have been here today?" (p. 247). So the experience of de-realization was, he concluded, like the experience of those wrecked by success, rooted in an oedipal wish to surpass the father. "A feeling of filial piety" (p. 248) had interfered with his wish to enjoy the journey to Athens.[2]

But why did Freud choose to present such an essay as a "gift" to Rolland? To make sense of this, it is necessary to remember that Rolland was a socially sanctioned representative of the Western religious culture, and Freud was not—although now, of course, he is. So it was as if Freud had said to Rolland, throughout his paper: "In all matters of complex subjective states, such as, for example, the oceanic feeling (which you think of as representative of humanity), or a confusing moment or experience such as I have had, which psychologically resembles yours . . . in all such matters, analytic knowledge is all we have—here, take it, if you can, because it is for this that I wish you and your Western heritage to remember me." Freud also emphasized how sad and old he felt at the age of eighty.

The Rolland episode portrays in yet another way a persistent and central theme in Freud's life and thought: his unconscious ambivalence toward pre-oedipal issues, as well as toward their cultural contexts. Consciously, Freud idealized Rolland and the religious promises which he embodied. But unconsciously as well as consciously, he also experienced disillusionment with these and turned to analytic modes of thought to make sense of his struggle. As in the Count Thun episode, so in the encounter with Rolland: the theory was oedipal and culture was disavowed as a potent psychological variable. Freud's reluctance to engage pre-oedipal, narcissistic issues analytically—he was quite comfortable with a moral stance toward these matters—prevented him from evolving a psychoanalytic psychology of the oceanic feeling and its cultural matrix, just as the same reluctance had prevented him from understanding earlier idealizations and de-idealizations (and disenchantments) of admired men (Breuer, Fliess, Jung) and admired social values (liberalism, Jewishness) and ambivalently sought-after illusions ("this one hope"). The investigations of this essay have sought to thematize this latent, unconscious, and split-off sector of Freud's life, thought, and social circumstance. But as I will point out shortly, this splitting was culturally and sociologically—and not psychologically—induced.

To return to the drama with Rolland: in it, as in the case of the earlier one with Jung, it seems clear that Freud wished to conquer religious modes of experience, so "humiliating" to have to live with, and to replace them with analytic knowledge. Perhaps his famous reference to himself as a conqueror or conquistador belongs here. Equipped with the resources of psychoanalytic technique and theory, Freud wished to conquer Western man's religious traditions. True to form, the night before he was to arrive in England in 1938, old, ill, and ready for death, he dreamt that he had actually landed at Pevensey, where William the Conqueror had landed in 1066 (Jones 1957, p. 228). Rome was no doubt the city of Freud's dreams, and just as surely Vienna was the city of his oppressions; but London was, I think, the city of his reality sense.

5 Freud's Mother, His Death Anxiety, and the Problem of History

This essay has lifted out the psychological theme of de-idealization and its cognates—disappointment, disillusionment, mourning, and disenchantment—from the complex data on Freud's life, thought, and social circumstance and has woven them into more recent studies, both psychoanalytic and historical. By deliberately avoiding the most creative period and centering instead on the time of Jung and the origins of the psychoanalytic movement, it has placed the accent primarily on the social. By glancing backward, it was possible to see the usefulness of the concept of de-idealization for understanding the influence of social forces on the most creative period; and by looking forward, to see the increasing centrality of culture for Freud's life and thought, understood as a force working against the historical novelty of his analytic theories and also as a challenge to analytic explanations of culture itself.

In the most sweeping sense, three closely linked issues have emerged from this study, two quite concrete and the third very general. From the relationship with Jung, the psychoanalytic movement, and Freud's turn to culture after 1914, there emerged the idea of a maternal presence: maternal transferences, the group self and the group illusion as a nurturing transitional object, and culture as the repository of shared, idealized maternal imagery. The developmental reality of a maternal presence in Freud's life and his intense and unconscious ambivalence toward it also shed light upon his periodic anxiety about his own death. Both were activated by the dynamics of idealization and de-idealization. But the idea of de-idealization also provoked the very general question of the relationship between psychoanalysis and history.

It is now possible to bring these issues to a more conclusive understanding by reflecting—once again backward and forward—upon two crucial instances in which Freud's death anxiety and his relationship to his mother were intimately associated. Both in turn bear upon the very general problem of psychoanalysis and history. But, as I will point out in a moment, the very achievements of the psychological and historical perspectives also constitute their greatest limitation. Even when joined together, the results lack a sociological grounding, without which both remain individualistic and idealistic. Let us, however, pursue these achievements a bit further, for it is also true that without them any attempt to formulate a sociological context for the origins of psychoanalysis is equally limited.

Freud fused the psychological idea of his own death with the historical fate of his psychoanalysis: were analysis not to be established in Western culture (were it not to achieve "immortality," so to speak), were the group/movement to fail, then that would have been the same as "a living death." The relationship between Freud's persistent anxiety about his own death and a developmentally real maternal presence/absence in his life receives further clarification from two events in his life: one, the death of his mother and his unusual reaction to it (he felt no current of mourning but could not explain why); the other, an exchange with his mother at the age of six, in which she demonstrated conclusively to him (he did not like the idea at all) that all people eventually die. These two events in Freud's life add some further evidence for my point, but I also use them as metaphors—perhaps even as parables—for my conclusion, in which I reformulate the relation between psychoanalysis and history. For anxiety about mortality and immortality has one of its genetic roots in the (developmentally specific) unconscious merger with the mother; individuation out of that merger into separateness (which includes de-idealization and structure building) activates this anxiety as well as making possible its mastery; and, insofar as such individuation proceeds, then the person becomes increasingly historical. So I conclude with a paradox: because psychoanalysis is the science of infantile life, it is also the science of the way in which a person becomes historical.

Freud's Death Anxiety and the Idea of a Maternal Presence

Moments after Felix Deutsch had examined Freud's "leucoplakia" in 1923, Freud asked him for help to "disappear from the world with decency" and then "spoke of his old mother, who would find the news of his death very hard to bear" (Jones 1957, p. 90). Later, in 1930, when he was vacationing in Frankfurt, Freud's mother died in Vienna. He was unable to detect a strong current of grief. He did not attend the funeral but instead sent Anna. He accounted for this unconventional decision when he explained his psychological reaction to his mother's death, first to Jones and then to Ferenczi. He reported to Jones that the event had produced an increase in personal freedom, "since it was always a terrifying thought that she might come to hear of my death." But he also wondered about the "effects such an experience may produce in deeper layers." To Ferenczi he said much the same thing: "I was not allowed to die as long as she was alive, and now I may." And he wondered again: "Somehow the values of life have notably changed in the deeper layers" (Jones 1957, pp. 152–53). So one must ask, Why was Freud "terrified" by the thought that he would predecease his mother? And what might have been the content of "the deeper layers"?

This fear symbolized a great deal, as anyone with analytic interests and sensitivity knows right away. It is also known that Freud proposed a simple, positive oedipal view of his own relationship to his mother, a view challenged by much current writing, which suggests that the relationship was far more primitive and ambivalent. If the latter is also correct—that is, if Freud's relationship to his mother was heavily overdetermined—then in his unconscious his anxiety about his own death and his anxiety about his mother's death were probably linked, condensed, maybe even interchangeable. If so, then "the deeper layers" contained the issue of a maternal presence and its absence and all the primitive ambivalence which that would arouse. In Freud's mature psychoanalytic theory death was, of course, a drive which polarized around the father, who, as a carrier of the cultural superego, in turn aggressed against each child's developing ego. But in his own experience toward the end of his own life, his psychological sense of his own death seems to have been more related to his mother and to have had a more complex meaning.

Although it is highly speculative to say, I think that an important clue to the genetic root of this linkage between Freud's fear of death and his unconscious anxiety about a maternal presence/absence lies in a dream which evoked a childhood memory in which he learned of death literally "at the hands" of his mother—she was his instructress in mortality. This dream immediately precedes the dream of Count Thun in *The Interpretation of Dreams*, and Freud offered both dreams as the best possible illustrations he could find of the relationship in the human mind between recent events and long-forgotten childhood experiences. Only one portion of the dream and Freud's interpretation of it is of concern here.

Tired and hungry after a journey, we are told (1900), Freud went to bed without eating and dreamt of food. Searching for pudding in a kitchen, he noticed three women, one of whom was twisting something in her hands as if to make a dumpling. The woman told Freud he would have to wait until she was ready, and he, impatient, "went off with a sense of injury." The three women may have been the Three Fates, one of whom was "the mother who gives life." The woman's twisting motion with her hands (as if to make a dumpling) in the dream produced a key association in Freud's mind, an early memory: "When I was six years old and was given my first lessons by my mother, I was expected to believe that we were all made of earth and must therefore return to earth. This did not suit me and I expressed doubts of the doctrine." His mother then rubbed her hands together and showed him the blackish scales of her epidermis "as a proof that we were made of earth." Freud was, he said, astonished, and accepted the idea then and there, although much later he acknowledged again the force of this idea in his appreciation of Shakespeare's famous line, "Thou owest nature [*sic*] a death" (1900, pp. 204–5).

So Freud's mother had confronted him, at the age of six, with the fact of death, to which he responded with a sense of narcissistic injury ("this did not suit me") and then with astonished acquiescence. "So they really were Fates that I found in the kitchen," he mused. In Freud's dream and in his interpretation awareness of death was associated not only with a mother, but with a mother who was withholding food, the "first nourishment" of "the living creature" (pp. 204–5). In this instance, Freud's relationship to his mother was not at all oedipal but rather narcissistic (in the dream, "I went off with a sense of injury"; in reality, "this did not suit me"). His parapraxis regarding Shakespeare's line is well known: Prince Hal told Falstaff, "Thou owest *God* a death," not nature. To the linkage, mother/awareness of death, Freud was able to add the idea of God only by way of negation, for "God" and "nature" are, in the history of Western thought, negatives of each other.

It is widely recognized that religious ideas register in the symbol system of a culture the wish for immortality and the denial of mortality. Yet Freud seems not to have associated his own sense of Jewish identity with either side of this issue. Perhaps this perception derives from the fact that scholars have, like Freud himself, always linked his Jewishness to his identification with male Jewish figures—Fliess, Breuer, Hammerschlag—and from there to his liberal, impecunious, Bible-reading father. I know of no studies of Freud's mother which center upon her Jewishness—that is, her religion—as a possible source of Freud's affirmation of a nondoctrinal Jewish identity. Could he have identified with her, and in doing so derived from her his "first lessons," and from these the unique pattern of idealization and de-idealization which so informed his tragic and ironic appreciation of the essence of life? In these passages Freud used the words "doctrine" and "belief" to characterize his mother's view of mortality. Her method of conveying her convictions about the fundamental meaning of life was certainly primitive and concretistic. Freud portrayed her here as well-nigh charismatic in her unshakable sense of certainty. Her method of instruction seems almost a parody of what Winnicott calls "good enough mothering," with its emphasis upon "holding," support, facilitation, and the process of gradually disillusioning the child. Of Amalia Freud, Ellenberger said: "Testimonies about her concur on three points: her beauty, her authoritarian personality, and her boundless admiration for her firstborn Sigmund" (1970, p. 426). Freud's gentle and rational brand of Jewishness, his lack of illusions about immortality, and his unique patterning of the universal experience of de-idealization may have been all that he cared to retain from his identification with what would seem to be a very irrational mother.

Psychoanalysis, History, and the Study of Freud's Person

In the very work of creating psychoanalysis and the tools for the psychological interpretation of history, Freud made history problematic for himself and for his followers. In Freud's thought there is, of course, no history of religion. Religion offered no new ideas or new experiences, but only the repetition of old ones. It was in fact pure repetition. Yet there is some question whether there is any history at all in Freud's thought. A theory in which social formations are all simply ever-widening displacements of the family romance makes institutions—even the "first" institution of the family—timeless, synchronic, and ahistorical. Freud set up the psyche of theory, just as he set up his own person at the beginning of the psychoanalytic movement, "in splendid isolation." So he created a dilemma: either timeless primary processes subvert all historical advance, in which case psychoanalysis is revenge on history, or the historian simply splits primary processes or illusion off from historical "reality," in which case history becomes revenge on analysis.

As we have seen, psychoanalysts and historians sensitive to psychoanalytic ideas have attempted to avert this dilemma by situating it in the context of Freud's person, and I have endeavored to revise this approach and extend it to the psychoanalytic movement and Freud's turn to culture in "the cultural texts." When that is done, the following operation is usually constructed. Initially, one encounters the lives of persons and their actions in the form of historical reports. Then one immerses oneself psychologically in these lives and their actions. In doing so, one enacts a kind of "trial identification," in the psychoanalytic sense. Subsequently, one begins to reflect on the data which that immersion has produced, and insofar as that reflection is successful, the trial identification is gradually broken down. The result is a double movement: in the initial phase one is "experience near"; in the phase of reflection one is "experience distant." This double movement is a kind of de-idealization all its own. As a result, one's sense of a figure's historicality emerges from one's sense of its psychologicalness. De-idealization is at once a tool for understanding Freud's person and the pathway to grasping his historical significance.

Therefore, psychoanalytic interpretation is a circular movement involving historical reports, empathic psychological involvement, reconceptualization and reflection, and subsequent conclusions, which are "more historical" because they are "more psychological." It is, however, incorrect to think of this process as a linear movement which could be represented as "history^A → psychological investigation → history^B," for two reasons. First, any investigator is always moving about at one or another of these points and only in a formal sense begins with the first. And second, all historical reports—no matter how "objective" or "scientific" or "empirical" or even "agreed upon" they are—are to some extent already psychological. So the psychological and historical dimensions are always relative to each other.

That this is so in the study of Freud's person appears more clearly when the psychoanalytic movement is understood as a group. Psychoanalytic self-understanding has the effect of constantly decomposing group formations. As psychoanalytic ideas became more and more diffused into the culture which surrounded them, the movement gradually lost much of its sectarian character. As diffusion increased, the movement became more and more a gesellschaft in which leaders executed the ego function of members and less a primary group in which leaders were experienced as self-objects. In this sense the movement was, as a movement, self-defeating from the start. On the other hand, genuine sects constantly engage in the reverse process, that of intensifying primitive group attachments. Religious sects continuously recompose themselves, and their historians regularly sing the praises of such activity. This also explains why genuine sects abhor psychological interpretations of their activities and their leaders and members alike rarely seek analytic treatment or study analytic theory. They have no need to, for they experience no anxiety. Psychological knowledge loosens group loyalties in the interests of autonomy and individuality. This deconstruction is a kind of de-idealization at the level of group life.

It should now be possible to connect the psychological and the historical in the study of Freud's turn to culture as well. I have proposed that discovering the psychological brings the historical into view and that psychological deconstructions of Freud's multiple, complex relationships within the group/movement made his person become less "larger than life," more lifelike, and as such more historical. The same can be said of the relationship between Freud's person and his cultural circumstances. As he de-idealized significant objects in Western culture, politics, and religion, Freud simultaneously undertook an aggressive effort to insert his psychoanalysis into Western culture. In doing so, he in effect proposed that modern man follow his own example and de-idealize his own Western past.

Freud was not the first man in the West to become intimate with his unconscious, but he was the first man to objectify that intimacy in scientific and literary modalities. As such, Freud was also the first man to realize in the fullest sense possible how small and infantile human life "in essence" really is. That made him also the first man to realize that the group formations of history and culture—especially those powerful entities known as politics and religion—derive their totalism and absolutism precisely from their members' denial of their unconscious sense of smallness. So Freud inserted his own mental organization, which was modified by knowledge of these very psychological mechanisms and which has been extended into the group/movement, into the unconscious symbolic processes of Western culture. He thereby conferred historical status on his own inner world and introduced psychological depth into the apsychological and purely moral cultural realities of Western politics and religion. In doing this, Freud created an entirely new vision of Western history— a psychological vision. Creating and recreating this vision was the continuing task of his cultural texts.

Freud's Death and Jones's Idealization of Freud

The creation and re-creation of Freud's vision of modern, Western man was also the legacy which he left to his followers, and none of those followers took that legacy more seriously than did

Ernest Jones. In a final effort to point out the theme of idealiza-
tion/de-idealization in Freud's social world, and in a renewed effort
to identify the psychological forces which activated the portrait Jones
painted in his three-volume work, I take the reader's attention away
from the above abstractions and direct it to a concrete event, Freud's
death itself, by way of several sentences at the end of Jones's funeral
oration, delivered to the mourners in September 1939, in London.
This is hardly the place to explore Jones's life and work psycho-
biographically, but one can hardly overemphasize the way in which
Jones was, in an extremely deep and intimate sense, "a part of" Freud,
psychologically, and that this unconscious merger is the key to his
famous biography, a key which every student of Freud's life does well
to have in hand. As he struggled to articulate what was paramount for
himself and for the others who had been intimately attached to Freud
and who had lost him, Jones's words unintentionally capture the
essentials of the idealization/de-idealization process, for mourning
and de-idealization are intertwined. Jones said (1957): "A great spirit
has passed from the world. How can life keep its meaning for those to
whom he was the center of life? Yet we do not feel it as a real parting
in the full sense, for Freud has so inspired us with his personality, his
character and his ideas that we can never truly part from him until we
finally part from ourselves in whom he still lives. His creative spirit
was so strong that he infused himself into others. If ever man can be
said to have conquered death itself, to live on in spite of the King of
Terrors, who held no terror for him, that man was Freud" (p. 248). In
these sentences one sees Jones mourning his intense attachment to
Freud and its life-giving quality. One can also sense the intimate
linkage between such attachments or identifications with a cherished other and the conviction that, as Winnicott has described one of
the results of a successful analysis, "life is worth living" or "life is
meaningful," which deep attachments often convey; the ameliorat-
ing effects of this sort of attachment on the fear of death and the wish
for immortality (a subdued reference to religion, no doubt, present
through its absence); and, to these I would add the thoroughly silent,
consciously absent, but unconsciously present, maternal presence,
which Freud must have conveyed to Jones and others through the
medium of the group/movement, alongside the better understood
effects of the "father imago."

With his theory of the three blows, then, Freud executed the first
psychological probe into Western man's unconscious cultural
heritage. And, through this analysis of the figure of Moses and of
Christian symbols, he probed the intrapsychic effects upon himself of
his own personal cultural heritage. The loss of the old ideals led first

to disappointment and then mourning and from there into new structures of appreciation, the most important of which was the new
science of psychoanalysis and its theory of culture. To continue: as
clinical theory the analytic situation is, in its most sweeping sense, a
process of mourning in which infantile objects, wishes, and feelings
are gradually renounced, their place to be taken eventually by psychological structure. As a theory of culture, analysis authorizes
mourning for the abandoned ideals, often unconscious, of the ancient
and archaic cultural heritage. Both are instances of the ability to
mourn. Without mourning there can be no growth, no historical
advance, no value change, no hope—the most valuable of all historical acquisitions, for hopelessness is little more than mourning gone
awry. These are the essential conclusions of this essay.

But it would be—and it has become—a bad mistake to think that
psychoanalysis inaugurated such a process. Rather, quite the reverse
is the case. The analytic theory of both the inner world and of culture
is itself the result of a long historical process of disenchantment,
instituted by complex social forces which anteceded the psychoanalytic movement by many centuries. It is time to turn to these
forces and understand them. Studying the 1906–14 period in Freud's
life and all that it entailed has placed us in an extremely advantageous position to do just that. It has set forth for all to see a great
deal of information and understanding about Freud's person, his
thought, and his social surroundings immediately following the "discovery of psychoanalysis"; furthermore, in this it has disclosed a
promontory, formerly thought to be nonexistent, from which one can
look back upon that mysterious event.

In order to comprehend what I here call "historical forces," it is
necessary to develop a sociologically grounded theory of culture in
which to situate more firmly and more deeply Freud's manifold sociality—which, as we have seen, he often denied—and also the
undeveloped allusions to mourning, disenchantment, and disillusionment in part 1. This fresh approach must now be formulated
directly. In particular, it is necessary to examine, in the light of a
sociological frame, what I have come to call the central axis of the
psychoanalytic project as a whole, both in Freud's life and thought
and in contemporary psychoanalysis as well: the self-analysis, the
movement, and the cultural texts. All this is the burden of part 2, and
the argument is set forth in detail there.

We will meet the stiffest resistance at the start, in the self-analysis,
in the form of the two received and regnant views of it: that "the
origins of psychoanalysis" is but a recent chapter in the history of

science or that it is chiefly the product of Freud's introspective genius or his enormous creativity. Both of these views are intrinsically psychological and asociological. So it is necessary to decenter or dispossess them of their totalism in a way that only a thoroughly social perspective can. Such a decentering is in effect a "narcissistic blow" to the solipsistic "fear of sociality" which characterizes the regnant point of view. But the following social analysis does not in any sense thereby destroy the psychological wisdom about "the origins" which has accrued. Rather, it actually illumines that wisdom further by placing it in its proper social and more fully human context. It is important to add that this "sociologizing" or "contextualizing" does not proceed by means of abstract argument but instead is demonstrated by empirical analysis which is supported by recent research.

Furthermore, only such an approach can link the psychoanalytic project as a whole, by reflecting backward, to its deepest roots in Western culture and, by reflecting forward, also show its interrelatedness to contemporary thought and life. For the society in which we all live is heavily psychological—perhaps even more so when this assertion is ignored or denied—and insofar as it is so, that is because it is the "heir" to the psychoanalytic movement and to the vision of culture which Freud announced in his cultural texts. These very far-reaching probes are taken up in part 3, for which part 2 is, in addition to the above, also a preparation.

II Disillusionment and the Social Origins of Psychoanalysis

6   Framing the Argument: Why Think Sociologically about Psychoanalysis?

> Man's characteristic privilege is that the bond he accepts is not physical but moral; that is, social. He is governed . . . by a conscience superior to his own, the superiority of which he feels. Because the greater, better part of his existence transcends the body, he escapes the body's yoke, but is subject to that of society. But when society is disturbed by some painful crisis or by . . . abrupt transitions, it is . . . incapable of exercising this influence.
>
> Durkheim, *Suicide*

> If left to himself, a neurotic is obliged to replace by his own symptom formations the great group formations from which he is excluded. He creates his own world of imagination for himself, his own religion . . . and thus recapitulates the institutions of humanity in a distorted way.
>
> Freud, *Group Psychology and the Analysis of the Ego*

Although Freud's thought and work were clearly devoted to the inner world of the single individual, it is also just as clear that, as the above citation indicates, he thought the inner world was socially located—in "the great group formations" of mankind. In this Freud agreed with the eminent French sociologist, Emile Durkheim, for Durkheim's idea of the social bond, which the individual feels and to whose superiority he is subject, and which is superintended by religious ideas and ideals, is simply the cultural superego. This double perception constitutes the principal methodological assumption of this second essay, which takes as its theme the sociological and historical—but not the psychological—side of Freud's life and his movement, and especially what Durkheim called "the painful crises" and "abrupt transitions" of society, which rupture the social bond and force upon its members anomie, the psychological word for which, it is now time to say, is neurosis.

However, when one turns from Freud's thought to his life, the social side of this double perception evaporates completely. As part 1 made abundantly clear, historical writing on Freud's life has repeatedly called attention to his intense isolation. This is the Freud of Jones, the Freud "unmoved by social circumstance." By introducing revisionist analytic perspectives, by focusing primarily on the formation of the movement and only then reflecting back on the self-analysis and by introducing more recent historical research, we saw a different Freud come into view. It became possible to see Freud struggling with loss and attachment: in relation to individuals (Jung, Abraham, and, earlier, Fliess, and, later, Rolland), but also in relation to particular historical forces (German political liberalism and his Jewish sense of community) and, more generally, with the sweeping, civilizational processes of disenchantment and rationalization. As Freud de-idealized and mourned for these persons, forces, and ideals, he turned in on himself. His creativity was stimulated, and he evolved not only original psychological ideas but also a richer, more psychological inner life.

Left to itself, the psychobiographical approach tells us a great deal about the inner significance of Freud's discoveries and personal relationships, about what "he came to," but it tells us far less about their social referents—"where he came from." In fact, it forestalls investigation of the latter. Historical studies go some distance in amending this by disclosing the ideals and ideas which confronted Freud. But it is an idealistic fallacy to think that anyone can de-idealize a conscious ideal without at one and the same time significantly altering his relationship to "the great group formations" of mankind, for these embody the ideal. This is especially so in the case of religion, which was so crucial to Freud's inner struggles. Conscious attachment to religious ideas and ideals represents the individual's unconscious attachment to the religious community, what Durkheim called the social and moral bond—"a conscience superior to his [man's] own." In short, psychological approaches convey inner depth but lack the social referent; historical approaches are social but lack psychological depth.

In order to understand more deeply and more broadly Freud's discoveries and, from there, the obscure interplay between his self-analysis, his work, his movement, and his composition of the cultural texts, it is necessary to have a clearer understanding of his social world. To accomplish this task, it is in turn necessary to reopen and reformulate the oldest, most central, and most hackneyed problem in social theory, which is also one of the most important issues in psychoanalytic thought, the relationship between *"das Ich"* and the social other. Talcott Parsons referred to "the convergence" noted above between the ideas of Freud and of Durkheim as one of the "truly fundamental landmarks of the development of modern social science" (1964, p. 19). I prefer the word "paradox" to "convergence" in order to emphasize the interface *between* the I and the social other and to deemphasize what is either "in" personality or "in" the social system, and this paradox serves as the sociological unit of analysis or tool which I use to link psychological and historical observations on Freud's life course and achievements.

The paradox is that analytic knowledge, the capacity to introspect empathically into one's inner world and its developmental infrastructures, is always generated at the margins of the social world of the other. Although I think this tension is a universal feature of social life, it acquired unprecedented depth and intensity in Freud's life. To put the matter the other way around: the more intense are a person's unconscious attachments to the great group formations which surround him, the stronger is the social or moral bond which joins him to "a conscience superior to his own" and the less likely will a person be to introspect in a depth-psychological way. When this formulation is directed to a historical situation in which "society is disturbed by some painful crisis" or by "abrupt transitions," then, under such cultural conditions the "ego will attempt to fulfill its organizing functions by increased insight into internal processes" (Hartmann, quoted in Weinstein and Platt 1969, p. 138). I formulate this paradox in detail below, along with the appropriate literature review, as the tension between analytic access and a common culture and make liberal use of the Durkheimian word "transition" to characterize the shift from culture to self, but I give the term a distinctly Winnicottian (1951) cast. Historical transitions, I propose showing, produce psychological transitions.

With these thoughts in mind, it becomes possible to reflect in a fresh way upon Freud's achievements. For example, his sad giving up of the ideals of political liberalism at the time of his self-analysis and the ensuing conflict between his earlier Jewish identity and an emerging psychoanalytic identity can be understood as the waning of a common culture and the consequent emergence of analytic access. The unexpected group cohesion of the movement itself owed much of its strength to its members' reparative attempts to constitute a common, analytic culture, and its later dissipation further illustrates the paradox just referred to: what flourishes at the margins (depth-psychological self-understanding) cannot exist at the center (the common culture) without being itself destroyed. In his cultural texts Freud sought to implement further the aims of the movement—to invade, as it were, the center—by creating psychological interpretations of, and thereby introducing analytic access into, the common cultures of the West (Judaism, Catholicism, and the modern state). As he became deeply disenchanted with the ideals which they had offered him, he proposed alternatives of his own.

Sociological reflection on psychoanalysis decenters the insistence of its received tradition on the uniqueness of Freud's achievement of a psychological perspective by adducing the analytic (but not psychoanalytic) category of social-structural change: changes such as these, and not only Freud's Beethoven-like genius, brought about in him marginality, anomie, and the anxiety-laden struggle to introspect. If this were so, then it would have to follow that Freud's introspective achievements were in fact independently duplicated in varying degrees by others. In the body of this essay I therefore compose vignettes (they are really sketches and not portraits) of three highly significant figures in Freud's movement—Carl Jung, Otto Rank, and Ernest Jones—in order to show that the pattern of their lives was in many ways similar to Freud's. They too were uprooted from a religiously formed common culture by industrialization and urbanization. Detached, anomic, and marginal to a heritage of received, common meanings, they too turned in on themselves and struggled to understand the depths of their own alienated sense of self-consciousness. They came to Freud and worked in the movement in order to enrich the self-understandings which they had organized, to clarify and augment their own "self-analyses." Like Freud, they were "in transition" from one set of common meanings to another, which was only beginning to emerge.

Studying the lives of these men in this way also allows me to carry forward another project begun in part 1, that of bringing into the light of day various "shadow figures" in Freud's movement. Although I am interested in the psychology of their personalities and in their place in the movement, I am even more concerned with the social forces and factors which shaped each man's unique search for a psychological point of view. So I consider each follower's pursuit of psychological self-understanding to be different from Freud's in degree but not in kind, and therefore characterize what I have been calling analytic access as an "ideal-type," in the Weberian sense—that is, as an ideal-typical patterning of a subjective state which can be found not only in Freud's life, or in the lives of those who populated his movement, but also for that matter in varying degrees in the works of creative writers in other places and other times.

Furthermore, this richer and fuller picture of the movement makes it possible to fathom far more precisely than heretofore why Freud turned to the writing of the cultural texts when he did and what the central issue in them really was, which the analysts' customary "applications" of psychoanalysis to the "scientific" study of society have so successfully obscured. The cultural texts were organic, psychological extensions of the movement, just as the latter was an extension of the self-analysis. So I first seek to explain the social forces which augmented this shift from movement to culture and then, second, go on to thematize the central leitmotiv of the texts themselves: Freud's intense ambivalence about the Western past and, in particular, its consoling, communal structure. Convinced that his creation "saw through" the mechanisms of culture (I call this view "the cunning of culture") and had thereby separated him and all who accepted his ideas irreparably from the consolations of the past, he also longed for and deeply mourned for the past. The cultural texts announce this loss, but they also attempt to heal and overcome it by relating developmental processes to historic form. Therefore, the psychoanalytic project, when it is taken as a whole, is a threefold one: the self-analysis, the movement, and the theory of culture. It is in fact safe to say that "the clinical Freud" was every bit as "cultural" as "the cultural Freud." When clinicians and humanists separate these two, they badly misunderstand the social context and the structure of psychoanalysis.

The usefulness of Weber's thought for a sociological understanding of psychoanalysis is, however, hardly exhausted by the concepts of disenchantment, rationalization, and the ideal-type. Weber always thought of the first two in the broader context of the historical clashes in the West between religion and physical science. That science, he said, disenchanted the religious world, and he modeled his own view of the science of society on its physicalistic approaches. So did Freud, such that the leading, distinguishing feature of psychoanalysis as a new body of thought came to be its scientific—that is, metapsychological—character. Freud thought that the metapsychology took on its critical, purgative power from its capacity to inflict a third blow to Western religious sensibilities. But he also assumed a purely cognitive and idealistic theory of science and thought in terms of a total and largely cognitive break between the religious past and the scientific present. This view was not only entirely asociological; it was also—and this may be just as important—apsychological in a number of ways as well. By overemphasizing science, Freud was able to underemphasize the social infrastructure in which he was embedded and, in particular, the complex and paradoxical part which his own religious tradition played in the origins of his work.

So, in the final chapter of this essay I explore the relations between psychoanalysis, science, and society by way of the work of Weber's well-known student Robert Merton on the role of Puritanism in the rise of physical science in the seventeenth century. Merton asked, How could devout Puritans create natural science and still be religious? He concluded that the Puritan ethos bore an internal, positive relation to science by means of which religious ideas actually facilitated a "breakthrough" into scientific discovery. I show that the origins of psychoanalysis repeated this pattern, and I think that this sheds a great deal of light on the still unresolved view that psychoanalysis was either a Jewish science or simply owed nothing at all to its Jewish past. Recognizing the plethora of Jews in the psychoanalytic movement and citing evidence for the unusually high statistical overrepresentation of Jews in contemporary psychoanalysis and psychotherapy, I develop a sociological account of the psychoanalyst's transition from his Jewish sensibilities, which were grounded in the common culture of Jewish faith, to the psychoanalytic point of view and its ideological essence, the metapsychology.

This account places me in an advantageous position to track the fate of the metapsychology and to explore the psychological and sociological meanings inherent in the claims of psychoanalysis to be scientific. The metapsychology collapsed in interwar London. Under the impress of further social-structural change and augmented by national mourning over the losses inflicted by the terrible war, it virtually withered away, to be replaced by clinical and theoretical concerns with attachment, loss, and the social world of patients, many of whom were soldiers and children, in striking contrast to Freud's hysterical (and largely Jewish) women. It comes as no surprise that, under these social circumstances, the psychology of mourning itself underwent great development and that the ability to mourn and the collapse of the metapsychology were closely related. I conclude that the metapsychology was an epoch-specific defense against mourning.

Then, in the final section of my essay, I refocus as concretely as possible much that has been said throughout about the origins of psychoanalysis, and especially the central construct, the tension between analytic access and a common culture, by examining the truly extraordinary similarities between Freud's life and work and Max Weber's. In particular, I explore the sociological and psychological roots of Weber's own "metapsychology," upon which I have relied so heavily, his idea of a value-free social science, and the closely related concept, disenchantment. After abandoning important attachments to his own religious past or common culture, which were mediated for him by an intensely ambivalent relationship to his deeply pious mother, Weber made that past into an intellectual problem, discovered in it its hidden, sociological significance, and formulated all this by means of his new ideals of disenchantment and value-free social science. Mourning was an important feature of his transition from his mother's piety to a sociological point of view. The essay concludes by extending the sociological perspective to the mechanisms of psychoanalytic healing.

The likenesses between the life and work of Freud and Weber allow me to propose that psychoanalysis belongs, in important ways, to social as well as to psychological science. They also refocus nicely the major issues of this second essay as a whole, especially the way in which "breaking with the past" became the central problem which Freud's (and Weber's) theory of culture made necessary but could not resolve. The final pages explain why and how part 3 is given over to putting to rest this issue.

How to Think Sociologically about Psychoanalysis

If psychobiographical and historical studies of Freud's life call for further exploration of his social world and that world's more sweeping historical context, then what sort of social theory is satisfactory for this task? Or, to restate the question in a more focused way so as to emphasize the origins of psychoanalysis, under what social conditions did psychoanalysis emerge when and where it did? The capacity of psychoanalysis to first attend in experience-near fashion and then reflect in an experience-distant way upon the evanescent surfaces of self-consciousness, such as dreams, forgotten childhood memories, slips of the tongue, and jokes, and then to trace these back into a hidden and forbidden unconscious matrix of wishes, desires, and objects or imagoes, and the capacity to do this in a manner which is more direct, less mediated, and less disguised by symbolic, cultural codes—all this sets analysis apart from the earlier, like-minded efforts of mystical, philosophical, artistic, and literary virtuosos, although by no means absolutely. It is the emergence of this capacity in Western culture which occupies us now.

A multifaceted approach is necessary in the case of psychoanalysis because it is a multifaceted phenomenon made up of new and original

ideas, a movement or community of men and women who investigated and lived out a new way of thinking about the relation between the
self and the social order, and an intellectual outlook which has powerfully and decisively shaped contemporary thought and experience.
The most effective sociological discussions of psychoanalysis have
all come from the sociology of knowledge, for good reason. All versions of this genre of thought manage to combine an emphasis upon
the social forces or conditions which give rise to new ideas with the
subjective states of individuals and their new relations to the surrounding world of everyday life while at the same time placing both
within the sweeping historical tension between tradition and religion, on the one hand, and modernity and secularity, on the other.

  The great strength of this genre is its comprehensiveness, but it
has an unfortunate weakness as well. Although all its proponents are
to some extent familiar with psychoanalytic ideas and practice, they
have little capacity to appreciate the subjective, experiential states of
mind which characterize the analytic situation. I begin by noting the
essential features of this theory and its roots in classic sociological
thought in order to identify it for the reader. In no sense do I attempt
to summarize it or defend it. In the next section I provide a brief
phenomenology of the ideal-type: the analytic situation, which I call
analytic access, and its sociological component, the idea of a common culture. From there I return to the matter at hand, Freud and his
followers, in order to explore further the social side of their work
together and especially how that work led to the cultural texts.

  All sociological theories of psychoanalysis are built upon four
heavily idealized stages of historical development, beginning with a
community-oriented medieval Christendom and ending with the
autonomy-oriented and fragmented modern society.[1] The outstanding feature of Western medieval life, they tell us, was not only its
amazing synthesis of nature and grace, in the work of St. Thomas
Aquinas, but also its even more amazing synthesis of the varieties of
person and station into a single, shared worldview in the workings of
the Roman Catholic church. Although highly differentiated and
stratified in many ways, social solidarity and ontological consensus
were, in medieval life, mutually supportive. Karl Mannheim characterized the Middle Ages as possessing "one, unambiguously
perceivable world order" (1936, p. 14). Peter Berger (1967) uses the
term "sacred canopy" to describe the fact that, despite diversity,
most men, women, and children could find essential aspects of themselves in the church's doctrines (theology and philosophy), moral
theology and casuistry (ethics), and cure of souls (pastoral psychol-

ogy). Weinstein and Platt think of medieval life as a common culture, by which they mean that "internalization of values occurs most intensively and extensively in relatively undifferentiated groups and communities" (1969, p. 32).

Reformation and Renaissance, Enlightenment, accelerating scientific discoveries, and technological advances culminating in the industrial revolution shattered the links between social solidarity and a shared sense of what was objectively true. Mannheim thought that vertical mobility was crucial. "Vertical mobility," as he said, "is the decisive factor in making persons uncertain and skeptical of their traditional view of the world" (1936, p. 7). Berger speaks of an initial transfer of scientific thinking to technological and economic activity, which later creates a "pluralization of world-views." Weinstein and Platt emphasize the primary role of industrialization in creating social-structural change: increased social differentiation forces upon men and women a growing split between public and private modes of experiencing. This split is one of the central hallmarks of modernity.[2]

These changes produced an increased strain on the personal sector, what I call the inner world. Whereas, before, problems of internal, social, and cultural adaptation were managed by the central, integrative institutional mechanism of the church, under conditions of increased social differentiation these tasks or activities became more and more forced back upon individuals, groups, classes, sects, and movements. Changes in the social fabric also brought about shifts in the way knowledge about the world was formulated: "After the objective ontological unity of the world had been demolished, the attempt was made to substitute for it a unity imposed by the perceiving subject. In the place of the medieval-Christian objective and ontological unity of the world, there emerged the subjective unity of the absolute subject of the Enlightenment—'consciousness in itself'" (Mannheim 1936, p. 66). Mannheim referred to this new emergent as an epistemology of the subject, and he thought that medieval preoccupations with theories of sin, despair, guilt and loneliness "were replaced by formalized entities such as the feeling of anxiety, the perception of inner conflict, the experiencing of isolation and the 'libido'" (p. 17). Weinstein and Platt cite the introspective, psychologically oriented themes found in the works of the Enlightenment philosophes as further evidence of a search for a new form of moral autonomy, one independent of maternally grounded, unconscious affective ties to ecclesiastical and political leaders who were, by definition, situated at the center of society.

The final phase of this development, in which strain on the personal sector underwent a transformation from the philosophical, literary, and religious elaboration of introspective themes into an objective psychological theory of the mind, chiefly in the form of its key concept, "the unconscious," has been the most difficult to comprehend (see also Berger 1965, in this regard). Like most sociologists, Mannheim and Berger are willing to grant phenomenological, but not epistemic, validity to the introspective explorations of depth psychology. Indeed, the first three stages which I have just noted (global social cohesion → social differentiation → marginal or "psychological" experiences) are grounded firmly in classic sociological theory. Durkheim's entire oeuvre is predicated on the passage from religious solidarity (community, inorganic solidarity), through differentiation (division of labor, individuation), to autonomy (organic solidarity and anomie). Weber's historical analysis of Western culture constantly emphasized the rationalization of persons' attachments to spontaneous, magical communities into empty and isolated personalities who inhabited a stifling bureaucratic structure. But neither of these originative sociologists, nor their innovative followers, saw fit to explore the sociological shifts they were describing so as to include the standpoint of the individual's inner world.

Weinstein and Platt have, however, offered an important but undeveloped explanation of the fourth step, the transition from mere strain on the personal sector, which was extremely high among introspective writers in the late nineteenth and early twentieth centuries (such as Dostoyevski, Tolstoy, Joyce, Kafka, and Proust), to the attempt of psychoanalysis to reflect in a systematic way upon the contents of consciousness released by the weakening of social cohesion. They propose a sociologically structured increase of flexibility in the repression barrier. Only in advanced industrial and urbanized situations, they point out, were fathers increasingly removed from the family and mothers segregated entirely into nurturant roles within the family. This increased differentiation of roles was less characteristic of preindustrial situations, where fathers were more nurturant and mothers less segregated. As long as fathers remained nurturant, sons would have neither the desire nor the capacity to rebel. But once industrialization drew fathers out of the family, sons could and did experience loss and anger and a subsequent wish to be included in the father's world, and not the mother's, by means of identification. As social-structural change reorganized the inner patterns of the family, fathers and sons gradually began to experience more consciously and reflect upon their newly acquired intense feelings about each other, and eventually some of them became able to develop theories to explain their experiences, both to themselves and to the world at large. In a moment I will reformulate this fourth step, and that theoretical innovation will open the way to rethinking the origins of Freud's discoveries.

No doubt there are mythic elements in this theory: even if it were spelled out in more detail, it would still be too smooth, and different narrators tell the same story over and over again. In its mythic dimension the theory is, I think, the myth of the origin of the sociologist. But myth can also be demythicized. Embedded in its mythic components are some valuable social and psychological elements as well. I find close to the heart of this theory the deceptively simple and actually profound principle that psychological thinking of the kind in which Freud engaged always emerges at the margins of a common culture. The best-known current discussion of a common culture comes from Talcott Parsons. Weinstein and Platt took their version of it from him and added to that the ego psychologies of Heinz Hartmann and Erik Erikson to link up sociological and psychological processes (they do not use, as I do, the phrase "tension between a common culture and analytic access"). Hartmann and Erikson of course took their ideas from Freud, and Parsons took his from Durkheim.

Parsons defines a common culture as "a commonly shared system of symbols" (T. Parsons 1964, p. 21) about which actors in any social system agree. The universality of common symbol systems derives from "the extreme plasticity and sensitivity of the human organism," which introduces "an element of extreme potential instability into the process of human interaction which requires stabilizing mechanisms" (p. 21). Weinstein and Platt elaborate this definition (the problem of instability in human interaction) in more detail by introducing the concept of the individual and his relations to specific group formations. These relationships are best characterized, they think, as object relations. They speak of "the ties that exist between and among individuals . . . and such abstract notions and collective arrangements as political authority and organizations, economic institutions, occupational groups, social statuses and rules" and "cultural ideals" (1973, p. 102). They then go on to point out that systematic-structural relations between the ego and social objects take on historical significance through the process of object loss, which is defined as the "state of being deprived of, or having to be or do without, some object (person, aspect of self, cultural abstraction) that is invested with affect and is culturally defined as valuable" (p.

102). From the individual point of view, the experience of loss includes "being hurt, disappointed, or neglected" and produces states such as sorrow, grief, depression, and hopelessness, but also "denial, relief, and the absence of feeling" (p. 103). This gradual process of modernization has produced "a growing capacity among individuals for making conscious, ego-oriented choices" (p. 73). It is understandable that Weinstein and Platt would cite with approval Roy Schafer's characterization of the new psychological point of view as one in which "individuals are able to review their thoughts and feelings and actions from several points of view, including the moral, rather than being overwhelmed by the moral point of view alone (p. 73).

Parsonian preoccupations with "system," "integration," and "convergence," however, along with ego psychology's view of personality as a highly individualized, synchronic, abstracted, and mechanical-like field of forces, obscure recognition of the dynamic and diachronic interface between the ego-subject and the social object, thereby denying the realization that it is precisely the interface between the two which generates what is then thought, by psychologists and sociologists, to be either "in the mind" or "in the culture." In an effort to avoid this pitfall, I reformulate the relation between the two as "transitional," in a sense which is initially Winnicottian (1951) but which also moves beyond that. I also think of the transitional space as existing not only between infant and mother or patient and therapist but also between individuals and representative persons in their shared common culture. Only this formulation can capture the enormously confusing blend of inner struggle, social structure, symbol formation, and symbol appropriation (but also symbol repudiation), self-transformation, and historical advance which characterized Freud's achievements. Consequently, I speak of Freud's "transition" from his political and religious common cultures, and in particular from the representative persons and symbolic objects in these cultures (these too are "representative"), to his achievement of access into the emerging inner or psychological world which the transition made available to him. This is, of course, what I have referred to above as "the fourth step" in the sociology of psychological knowledge, and it can now be described.

The speculation of Weinstein and Platt, that social-structural change produced important shifts in the psychological organization of the family over time, can easily be confused with the old debate about the nuclear family: an "extended family" characteristic of preindustrial times was shrunk by industrialization to become the "nuclear family" of contemporary Western life. More to the point, their concept of an "increased flexibility of the repression barrier" has a kind of sui generis quality and ignores the crucial interactions which so often occur between individuals and representative persons in the community at large, which both inhabit, and the way these patterns can change.

I assume that the European family in preindustrial times was also nuclear, as Mitterauer and Sieder (1982) and many others have pointed out, but I also think that industrialization—wherever it occurs—has the psychological effect of diminishing the capacity of individuals to invest representative persons in their communities with the same quality of primitive and unconscious affect which, today, tends to be associated with the nuclear family. In other words, there has been over time a gradual withdrawal of psychological energy from such representative persons, and this has "raised the psychological temperature" of life within the family. It has also reduced the psychological temperature in the culture at large. Such withdrawal can also be formulated psychoanalytically as a kind of "delibidinalization" of representative persons in the surrounding preindustrial social and cultural world. As industrialization and the technologizing of nature progressed, and as mechanical and material objects acquired ever greater social ascendancy and visibility, it became—and still continues to become—increasingly difficult for persons to invest such representative figures or objects with primitive, unconscious affect.[3]

In the more immediate and face-to-face sense, the word "transition" refers to the psychological space which exists between the objective, taken-for-granted social world and the subjective psychological world of unconscious wishes, drives, and objects. Whenever creative activity occurs, it takes place in this space, which Winnicott characterized as the place or space in the mind for culture, what he called "the location of cultural experience." Winnicott said (1967), rightly I think, that Freud could find no place in the mind for culture. In what follows I also speak of Freud's transition in terms of disillusionment, as well as of de-idealization and mourning. Furthermore, I reformulate the unavoidably static and reified concept of a common culture along the more dynamic and historical lines of "a sense of community" or "a sense of belonging." Much later (in part 3) I pick up the trail of this concept and rework it along more constructive and creative lines, making especial use of the idea of "a collective memory."

Before turning to Freud's self-analysis and his movement, however, it is necessary to demonstrate more clearly and with far greater specificity how and why psychological self-understanding or analytic access and the common culture in which it is embedded and which always gives it its particular shape are in conflict—for none of the accounts of psychoanalysis which I have reviewed (either here or in part 1: psychological, historical, or sociological) have recognized the centrality of this tension, especially when it is cast in the heuristically advantageous format of an ideal-type.

The Essential Tension: Analytic Access and a Common Culture

Historical studies of psychoanalysis trace and track the appearance of Freud's ideas about mental life in relation to various traditions of inquiry, chiefly philosophical and scientific, existing at the time. Psychobiography centers upon Freud's personal experiences of these traditions. Sociological approaches emphasize shifting social-structural change. Like the psychobiographers, I think that the essence of psychoanalysis is the capacity to experience in a highly direct way the reality of unconscious mental processes, as well as the ability to reflect upon these, gradually formulating introspective aperçus into a coherent explanatory frame of ideas. Psychoanalysis means closeness to or "access" into depth-psychological events. But like the sociologists, I also think that psychological ideas are generated by social forces, and for that reason facsimiles of Freud's allegedly unique achievement can be found in the lives and works of others and not only in the life of one great man, although he may formulate these more cogently or more convincingly than others. If both propositions are true, then it becomes necessary to think about psychoanalysis and about its origins in a way which accounts both for the uniqueness of one person's individual, psychological experience and for its socially shared or typical features.

For this reason I use the concept of the "ideal-typical," adapted from Max Weber (1904, 1904–5). I think that the capacity for depth-psychological self-understanding was shared by many, beginning roughly with the turn of the century, and has increased over the years—hence the contemporary so-called psychological culture of psychological man (Rieff 1959) and the even more recent so-called culture of narcissism (Lasch 1978). It is a type of experience. Furthermore, because analytic access contains an experience-distant component which is supported by the view that it is a science (a view I progressively criticize and disenchant as this essay develops), the discoveries of Freud and of other modern psychologists have to be distinguished, at least for the moment, from those of earlier psychological virtuosos such as, in theology, St. Paul, St. Augustine, and Kierkegaard; in philosophy, Montaigne, Rousseau, and Descartes; in medicine and psychology, Charcot and Fechner; and in literature. The insights of these writers were, from the psychoanalytic point of view, sporadic and idiosyncratic. They did not really penetrate the repression barrier as completely as did more recent efforts, and hence they did not represent accurately infantile developmental processes in a systematic way.

By ideal, in the concept ideal-typical, I wish to convey the presence of a formal pattern of structure but not the idea of perfection, whereas typical suggests that the pattern is really a type which is shared by others, although it is not necessarily average. In taking analytic access as an ideal-type, I do little more than the student of genre or folktales who seeks to establish a representative text in preparation for interpretation. One cannot analyze every tale (one cannot describe completely or exhaustively every analysis, or even one analysis), nor can one create a composite tale which contains all the key elements of all tales (nor can one abstract from many analyses an average or typical analysis). Instead, confronted by endless plurality but convinced nonetheless that continuity and a common structure exist across the cases which one observes, one momentarily turns away from them and into oneself, drawing upon one's own imagination in order to return thereby to the data with a construction—that is to say, with a projection—of an ideal-typical version, one which has never existed historically and which can never and will never exist as such. Only in such a construction can the historical forces and forms which one is studying find themselves. Freud understood this approach well when he said of his interpretive efforts to "glimpse a new meaning" in Michelangelo's statue of Moses: "In imagination we complete the scene of which this movement . . . is a part" (1914*a*, p. 224).[4] In so saying, Freud in effect sought the ideal-typical elements in Jews' experiences of their highly esteemed and socially shared cultural symbol, the historical and legendary figure of Moses.

The indisputably outstanding mark or feature of analytic access is its claim (to be disputed later) to be utterly prepolitical, preethical, and presocial in character. In order to probe in depth one's inner world, one must withdraw from the real world of everyday social life, which is so convincing, at least while one is in it, that it forestalls any attention to the inner life. This retreat is augmented by the patient's couch, which deprives him of the most ordinary social distractions and reduces the social stimulus value of the analyst; by the analyst's double doors, which keep out the voices of other people, who are engaged in social transactions; especially by the analyst's insistence upon listening and upon refusing to make conversation, which reverses the rules of ordinary social intercourse in a truly disturbing way; but most of all by the basic rule (one must say whatever comes to mind), which is an affront to the essence of social structure, the repression barrier. All these circumstances facilitate the gradual turning in of consciousness to the inner world of personal desire and memory. The truth claims of psychoanalysis always refer back to these circumstances, and Freud's concepts and the evidence he offered to support them derive their cogency from these phenomenological realities of the analytic situation. Opponents of Freud's theories are often unable to repeat in their own imagination this outstanding mark or feature of analytic access, and it is understandable that they should, for this reason, reject his views.

The central "location" of analytic access is between biology and society or between nature and culture, or —as Freud put it—the "I" exists between instinctual drives and social forces. The psychical is precisely this intermediate or transitional sector known as the individual mind. It follows that the goal of analysis is individuation or development or psychological structure building. The organism accomplishes this by progressing from the largely unconscious deep dependency of the infantile situation, through primitive relationships with significant objects and roles, to a state of relative independence by means of identifications, internalizations, introjections, and projections. Neural and social components combine in the synthetic activity of fantasy, and it is fantasy activity that analytic access gives access to. The fantasy is the unit of analysis in psychoanalysis. As such, fantasy is the form or model for the mental contents which analysis analyzes: dreams, free associations, faulty actions, and, of course, transferences. Because fantasy bridges between nature and culture it is an essential component of "the category of the person" (Mauss 1938).

Transference is the principal means or medium for facilitating analytic access. When the usual definitions of it are formulated socially, transference can be seen as the creation or re-creation of a false and archaic sociality on the basis of distorted infantile wishes, desires, and object relations. Transference is the essential paradox of analysis, for only by allowing a false sociality to exist and claiming it to be true can a genuine sociality eventually be built up. Although it is an illusion, the false and archaic sociality must be believed for a while (it *is* true), if it is to lead back to self-knowledge (it *was* true) and forward to integration and self-transformation (it continues to "exist," but only in the form of illusion and memory and can be to some extent relinquished).

Dreams are really internal or intrapsychical transferences from the unconscious to the realm of conscious thought and experience, and they show with special clarity how the analytic situation is a retreat or withdrawal from the social world, for dreams are "the royal road" to the unconscious. Dreams are the most personal, private, and individual of mental actions. They occur under conditions of physical and social withdrawal. One's dreams can be told only to another, and even telling them asks an imaginative leap from the hearer, who cannot experience them directly. Social propriety forbids the telling of dreams in public life, and remembering dreams during the day varies inversely with the intensity of one's participation in the everyday social world. Only at night, when one is unconscious, does the unconscious become conscious, and it makes its appearance in dreams.

Different analytic writers have formulated the goals of treatment in different ways: Freud emphasized insight, psychological truth, and self-knowledge; the ego psychologists prefer neutralization of drives and expanded, more autonomous ego functions; self-psychology speaks of the analyst's capacity to promote a situation of optimal frustration or disillusionment or de-idealization of archaic imagoes and the consequent building up of psychological structure. But all agree that a common pathway to their respective goals is an enhanced capacity not simply to appreciate the fine points of one's own developmental reality but also to accept in a self-empathic way the reality or existence, as such, of unconscious developmental experience. The "I" which introspects upon developmental reality is both near to it and distant from it.

So understood, the achievement of analytic access, though always a more or less relative one, constitutes a radical revision of the relation between self and society in the history of Western culture. On the one hand, it is virtually synonymous with detachment, working unabashedly against massive identifications and the ad hoc internalization of the social norms which those who superintend a common culture love to celebrate. But analytic access is not individualism or deracination or the search for a metainstitutional self. Dissolving the false sociality of the transference paves the way for the building up of psychological structure and a consequent rapprochement with society based on an enhanced tolerance for the inner world—as that world exists both in the self and in the social other.

Since this rapprochement lacks the driven, blind, and compacted character of most attachments to a common culture, it also authorizes as permanent a deeper split between the private and public reality than was ever possible before the historical emergence of depth psychology.

In these several ways, analytic access brackets the social world, but that world is best understood as rooted in a common culture. It consists primarily of intense, unconscious shared attachments and the ideas, ideals, and symbols which in turn represent (in the sense of re-present) these attachments. Such attachments have principally to do with issues of self and identity, understood as a process of primary self-definition. A common culture can refer to virtually all levels of a social world or simply to the least differentiated core of an otherwise pluralized social order. Durkheim's descriptions of primitive solidarity (tribe and church) and Mannheim's idealization of the medieval community indicate that religiousness and ethnocentrism, along with language and race, remain the strongest components of a common culture. Most important of all, as one moves from the periphery of a common culture toward its center, one becomes less and less psychological. A chilling analogue to this principle lies in the contrast between democratic and totalitarian societies. The former make room for a thick margin of psychological activity at the periphery, in which unconscious thoughts and fantasies are tolerated and allowed to exist in the thinking of its citizens, but this also makes forming a cohesive social center more difficult; the latter forbid any such recognizable margin of psychological activity to exist, in the interest of greater collective stability and reliability. It follows from this that psychoanalysis has existed only in democratic sociopolitical systems and is always persecuted in totalitarian ones because the mere thought of analytic access terrifies those in power by consciously calling attention to their own unconscious inner worlds and to the separateness which such attention facilitates.

Finally—a direct correlate of the above—analytic access is not the only consequence of object loss and disappointment in the face of a weakening common culture. Its reverse or inverse, persecutory anxiety (the fear of being persecuted and the wish to persecute others) and annihilatory anxiety also make their appearance at such times. In this latter case genuine structure building also takes place, but largely "on the outside," so to speak (that is, not in the inner world but in the outer one, composed of social symbols). This structure building takes the form of new revitalized group formations and new systems of ideas, such as are found in sect formations, ideological rigidity, and massive remythologizations. As I have already shown, and will shortly show in far greater detail, the original analysts sought the first but were by no means immune from the second.

Let us now conclude this phenomenology of analytic access by recapitulating its outstanding features and drawing them into a structural or ideational pattern such that, when the two are taken together, they constitute the process and structure of the ideal-type. Speaking descriptively, the analytic situation is intensely presocial (and preethical and prepolitical); it takes fantasy as its unit of analysis, thereby linking together biology or nature and society or culture; it analyzes the transference, understood as an archaic or prehistoric sociality; to do this it centers in a privileged way upon dreams; it gradually produces the conviction that unconscious, infantile processes powerfully organize current living; and through its work it prepares the way for a more individuated and more self-constituted rapprochement with the patient's surrounding common culture.[5]

But what is the pattern or structure which underlies this descriptive, processual account? All forms of analytic access betray a common structure composed of four leading elements, in the form of tensions, which might be called "ideas" or even "unit ideas" of "the psychological tradition" (Nisbet 1966). These elements can be found in each of the descriptive phases of analytic access. As the analytic situation is engaged, it inevitably generates particular forms of thought or tensions. They are the tension between conscious and unconscious mental life (internal), the tension between childhood and selfhood (developmental), the tension between ego and social other (sociological), and the tension between experimental and experiential modes of validation and conviction (practical or methodological). Arching over and informing these elements and uniting them with the process of analytic access is the highly privileged phenomenon of fantasy and its sister phenomenon, illusion. Analysis begins with "reality," social reality; it proceeds to deconstruct that reality by way of engaging fantasy processes and makes the discovery of the archaic sociality, which seems for a while more real than the initial reality; and it ends when that "more real" reality and its fantasy structure are accepted as an indestructible illusion; that acceptance facilitates "return" or rapprochement, with the social world, by means of disillusionment and mourning for the archaic. Rapprochement occurs by means of the reappropriation of culture, but understanding how that process occurs must wait for part 3.

I now propose to show how the ideal-type of analytic access (the essential tension) finds a most visible and convincing example in

Freud's self-analysis and how the first analysts attempted to institutionalize the ideal-type in the form of the psychoanalytic movement, and I explain why the attempt failed. From there I go on to show that the lives and works of three followers, Jung, Rank, and Jones, also instantiated the ideal-type and this quite apart from and before their contact with Freud in the movement. Then I examine Freud's attempt to introduce his analytic ideas into the political and religious common cultures which surrounded him and argue that these attempts, the "cultural texts," are an essential part of Freud's work and of the ideal-type. Finally, in the last chapter, I explore the sociological and psychological roots of Freud's claim to science and the heart of this claim, the metapsychology, and deconstruct that claim by contextualizing it in relation to the common culture of his time and place.

7 The Sociology of Freud's Self-Analysis and the Psychoanalytic Movement

Sociological Reflections on Freud's Self-Analysis

Sociological reflections on Freud's self-analysis will search out what he shared with or had in common with others, the ways in which he was "a part of" rather that "apart from" a social whole. I have already noted his own psychological definition of identity (the idea of "a common psychological structure") and have cited with approval Klein's description of Freud's "Jewish identification" and "Jewish conscience." But Freud's Jewish identity, which was fundamental to his concept of himself as a person, took its shape and strength from a feeling of belongingness, a feeling of community. And so one must ask, In what did such belongingness and community consist?

A large part of the answer to this question is found virtually tailor-made in the work of Marsha Rozenblit (1983) and William McGrath (1986). Rozenblit has written a quantitative study of Jewish life in Freud's Vienna, and from it one can conclude that Freud was, on all major measures, a typical Jew. McGrath has shown how powerful political and Jewish ideals of identity were mediated for the young Freud through family and teachers and especially through the Hebrew Bible. McGrath has traced Freud's appropriation of these ideals to his most intimate thoughts and dreams, arguing that his disillusionment with these ideals in the late 1890s stimulated his self-analysis and psychological discoveries in a central way. But McGrath does not give an account of how this could have happened. After briefly reviewing these two studies, I draw upon them to propose my own sociological explanation of Freud's discoveries, the "origins" of psychoanalysis.

Although she is interested in eminent Viennese Jews such as Freud, Arthur Schnitzler, Stefan Zweig, Gustav Mahler, and Arnold Schönberg, Rozenblit devoted her energies to "ordinary Jews" through quantitative analysis of birth, marriage, and tax records. To her, "Jewishness" simply means "a sense of belonging to the Jewish community," the capacity to possess a "group identity" (chap. 1). Migrating to Vienna during the second half of the nineteenth century, the Jews sought to preserve their group identity in the face of the inevitable pressure to assimilate. To some extent they did, by adopting the cultural mores of the general society: dress, recreational tastes, economic patterns, language, and political views. But they preserved their primary attachments, remaining within their own group with regard to friendships, personal associations, marriage, and family ties. They regularly associated with each other on four major measures of group identity: occupation, neighborhoods, education, and organizational networks. And they avoided the two activities most destructive of group solidarity, intermarriage and religious conversion. Contrary to some accounts, the Jews of Vienna did not assimilate; their sense of group identity remained solid until it was destroyed in the Holocaust.

In all these many ways, and especially with regard to the four principal measures, Freud was a typical Viennese Jew. He grew up in the Leopoldstadt (District II), which contained the largest Jewish population of the nineteen districts. It was at least 25 percent Jewish in 1900, when Jews composed only 9 percent of the total population. Clark simply referred to this district as "the mainly Jewish quarter" (1982, p. 16). In the gymnasiums of the Leopoldstadt 40–80 percent of the students were Jewish and "non-Jews were the outsiders" (p. 124). Jews in Vienna abandoned "the old Jewish occupations in trade" for "a new typically Jewish pattern of occupational preference" (p. 49). Most became clerks and managers, but some also entered the professions (medicine, law, and education), although not in large numbers.

When Freud finally married Martha Bernays, he chose to live with her in the Alsergrund, District IX, second only to the Leopoldstadt in Jewish representation. The Alsergrund was "the proper address for the new breed of urban Jew" (p. 85), young, middle class, and professional, and Bergasse was a wealthy Jewish street where more prosperous taxpayers lived. Of great importance is Rozenblit's observation that economic expansion, industrialization, and modernization during the period 1872–1900 in Vienna "led to the general (but not complete) replacement of artisanal workshops with factories" and established districts such as the Alsergrund "as middle-class residential areas, areas in which residence and work were increasingly separated" (pp. 72–73). When Freud joined the B'nai B'rith in the midst of his self-analysis, he turned to one of many organizational networks Jews formed in Vienna to preserve Jewish identity. In all respects, then, Freud was—in addition to being the unique and creative individual who was "the first psychoanalyst"—a very typical Viennese Jew.

But this sense of belonging was mediated for Freud in a very personal and intensive way. Historians have taken a long time to see the simple truth, so sincerely stated, of Freud's own account of this mediation: "My deep engrossment in the Bible story (almost as soon as I had learned the art of reading) had . . . an enduring effect upon the direction of my interest" (1925, p. 8). Making extensive use of Freud's dreams, his letters, other autobiographical statements, and his psychological writings, McGrath has shown that "the Bible story" not only moved Freud emotionally but that it was also a source of self-definition. Freud identified with Joseph, the Jew who moved skillfully and tactfully within a variety of hostile anti-Semitic situations by means of his ability to interpret the dreams of his enemies. On the other hand, Moses was a forceful leader who set the Jews—and himself—apart from alien cultures. Jacob Freud's Bible was the Philippson Bible. It presented Jewish history in terms of naturalistic and assimilationist values and emphasized freedom, independence, and imagination as Jewish ideals: God exercised his guiding influence over his people through dreams. Freud did not simply "have fantasies" about Joseph and Moses. While the Bible stories depicting these persons were in one sense tales, they were not stories like those of the Grimm brothers, for fairy tales do not produce internalized images of enduring social self-definition. Rather, these Biblical narratives conferred social identity, as is seen in the socially rich cliché that the Jews are "a people of the Book." In such narratives, religious and political issues are inseparable, for both address the freedom which one group loses because of the oppression of another group.

Freud remained preoccupied with these ideals and values during his first years at the University of Vienna, which he entered in 1873 at the age of sixteen. For a while he belonged to a politically active fraternity. Gradually, however, "the political radical" was transformed into a "revolutionary scientist" (McGrath 1986, p. 94): Freud studied with Franz Brentano, read the works of Feuerbach, and became more and more committed to the scientific materialism of Helmholz and Brücke. McGrath calls this shift the first of a series of "disillusionments."

Disillusionment is in fact McGrath's main descriptive term for Freud's transition from the religiopolitical common culture of Viennese Judaism to the discovery-generating self-analysis. Freud's father embodied many Jewish ideals, and Freud himself noted the centrality of his father's death, toward the end of 1896, to his great work (the book was "a portion of my own self-analysis, my reaction to my father's death" [1900, p. xxvi]). To this McGrath adds the election of Karl Lüger, the anti-Semitic mayor of Vienna, in the spring of 1897. Lüger's election meant that the liberals had abandoned the Jews, and Freud was passionately committed to liberalism. Under the impact of this double disappointment, "Freud was determined to free himself from the power of his political past. . . . It was to the inner world of the psyche that he turned in the face of deep political disillusionment" (p. 264). Let us probe the social mechanism of this turn.

As long as he was in the grip of powerful, religiously toned political aspirations and loyalties, Freud could not reflect upon them psychologically. However, once he abandoned these, he was able to realize that these hopes and ideals, and also the forces opposing them, were both driven by fantasies and wishes, and the self-analysis was nothing less than a search for, and finding of, the phenomenological reality of fantasy and its psychodynamic, infantile role in adult mental—and political—life. In such fashion did "political disillusionment" produce a radical kind of psychological discovery. McGrath uses other words, such as "movement," "transfer," and "translation," to characterize Freud's shift from politics to psychology. But these descriptive terms lack the depth and structure necessary to explain why and how such a shift took place, and therefore at this point I wish to reintroduce the word "de-idealization."

To understand Freud's shift from politics to psychology more fully, it is necessary to understand in greater detail the process of de-idealization itself. Its essence captures much that is also the essence of psychoanalysis as well, and this can be seen in the lowly parapraxis, which Freud actually took as the model for all psychoanalytic inquiry. Immediately after one has made a slip of the tongue, two possible courses of action open up. One can simply disavow or deny that anything untoward has occurred at all and pretend that nothing has happened—something akin to *"la belle indifférence"* of the hysteric. Or one can allow the appropriate amount of painful shame to enter consciousness, tolerate the ensuing loss of self-esteem, begin to "own" the action, and then to reflect, as if to say to oneself: At first I think I intended only X, but now I realize I also intended Y; indeed, I may have actually intended Y instead of X all the time. Thus an investigation of one's deeper motives and a search for access into unconscious wishes and fantasies begins. This is essentially a de-idealization process because one deconstructs or de-idealizes one's "perfect" ideal and idealized self-consciousness—that one exercises total mastery over one's mental life—and, as investigation proceeds, one recovers self-esteem "on the other side," so to speak, of the operation, as if to say to oneself: Yes, it is I who am so flawed, but now it is also I who know about the unconscious. In so doing one also builds a little bit of psychological structure.

What I have called the marks of analytic access—presociality, dreams and transferences, the acceptance of developmental reality, and subsequent rapprochement with the social world—are all present only in a fleeting and rudimentary way in the parapraxis, but they appear in bold relief in Freud's self-analysis and as such constitute its essential structure. Let us recall one more time Freud's most creative phase, established by psychoanalytic biography and described in part 1, and let us now situate it in the social, political, and religious realities just noted:

(1) Freud thinks intently about a research problem, the nature of neurosis

(2) He enters into an intense relationship with another man (Fliess), and the relationship becomes increasingly conflicted

(3) Freud introspects about this relationship (self-analysis) within the context of creating a significant psychological work, *The Interpretation of Dreams*

(4) A psychological discovery is made (the infantile unconscious), the work which embodies it is completed, and the relationship with the significant figure is dissolved

This sequence of mental events did not take place "in splendid isolation"; instead, it took place in relation to a string of intimate personal relationships with Jewish men characterized by an initial period of idealization of them and then a subsequent (sometimes only partial) de-idealization or object loss: Hammerschlag, the revered Bible teacher of his youth (Freud never de-idealized Hammerschlag, but he did become deeply disappointed with the values which he represented); his father, who could not comprehend the religious, political, and intellectual conflicts which surrounded his son; Breuer; Fliess; and finally, the brothers of the B'nai B'rith. In turning away from these men, Freud also turned away from the ethos or cultural ideals and promises—what he himself later called "the great group formations"—which they set forth and represented to him. He turned into himself to search for something more which lay hidden within and beneath the surface networks of group identity and a feeling of belongingness. Each of the marks or elements of this search expressed in a concrete way the essential tension between loyalty to a common culture and analytic or depth-psychological self-understanding. A truly formidable struggle was at work.

Freud's self-analysis was not only presocial; it was—again, paradoxically—a preeminently social experience as well. In it Freud created for himself a piece of social space in Viennese society for a transference relationship to Fliess in spite of the fact that no such space was allowed to exist at the time. Masud Khan (1970) has described the self-analysis best of all as Freud's "epistemology of self-experience," the discovery that a person can observe himself only through the medium of another's presence: "In self-experience, the role of a specialized human object-relationship is very necessary; otherwise a purely mental apprehension of self leads either to ethics or metaphysics" (p. 109). None of the customarily celebrated earlier probes into psychological depth in Western culture—for example, in philosophy, Montaigne and Descartes; in theology, St. Augustine and Kierkegaard—could match Freud's, for these men had no such "other" in the same way that he did. In the transference to Fliess, which Freud created, he discovered the archaic sociality which Viennese politics and religion had exploited, masked, recoded, and then valorized.[1]

The instrumentation of this process was almost entirely that of the dream and its derivatives, fantasy and free association. Freud did not simply introspect on the presocial mass of his inchoate subjectivity, as philosophers in the phenomenological and existential traditions did, nor did he elaborate his subjectivity into pleasing imaginative works, as artists and poets before him had done, although both of these examples also presuppose a certain amount of regression. Rather, Freud worked with specific "mental materials," breaking these down into their elements, comparing them, studying them in relation to the dreams of others, and so forth. Through this work he broke decisively not only with the biological-scientific views of his day, which understood dreams as epiphenomenal, but even more so with what I call the "folkish" dream books. These *"Traumdeutung"* offered their readers spiritual, predictive, and prophetic explanations grounded in the shared wisdom of a common culture. Accepting such explanations presupposes that one is a part of the community which proffers such wisdom. Instead, Freud assigned the genesis and significance of the dream to the infantile unconscious of the individual and called upon persons to own these avowedly social constructions, just as he had done.

The theoretical yield was spectacular. Khan's phrase, epistemology of self-experience, captures well the distinguishable but inseparable character of experience-near and experience-distant components in analytic access: Freud's self-experience did eventuate in a form of knowledge. As he permitted himself to elaborate his dreams, wishes, and fears, he gradually gained perspective on his subjectivity. By freely subjectifying in relation to a special other, he could objectify in relation to himself. But the scientific character of the "experiment" derived its validity entirely from the socially constituted interface between the two men. "Freely" does not mean morally or politically free, the "right" to say things in public to a separate and distinct social other, things which he and others like him disapprove of; it meant the immediate and intimate free-flowing of wishes and fantasies which anteceded the rules and grids of the social world, mental activities which generated thoughts. The result was the inner conviction of the reality of psychological development, of unconscious childhood experience and of "the inner world" which exists alongside and beneath the social world. Concepts like secondary process and reality principle served to reify the frightful and anxiety-laden immediacies of Freud's concrete and specific sociology, the oppressive and anti-individualistic religion and politics of Vienna in the late 1890s.[2]

The practical yield was also impressive. Analytic scholars have not paid sufficient attention to the complex and contradictory character of the kind of sociality that virtually constitutes the analytic situation and its historical prototype, Freud's self-analysis. In the polite and mannered language of phenomenology, the self-analysis "bracketed" the social world in the interests of forms of self-understanding which that social world had forbidden. The depth-sociality of the transference, judged a false one by the rules of society, generates an archaic sociality which is "more" real and "truer" than the outer one approved by society. Only concepts like illusion and paradox can grasp these swings and shifts in meaning. Eventually, there is a return to that outer, social world which I have called rapprochement. It was certainly so for Freud. As his self-analysis drew to a close, he became sufficiently free, inwardly, to make his Rome journey. There, he saw for the first of many times the Moses of Michelangelo, which condensed artistically the Jewish and Catholic forces and ideals from which he had retreated so massively at first. He also intervened actively on his own behalf for a university appointment. Most important of all, he was inwardly fortified for movement.

Paradox and illusion are the right words to describe Freud's self-analysis because it was transitional in the strictly Winnicottian sense. By this I mean that Freud created psychological space mid-way between the objective world of social fact, which he himself later called the reality principle or secondary process, and the uncon-scious inner world of object representations, which he called the pleasure principle or primary process. My sociological concerns iden-tify this objective world of social fact as the common culture of his day. But the genetic prototype for any common culture is the infant-mother relationship and the infantile omnipotence which inspires it with an aura which, it is interesting to note, has been represented religiously in Christian iconography as a nimbus. As this aura fades, under the impress of disillusionment, the infant—and the creative figure as well—fills the "space" thereby created with transitional objects of its own making. In Freud's case the transitional space was filled with metapsychological reflections and speculations, which framed adequately for him, although not for us, the realities which he was discovering. Did he not refer to the metapsychology as "our witch"? And is not a witch the residue of a denying, persecuting maternal presence that destroys social relatedness by breaking it up into discrete objects? In such fashion did Freud transform the curse of isolation into the very mixed blessing of psychological self-understanding.

This process had a definite bodily dimension to it, which is con-sistent with the psychoanalytical view that thought or the mind itself is rooted in its somatic matrices. Freud of course later observed that the ego was first and foremost a body-ego, and it is important not to forget Jones's astute observation that Freud thought of psycho-analysis after the fashion of a product of his own body. In May 1899, as the self-analysis and the dream book both drew to a close, Freud said of the latter to Fliess, "None of my works has been so completely my own as this; it is my own dung-heap, my own seedling, and a *nova species mihi* [sic]" (1954, p. 281). In so saying, Freud acknowledged the intimate relation between body and mind and also that in creat-ing *The Interpretation of Dreams* he had reproduced and trans-formed—in fact, re-created—the very essence of himself, a *"nova species mihi"*—in other words, a new form of himself.

In referring to the metapsychology as a witch, Freud was even more right than he thought, but in a different sense, for the scientific status of psychoanalysis has haunted and vexed or "hexed" psycho-analysis, and it has yet to awaken from the spell of the metapsychology which Freud cast upon it. Up to this point at least, the self-analysis seems no different from any other form of artistic creativity, yet Freud insisted that his ideas about the mind, which were embodied in the self-analysis, were scientific and not artistic. Paradoxically, only a sociological discussion, and not one based on the philosophy of science, can break this spell. There have been many excellent philosophical discussions of the scientific status of analysis, but none has resolved this question satisfactorily.

Marion Milner, a British psychoanalyst, has observed that both artists and scientists "acquire a special experience of life" and as a result both negate "the common ego or the common social world." They thereby refashion "these worlds to include the new experience" (1955, p. 105). The artist does so affectively, the scientist perceptually. The artistic component in Freud's work is very strong. But I wish to understand his claim to science, which consisted chiefly in the claim to have observed lawlike features, what he called psychological determinism. The claim derives from the fact that the dyadic self-analysis took place within the context of the scientific culture of biology, physiology, and neurology of Freud's time. As his attachments to the common social world weakened, he withdrew more and more into isolation, and, as a result, his more archaic mental potentials made their unwelcome appearance. In the face of this Freud did not abandon his commitment to his scientific culture and it continued to support the experience-distant component of his self-scrutiny. So there was a kind of transfer of assumptions and methods from the scientific culture of his day to the materials of his increasingly alienated and regressed mental life. To put the matter in a more generalized way: science, especially when its principles and values are applied to the conscious, idealized, contents of one's own self-consciousness, always de-idealizes, and Freud had a precociously strong "scientific ego." When applied specifically to human mental life, science forces that life to split itself even more gravely into experiencing and observing portions than the prevailing religiously inspired common culture permits. In Freud's hands science became a principle of negation and alienation, of distance, and later even a principle of transcendence. But this process had a crucial social side to it, beyond these psychological-epistemological observations.

Conditions of retreat or object loss in relation to a shared common culture, I have proposed, produce a heightened sense of self-consciousness and the irruption of ego-alien material. Under such conditions, the ebb and flow of these "mental materials" within the analytic situation take on an unmistakably lawlike character. They do so because neurologically grounded fantasy (and therefore lawlike) material is given freer rein because of the partial relaxation of cultural controls. It becomes possible for biologically shaped fixed sequences to assert themselves. The presocial character of the self-analysis produced regression and transference, and Freud was able to track and formulate connections between his dreams, associations, and wishes and his irrational feelings toward Fliess. Under these conditions he could claim with some genuine justification something of the order of psychological determinism. But, outside the analytic situation, when one is more a part of culture, such determinism fades, or, if it does show itself, it is classified by social convention—and by social science, as well—as deviant or anomalous and either discarded or renamed. To put the matter in the language of one of today's most eminent cultural scientists, Claude Lévi-Strauss, who understands the person as a product of a continuous series of transformations between nature and culture: under the conditions of analytic access, one moves, for a little while at least, as Freud did, a bit closer to nature and a bit further away from culture. Freud's investigations took as their object the fantasy structure of mental life, and fantasy became the unit of analysis of psychoanalysis.

Freud's achievement of analytic access should not be separated from its inverse, his neurosis. The more compacted and undifferentiated is a segment of society, the less likelihood is there of either neurotic conflict or the capacity to objectify it in the form of psychological access to it. Firm attachments to a common culture mercifully tend to forestall both. On the other hand, when social-structural change weakens such attachments, the potential for both increases. This is so because neurosis and analytic access share the same experiential matrix—the latter is simply a more successful resolution of the former. The history of neurosis, as that has been described by Lopez Pinero (1983), for example, is not at issue here. What is at issue is the fact that, because the writing of *The Interpretation of Dreams* was inseparable from the self-analysis, Freud's neurosis also has to be seen as a crucial part of his creative process. As his book became more and more widely known, it became a part of the cultural world. But the book "contained" his neurosis. So his neurosis also gradually became a social and cultural object. In this way neurosis too, along with psychoanalytic theory, became a cultural, and not only a clinical, category. It is a mistake to separate neurosis from the new ideal-type of experience which was taking shape.

The double view of neurosis taken here is in agreement with Kohut's conviction that neurosis is a first, albeit abortive, step in "the search for the self": "I believe that these psychic conditions (the psychoneuroses), which are generally conceived as diseases and which are indeed the cause of much intense suffering and unhappiness, should in certain respects be understood as man's grasping toward the enlargement and intensification of his inner life . . . these miscarried attempts should be evaluated as more courageous, and potentially more creative, than some of the forms of psychic equilibrium that make up the area of emotional normality or health" (1973b, p. 541).

Recognizing the intimate relationship between analytic access and neurosis will enhance the further understanding of Freud's movement, to which I now turn, for its members were, in many cases, deeply neurotic and socially alienated men who came to Freud for some kind of a solution to their plight. However, before taking up the lives and works of Jung, Rank, and Jones, I reanalyze some of my earlier psychological and historical observations on the psychoanalytic movement, understood as a group, in order to create a sociological explanation of its most contradictory feature. If psychological self-understanding tends to free one from being bound to a common culture, why then, I ask, did the first analysts create a social organization which evinced the two principal features of a common culture, a symbolic-ideational system which powerfully organized group cohesion?

The Psychoanalytic Movement as a Psychological Culture

Freud's isolation, neurosis, heightened self-consciousness, introspection, and so forth—in short, the curse of isolation—called for amelioration and support. Both were forthcoming, first in what should be called the protomovement, which took shape during 1901–6, and then, in much greater force, in the first period of the movement proper, 1906–14.

The purpose of the Wednesday night meetings, all twenty members of which were Jews, was to give Freud a forum for his new ideas and to provide members with a chance to hear him out. This was indeed, as Jones said, a "circle" or salon or gathering, and not a group or movement. I have already reviewed the circumstances leading to the second phase: vitriolic quarrelsomeness; Freud's growing apprehension that his psychoanalysis would be perceived by others as a Jewish national affair (that is, as a religion); the sensible remove to Zurich; the hope-filled idealization of Jung; and the formation of the movement, with the psychological characteristics of a group. Given the social and cultural background of the self-analysis, it is readily understandable why Freud was both impatient with and fearful of his new-found colleagues. He had progressed a considerable distance along a new path, whereas they were just beginning the journey.

To all this there can now be added the observation that the new entrants were from very different cultural backgrounds politically, socially, and religiously. The exclusivity of the Jewish circle was broken up by men of different psychological structure. Furthermore, the highly creative men who were most committed to movement— in particular, Jung, Rank, and Jones—were in the midst of rapidly de-idealizing their own common cultures. Above all else this factor explains their loyalty, seriousness, excitement, rebelliousness, and unconscious hopes. These men shared with Freud not only ideas about the mind but also a social life course in which they turned away from a cultural tradition and toward psychological self-understanding. But there were important differences as well.

The intense sense of loyalty which bound Abraham and Freud together stemmed in great part from their shared Jewish heritage. It smoothed the way for shared identifications, thereby permitting analytic and Jewish sensibilities to exist side by side with a minimum of perceived conflict. Rank's poignant idealization of Freud and his ideas was rooted in his search for a redemptive vision for the Jew in Western culture, a vision which, he bitterly thought, his own past had denied him. Jung idealized Freud's scientific rigor, only to break with him and then reconcile his newly formed psychology with his abandoned Christian roots. Upon all this the cool and distant Jones gazed with both curiosity and skepticism. More than the others, he had renounced the consolations of his rural, Welsh, and Baptist culture, but not as completely as he thought, and this oversight accounted for much of his ceaseless organizational activity and most of his love of doctrine.

If clashing common cultures in varying stages of dissolution set the stage for the first analysts' coming together, how is one to account for their being swept up into unmistakable unity and cohesion? If analytic modes of experiencing and thinking break down identification with, and internalizations of, a common culture, how can they promote community? I think the group/movement formed as a result of a shared attempt to construct—really to reconstruct—a new analytic common culture, one based on psychoanalytic rather than traditional ideas. Up to this point I have explained cohesion and unity of the group/movement by means of the psychoanalytic concept of a group illusion, but a group illusion is only the essential psychological core of every common culture. When that illusion is codified into precepts and myths, it solidifies and spreads out into a pervasive and all-embracing sense of belonging. As the first analysts' ties to their historic values gradually eroded, they became more susceptible to, and more in need of, new modes of thought and experience which were capable of clarifying their new existential situation. Each had already achieved some genuine psychological understanding of the inner world before coming to Freud, and each rightly sensed that Freud's ideas applied especially to him. But the analytic access which fate accorded to them could hardly assuage the full force of their disenchantments or support the heroic ideal of autonomy which they felt it promised and which they thought they saw in Freud's person and work. The transition away from the historic past took place with overwhelming rapidity.

From this point forward, and for those reasons, analytic ideas took on a distinctly ideological cast. By this I do not mean that they were untrue—or, for that matter, that they were true. Rather the first analysts endowed these ideas with a sense of total conviction and unshakable correctness; as such, analytic ideas came to serve as a container or canopy, the sociological function of which was to confer a sense of group cohesion and community upon those who espoused them. And so the most fateful of all the many marks of a common culture took root in the little group: a hidden, intense, unconscious, and internal relation between ideas and group-social solidarity. To question these ideas did not only mean challenging a delimited sector of theory, evidence, or clinical experience; it also meant jeopardizing one's position or status in a complex web of unconscious social attachments.

Consequently, the first analysts began to feel that analytic ideas could explain everything the way a weltanschauung, or worldview, does. So they wrote audacious treatises on virtually every aspect of culture—morality, art, history, and religion. They were convinced that their new appropriations of analytic access and in particular its essential structure, the unconscious dynamics of fantasy, could be discerned as a kind of hidden infrastructure embedded in the superstructure of cultural figures and symbols. In doing so, they turned back to the common cultures from which social change had uprooted them—each man invariably turning back to his own particular common culture—there to see writ large what they had come to see writ small in themselves.

Several observations clarify further this transformation of psychological ideas into an ideology. Most important of all was the first

analysts' inability to recognize and then modulate the powerful narcissistic processes which their disenchantments with historic ideas
and values had released. Knowledge of the prestructural level of mental functioning has only gradually become available in the history of
psychoanalysis. It would be deeply moralistic and righteous to insist,
in retrospect, that the first analysts "should have known" about such
things. But it is possible to track these features and to observe their
effects in the interest of greater historical understanding. Furthermore, the experience of achieving genuine psychological insight into
a once-opaque sector of mental life—an experience which all the first
analysts had achieved before coming to Freud—is often in and of
itself exciting and can activate further archaic grandiosity and a sense
of omniscience, thereby ironically subverting the original goal of
such insight.

Second, the first analysts lacked the crucial social support for self-
exploration which is part and parcel of the conventional analytic
situation of today, both in the consulting room and in the institutes.
These strict social arrangements serve to monitor and make manageable too rapidly acquired analytic access. It must be remembered that
at the time of the movement the analytic situation had not been
institutionalized. Freud handled the "psychological flooding" and
acting out which he encountered in the group/movement with the
dispatch of a confident group leader, that is, by moral means, thereby
becoming—as Ronald Clark (1982) has made so clear—the "com-
mander-in-chief."

Finally, the first analysts completely disregarded the way in which
loyalty to the historical values of a common culture unconsciously
persists, even in the face of intense introspective experience. Instead,
each in his own way adopted a "total break" theory of the relation
between psychoanalysis and Western culture. Each resolutely turned
his back on the past but failed to recognize how tightly the hand of
the past continued to grip his life. To put the same point in a very
different way: the totalistic and ideologic ethos of the group/move-
ment was indeed "like a religion," not because its members were
"really religious," but because they did in fact engage together in an
open, direct, and intimate way the same powerful emotional forces
which attachment to a common culture always monitors symbolically and always places at a safe distance: envy, murderous
hatred, vaulting ambition, sexuality, incest, jealousy, fear of death—
in short, "existential anxiety."

8 Tracking the Ideal-Type: Disenchantment and Psychological Discovery in the Lives of Three Followers

I now turn to several individuals in the movement to expand and deepen its social meaning by taking their lives and works as further instances of the ideal-type. This approach identifies these analysts' relationships to their common cultures and takes it as a decisive clue or index to their behavior in the movement. It claims that the degree and quality of distance or detachment from their common cultures—in particular, the nature and quality of their de-idealization of it, especially its rapidity—shaped their loyalty to Freud and his ideas, to the extent that they were willing to remain involved in the movement and the character of their creative work. At each stage in their careers—premovement (childhood, adolescence, and early maturity); entry into the movement; activities; exit from the movement and creative works—each sought, found, at times lost, and at times elaborated versions of analytic access, such that each man's unique and distinctive life provides further historical evidence for the ideal-type. The life course is taken here as a social unit.

Abraham, Jones, Jung, and Rank were all central to the movement. Each came to Freud seeking further psychological knowledge and self-understanding, each worked vigorously in behalf of the movement, each was a practicing psychoanalyst, and each wrote creative, original clinical and cultural studies. Two remained loyal to the very end (Abraham and Jones); two "defected" (Jung and Rank). The most rebellious and innovative (Jung and Rank) were the most conflicted about their religious heritages and the most intrapsychically conflicted as well. They were also profoundly influenced by Nietzsche (Abraham and Jones paid no attention to Nietzsche). And they were also the ones most interested in elaborating psychoanalytic ideas into some sort of religious or world-historical synthesis, and their creative works gave expression to this concern. The least rebellious (Abraham and Jones) were more at peace with their historically received values, and they were more attentive to clinical issues, although all the first analysts speculated to some extent about history and culture.

With the exception of Abraham, there exist good studies of these men which discuss their psychological characteristics and their activities in the movement, and I draw upon these in order to advance my own views. I take these followers up in order of ascending loyalty to Freud and his movement and note only the barest social facts about them, chiefly their ties to the past, formative intellectual influences, their personal struggle with both, their entrance into the movement, and their creative ideas. In no sense do I strive to create complete portraits of them. There are times when a sketch, vignette, or even a series of snapshots is far more revealing than a portrait, which embeds its protagonist in a timeless and noble frieze. In the case of Jung, who has been studied the most, I draw upon my previously published literature reviews and psychological observations of his childhood and youth (Homans 1979*b*) and begin citations and more detailed study only at the time of his university work, especially his encounter with Nietzsche; in the case of Rank, who has been studied less, I cite primary and secondary sources more frequently; and in the case of Jones, who has received even less attention, I delve deeply into his life and thought, chiefly as found in his autobiography. Thorough analyses of this text as a whole are for the most part still lacking.

Each of these men achieved analytic access in his unique way and on the basis of that sought to transform Freud's ideas into a fresh psychological vision, anticipating the three major stances which psychoanalysis continues to take toward itself and culture: psychoanalysis as hermeneutics (Jung), as art (Rank), and science (Jones), although none of these men are usually recognized today as having laid down these foundations.

Carl G. Jung: Psychoanalysis as Hermeneutics

Freudians and Jungians have always pointed to the strikingly different ideas which separate their two authorities. To this has been added, more recently, an emphasis upon the very different structures of their personalities. A sociological approach discloses an unsuspected commonality: both men became disenchanted with their religious heritages, turned away from them, and thereupon achieved psychological self-understanding. Many of the time-honored differences between the two can be traced back to the quality of their turning away, their respective de-idealizations. Jung certainly achieved considerable psychological self-understanding before he came to Freud. And after he left the movement, his grasp of unconscious psychological depth surpassed Freud's in certain respects. These observations alone suggest that the events surrounding Freud's discoveries were not unique, as psychobiographers and historians believe, but were, instead, in some sense typical—that is, common to others or shared by others.

Jung spent his infancy and childhood in a small Swiss village, remote from any town or city, deeply embedded in the severe Protestant traditions of his time and place (Homans 1979b, chap. 5). His father was a pastor, as were several uncles on both sides of the family. As far back as he could remember, Jung struggled repeatedly, unsuccessfully, and with a persistent sense of resentful disappointment to acquire the socially preferred religious view of things. A second struggle accompanied the first. Jung was beset by dreams, fantasies, and visions which, because they both attracted and terrified him, he sought to explain to himself and understand. His parents were self-absorbed and unempathic—his father weak and well-meaning, his mother stronger but also mysterious and inscrutable. Alone, alienated, and without companions, the young Jung was unable to connect with his surrounding social world. He could not idealize or internalize much of it or its socially appointed representatives, parents and community leaders. Above all else, Jung's infancy and childhood were characterized by an unbearably sharp and chronically painful sense of self—a self which did not, however, have much structure to it in the early years.

But Jung was also a psychologically precocious child. His self-absorption stimulated curiosity and a desire to know about "the psyche." His childhood dreams, visions, and fantasies became occasions for an elementary form of analytic access, and he later imposed upon those mental productions his own unique construction, such that his entire approach to psychology was prefigured in his early years. As he became more introspective and empathic toward himself, he devised a rudimentary psychological typology. People, he decided, were composed of two personalities: an outer, number one, and a hidden inner, number two. In this way he could name and to some extent control the confusing and threatening forces in his own inner world and relate himself to the surrounding social world. Very early in life, Jung had decisively split experience into public and private. The mature Jung gave sophisticated form to this classification by making it the basis for his theory of the conscious and unconscious psyche and its structures, the ego and the self.

When Jung was eleven, his family moved to another village within walking distance of the city of Basel. There he continued to go to school and later studied university subjects and medicine. Gradually, he was able to overcome, to a considerable degree, much of his earlier self-absorption, low self-esteem, and narcissistic vulnerability and to exchange these for a more autonomous and independent sense of himself. Daily exposure to a cosmopolitan city relieved him of much introversion. He talked out and thought through his bitter frustrations and disappointments with his father's religious values and beliefs, gradually putting them aside. Stimulated by his university studies, he made friends and joined a fraternity, and even gave several lectures to its members on psychological and theological subjects. His major interests were general science, the empirical point of view, and in particular evolutionary theory and comparative anatomy. His favorite philosophical authors were Kant and Nietzsche. Toward the end of this period he became more and more comfortable with his new-found modern and secular identity and abandoned his father's need to locate life and experience in some sort of grand, cosmic, and theological scheme of things.

Jung's encounter with Nietzsche was decisive in several important respects. It consolidated further his evolving psychological self-understanding, it was a crucial element in his choice of psychiatry as a specialization, and it clarified further his attitude toward his own secularization, his break with his Christian past. Nietzsche had held an appointment at Basel years earlier, and his work was widely read and discussed there but in largely negative and critical ways. Some of this criticism was directed at his personal manner, which had isolated him from the social world of Basel. Nietzsche had also relentlessly attacked the bourgeois values of family, state, and religion. For these very reasons Jung was attracted to Nietzsche, but he also postponed reading him. He feared that an identification with Nietzsche might overtake him ("But I was held back by a secret fear that I might perhaps be like him" [1961, p. 102]). This fear was based on the shared characteristic of profound social isolation ("I feared that I might be forced to recognize that I too was another such strange bird . . . like me, he was a clergyman's son" [p. 102]).

This fear was so intense that it included the fear of madness. When Jung finally read Nietzsche, he found Zarathustra especially appealing ("a tremendous experience for me" [p. 102]) and he identified with Zarathustra ("my No. 2 now corresponded to Zarathustra" [p. 102]). But it was also clear to Jung that Zarathustra "was morbid," and Jung therefore wondered whether it followed that this secret part of his own personality was also morbid. These thoughts forced him to reflect further upon himself, and he concluded that Nietzsche had, like a child, poured his no. 2 (what Jung later called the unconscious is, in the parlance of the theory of object relations, the true self) onto the unsuspecting and intolerant social world and its compendium of conventional values. He flooded it with his own hatreds, idiosyncrasies, and unique perceptions (Nietzsche "did not know his way about in this world and was like a man possessed" [p. 103]). Jung concluded that Nietzsche was unable to distinguish clearly between the social world and the inner psychical world and was therefore unable to recognize the animosity of the social world toward his revolutionary views; so he went mad. But Jung also concluded that he himself had been able to tolerate the social alienation which access into the unconscious produces through psychological self-reflection and thought. This was a talent which Nietzsche lacked. And he sadly realized that "people" will accept new ideas only when they are posed in the form of facts. This realization led him still further in the direction of empiricism and medicine.

Reading Nietzsche not only forced Jung to define more sharply his own identity and his relationship to the past; it also facilitated his choice of psychiatry—in fact, the three were closely related. Toward the end of his medical studies Jung became indecisive over the question of a speciality. He knew he wanted a scientific career, but he was also unwilling to let go of the psychological depth he had experienced earlier in the form of his childhood fantasies and visions and in his encounter with Nietzsche. The science of his time clearly precluded these. His preoccupation with psychical processes led him to study spiritualistic and occult phenomena (later to be called parapsychology), and he wrote his dissertation on the subject. Then, while skimming a textbook on psychiatry by Krafft-Ebing, Jung suddenly sensed the import for himself of its author's suggestion that the psychoses were "diseases of the personality." This meant that they had a subjective psychological element in addition to their objective, physiological, and neurological components (pp. 108–9). He thereupon decided ("My heart suddenly began to pound . . . my excitement was intense . . ." [pp. 108–9]) that psychiatry would allow him to approach both biological and spiritual phenomena, the antithetical worlds of nature and spirit, empirically.

The decision for psychiatry, and especially the formation of his own version of that discipline, consolidated Jung's identity as a professional, upwardly mobile man who had broken his ties to the past. For example, in anticipation of his residency at the Burghölzli in

Zurich in 1900, Jung paid his respects to an old aunt ("she was the last breath of a vanishing, irretrievable past"); this visit was "a final farewell to the nostalgias of my childhood" (p. 111). And he said a painful good-bye to his mother and sister, who shared a sheltered life together, and was glad to leave Basel ("where the pressure of tradition was too much for me" [p. 111]). At the Burghölzli he anticipated studying mental disease as "a biological reaction." But he could not connect with the rationalized, professional, and bureaucratic world of institutional medicine and its representatives, to which he had turned. He found the work dull and banal, for it excluded everything extraordinary and significant. As for his colleagues (the "psychiatric mentality"), he approached them with the same grimness which he displayed toward his patients. Disenchanted with the past but unsatisfied with the present, he was at this time well prepared for an intense, intimate relationship with an inspiring man, for strong psychological ideas, and for a community of like-minded men which could claim his vagrant, objectless energies.

Let us briefly review the major psychobiographical and historical features of Jung's entry into the psychoanalytic movement, already noted in part 1. Shortly after its publication, Jung was asked to report on *The Interpretation of Dreams* to the Burghölzli staff. Soon after that he was in correspondence with Freud. Exchanges of writings and personal meetings followed, and Jung took on his well-known publishing and administrative activities in behalf of the movement. An intense idealization composed of strong feelings of affection rapidly developed, lending psychological depth to the intellectual exchanges. After their return from America in the fall of 1909, Jung shared psychological insights about himself with Freud and also expressed an overriding interest in understanding mythology and religion—the symbols of the past—psychoanalytically. Freud applauded and then went on, a few months later, to say that he himself had, in a "flash of inspiration," discovered "the ultimate basis of man's need for religion" in infantile helplessness, associated with the ego instincts rather than the sexual instincts. Then, less than a month after that, Freud broached the question of affiliating analysis with an ethical fraternity, and Jung offered his view that analysis could only serve to revitalize the religious past. From this point on the relationship gradually deteriorated into its well-known conclusion.

Psychobiographical explanation traces all this back to Jung's unconscious, infantile past. Unable to idealize his father, he later idealized Freud and then the entire movement, elevating it, so to speak, "into a religion." Freud, however, rejected this proposal, and that precipitated Jung's excessively rapid de-idealization of Freud and the movement. Jung's attempt to transform the movement into some sort of utopian situation infused with charisma ("nourished by the deep instincts of the race. . . . Religion can be replaced only by religion") was also an attempt to refind or regain contact with the common culture of his own community of origin by means of psychological ideas. When Freud's rebuff deprived Jung of these attachments for a second time, he drove Jung back into his own psyche with great intensity.

Freud's social situation differed from Jung's in two ways, and this explains much of their very dissimilar behavior and antagonism in the movement. Freud's disenchantment with his religious heritage was a gradual and progressive one, whereas Jung's was precipitous and excessively rapid. Although he never adhered to any formal religious orientation or organization, Freud's sense of Jewish identity and his need for belonging to a community inspired by Jewish men and ideals remained strong. Freud's father thought of Jewishness as deep affection in the family and, especially for his son Shlomo, respect for the scriptures as a source of inspiration and wholeness (that is, as a source of a common psychological structure) and as the gradual expansion of all this into a sense of belonging which would include Jews in common humanity. Jacob Freud had no interest in doctrinal truths or in ritual observances. From early childhood Freud was exposed to an urbanized, scientific, and humanistic culture, and the revered Hammerschlag's biblical instruction was consistent with the ethical and communal emphasis of the liberal, assimilationist Jewish community. Even the self-analysis, into which so many issues of de-idealization were telescoped with great intensity, was gradual, taking place over a span of several years and in the context of considerable support: a loving wife and stable family, a devoted friend and colleague (Fliess), a supportive older man (Breuer), and an admiring group of "brothers," the B'nai B'rith—all Jewish. These people permitted the self-analysis to proceed bit by bit, so that Freud's ego was never completely overwhelmed by the unconscious forces, the emergence of which his social isolation had fatefully authorized. Furthermore, Freud never completely de-idealized his religious heritage. He retained a sense of belonging to it, although in his final years he attempted, again without complete success, to penetrate the character of this social bond psychoanalytically by writing about its cultural-symbolic embodiment, the idea of one God, in *Moses and Monotheism*.

Such gradualness and support were both denied to Jung, and therefore his finding and charting of the inner world simply had to take a form different from Freud's. At the beginning of their relationship, Jung had allowed many of his ties to the Burghölzli to weaken, especially his association with Bleuler, in the interests of total devotion to the movement. After his exit from it, he severed not only all personal, theoretical, editorial, and administrative loyalties to Freud and his group but also his teaching responsibilities at the university. Then he entered into a lonely, psychologically stressful period of several years duration. It ended spontaneously, and shortly thereafter he produced most of what are known today as distinctly Jungian ideas, and he took up the leadership of his new school of analytical psychology. The psychology of these events has been well discussed. Ellenberger thinks of it as a creative illness. Gedo and Stolorow and Atwood emphasize self-fragmentation and narcissistic vulnerability. My own study also took up these issues but centered primarily upon the linkage between a personal struggle with pre-oedipal, narcissistic themes and a later psychological-theoretical formulation of a theory of the self, in contrast to Freud's interest in the ego. Jung was, I continue to think, the first psychologist of the self in the history of psychoanalysis. However, social considerations place this stressful period in the wider frame of a tension between analytic access and an unsupportive common culture, and this perspective observes that Jung's mature theory conceived of the mind as a vast storehouse which contained the lost objects of cultural tradition in the form of internal mental structures: the archetypes of the collective unconscious. As the mind mourns the objects of the tradition which it has lost, it reconstitutes that tradition by creating convincing symbolic representations of it. The objects of religious belief were recovered, after the disillusionment process, in the form of psychological theory. What is lost through absence becomes present once again, by means of absence. This observation is to some extent reminiscent of Freud's well-known remark in *The Ego and the Id* (1923): "The ego is a precipitate of abandoned object-cathexes" (p. 29). Let us look more closely at the lonely, creative period.

Jung's time of stress following his remove from the movement was inaugurated by a thoroughly sociological perception entirely of his own making. First, he decided to assess the progress and direction of his life thus far. He had, he said, just written a book, *Symbols of Transformation*, of which Freud had been highly critical, in which he explained peoples' myths of the past and the psychology of the hero. As for the present, he concluded that men still lived in the Christian myth. But then he asked himself, "Do *you* live in it?" He had to admit that he did not ("For me, it is not what I live by" [1961, p. 171]). Pressing the point further, he then asked himself, "But then what is your myth—the myth in which you do live?" He could find no answer ("At this point the dialogue with myself became uncomfortable, and I stopped thinking" [p. 171]). This forthright, conclusive recognition that his religious past was no longer a resource for him produced a period of fantasy, dreams, and visions which only gradually subsided after several years of intense introspection on them. His struggle with these mental materials proved enormously fruitful. It was a form of self-analysis. By means of it Jung was able to formulate coherently and in communicable form his own mature version of analytic access.

He referred to the capacity to have such fantasies, dreams, and visions, without either denying them or merely submitting for them, as the capacity to entertain "immediate experience." They had their roots in the unconscious, which "corresponds to the mythic land of the dead, the land of the ancestors" (p. 191). He approached these imaginative structures by means of what he later called "the method of amplification," only somewhat similar to free association, in which one consciously links the fantasy materials of immediate experience to ideas, figures, and images in the history of culture—the "texts" of art, philosophy, and religion—allowing these first to structure experiencing and then in turn to stimulate further experiencing. When these evolving images recurred with sufficient frequency and form, Jung called them archetypes and sometimes talked to them, referring to them as "the little people." "The essential thing," he said, was "to differentiate oneself," through interpretation, "from these unconscious contents . . . and . . . to bring them into relationship with consciousness" (p. 187), what he called the process of individuation. Toward the end of the stressful period Jung was able to realize that his techniques facilitated the building up of the self, which he defined as "the wholeness of personality" and the achievement of which he designated "the goal of psychic development." The self announces its presence to the conscious ego, he thought, through the medium of dreams about centered, four-sided structures or mandalas, which represent the emerging psychological wholeness. But the emergence of the self is also accompanied by a new sense of sociality. Earlier, he had said of his struggle to find a vocation, "My old wound, the feeling of being an outsider and of alienating others, began to ache again" (p. 109). But with the discovery of the self, which included Jung's discovery of his own self, the stressful period came to a close, and so did his isolation: "That [finding the mandala as an expression of the self] was the first event which broke through my isolation. . . . I could establish ties with something and someone" [p. 197]). This was his rapprochement.

Throughout the rest of his life Jung elaborated these sketchy notations into the complex systematic psychology which constitutes his *Collected Works*. Of this psychology it is necessary to note here only that the social pattern of Jung's life course made itself felt in his works as well. The common culture from which he had so decisively retreated in the first half of his life returned, so to speak, in his mature theory of the mind. In this theory the unconscious portion of the mind is composed of a series of biological-psychological structures which have shaped and energized the artistic, mythic, and philosophical products of man's history and culture. All people have these structures in common, although each person's culture shapes them differently. In the midst of these many structures stands the unconscious archetype of the self, which authorizes the search for and achievement of personal uniqueness and identity. So Jung repeatedly probed his own past, the Christian past, and concluded that the figure of Christ was the archetype of the self. He had first lost and then found the centerpiece of his own Christian common culture.

These observations support the conclusion that Jung's life and work together bear all the essential marks of the ideal-type. For historical-structural reasons Jung detached himself from a religious heritage; he engaged in profound and disturbing introspective probes, which required great courage and brilliance; these probes were directed to the unconscious nature of fantasy and dream; he formulated a theory based on his experience; he generalized these into a global, grand theory of culture; and he had little awareness of the complicity of social forces in the formation of his discoveries.

Otto Rank: Psychoanalysis as Art

No two members of Freud's movement would seem to be more different than Rank and Jung. Rank came to Freud with only a technical high school education; Jung had a university degree and was a medical doctor and psychiatrist. Rank grew up in Austria's Vienna, Jung in a small Swiss village. Rank's roots were Jewish, Jung's Christian. After they left the movement, Jung became the world-famous leader of a school of psychology; Rank did not. On the other hand, both men idealized Freud and the movement intensely (consciously and unconsciously), both struggled desperately with prestructural, narcissistic conflicts in their personal lives, both explored issues of self and the pre-oedipal mother in their later works, and both devoted their postmovement energies to the psychology of culture and religion. Furthermore, both men struggled—again, desperately—with their religious traditions, saw the movement to a great extent as the locus in which that struggle could be worked out and resolved, and later, after they had left the movement, both men used their own versions of psychoanalytic ideas to advance a religiously toned ethical vision of the person, society, and history. This last feature concerns us the most, although the psychological commonalities are the place to begin.

Stolorow and Atwood (1976) have studied Rank's life and work and think that his immersion in narcissistic themes links the two together, thereby providing an overall sense of his significance. In *The Trauma of Birth* (1924), the book which marked his departure from the movement, Rank stated that the experience of birth is charged with intense anxiety, which then undergoes primal repression and subsequently makes its reappearance in symptoms and the transference, both of which disguise the unconscious desire to reestablish an intimate bond with the mother and especially with her body. The principal task of the analyst therefore consists in working with this transference or "mother fixation" so as to facilitate separation and self-differentiation. The authors conclude that Rank appears to be describing, with the biological metaphor of birth, the resolution of a narcissistic transference and the necessity of building up psychological structure, as these have been described by Kohut. They then extend this interpretation of Rank's key book to other conceptual themes in his work as a whole (the theme of the hero, the theme of the artist, etc.). In the second half of their study they review Rank's diary entries and letters, as these appear in Taft's biography, and find there rich evidence for narcissistic disturbances (mood swings, interpersonal isolation, reparative trends, etc.), although they conclude that Rank was a creative genius whose ego was sufficiently strong to master the claims of the grandiose self.

Their study also illumines, they think, Rank's relationship to Freud and his movement. Freud was, literally, the only man Rank had been able to idealize in a thoroughgoing way, and his poorly bounded ego made a psychological merger with the group/movement necessary. Then, when Freud gently but firmly disagreed (by this time he had learned to soften his criticism) with the ideas in his book, Rank's needs for mirroring and support were massively frustrated, he became rapidly disillusioned with Freud, and bitterly withdrew into isolation. The pain, loneliness, and difficulties which followed, as

Rank tried to establish himself as an analyst and author, first in Paris and then in New York City, are more understandable in the light of these psychological considerations. The parallel to Jung's life and work is obvious, and in the next section I will propose that Ernest Jones too shared many of these same psychological conflicts.

Psychobiography cannot, however, illumine that portion of Rank's life and work which did not belong to Freud and his movement, and when this portion is brought into the light of day a fuller and richer figure appears. Indeed, so understood, even the received meaning of Rank's work in the movement itself shifts. This portion of Rank's life took shape during the years directly preceding his entry into the movement, and its full realization occurred only after he left it. At this time (1903–5, ages 19–21), Rank engaged in a truly formidable struggle with his Jewish identity and the heritage in which it was grounded. He hated this heritage deeply—and virtually everything else in his purview as well—but he had no alternative context in which to anchor his self-concept and the experiencing which it supports. As he struggled, he became increasingly introspective and gradually achieved a genuinely psychological orientation, organized around a sense of himself as an artist, which virtually erupted during this short period. To facilitate his search for identify, he kept a diary. To support his struggle against the past, he read Nietzsche and later Freud, using these two men as guides, for Rank's inner search was both personal-psychological and social-intellectual. This tremendous struggle for self-definition culminated in the writing of *The Artist* (begun in 1905 but not published until 1907). This work also gained him admission into Freud's group. But *The Artist* was in fact the introduction to a second essay, *The Essence of Judaism* (1905), and the two are inseparable. In the latter Rank made generous use of his own psychological concerns with art, culture, and psychoanalytic ideas in order to assert that the Jews as a people had privileged access into the unconscious and were, therefore, in a unique position to heal mankind of its neuroses, brought about by the repressions of civilization. Klein thinks (1981) that "it is clear, just from his use of *Der Künstler* as an introduction to the essay on Judaism, that Rank regarded Jews as an integral part of the psychoanalytic movement. Indeed, as an event in his intellectual development, the essay ("The Essence of Judaism") brings out the central significance of his Jewish consciousness in his growing devotion to Freud and to the movement" (p. 129).

None of the best-known psychological authorities whom I have consulted on Rank (Taft 1958; Stolorow and Atwood 1976; Menaker

1982; and Lieberman 1985) even mention the essay on Judaism. None of the psychoanalysts (Stolorow and Atwood, Menaker) consulted the diaries, which are so rich in social reference. So it is necessary to enlarge the picture of Rank developed by the psychologists by taking it for what it is, a kind of foreground study, and place it in the context of its foundational social background—Rank's Jewish self-identity and the common culture which had first formed it and from which he became so alienated. Only when this is done will it be possible to understand correctly the origins of Rank's psychology and—even more important—the fact that, like Jung and Jones, he arrived at a genuine dynamic psychological point of view before he ever met or even had heard of Freud. Like the others, Rank too belonged to the ideal-type.

Rank (Otto Rosenfeld) grew up in the Leopoldstadt (District II) of Vienna at the turn of the century. He was fifteen in 1899, the year Freud published the *Interpretation of Dreams* at the age of forty-three. Rank was the youngest in a lower-middle-class family of four, in which the father (Simon Rosenfeld) was an artisan-jeweler. Like other assimilating Jews, the family attended synagogue and observed Jewish customs, but "they were for the most part unaffected by the traditional or moral imperatives of the religion" (Taft 1958, pp. 10–11). At his father's insistence Rank did not attend a gymnasium but instead took technical training, after which he worked as a locksmith's apprentice and earned a diploma from an advanced technical school in 1903. From 1903 to 1905 (ages nineteen to twenty-one) he worked in machine factories. This period was crucial, for during it Rank turned into himself, engaged in creative and original depth-psychological self-explorations and formulations, discovered (perhaps it would be better to say, created) his self-identity as an artist, and made his transition to psychoanalysis. His diary entries (Rank 1903–5) cover this period and serve as a window into the origins or genesis of a unique psychological perspective.

Rank began his diary, which should really be called a "daybook" (*Tagebücher*), on January 1, 1903, with a very clearly defined purpose: "I begin this book for my own enlightenment. Before all else, I want to make progress in psychology . . . the comprehensive knowledge of mankind which explains the riddles of our thinking." To accomplish this goal, he said, "self-observation is necessary . . . to fix passing moods, impressions and feelings." Such observations would permit him "to trace the inner connections and external incidents of my development." He divided it into four parts, but the first (covering roughly the year 1903) contained all the essentials: bitter scorn and derision for religious customs of any sort, but especially for those of the Jewish past; for the middle-class round of life which he was being forced to enter; contempt for emotionally cold and unconcerned parents; self-isolation and an almost nonexistent sense of self-definition; and, at the end, a triumphant self-discovery of a genuine self-identity as an artist. The next two books (covering most of 1904 and the early months of 1905) continue the theme of alienation, but the sense of self-identity grew stronger and stronger, an interest in dreams became apparent, and there are passing first references to Freud's *The Interpretation of Dreams;* the final book (middle months of 1905) contains notes for *The Artist* and is almost devoid of personal reflections. In what follows, I only note these central themes, calling upon Rank to speak for himself; in no sense do I attempt a detailed and comprehensive analysis of the daybooks. Following this, I turn to the development of his thoughts, its self-integrating function and the turn to the psychoanalytic movement.

After a page or two of scattered aphorisms, Rank launched in detail into the most important issue which was on his mind at the time. He had looked out of his window and seen "a pompous Catholic funeral." This stimulated a long, rambling, and scathing denunciation of funeral practices generally ("expensive, hypocritical and in bad taste . . . embarrassing for the passers-by"). Rank thought he was suffering from the beginnings of what he called (but did not describe) "brain paralysis," and he wove this personal concern into his meditation, which shifted to the topic of immortality and to the "uncertainty and brevity of human life," from these to the way societies honor their dead, cremation as a more civilized custom, and, finally, the way society denies the reality of death while seeming to acknowledge it. Protestant and Jewish funerals were, he then noted, a bit less offensive. These reflections crystallized the real issue for Rank, how a Jew could live in the modern world. The real problem for "the modern Jew" was "the struggle between the customs, ceremonies and precepts as tradition teaches and real life." The old ways were "quite impossible": "the last 'Jew' is already dead; and still his descendants, with a mixture of defiance, pride, malice and conceit peculiar to their race, cling to the laws and advantages bequeathed by them" (July 20, 1903). So, Rank began his search for psychological knowledge with a meditation on the hypocrisies of religious traditions, on immortality, and on the finality of death.

He did not, however, restrict his scorn to religious heritage alone. He extended it to include the conventionalities and institutions of the bourgeois forms of life which impinged upon his emerging adolescence with greater and greater force. For example, he denigrated "woman, the Earthspirit," who "has triumphed for now in the fierce way between the sexes . . . the art of deception is woman's chief weapon." This view included "the much prized mother love," of which he was particularly derisive. To counteract woman's triumph, he proposed "powerful men, as in the Renaissance . . . to save a Europe becoming decidedly feminine." Romantic love, marriage, childbearing were, however, the real hypocrisies: the man "wants a housekeeper," and the woman is curious "about sexual love" and turns her later boredom into "mother-love." Both disguised their self-serving needs. At the end of a brief meditation on Darwin's works, Rank concluded that rejection of their obvious truths could be due only to "the deeply rooted prejudices of the people" (July/August 1903).

These diatribes culminated, in October 1903, in a remarkable parody of the Ten Commandments, the heart or essence of Jewish faith. Taft describes this parody morally, as one of "bitter cynicism." But if one attends carefully to the tone of the "Rankian Decalogue," it is easy to see that it was, consciously, a witty and scornful derision, and, unconsciously, a painful de-idealization. Five of Rank's ten "laws" read:

1. Thou shalt have no God
2. Thou shalt not suffer any other besides thyself
5. Fathers and mothers: Honor your children and love them so that you do not beget them if you are not able to support and educate them
7. Thou shalt not contract marriage
9. Thou shalt not desire thy neighbor's wife, for there are plenty of others

With a few easy strokes of the pen Rank was able to symbolize his withdrawal from the sense of community which his Jewish heritage had proferred to him by denying to it the existence of that community's capstone, the one God; to censure with a severity that belongs only to religious authority his parents for their neglect of him; and to affirm his unconscious, grandiose self and its refusal to allow the reality or existence of another person to modify it. Parodies of the Decalogue are interesting from a psychological point of view, for through them an author arrogates to himself the omnipotence and omniscience which members of a religious community ordinarily deny to themselves and with which they instead endow a transcendent being. Such parodies afford a glimpse into atheism—it would be more correct to say, skepticism or even cynicism—as a psychological, rather than a philosophical and theological, activity.[1]

Having sketched out his sense of the world as a whole, Rank turned to more immediate, personal concerns. Only two weeks later he drew up what was virtually the centerpiece of the first daybook, an autobiographical sketch (he called it an "autobiography") running just under ten pages. It tells a great deal about his family life and his inner responses to it. His bitterness still very much intact, he said with characteristic irony that his was "an idyllic family life." "My father . . . bothered himself little about me . . . and my mother found her satisfaction in the fact that we at least 'lived'; that is, ate and went 'decently' clothed. So I grew up, left to myself, without education, without friends, without books." The "lack of friends" was "very painful" for many years. But most psychologists would argue that the crucial emotional issue for Rank was his relation to his father: he was "a quiet drinker" but at times could be a terrifying man: on one occasion "I was alone with him in the house and still remember clearly how he bellowed hoarsely and struck his hands against the table til they bled, while I sat motionless in a corner, as if not alive but turned to stone and followed him with my eyes." In sum, "almost no word was spoken in the house, but . . . every one of us had a deep rage inside."

Within his inner world Rank's most fundamental problem was a lack of any sense that life was meaningful. An opening reflection in the first daybook asked, "What do I think of myself? Nothing! I shall live in vain." He referred more than once to "the accident of birth" and "the aimlessness of life." Toward the end of the first daybook he admitted: "There are days in my life to which I can assign no meaning, in relation to my mental development. And that I find painful" (February 5, 1904). Months later, while working in a machine shop, he noted "the terrible aimlessness and emptiness of my occupation" (April 24, 1904). There are a number of references to suicide in the daybooks, and, only a few months after the long "autobiography," he wrote a will, several pages long. In it he prescribed the manner in which he wanted to be buried: "I wish to lie alone outside of all cemetery walls and boundaries, in a quiet place if possible on the edge of a forest . . . as a grave marker, I would like a rough, unpolished block of stone of medium height" (January 1904). Just as Rank found it impossible to live in the presence of others, he could not imagine being dead in their presence, either.

But these gloomy things were not the whole story. During this time Rank was not only tearing things down, but he was also building them up: he was reading voraciously (Dostoyevski, Schopenhauer, Darwin, and Nietzsche, along with many lesser-known writers); he was attending (and enjoying immensely) plays, operas, and concerts (Wagner, Meyerbeer, Mozart, Beethoven); he was writing his own creative reflections and interpretations of these works; and he was also creating works of his own ("I am occupied with the following plans, of which I have already outlined some: a novella, a novel, four dramas, eight poems and three essays" [January, 1904]). These efforts, however, carried with them anxieties of their own. After writing his will he said, "I cannot bring myself to share my manuscripts with anyone. Also, I have no one. No person knows that I write" (January 26, 1904). In addition to these activities, he developed ideas about how writers produce their thoughts and works. Rank's "autobiography" ended with the observation that in order to understand an idea or an event in one's own life, one must "experience it fully" and at the same time gain "distance" from it, and close to the end he cited an unidentified author's aphorism, which he applied to himself: "I congratulate you on a new life-course" (October 27, 1903). That is to say, he wrote about the way writers write, to explain himself to himself. He was, in Kierkegaard's words, becoming who he was. So the reader should not be too surprised to learn that the first daybook ended on a note of truly remarkable psychological synthesis and identity formation: "I am an artist, even if I never succeed in bringing forth a single work of art . . . there are moments in which I believe firmly in my high endowment and therein that I belong to those who, even if they are not immortal, still live on for several centuries in their works. In such moments I have an indescribable feeling of happiness. . . . If I have erred, there will come a disillusionment so frightful that I shall never overcome it" (February 1904).

Unlike the first daybook, which reflected back on the Western cultural past and then forward through deep personal alienation and into a new personal sense of identity, the second and third books virtually abandoned the first concern in favor of an increasing sense of progress. One could say that Rank's feelings of betrayal by the past "withered away" or simply dropped out of the picture. Instead, these two books herald the following advances: continued states of self-alienation but also rapid recoveries from them; practical, realistic insights into himself and others (especially his father); consolidation of intellectual issues; and, of course, the initial intellectual encounter with Freud's *The Interpretation of Dreams*. After briefly noting these trends, I turn to Rank's intellectual development, which resolved the personal struggles, and especially to the place of Nietzsche and Freud in this resolution. Then I offer my interpretation of the social-structural mechanism which called into existence this unique depth psychology.

Rank's deep sense of self-alienation was by no means immediately or completely resolved by the consolidation of his identity ("I am an artist"). The meaninglessness of his life continued to disturb him, largely in the form of suicidal thoughts. Shortly after taking a position in a Vienna machine factory (on March 19, 1904), he noted: "When I wake up now in the morning, the first thought that enters my consciousness is the hollowness, emptiness and aimlessness of my present life. The feeling is awful! I would like to go to sleep again at once and forever" (March 30, 1904). A month later, again citing "the terrible emptiness and aimlessness of my occupation," he could say: "I came near to killing myself. I see no other way out. Why didn't I do it?" (April 24, 1904). Then, three weeks later, he provided the answer to his own question: "Today I bought a weapon to kill myself. Afterwards the highest lust for life and the greatest courage of death grew up in me. What do I know!" (May 14, 1904).

Rank's "lust for life" and "courage" were gaining the upper hand. At the end of April he drafted a long letter (five pages) which was, in essence, a request for employment as a writer. It is not known for whom it was intended or whether it was ever sent, although the putative recipient was obviously someone of position and authority. The letter is courteous, thorough, specific, and dignified. In the beginning he confessed it was difficult to write it ("there is nothing more painful for a person than to have to reveal to a stranger . . . his innermost thoughts and feelings"); he then described his occupation ("I have won the firm conviction that I am a poet") and mentioned the works he had written which he would include with the letter as examples of his abilities; he chronicled his personal and intellectual development briefly and explained why his current work was unsatisfactory ("the aimlessness and nothingness of my shop activity"); he announced his new plan ("I shall give up my position as soon as possible, leave my parents . . . and begin my own course as a writer"); he concluded by asking for support ("a loan that I would repay with thanks just as soon as I am able to do it"); finally, he noted the skills he could offer the employer (translations of French psychological works and the teaching of German) (April 29, 1904). Rank had become strong enough to test what he had won in the realm of a fantasied identity in the world of practical reality.

This readiness to commit himself to the world of work was accompanied by a more accurate sense of his own inner world. He wrote a long description of the similarities and differences between himself and his father (how "my development proceeds out of the tendencies of my father"); he wondered about a psychological merger with another man ("Man experiences a strange aversion before the thought of having to merge his individuality with another. I think no one would do it" [March 5, 1904]); and he recognized his inability to idealize another man ("Up to now I have known no living man whom I would have considered more complete (mature) in every respect than myself, when I experienced a deep need for association with another man" [May 14, 1904]). A bit later he was able to link the activity of creativity to the pleasures of psychological "self-observation": "The most exciting is introspection and the feelings of joy that streams through me at such moments . . . at every such moment I feel myself tremendously grown" (January/February 1905). Perhaps most important of all, at this time he analyzed in some detail his relation to three friends and concluded that "What I lack, that I love in the three" (January/February 1905).

This linkage between identity formation ("I am an artist") and an increased capacity to adapt more realistically to inner and outer actualities is a striking example of the central psychological theorem of Erik Erikson's entire psychology, that identity formation is the "developmental a priori," so to speak, of the entire human life course or life-cycle. In Rank's case, he discovered his identity as a creative writer by writing creatively about the creations and creativity of great artists and writers whom he admired. He poured himself, his very soul, into his daybooks, then reflected on these outpourings, and gradually put the two together. So the daybooks were tantamount to a self-analysis or creative illness. But, impressive as this may appear, it was not enough to consolidate in a permanent way a firm sense of self-identity and self-cohesion. To complete the process, Rank had to decide, not just to be a writer, but what to write about. Again in Erikson's terms, identity and ideology cannot be separated. Strictly speaking, this question takes us away from Rank's person and to his thought, the subject discussed next. But in a wider sense it also returns us to his inner world one more time, for we have also learned that any so-called self-analysis or creative illness never takes place in isolation but instead in relation to an important and intimate "other." So, who was "the other" in Rank's case? The answer is, first Nietzsche and then Freud. These two creative writers were, for Rank at least, both "objects" in the strict psychodynamic sense (more precisely, "good objects") and at the same time representatives of the world of culture from which he appropriated his ideology. Let us note these briefly before turning to an explanation of the process, taken as a whole.

Toward the end of his first daybook (in February 1904), Rank came to realize that his central interest was the artist and the artist's relation to culture. Culture meant many things to him: the Jewish heritage (common culture) of his past and "the past" generally, current intellectual figures, customs (social structure), and the shared world of imaginative or artistic forms. Rank wanted to know how the artist and culture were related. This was the intellectual side of his own personal quest: How did he himself fit into the social and cultural world of his everyday life, from which he had so massively withdrawn? So the issue was twofold: detachment but then also return or rapprochement. Detachment had produced the question (What is the artist's relation to culture?). The first hint of an answer came a month later. Rank's interest turned to the relations between dreaming and sleeping, life and death: "The dream is the same in sleep as life in death" (March 9, 1904). Art and dream had to be related, he began to think, but how? In October, the first reference to Freud occurs—to the concept of the unconscious in *The Interpretation of Dreams*. The remaining one-third of the second daybook contains, increasingly, references to Freud's theories. It is the psychology of dreams and the unconscious which links the artist and art to culture: "When the [dream] thoughts become oppressive inside, then also art begins" (November 24, 1904); "art is life's dream interpretation" (December 3, 1904); "the dream is built up like a drama" (December 8, 1904). But there was one difference between his ideas and Freud's: "In the dream the wishes are the driving element, in life the will itself" (December 26, 1904).

As the last two daybooks progressed (January–July 1905), they centered more and more on these themes: to art, dream, and will, Rank added only "the hero." His own introspective observations on the personal significance of daily events gradually dropped out of his entries. He began to put together his four interests, but especially the concept of the artist, more and more through the use of Freud's ideas of the unconscious, the instincts, and repression. The passages take on the character of paragraphs from a book. He was working on *The Artist* (1907). At the beginning of the final daybook he announced that "it is actually quite unnecessary to keep a daybook" (April 10, 1905). At the end he explained why: "Now I see everything clearly: the world process is no longer a riddle; I can explain the whole culture, yes I can explain everything" (May 13, 1905). It is also interesting to note that he identified God with the unconscious (June 12, 1905). It was *The Artist* and *The Essence of Judaism* which "explained everything" about the "world process," which is to say, made sense of the world, made life meaningful. How did this integration between "person" and "work" take place?

Rank's path out of his early search for self-definition and into his mature vision of the dynamics of culture led, like Jung's, through the works of Nietzsche and Freud, those two champions of the modern individual, and from there to idealizing Freud and fitting comfortably and gratefully into the group illusion of the psychoanalytic movement. Nietzsche became for Rank his "first truly inspiring teacher" (Klein 1981, p. 114). In the "Autobiography" section of Daybook 1, Rank accorded Nietzsche exceptional significance: "To him I will . . . set up a special memorial, for he was to me at once ideal leader and guide" (October 26, 1904). Rank internalized and identified with Nietzsche and his ideas, treating the philosopher as if he were a living person with whom he was studying. "Whence would I have had my practical and psychological knowledge," he said, "if I had not been guided to it by J.F.N.? The mixture in me is above all the most wonderful that I know" (January/February 1904). He "bathed . . . in Nietzsche's spirit" (October 26, 1904). The idea of "a mixture in me" suggests some sort of psychological fusion. Reading Nietzsche also helped Rank set aside "the most earnest thoughts of suicide" (October 26, 1904). When he learned that Nietzsche had died of syphilis, Rank said "the information shattered me" (November 28, 1904). Rank idealized Nietzsche with extraodinary intensity.

Klein has pointed out that several leading ideas in Nietzsche's works were of special value to Rank (1981, pp. 108–18). Nietzsche's contempt for the exhausted liberal values of family, education, politics, and religion appealed to Rank's irrevocable sense of separateness from the past. The philosopher's conviction that regeneration and renewal had to be worked out internally, in the immediate psychological world of each person, gave validity to Rank's extremely sharp and painful sense of self and his inability to effect a release from his persistent and prisonlike preoccupation with his own inner mental processes. Nietzsche believed that the individual could best accomplish renewal through the medium of an educator, and this no doubt activated Rank's "deep need for association" with "a man more complete than myself." Furthermore, the philosopher had said that such transformation could take place only within the context of a strong organization or heroic minority, a "mighty community" held together by a fundamental idea. Rank had never been able to enjoy the pleasure of belonging to a group—be it a clique, a fraternity, or an institution such as a school or college. Finally, Nietzsche called for the consecration of culture as a whole, and Rank never separated his personal searchings from the past and future of mankind. In sum, Nietzsche's program for individual and cultural renewal appealed to Rank's need for what Klein calls "meaningful religious satisfaction," for "a religion to which he could cleave" (p. 116). Having incompletely repudiated the social support of a traditional religious community, and on that account inwardly conflicted, Rank yearned for a theory of the whole which would reduce his inner conflict and restore him or guide him to what Durkheim called "a conscience superior to his own." Rank yearned for what Erich Fromm has called "a frame of orientation and devotion" (1955, pp. 63–66).

But Rank's idealization of Nietzsche was not, in and of itself, enough to consolidate his life course and his need for a view of the world. He also required "emotionally immediate contact," "direct stimulation and discipline," "direct inspiration" (Klein 1981, pp. 119–20)—which is to say, psychologically, that he needed a real person to embody in concrete relation to him the exciting ideas and ideals which he had been studying and creating. Klein's use of the word "inspiration" is, I think, correct, in the sense that it contains the implication of one person "breathing into" another person a life-giving essence which could shore up into some sort of unity fragments of self. Rank's desperation and neediness in 1903–5 suggests that he may have unconsciously felt that there was some part of himself that was dead. His frequent suicidal thoughts, his elaborate and carefully thought-out fantasy of his own burial, and his many references to the emptiness and meaninglessness of life all support this observation. His scorn for ancient ways and views and his bitterness in the face of massive parental neglect was, doubtless, the major source of this conviction.

It is important to realize that in all this Rank did not consider himself ill or in need of assistance. He did not want a doctor, and he had never heard of psychotherapy, for it did not at the time exist; he wanted a teacher. But Rank had many physical ailments and in one visit to the family physician, who we now know was none other than Alfred Adler, his doctor showed him Freud's *The Interpretation of Dreams*. "I read [the book] through," he said, "and was completely inspired" (Klein 1981, p. 121). As I have pointed out, from this point on Rank began to rethink many of the problems and issues which had occupied him in his diary in the light of Freud's theories. Art, his principal concern, and especially the music dramas of Wagner, whose beauty had moved him deeply, could be understood as a kind of dreaming, rooted in the unconscious. This would make the artist a kind of culturally appointed dreamer. Culture would then in turn have to be thought of as a repressive process, the embodiment of neurosis, over against which the artist stood and struggled. In such fashion did Freud's theory of neurosis and its healing through the interpretation of unconscious dream symbols provide the much-needed psychological link between Rank's own creative reflections on art and culture and the Nietzchean program for the renewal of culture.

As Klein has pointed out, the year 1905 was a time of decisive integration for Rank's life and work (1981, pp. 127–28). In January and February he began to develop ideas for *The Artist* and started writing in the spring. In May he wrote an eight-page letter to Freud which he never sent. In August he referred to his "personal contact with Freud." In December he wrote a three-page essay, *The Essence of Judaism*, which he considered to be a companion piece to *The Artist*. By October 1906, when he attended his first psychoanalytic meeting, he moved out of his family home to an apartment "not far from Freud's residence." He became the salaried secretary for the Wednesday night meetings, and *The Artist* was published in 1907. At Freud's urging he attended gymnasium, graduating in 1908, and went directly on to the University of Vienna for his doctorate. He legally changed his name from Rosenfeld to Rank in 1909 (Klein 1981, p. 110). In addition to fatherly guidance, Freud offered financial support.

In *The Artist* Rank stated that mankind has gradually evolved from an original state of primitive and unchallenged sexual gratification to one of repression, neurosis, and hysteria. The artist is able to forestall complete repression by giving expression to the unconscious while still remaining part of the repressed society. But only by becoming a healing artist, one who carefully attends to the unconscious and its modes of action, can the artist really cure neurosis. So understood, the artist is a "new vanguard of universal artistic redemption" (Klein 1981, pp. 128–29). *The Essence of Judaism* completed this line of thinking by identifying the specific historical circumstances of this universal "world process." In his second essay Rank proposed that the Jews, more than any other people, had remained in a state of primitive sexuality ("the essence of Judaism is its stress on primitive sexuality" [1905, p. 171]) and are therefore less vulnerable to the processes of cultural repression. It follows that "Jews thoroughly understood the *radical* cure of neurosis better than other people" (p. 172). Clearly, *The Artist* and *The Essence of Judaism* were complementary documents. And, just as clearly, Rank found in psychoanalytic ideas a redemptive vision for mankind and in Freud's movement a context for the historical realization of that vision.

It is also very clear that Rank made a transition from a waning sense of Jewish self-identity to psychoanalysis during the years 1902–6 and that this transition was determinative for his life. But it is still not at all clear how he made this transition. Klein has shown that Rank's essay on Judaism embodied themes which preoccupied other Jews of the time, such as assimilation and anti-Semitism. Like many other Jews, Rank also retained an inner sense of having belonged to a distinctly Jewish heritage. As a historian Klein rightly eschews efforts to explain how Rank went from the waning "ideal of Jewish existence" to his psychoanalytic writings and his postmovement, mature works. In these works the religious reference is more diffuse but nonetheless distinctly present. The psychologists on the other hand describe his inner world—what "he turned to"—but eschew entirely Rank's religious background and his essay on Judaism, which are in effect accounts of "where he came from."

The two are, however, intimately related, and the link between them which is missing in the above accounts illumines each one further. The link is the character of Rank's disappointment with the first and the way that shaped the second. I have already pointed out that the daybooks begin with a de-idealization of the sociological "essence" of Judaism, the Decalogue, and of the religious community which it symbolized and integrated. Rank consciously ridiculed the holy laws in a gloating and triumphant way. From a psychological point of view these conscious thoughts had to have activated an unconscious recognition of separation and an unconscious invitation to psychological self-understanding and the building up of psychological structure. Rank's response to this mandate was a unique amalgamation of art, psychoanalysis, and religion. He built up and clarified these elements, fleetingly alluded to in the daybooks, and made them the centerpiece of *The Artist*, the work which consolidated his life course. Two paragraphs in this work deserve careful attention because they set forth in an unusually forthright way the progression I have just described. In the beginning of chapter 2, Rank gave a religious description of the fundamental problem of "all human knowledge": "The external God with his praise of Creation—

and behold it was good—was a grave mistake, an expression of that 'monstrous displacement of affects' with which all human knowledge begins . . . the human will is the long-sought God who directs and guides everything and now man dares to bring down judgment on the world—and behold it was bad" (Taft 1958, p. 53). In the final paragraph of his book Rank announced his artistic and psychoanalytic solution for "the future of the human race":

> And now as the condition for the cure of neurosis has been given, there is opened up a broader outlook on the future of the human race. Humanity may face hysteria, the inevitable end of every cultural development, with hope, for now, if it can surmount this ending, it may be able to construct a way out, and if formerly people came to grief in the neurosis, now they will go clear through it and thereby become enlightened. But only when a complete change of attitude toward everything psychic has come of pass, the whole unconscious become conscious, then will the "unartist" asexual man stand in the midst of life, light and strong like a God, and direct and rule his instincts with a sure hand. (Taft 1958, p. 53)

These paragraphs show with clarity what Rank meant when he wrote in his daybooks, at the time when things were coming together for him, "Now I see everything clearly. . . . I can explain the whole of culture, I can explain everything." These words must be taken as emblematic of his entire life course, foreshadowing especially what he turned to.

But the transition was not a smooth one. Instead of undergoing a gradual and progressive de-idealization and subsequent structure building, Rank negotiated these conditions very rapidly and only very incompletely. The result was that he had to confront more directly his own narcissistic vulnerability and, in particular, his normal, human propensity for totalism and absolutism, without the softening benefits which a common, sociosymbolic context confers. To return again to the historical idiom: the redemptive vision was shorn of its ancient contexts, and Rank filled the empty space with new contents drawn from Nietzsche, Freud, and others. He transferred his unconscious search for a truly authoritative object of idealization to Freud's theories and, later, his person and his group. The remainder of his life was given over to the clarification and elaboration of the rudimentary vision laid down in 1905 in *The Artist* and *The Essence of Judaism*.

Rank's relationship to Freud, his progress within the movement, and his subsequent break with both in the mid-1920s have been well discussed (Stolorow and Atwood 1976; Taft 1958; Roazen 1975). All emphasize the mutual affection and the intense dependency and dutifulness of Rank throughout, roughly, the first ten years (1907–17). He worked industriously at his assigned task: the nonmedical "applications" of psychoanalysis. For example, *The Myth of the Birth of the Hero* began with what became Freud's short paper, "Family Romances" (1909), and then extended this theory—the child's fantasy of two sets of parents—into the myths about the parentage of the hero, understood as a type in history. The intense and unconscious ambivalent affection between the two men is seen in the fact that Rank sometimes interpreted Freud's dreams to him, to Freud's satisfaction (Taft 1958, pp. 78–79), and Freud often thought of Rank as a the truly ideal heir to lead the movement, once Jung had departed.

By the end of the First World War Rank had achieved considerable separation from Freud. He had lived in Cracow, where he edited the official publication of the Austrian army, and when he returned to Vienna he was accompanied by a beautiful and talented wife. By 1920 he had begun to see patients regularly. In his work as a psychoanalyst Rank noticed many references to mother transferences and identified a "mother fixation," rather than an unconscious preoccupation with the father, as the essential element in "the transference." To this innovation in clinical theory Rank also added a new principle of technique: he thought that emotional release, not insight, was the truly effective element in analytic healing. These two ideas became the basis of his new book, *The Trauma of Birth*, already discussed above, which separated him completely from Freud.

Psychobiography (Stolorow and Atwood 1976) says that the determinative factor in this bitter separation was Rank's narcissistic vulnerability: his need to idealize Freud and his need for Freud's gentle, warm, and empathic mirroring of the creative products of his mind were both frustrated. By disagreeing with Rank's ideas, Freud asserted himself as a self, separate from Rank's self, and the narcissistic union was broken. Rank's inner sense of self-cohesion was fragmented; he responded with rage and became socially isolated, setting out on his own and looking back in anger. Taft (1958) takes a more characteristically Rankian view and argues that what could be called Rank's structure of experience was so different from Freud's that a break was really unavoidable. In her own way, though, she deals with issues of self. Roazen's history of the psychoanalytic movement (1975) charts Rank's intellectual modifications of psychoanalytic thought, which led him away from Freud. Unfortunately, Klein does not discuss Rank's life and thought beyond his entry into the movement in 1906.

To complete this picture it is necessary to track Rank's Jewish vision of renewal or redemption, embodied in *The Artist* and *The Essence of Judaism,* into the movement and from there into his mature—that is, post-Freudian—works, for this vision was a central, creative element throughout, although it underwent continuous modification. In the psychoanalytic movement Rank's earlier account of the regeneration of culture and history by means of the work of the healing artist became muted. These years were a kind of latency or moratorium, in Erikson's (1958) sense of the term. Rank enjoyed Freud's intimacy and warmth, the support of like-minded men, and the intellectual challenge to advance psychoanalytic thinking. His previously frustrated needs to idealize were once more allowed to flourish, and he was occupied enough—or comfortable enough—to neglect the problems of cultural renewal in favor of more interpretive and exacting analytic work.

In *The Trauma of Birth* Rank struggled with pre-oedipal issues in the manner of idiosyncratic insight—that is, his theories there were not worked out analytically. Freud was highly critical of this, although it is probably just as true that he would not have been interested in this sector of mental life no matter how clearly and effectively it might have been put to him. But his new book also reopened Rank's search for a vision of cultural renewal and redemption. The moratorium was over. The birth experience was a biological symbol for the psychological genesis of the individual, the experience of self-creation. Rank was able to weave into his own and new psychoanalytic formulation his earlier concerns with the regenerative and redemptive function of the artist. The patient had become his own artist, or the artist had become his own patient. In his short book, which combined clarity and simplicity, Rank revisioned the whole of psychoanalytic theory, technique, and nosology in the light of the spiritual, philosophical, and artistic dimensions of the history of culture, under the control of his one great idea. Once again he was able to exclaim, in effect, "Now I have explained everything."

Rank's thought after his departure from the movement represents the fulfillment and integration of his earlier work before and during his stay in the psychoanalytic movement. In what should be called his mature works—*Truth and Reality* (1929), *Will Therapy* (1931), and *Art and Artist* (1932)—Rank was able to recast his earlier concerns with the regeneration of culture, the artist, and psychoanalytic theory into a lucid, complex, learned, and by every measure global philosophy of Western history and culture. The earlier vision, constructed before he read Freud, remained determinative, although it underwent constant modification. It is of crucial importance to remember that even in 1904–5, when Rank read Freud for the first time, he rejected important parts of Freud's theory: "Wishes are phenomena of will. . . . In a dream the wishes are the driving element, in life the will itself" (December 18 and 26, 1904). Klein notes further that even at this time Rank thought Freud's theory of dreams was a form of scientific disguise, that it "demonstrated the temptation of withdrawing into reason and resolution too quickly" (1981, pp. 127–28). So Rank did not simply "rebel against Freud" in a reactive way. Rather, he rebelled in order to retrieve his earliest ideas, give them deeper, more idiosyncratic depth-psychological formulation, and restate them in still more compelling and articulate ways. In these final works, the idea of the will acquired the prominence which Rank always thought it deserved but which he could not formulate until much later in life.

The building blocks of Rank's mature works were present in his earlier writings: the development of culture as the increase in repression, the artist a the prototypical healer or redeemer of culture, and the psychoanalysis of dreams as the concrete implementation of healing. But these elements lacked a coherent relationship to each other and to a theory of the development of culture as a whole. The mature works organized Rank's earlier ideas around a new and truly precipitous conception of historical progress or advance and, further, placed Freud and psychoanalysis (and Jung and Adler as well) in this progression. As long as Rank remained in the movement, he thought the movement itself constituted the point of greatest historical advance. But, in the mature works, he concluded that the movement had become part of the problem, to which his own unique brand of psychology and historical analysis was the solution.

So Rank spoke of the stages of Western art, philosophy, and religion (for example, primitive art, classical art, modern art; or, Jewish, Greek, and Christian spiritual development). These culminated in a modern, individualized man, the result of the increasing extension and expansion of self-awareness in humanity. To provide focal points in his sweep, Rank spoke of types of people: the artist, the average, the neurotic, and the productive. The modern type was characterized by a heightened sense of self-consciousness and, related to this, a sharp sense of separateness from the ideologies, largely religious, which had formerly provided individuals with stability. The result was the creation of the neurotic type, who could not adapt creatively to culture, and the average type, who could only adapt to culture in a mode of compliance, thereby surrendering individuality. Freud's psychoanalysis worked at this second level: it converted the neurotic into the average. By conveying to the patient scientifically informed insight, it fostered adaptation to conventional society and therefore was the functional equivalent of earlier ideologies. The real solution, on the other hand, was to enhance and deepen the neurotic's quality of experiencing in order to bring out the latent capacities for creative willing. What Rank called "will therapy" accomplished this task. In it the therapist facilitated the conscious struggle for creative self-expression and self-realization. Freud's preoccupation with making conscious the conflicts of the unconscious through insight only forestalled this process. The prototype for creative self-expression was the artist's struggle to create works of art. Formerly, the artist healed culture through creative self-expression; now historical advance had created the neurotic, and Rank called upon him to heal "the culture within" by helping him become an artist unto himself.

In his emphasis upon the creative struggle to realize one's innermost essence, one can see the final resting point of Rank's early vision of regeneration. Although now clothed in a new psychology of experiencing and a new history of culture, and considerably modified by these, its original shape is still recognizable. With remarkable self-consistency Rank entitled the final chapter of *Truth and Reality*, which is, along with *Art and Artist*, perhaps the clearest and richest of his mature works, "Happiness and Redemption."

Ernest Jones: Psychoanalysis as Science

When Jung and Rank wrote about their own lives, they did so from the point of view of the unique and original psychological theories which each had created. Jung's *Memories, Dreams, Reflections* is an autobiographical statement of the process of individuation, and Rank's diaries set forth his own life as an exemplary instance of his idea of the artist. In his letters to Fliess and in *The Interpretation of Dreams*, Freud used his oedipal model, and when Jones wrote about Freud's life he too used the master's theory. But when Jones turned to his own autobiography, he announced in its opening pages a surprisingly different but equally universal life theme: the essence of his life, he said, and for that matter of every life, could best be described as "the gradual taming of the grandiloquent hopes and fantasies of infancy . . . the narcissism of childhood" (1959, pp. 11–12). To this universal principle he added, with an air of deliberate mystery, a very particular one of his own, that of a "double allegiance," which was far more sociological than psychological. By "double allegiance" he meant that "the essential story" of his life lay "hidden" in the very social fact that he had been born in the ancient Welsh kingdom of Gower but that Gower had belonged to two different counties (Glamorgan and Caemarthen)—his father came from the first, his mother from the second—that as an adult he always felt a tension between Wales and England, and that, in his lifelong occupation as a physician, he felt caught between an allegiance to medicine and to psychoanalysis. He could have added others, such as England and Canada or London and Vienna, for Jones was indeed "a man between." But as he developed the story of his life, Jones quickly lost sight of this perspective, for he had no wish to understand precisely how he moved from his social embeddedness in his land of origin to the individualizing world of psychoanalysis.

In the account which follows I make explicit and central what Jones left implicit and peripheral in his, since his disavowal of the social in favor of the psychological in his biography of Freud was as complete as it was in his own autobiography: the gradual, lifelong transition from the commonalities of a rural, ethnic, Christian village (what he "came from") to the autonomous, professionalized, urban-industrial, and highly individualized preoccupations of the psychoanalyst with the inner world (what he "came to"). The quality, rapidity, painfulness, and character of this transition shaped Jones's capacity to appreciate Freud's ideas and to remain loyal to them, for it was a gradual and—to a considerable extent—conscious one. These observations also help explain why Jones's approach to the movement differed so much from Jung's and Rank's—their "transitions" had been rapid, chaotic, and partial—and why it resembled Freud's which was also gradual. Furthermore, knowledge of Jones's transition sheds light on the three central interlocking features of his life and thought: his dedication to revolutionary social change, his constant preoccupation with the conflict between religion and science, and his own special capacity for depth-psychological self-understanding, which culminated, later in life, in an effort to probe more deeply than did Freud the psychology of mourning.

The rural round of life which embraced and contained the childhood and adolescence of Ernest Jones consisted in a profound appreciation for the natural beauty of the land, a strong loyalty to Welsh ethnic-national identity, and a sincere, idealizing attachment to the family's Protestant (Baptist, but later Anglican) Christianity.

Whenever he was lonely as a boy, Jones took consolation from long, solitary walks through hills and along the edges of bays and cliffs. He bore a lifelong grudge against his school masters for not teaching him Welsh. And he always considered the English foreigners ("The English are notoriously hard to understand—they really are a peculiar people" [1959, p. 45]), although he felt he could enter their world. On the other hand, he also found the Welsh narrow and parochial.

Jones's parents were both religious, his mother more so than his father, and they took their children to church regularly. He described his mother as a quiet but affectionate woman, a pious reader of the Bible and religious magazines. She read him Bible stories when he was a child, and she hoped that he would become a clergyman. When Jones was quite young, his father struck him as emotionally restrained by a deep inner reserve related to a conversion to the "rigid principles" of the Baptist church (1959, p. 21). He gradually grew away from this orientation, first by becoming an Anglican and still later by dropping that. These shifts were accompanied by advances in his work (he began as a clerk in a coal mine, later became an engineer, and after that was promoted to manager—"he evidently felt that strict attendance to his new financial duties absolved him from the need for further Sabbatarian obligations" (p. 24)—and by an increasingly more tolerant attitude toward himself and others. Rounding out this family picture was a fanatical nurse who mixed religious punishment ("She inspired me with a dread of what was euphemistically called 'the burning fire'" [p. 29]) with sexual stimulation ("She taught me two words to designate the male organ, one for it in a flaccid state, and other in an erect" [p. 30]).

This picture of rural life and its principal elements of land, ethnicity, language, and religion is so easily recognizable that it can actually obscure recognition of the ways in which it provided a conscious and unconscious sense of belonging. In Jones's case this sense of community was mediated for him primarily by his relation to women—his mother, his wife, and his daughter, all of whom Jones loved deeply. He believed the tie to the mother to be more basic than to the father ("A mother's influence, though more profound, is less tangible" [1959, p. 26]), he felt he was her favorite ("She was . . . completely devoted to me" [p. 26]) and that this had influenced him decisively ("An early relationship of this kind, as Freud has truly remarked, provides an unshakable basis for self-confidence in later life, and that I have never lacked" [p. 27]). But Jones's mother also spoke Welsh (his father did not). He could not forgive his father for naming him Alfred Ernest, after Queen Victoria's second son, for he "would have much preferred his mother's choice of Myrddin" (Davies 1979, p. 17). Many years later Jones married a Welsh woman, Morfydd Owen ("It was irrational, but something in me strove against marrying an English woman; it seemed so commonplace" [1959, p. 253]). He named his first daughter by a second marriage Gwyneth, and when Morfydd and Gwyneth died tragically, Jones searched his inner world more deeply than at any other time in his life (Brome 1983, p. 165). And upon his death his ashes were preserved "in the grave of his daughter Gwyneth at the village of Chariton, which is the next village to Llanmadoc where stood the cottage Ty Gwyn to which he so often returned in life to. . . . recover the peace of his roots" (Brome 1983, p. 218).

Jones's attachment to his mother and to other women, and from there to "things Welsh" and to "Welshness," was all of a piece with his mother's religious orientation, and it was from her, according to Davies, that he acquired his capacity to engage his inner world. In contrast to his father, who emphasized the need to change material conditions in order to improve conditions of living, Jones's mother believed that inner change was more important and that it occurred "through a process of 'internal' regeneration." Jones's later rejection of religion "did not deter him from acknowledging that in these things his mother's ideas were nearer to his than were his father's" (Davies 1979, p. 17). In the next chapter I clarify the way in which a religious orientation can actually produce a psychological one despite the fact that the two are, on the surface, antithetical to each other. There I discuss Freud's transition from "Jewish-religious" to "psychological" as an instance of Weber's view that historical change occurs when idealistic-religious ideas "break through" to material conditions.

I have already noted the view that massive industrialization was an essential social-structural precondition for the emergence of psychoanalytic ideas in the West. Industrialization forced fathers to abandon the more nurturant role they formerly played in preindustrial families. That in turn stimulated sons' hatred for fathers but also the wish to identify with the father and to be included in his world. This was certainly so in the case of Jones and his father. Gower was in the midst of industrialization. Jones called it a "newly rising industrial village" (1959, p. 41). Coal mining had been first. There was a village slaughterhouse. And to the opening sentence of his autobiography, already noted ("The essential story of my life lies hidden in those sentences" [p. 11]), Jones immediately added that, although he had been, strictly speaking, born in the village of Rhosfelyn, the Great Western Railway "rechristened" it as Gower Road and that only later did his father arrange for the name of Gowerton.

Jones's father was very much in the midst of Gower's industrialization. As I have already noted, he had advanced from clerk to engineer to manager. He grew to value science above all other forms of knowledge, and under the impress of these developments his religious attachments had gradually withered away. His social views became more liberal and progressive. Above all else he was a practical man concerned with the affairs of the world. At the end of his life he resembled in all its essentials Max Weber's portrait of the Protestant entrepreneur: "He became less idealistic, less serious, more mundane, and perhaps more commonplace—more bourgeois. This tendency increased with the years as he rose in the world until at the end he could be distinguished from the average industrialist only by a certain air of distinction, a special high standard of integrity" (1959, p. 25).

Just as the Great Western Railway drew the men of Gower out of rural embeddedness and into the industrializing world, Jones's positive oedipal identification with his father drew him out of the social rhythms of that common life and his attachment to his mother and into the new, urban-industrial world. There he found it necessary to adopt new rules and values, such as autonomy, emotional restraint, asceticism, the manipulation of abstractions, and professionalism. Jones's desire to become a physician, felt early in life, had the foreordained and spiritual quality of a "calling," as did his desire to take up the university studies which it presupposed. Even more taken-for-granted was his deep inner conviction that a city was the only place where life—regardless of the particular opportunities it afforded—could best be realized: "London had from childhood meant for me more than a place; it was the prime place from which life could best be explored, and no provincial capital, not even that of my native land, could serve instead" (1959, p. 116).

In 1895, at the age of sixteen, Jones entered University College, Cardiff, where he studied medical and humanistic subjects. He began his practical training (internship and residency) in London in 1898 and was licensed in 1900, with a strong preference for neurology. During the next six years he gradually shifted to psychiatry and from there to psychoanalysis. He came across Freud's works for the first time in 1898, began "practicing" Freud's "method" in 1906, and then entered the movement, meeting Jung first in 1907 and then Freud in 1908.

When Jones finally turned to psychoanalysis, Freud, and the movement, his propensity to take up a great cause was in fact already well established. That readiness was really the endpoint in a series of personal experiences and intellectual shifts which I have called his transition: a gradual disillusionment with his childhood and adolescent round of life and an increasing psychologization of his adult urban identity. If we take Jones at his word, the intellectual components of this transition were of great importance, but I think that they were also the surface of deeper personal and social experiences. At the center of this transition lay his lifelong preoccupation with the conflict between religion and science. Paradoxically, the stimulus to this conflict came not from psychology and personality theory but from "society." Jones's transition breaks down into three movements: his intellectual struggles at Cardiff, ages sixteen to nineteen, in which he moved away from religion to philosophy; a grandiose, revolutionary scheme for the transformation of society, concocted with his best friend, Wilfred Trotter, the only man he ever felt close to in addition to Freud, during the early London years (age twenty-six); and, following that, his theory that psychoanalysis was the key which could unlock the secrets of a disordered society by identifying "the inherited elements of the mind" (1959, p. 143). The intellectual struggles precipitated the revolutionary scheme, and the psychoanalytic theory of culture consolidated it.

When Jones passed his examinations in medicine with first-class honors, he said he was so elated that his success had to have activated his "omnipotence complex" and that this experience contrasted sharply with "my earlier years of burning self-criticism, with its sense of guilt in the spheres of religion and sex" (1959, p. 105). These childhood psychological conflicts formed the emotional base for his first two years at Cardiff, "the most stirring and formative" years of his life. Of them he said: "The starting point was the problem of religion, which covered more personal sexual ones. Since the age of ten I had never been able to give my adherence to any particular creed, but my conscience troubled me badly and impelled me to seek in every direction for enlightenment. I prayed earnestly, frequented the diverse religious services available, and read widely on both sides. From that time dates my lasting interest in religious phenomena and the meaning of their important to the human soul" (1959, p. 57). Mixed into these personal preoccupations were readings in Hume, Bergson, Huxley, and Russell, the mind-body problem and the controversy over evolution. At the age of seventeen Jones became a philosophical materialist by refusing "to believe that mental processes, or beings, can exist independently of the physical world," and "a confirmed atheist," by which he meant "not one who denies any possible existence of a deity, but one who sees no good reason for believing in the concept" (1959, p. 59).

These thinkers and their ideas fired Jones's imagination and turned him away from his religious concerns. But the process which brought about this shift was psychological as well as cognitive, and Jones overlooked its central mechanism. The decisive moment, "when I gave orthodoxy its last chance," he explained, was a lecture on agnosticism by a famous Biblical scholar. At that time Jones presumably held some hope that his religious concerns might still prove to have some validity. But then, he said, "my disappointment" with the lecture "turned to scorn" (1959, pp. 59–60). And so one must ask, What produced the disappointment and what psychological process brought feelings of scorn rather than sadness into awareness?

For years Jones had struggled to believe in the existence of (to idealize) a realm of clear and absolutely binding moral principles which were accessible to consciousness and the will, which conferred a sense of self-control over sexuality, and which supported self-esteem, a global feeling of being a good person. Although the psychological cost of this belief was considerable ("burning self-criticism . . . a sense of guilt"), its purchase also assured him of an enduring but unconscious sense of attachment or belonging to a community of like-minded elders whose collective religioethical endeavors guaranteed that deeper sexual wishes and feelings of shame, badness, and low self-esteem would remain safely at bay. Although drives and in particular the sexual drive were a life-long personal preoccupation for Jones, the process of idealization and its vicissitudes were easily as important, even if he did not choose to attend to it.

As he listened to the famous biblical scholar's lecture, Jones consciously gave up the religious ideals of his childhood and adolescence (this was his "disappointment"), and his conscious response was one of narcissistic anger (his disappointment "turned to scorn"). To have been more complete, the disillusionment would have had to eventuate in a genuine sense of sadness, mourning, and longing, imbued with an elegiac emotional tone, in which strife was for the most part absent. But Jones remained angry and was consequently left with an unconscious need to idealize a new person or idea and an unconscious surplus of anger to be directed at the new person's critics. He still needed a "creed" to "adhere to."

The next three sentences of his autobiography which describe this incident provide further support for this interpretation. In an effort to clarify his disappointment and scorn, Jones immediately digressed in order to inform his reader that Huxley was the only man who had ever influenced his mental development and that he "must have" unconsciously identified with Huxley. Indeed, Jones himself had designated Freud as the "Darwin of the mind," and he proudly concluded that he had fought for Freud exactly as Huxley had fought for Darwin: "We were both 'bonny fighters'" (1959, p. 60). In such fashion did fate transform Jones's inner, guilt-laden consciousness and its latent persecutory potential into a secular, intellectual problem.

This transformation can be rendered metaphorically without completely losing its psychodynamic significance. In Francis Thompson's well-known poem, "The Hound of Heaven," God persecutes or "hounds" the person who no longer wishes to believe in his existence, creating a terrible inner sense of badness and fear of self-fragmentation and loss of social support in the subject. Jones's dilemma was typical for many of his time. He decided against God and for a secular point of view but in doing so transformed the unresolved portions of his unconscious conflict (the need to control sexual wishes and the need for a sense of belonging or group self) into the psychoanalytic movement. In terms of the central image of the poem, the Hound of Heaven became the barking (and sometimes biting) bulldog of psychoanalysis, for just as Huxley was "Darwin's bulldog," Jones thought of himself as "Freud's bulldog."

This transformation inaugurated Jones's lifelong concern with social problems: "From religion one passed naturally to philosophy, ethics and sociology," he said, and so he studied the works of Saint-Simon, Fourier, and Marx over a period of ten years (1959, p. 60). But there is nothing "natural" about such a passage; its only logic is "psychologic." One would "naturally" take up a challenging and adversarial attitude toward an existing social order only if one had become disappointed with an earlier, unquestioned, and taken-for-granted sense of it. At this time Jones became convinced that the "arrangements of society" were "highly unsatisfactory." This conviction propelled him in the direction of psychoanalysis, and he devoted much of the rest of his life to the psychoanalytic study of society. We see here a fragment of the psychology of the social reformer or revolutionary.

These preoccupations with unsatisfactory social arrangements, begun at Cardiff, were never really interrupted by Jones's medical studies and his need to establish himself professionally. For the two years following completion of his medical studies in 1901, Jones enjoyed successful appointments as a house physician. These were followed, however, by several devastating rejections, and these consolidated further his sense of bitter dissatisfaction with "society." He could not connect or fit in with others and began to drift. In order to stabilize his career, he decided to set himself up in private practice in 1905 with his eminent friend Wilfred Trotter. This relationship catalyzed his thinking about himself and life and strengthened his wavering interests in psychoanalysis, making possible the final step to Freud and the movement in 1907. Psychoanalysis provided Jones with the theory of the social world which he himself lacked, along with a place in that social world into which he had been unable to fit. As he explained: "My interest in psychology did not begin . . . from concern about some personal individual problem so much as from a wide interest in general social problems. . . . It was thus the injustices, stupidities and irrationalities of our social organization . . . that impelled me to learn something about that curious thing responsible for it all: human nature" (1959, p. 153).

Jones described himself as an extraordinary ambitious young man whose first professional experiences were "imbued with the magic of glittering success" (1959, p. 94). He attributed this to the persistence into adult life of his infantile narcissism ("A certain spoiltness in my nature, assuredly derived from my relations with my mother" [p. 94]). When an application to a prestigious hospital was rejected, it produced a cycle of further rejections. Jones found that he could obtain no appointment at all which he really wanted and that he had become, in a short time, "a marked man" in London medicine (p. 115). The experience was a devastating blow to his self-esteem ("Fate hammered one hard blow after another" [p. 94]). His explanation for these events was both moral and psychological. Reflecting on the way in which nurses, students, and especially senior physicians had taken offence at "my passion for the highest standard of work," Jones concluded that "I had a tongue. And a young man may be so filled with righteousness that he can see no reason for restraining his tongue when his virtuous endeavors meet with opposition." He was, he said, "opinionated, tactless, conceited" (p. 96). His genetic explanation was "a deep feeling of insecurity and inferiority" due to a combination of "internal factors," premature weaning, and early ill health (p. 115).

This description anticipates in a rudimentary way Kohut's portrayal of an insufficiently modified archaic, grandiose self struggling unsuccessfully with a confusing and painful sense of shame. Jones's grasp of narcissistic issues was truly remarkable, even when one recognizes that he probably drafted the notes for this portion of his

autobiography in 1944. But these psychobiographical and moral reflections deflected his attention from a fundamental social fact: Jones
had become marginal to medicine and neurology, could not fit in, and
had begun to wander. His disillusionments reached beyond the
boundaries of the ego and into the disappointing social order upon
which he gazed with an even sharper sense of discontent than that of
his Cardiff days.

To repair this situation Jones seems to have tried everything: public health, pediatrics, tropical medicine, tutoring medical students
for examinations, administering the examinations, and delivering
occasional lectures for hospital programs. He mastered new spe-
cialties quickly and read endlessly in others, carried along by
inexhaustible currents of restless, almost feverish, energy. Two other
episodes consolidated further his drift away from what he had earlier
thought would be the center of his life. In 1905 he was arrested on a
charge of molesting two young children while administering a special
test. Although he was acquitted, he spent a night in jail and there was
a scandal. In 1908 he was asked to resign from the staff of a hospital
because he had discussed sexual topics with a young female patient.
Jones entered adult life with the desire to make a mark on the world
by doing something lofty for mankind, but he felt poorly prepared for
this: badly educated, without particular endowments, and "destitute
of any cultural refinement" (1959, p. 64). This series of circumstances
between 1903 and 1908, characterized by self-doubt and social alienation, led Jones to Wilfred Trotter and their revolutionary social
scheme, which in turn led him to psychoanalysis.

Trotter was a highly admired, successful surgeon, seven years senior to Jones. They had met during his hospital days, but only in 1905
did they become close. Like some other physicians of his generation,
Trotter interested himself in subjects wholly unrelated to his profession. For example, he was the author of a well-known book (1916) on
social behavior, *Instincts of the Herd in Peace and War*. Alongside
his more obvious traits of wittiness, skepticism, and a profound commitment to the scientific attitude, Trotter was "the most extreme,
and even blood-thirsty, revolutionary in thought and fantasy that one
could imagine" (1959, p. 101). He had "a strong Savior complex" and
a "flaming passion to arouse mankind from its slumbers." Trotter
"yearned to do great things, and felt he was destined to redeem mankind from at least some of its follies and stupidities" (p. 127). He was
widely read and his favorite author was Nietzsche, with whom he
shared "the idea of breeding a better race" (p. 130). But Trotter was
not politically active, and from 1910 on he abandoned his revolution-

ary feelings and attitudes and became highly conventional, aloof, and inhibited.

Jones described Trotter as "my best friend and apart from Freud, the man who has mattered most in my life" (1959, p. 101). In addition to sharing a house, they ate their dinners, spent the evenings, and took long walks together, several times a week. Jones's sister kept house for them, and in 1910 she and Trotter married. Jones looked up to Trotter, who embodied in living actuality the ideas and ideals he felt stirring in himself. Most of all Jones admired Trotter's unique combination of "philosophic calm" (a "profound grasp of the essentials of the scientific attitude . . . together with the all-embracing skepticism it implies" [p. 102]) with intense social-revolutionary feelings. Jones was able to live out vicariously, through Trotter, his own emotional hatred for an unforgiving social world and still satisfy his profound psychological need for inner calm and control through a commitment to science. In this relationship we can also catch a glimpse of the interesting psychology of skepticism, to which I return in a moment, the way in which a particular conception of science serves an emotional need. Intimately related to this was Jones's sense of himself and his work, especially his approach to science and his later view of psychoanalysis as a science. That view is captured well by his own phrase, his "intolerance of illusion," a trait he also shared with Freud. Jones was later able to idealize once again these features of Trotter in the life and works of Fred, and his relationship to Trotter constitutes a crucial fragment in the genetic reconstruction of the values Jones used to frame his world-famous subject.

Jones and Trotter together objectified their close emotional relationship and the ideals which cemented it in the form of a revolutionary scheme to transform existing society. In the new utopia each was to have a central leadership role. They agreed completely that "the organizing of life in a community" had to be based upon "full knowledge of the biological, including psychological, motivation of man" (1959, p. 128). They planned a book which Jones called their "campaign." It was to begin with "a detailed . . . scathing indictment of the maladies of civilization" and would conclude with "the way in which the most promising remedies are to be found" (p. 128). Jones did not say what the maladies and remedies were, but the leadership was not in doubt. Trotter thought there should be five leaders and, "in his more megalomaniac moments," that "the five great cities of the world would be re-named after them, just as Petrograd became changed to Leningrad" (p. 129). The allusion to Marxism did not escape Jones, nor did the less obvious allusion to the Committee, which this grandiose plan anticipated: "Perhaps it was from this number (five leaders) that I, years later, made the committee of five as Freud's bodyguard" (p. 129). What did escape Jones, through disavowal, was the social-revolutionary context of the Committee. Here one gains further understanding of why Jones could reduce a powerful, driving intellectual movement to a mere "circle" and why he found Freud's allusion to "the psychoanalytic movement" to be "not a very happy phrase" (1955, p. 67). Revolutionary fantasies are the precipitates of profound disappointments; one way to disown the disappointment is to disown the fantasy. Beneath both lies the unconscious struggle to mourn what has been lost and the equally unconscious struggle to reconstitute oneself along the lines of a new social formation.

In addition to providing him with the emotional support tantamount to a narcissistic transference, Trotter also provided Jones with practical guidance. He introduced Jones to Freud's writings in 1898. They read psychology together (James, Meyers, Prince, Janet), and Jones began to practice Freud's method in 1906. When Jones wavered at the last moment from committing himself wholeheartedly to psychoanalysis, Trotter urged him on. He met Jung in 1907 and Freud in 1908, the year he left London for Canada. These events augured well: "I was bound for a new world, charged with new ideas" (1959, p. 171). Contact with Freud and his ideas had stabilized his doubts and drift and channeled the energies which doubt and drift invariably released into a new and powerful sense of direction, a calling: "There might still be a future worth having" (p. 171). Psychoanalysis had finally brought things together for Jones, just as it had for Jung and Rank.

Let us summarize before moving on. It is abundantly clear from his autobiography, which is a kind of bildungsroman, that Jones understood his journey from his rural Welsh origins into the highly urban and differentiated world of neurology and psychoanalysis primarily in terms of cognitive and emotional factors. On the one hand, there was the intellectual search for ideas which would both comprehend and transform "unsatisfactory social arrangement." It began in the Cardiff years, was augmented by the disappointments inflicted on him by the medical profession, restated itself in the grandiose, social-revolutionary vision shared with Trotter, and was finally consolidated into psychoanalytic form. On the other hand, Jones emphasized the psychological. Under the guidance of Trotter ("our thoughts were working in much the same direction" [1959, p. 154]) he realized that "the secrets of the human soul were to be apprehended and understood only in connection with suffering: through being able to suffer

oneself and thus entering into contact with the suffering of others."
"The majority of mankind," they concluded, "flinch from being
deeply moved" (p. 154). Trotter divided mankind into two groups, the
sensitive and the insensitive, but Jones simply used the terms "psychologically minded and unpsychologically minded" (p. 154). One
recognizes in these observations, as well as many others, Jones's own
unique rendition of analytic access, acquired well before he came to
Freud.

But Jones's exclusive preoccupation with the inner world spared
him having to recognize the extent to which that very suffering was a
response to forces in the actual world. Those forces insisted that he
give up the consolations of belonging derived from his childhood and
adolescent experiences of religion. Jones's psychological self-understanding led him to disavow the social world. It could not occur to
him that the religious ideas and ideals which he gradually set aside
were in fact also potent social objects in his life world, symbolic
representations of complex and meaningful webs of social solidarity
which bound and structured his internal needs. By thinking only in
terms of structural psychology, Jones was able to ease, but only somewhat, the deeper psychological pain of "parting from" what he had
been "a part of" in an intimate sense.

These investigations into the social roots of Jones's life and
thought now bring into view their deepest components, a polarity
or tension between a powerful intellectualizing and rationalizing
trend and an equally strong capacity for introspection and depth-
psychological self-understanding. This tension captured in a seemingly contradictory way the answer he found to his central, lifelong
search for the right relations between the ego and the social order. In
the first we find Jones the psychoanalyst, the champion of "analytic
reason," of the metapsychological point of view, and that leads to his
positivism, his skepticism, his intolerance of illusion, and his reification of the unconscious. These in turn lead to what I now suggest was
his use of science as a defense against the perception of deeper psychological and sociological factors. In the second we see a man of
great psychological honesty and courage mourning for a wife and
then a daughter, probing in the midst of that despair the deepest
meanings of his life. In these moments he caught a glimpse of "the
psychological" and "the sociological" as they momentarily came
together for him in the human experience of mourning through
which, he thought, all men are united, however briefly.

Jones was so thoroughly disillusioned with his religious past that
he felt it absolutely necessary to adopt a stance which was com-

pletely contrary to its essential identity: skepticism and positivism. He clung to these with an intensity which could only have derived from an overriding unconscious persistence of the earlier commitment into the later one. This strategy accounts for what he said was his central intellectual trait, an all-encompassing "intolerance of illusion" (1959, p. 63). This severe thought meant to him that once one had brought a specific psychological conflict into the conscious arena of the ego, it simply had to stay there. He knew that some patients—and even some analysts—forget their hard-won insights, reremembering and reforgetting them from time to time. But he said that such forgetfulness was "so alien to my temperament that it has always needed an effort to comprehend it" (p. 63). And he cited Jung's retreat from psychoanalysis as the most extreme instance of it, although he certainly included Rank as well. But Jones's intolerance of illusion was supported by an agitated and uncomfortable state of mind consisting of the emotions of contempt and scorn, the by-products of an incomplete de-idealization. As I have already pointed out, Freud spoke of these sorts of psychological issues, especially the psychological status of illusion, in terms of infantile narcissism and the omnipotence of thought. He relegated them to the rudimentary and pre-oedipal ego's relation to reality. But in Freud's view such processes had been "surmounted" and overcome, and therefore they did not constitute an analyzable issue. Today such issues are often referred to as belonging to the sphere of the "primitive psyche," and infantile illusions, for example, are considered to be, when properly modified, a valuable developmental acquisition. For this reason I think that Jones's intolerance of illusion probably belonged to a period in his life in which the religious illusions of childhood were not only tolerated but even positively valued, probably by his mother and her acceptance of religious images, for example, when she read her very small son Bible stores. In adolescence they were massively disavowed, shaping in turn his adult view of the world and the mind.

Jones's intolerance of illusion was all of a piece with his highly reified view of the unconscious, which took the form of the metapsychology. He thought of the unconscious as a kind of "place-thing" which contained unconscious impulses. Or, to shift the metaphor, Jones thought of the metapsychology as a kind of psychological version of the atomic table: once a derivative of the unconscious had been demarcated and analyzed, it could no more be forgotten than could an element in the realm of matter "be forgotten" once that had been discovered. Jones's intolerance of illusion and his reification of the unconscious were all of a piece with a more general, powerful, and dominating intellectualizing trend. By intellectualization I refer to a mental action in which, as soon as an unconscious derivative makes its appearance in consciousness, mental effort is initiated which immediately and rapidly assigns a genetic or economic or dynamic significance to it, and one then holds fast to this meaning. Such effort has the deeper psychological consequence of warding off any further deepening or painful tensions, and for this reason it is closely related to the defense of isolation and the "blowing away" of unwelcome affects. The model for this process is the joyful éclat which accompanies the climax of a successful joke. At such moments the unconscious perception momentarily breaks into awareness and is recognized but is then immediately "blown away" or disavowed by the ensuing gust of laughter. In this way the realization that one accepts a specific illusion, in spite of its factual irrationality, can be blown away and kept away by a scientific frame of mind.

Jones's intellectualizing tendencies came to highly practical fruition in the way he tenaciously fixed his own and others' minds on what he liked to call the "tenets" of psychoanalysis (1955, p. 152; 1959, p. 162), such as repression, the existence of the unconscious, infantile sexuality, and so forth. When Jones proposed the Committee to Freud, he also suggested that its principal function consist in supervising loyalty to these several tenets. The dictionary defines a tenet as "a doctrine, dogma, principle or opinion, in religion, philosophy, politics, or the like, held by a school, sect, party or person" (*Shorter Oxford English Dictionary*, 3d ed., 1955).

It is but a short step from these considerations to the idea that a particular conception of science can itself became a defense against deeper layers of unconscious subjectivity, in this case largely narcissistic processes, by rationalizing them with excessive rapidity and then encasing them in mechanical models. Mechanicity is an essentially nonpsychological, even antipsychological, model. It splits facts from fantasy. For men of Jones's time and place, with their epoch-specific, incomplete transitions from a religious to a psychological orientation, this conception of science was unavoidable, and it continues to be of great historical interest—and, I would also add, of great psychological interest as well. Freud too shared this conception of science with Jones, and it set both of them apart from Jung and Rank. Indeed, Max Weber also took the very same view when he created such stark and forbidding juxtapositions as those between value free and value laden, rational and magical, bureaucratic and charismatic. This will come as no surprise if one recognizes, as I will point out in the next chapter, that Weber also underwent a transition from a religious to a scientific point of view and that this view was, in its principal sociological and psychological features, virtually identical with Freud's and Jones's. For all three men the ego had become so strong—or so rigid—that it foreclosed rapidly or split off the gratifications of their religiously informed and primitive infantile and virtually "prehistoric" contexts. In the adult intellectual constructions of these men the category of religion returned—after the fashion of "the return of the repressed"—in the form of the split-off, ego-alien "other" whose earlier gratifications were later forbidden. Having suffered a massive renunciation of these gratifications, which was forced upon them by social-structural changes and by an epoch-specific concept of science, these men were able to see new things. But they also paid a heavy price for their bold and defiant visions. These very visions forbade the seeing of other things.

This particular view of the relation between the ego and illusion, in which the ego simply cannot tolerate illusions of any sort, has undergone considerable development in contemporary psychoanalysis, where the problem of illusion has acquired increasing clinical importance. Workers like Kohut and Winnicott, and especially Marion Milner, think that successful treatment does not necessarily eventuate in the simple destruction of illusions. For them, the capacity to generate illusions, to comprehend them experientially, and to understand them psychologically contributes in an essential way to a wholesome adaptation to social and especially to cultural reality. They have thus added the culturally supported social world to the natural, timeless, abstracted, and synchronic world of the reality principle, understood as that which stands starkly over against the ego. Both discussions are essential. But these innovations must also be seen as advances—and, paradoxically, as scientific advances—rather than as retreats to a prepsychoanalytic religious residue, for they presuppose the views of men like Freud and Jones, of whom fate decreed that they break things down in order that others could later recompose them. In the following chapter I not only discuss in detail the relations between "classical" physical science and the metapsychology of Jones and Freud; I also trace the gradual dissolution of the latter in the current of discussion in interwar London, where object-relations theory was formulated for the first time.

Jones's intellectualizing and all that it implied must not, however, be construed to mean that his experiential grasp of analytic access was meager or twisted. On the contrary, alongside this trend in his mental life, there also existed a second one, his unusual capacity for introspection and empathy. In fact, Jones's intellectualizing trends were in constant tension throughout his life with more genuine or primary mode of self-exploration. This is nowhere better seen than in what were undoubtedly the two most painful events of his life, his struggle to mourn for his first wife, Morfydd, in 1918, and for his daughter, Gwyneth, born of his second marriage, who died at the age of eight in 1928. Because he thought of all his intellectual constructions as scientific and therefore devoid of emotion, Jones could not consciously mourn the deeper layers of his social past, although he did so unconsciously. But in his personal familial relations he did indeed possess "the ability to mourn" in the more easily recognizable sense.

In 1918, when the war was over and Jones was well established in the psychoanalytic movement, he found himself in a more optimistic mood and decided to marry. But his matchmaking friends continually came up with English candidates, and they were not interesting to him: "Marrying an Englishwomen . . . seemed so commonplace" (1959, p. 253). Then he met Morfydd Owen, a beautiful, young, and highly acclaimed Welsh musician, and proposed to her at their third meeting. As might be expected, he reflected analytically on this seemingly hasty decision: ". . . a deep affinity, based . . . on profound emotions emanating from early impressions of childhood . . . linking her with my young mother" (p. 253). And on his bride: while she was "singularly mature," she was still embedded in her Welsh culture, she was deeply attached to her father, and she was religious ("Her faith and devotion, so admirable when related to her country and her people, were also unfortunately attached to very simple-minded religious beliefs" [p. 254]).

Only eighteen months later, still enraptured with Morfydd, Jones took her to Wales to visit his father and his land of origin ("I was looking forward to taking her over my familiar Gowerland" [1959, p. 254]). Morfydd developed appendicitis. On the phone trotter advised Jones to use a local surgeon, who then botched the simple operation, and she died: "The grief I then had to endure was the most painful experience of my life. . . . The acuteness of the pain had the effect of bringing out all the gentleness and kindliness in my nature. I felt that with such possibilities of pain in the world it behooved everyone . . . to be as kind as they could be to their fellows. If only mankind could learn that lesson!" (p. 255). So Jones linked the universal experience of mourning, the loss of an important attachment, to the appearance of a cosmic ideal of tolerance for all mankind which mitigated and even dissolved hate and which can be understood as a new kind of attachment, membership in "the family of man." In this paradox of loss and gain, he momentarily and simply glimpsed what was in effect an answer to his lifelong search for a solution to the human hate which fueled "unsatisfactory social relations." Then, only moments later, this loss and these reflections opened up an old narcissistic wound, for they reactivated his earlier conflicts with religion. It was as if his old enemy, the Hound of Heaven, still prowled about in the woods of "my familiar Gowerland." So he bitterly concluded: "At least I was spared one agony, that of having to reconcile such a loss with belief in a benevolent Deity." The two were incompatible. As he explained: the believer accepts the loss (agrees to decathect the loved object) in order to submit to the deity's unfathomable but wise plan; the atheist, unsupported by a socially sanctioned internalized God imago, and thereby bereft of a key illusion, is forced to feel the loss more deeply, more poignantly, more shatteringly. In fact, Jones concluded, if human love is strong enough, it will entirely override the idea of a deity. He cited as a telling example Morfydd's father, who was a devout believer. In the same year, he lost his wife and all his remaining children. At the end, his faith had "broken under the strain." In such fashion did Jones seek to explain his misery to himself and relate it to the central experiences and thoughts of his life.

Eight years later, the second most painful event also stimulated thoughts about the psychology of mourning, but this time there was no religious referent. The event and Jones's thoughts about it are contained in several letters to Freud. In February 1928, Jones's eight-year-old daughter, Gwyneth, died of pneumonia. Over a period of ten days there had been seven doctors, drugs, and transfusions, but to no avail. "I cannot picture to you," he wrote, "the agonies of alternating fear, despair and painful hope we experienced but it left us little able to bear the final blow" (cited in Brome 1983, p. 163). Jones had expected some consolation from Freud, on the basis not only of their intimacy but also of the parallel between his own loss and Freud's loss of his daughter Sophie in 1920. But Freud had problems of his own. He could only coldly suggest that Jones write a paper on Shakespeare to distract himself. Several months later he wrote again, this time in a metapsychological vein, probing further the relationship of grief to the unconscious. He first dutifully rehearsed Freud's theory: "The Unconscious cannot conceive of another person's death except in terms of murder. . . . We know in this connection the guilt that often follows death" (cited in Brome 1983, p. 165). But the next thought was a nonsequitur. He understood Freud's theory even more clearly, he said, "because my attitude towards my daughter was a purer non-ambivalent love than in any of my other experiences" (cited in Brome 1983, p. 165). In "Mourning and Melancholia," Freud had emphasized unconscious ambivalence as the sine qua non for an analytic understanding of mourning.

I think that in these remarks Jones was probing a deeper layer of the unconscious mind, one populated by a congeries of internal objects and associated with the mother, who is experienced unconsciously as an object of attachment and not only as an object of instinctual gratification. It was as if Jones were thinking to himself: My experience of my daughter's death tells me that there must be something more to mourning than I currently know . . . but what could that be? Freud's drive-centered, asocial, and scientific metapsychology of mourning could not answer this question for Jones. But unconsciously he sensed that there was something more important still to be learned. Only two years before he had invited Melanie Klein to settle in London, only in part so that she could analyze his children. And later he was on friendly terms with D. W. Foulkes, who became the founding figure in the psychoanalysis of groups. Jones's contribution to psychoanalysis consisted not only of his key role as a defender of Freud, science, and "the movement"; he also provided a powerful stimulus to object-relations theory and group theory. This second contribution derived from his unique understanding of analytic access, which was, essentially, in his experience but not in his thought, very different from Freud's.

To sum up. These social notations on Jones's life and thought deepen our understanding of his approach to the movement, to Freud's person, and to his ideas, especially his conception of analysis as a science. In a conscious sense Jones came to Freud with his transition complete in all but one respect. In Freud's biologically grounded psychological theory of the unconscious Jones found the convincing theoretical-scientific fulfillment of his own earlier search for the roots of "mankind's unsatisfactory social arrangements," elaborated first in his Cardiff years and later in association with Trotter. Within psychoanalysis these took the form of a search for "the inherited elements of the mind" ("Scientific knowledge concerning heredity is of the utmost importance for the founding of any stable social organization" [1959, pp. 142–43]). In Freud's person and especially in his positivism, his devotion to science, his intolerance of illusion, and his skepticism, Jones found the "ideal" replica of his intimate and admired friend, Trotter, a man of sufficient substance (strong-enough self) to receive the full force of Jones's unconscious needs in this regard. And in Freud's movement Jones found the opportunity to give himself over to powerful social attachments which could to some extent replace his lost childhood world of belonging.

However, Jones also brought to psychoanalysis the incompleted portions of his transition, in particular his disavowal of the social realm. This disavowal made it possible for him to participate unconsciously in the construction and maintenance of a group illusion while at the same time consciously denying its reality. Consequently, Jones did not see in the psychoanalytic movement what others outside it have so easily noticed: its rigidity, its ideology, and so forth. In page after page of his autobiography and the *Life and Work of Sigmund Freud* Jones lamely tried to account for these features by repeating Freud's theory of resistance to psychoanalysis. This disavowal had its roots in Jones's intellectualizing trends, his characterologically grounded hypercathexis of the autonomous, individual ego, which necessarily depreciated any deep dependency upon "the other" as a social object and especially upon the social world as a powerful, experiential reality with unconscious dimensions.

To Jones's intellectualizing trends we owe the most outstanding characteristic of his treatment of Freud's thought. His summaries in the *Life and Work* are dry and dull, devoid of Freud's tolerance for ambiguity and his literary brilliance in conveying to the reader something of the quality of his own primary process and his audacious attempts to engage the primary process of the reader actively. Jones's summaries read like dated encyclopedia articles on the history of physics or astronomy. And it is worth repeating that Jones's account of the origins of psychoanalysis portray a Freud unmoved by social circumstance and devoid of powerful social attachments, especially religious ones. For that is the way Jones saw himself. But his study of Freud's life, in contrast to his treatment of the master's theories, is rich, animated, and complex. Here Jones was at his best. Indeed, even his own psychoanalytic papers are also tedious, devoid of emotion and painful to read. Freud the man was, to put it as simply as possible, the light of his life.

But is it really correct to say that Jones "read himself" into Freud's life and work? Might it not be more correct to put it the other way around: Jones read Freud back into Jones's "life and work"? There is certainly plenty of evidence for both of these views, as one reads in and out of the *Life and Work* and *Free Associations*. And Jones would certainly agree with both. It is best to break off by saying only that their respective social transitions, which were so different in so many obvious ways (religion, nation, class, parents' personalities), also shared a similar structure.

Both began with high hopes of many kinds; these were followed by disillusionment and disenchantment with the past, understood not only as a body of lofty and inspiring ideas and ideals but also a cohesive community of which they had been a part; there followed marginality (isolation, alienation, and anomie), drift, and neurosis; that in turn eventuated in a mandate to introspect, in the context of science and medicine; it yielded up access to the inner world, which was formulated in an experience-distant way; these discoveries and the need to share them authorized a coming together. Indeed, the same can be said of Jung and Rank, who underwent similar transitions, so different in many details but so alike with regard to the basic pattern. Propelled by powerful emotions and ideas which convinced them that the contours of the inner world, thrust upon them by sweeping social forces which they did not recognize as such, could in fact be charted, the first analysts came together and did their work. After briefly noting the dissipation of the movement, its role in Freud's turn to culture (the writing of the cultural texts), and the central themes of this body of work, I go on to draw into a more substantial sociological frame this ensemble of social and psychological vignettes.

The Dissipation of the Movement and Freud's Turn to the "Cunning of Culture"

I have pointed out some of the more significant ways in which Jung, Rank, and Jones found their ways to Freud and how, together with him, they formed the psychoanalytic movement. I have also noted the shared group illusion, the ideologizing of psychoanalytic ideas, and the attempt to construct a common analytic culture. This puts me in an advantageous position to view the conclusion or final disposition of the movement, what I call its dissipation or waning, which took place between the war years and Freud's death in 1939. As the movement gradually weakened over time, each weakening had the effect of stimulating Freud's search for hidden psychological meanings in the cultural contexts of his own life. The relation between the two was not, however, an arbitrary one. Rather, an internal connection between the first, or waning of the movement, and the second, or turn to culture, accounted for the shift. For this shift (waning of the movement → writing of the cultural texts) simply expressed, on a wider and more social scale, the more primary pattern of Freud's creativity, in which the circumstances of personal and social isolation drove him into himself and stimulated painful/joyful creative activity.

The years following the formation of the movement can be divided into three periods: the war years (1914–18), the postwar years (1918 to mid-1920's), and the final years (mid-1920s to 1939). Thus, during the war, publications and communications among members of the movement were virtually suspended. This isolated Freud further and he produced—paradoxically—the well-known metapyschological papers but also what I will call the little-known but highly significant "protocultural texts." After the war publications and communications were restored, but toward the end of the postwar period the Committee was dissolved, and Freud's illness and many tragic personal losses isolated him further. I include as further instances of Freud's personal situation not only his declining health after 1923 but also, before that, the progressive unleashing of his speculative tendencies from 1918 onward. As he came to realize that he had completed a significant body of clinical and theoretical work, and stimulated by the personalization of death which aging invariably brings to all, Freud abandoned his scientific rigor and turned to the contribution he thought he could make to the universal problems of mankind, producing the better-known cultural texts. Then, in the final years, his social world disintegrated completely under the impact of the political and religious persecution of the Jews and psychoanalysis. At this time and under these circumstances, he created what I believe to be one of the most important and least understood of his works, *Moses and Monotheism.* This book fused his own personal essence or soul with the principal world-historical idea in Western culture, the idea of God. Mediating between the two was the figure of Moses.

All the external evidence suggests that Freud accomplished these feats alone. But let us recall Masud Khan's view of the self-analysis, that through and in it Freud constructed his "epistemology of self-experience," the view that psychological discovery always takes place in the context of "another." The creativity of the interwar years was stimulated by Freud's relation to Jung; Rolland played an important part in the writing of *Civilization and Its Discontents*; and Freud's "internal dispute" with the image of Moses, which was highly personalized (it was a special kind of object relation), drove him to write the great essay of monotheism, which articulated a psychoanalytic theory of Western history. That essay has to be seen as another "blow" to the narcissism of Western man, in which Freud boldly took himself as the prototype of Western man upon whom there was forced yet another renunciation.

In addition to the central theme of isolation, both personal and social, there was also what should be called simply "the fortunes of psychoanalysis," a social-structural issue beyond Freud's personal control. Not until the end of he war did it become evident that Freud would be famous and that is creation or "child," psychoanalysis, would not perish. As the European and American public at large started to embrace psychoanalytic ideas and practice, the institutionalization of psychoanalysis began. This had the effect of diminishing the need for the movement, and for this reason as well it dissolved or withered away. But these events played back, so to speak, on Freud's isolation. As he became increasingly famous, he had to face an entirely new reality—an anonymous public—and that in turn forced him into a new kind of isolation. Furthermore, he was never admired in Vienna as he was in the countries to the west of it, and as the final years approached, the cold Viennese world could not but heighten in a fresh and different way his anxieties about the future of his work, despite the evidence of fame.

As for the texts themselves, there are for the most part two conflicting views of their significance. On one hand, these books are taken (chiefly by analysts) as foundational studies for a psychoanalytic science of society. They are thought to be "detached," "objective," and "scientific" treatises on the unconscious psychological dynamics of culture, in exactly the same sense in which the metapsychology is thought to be a scientific theory of the way the mind works. On the other hand, Freud's books about culture are also sometimes taken (chiefly by critics of analysis) as bad sociology and bad anthropology, riddled with historical errors predicated upon a fatal individualistic bias. In this sense they are seen as the subjective preoccupations of a man who simply universalized the particularities of his personal and clinical insights into a project which would, like Rank's, "explain everything."

In what follows I place Freud's cultural texts in relation to the social processes which characterized his self-analysis and the formation of the movement. In doing so, I argue that these books were still further expressions of Freud's lifelong attempt to explore his inner world and, this time, to relate its contents in a much more explicit way to the realms of social circumstance from which his psychological explorations had necessarily separated him. Earlier in life he had retreated massively from these realms in order to make his discoveries; later in life, older, accomplished, with new increments of psychological structure, and less isolated, he turned back to these realms, where his isolation took fresh and different forms. In this sense the cultural texts were expressions of Freud's search for a rapprochement with the social world, an attempt to overcome the curse of isolation which had previously so overcome him. They were further attempts on his part to build psychological structure and facilitate his individuation by thinking and working through in a very personal way the complex relations and contradictions between himself and his social world and, on a theoretical plane, between the individual and the social order. Freud's explorations of the inner world had separated him irrevocably from his sense of belonging to his common culture, heightening his alienation from it. That having happened, he sought to recapture what had been lost historically in the intermediate, mediating, or transitional realms of cultural symbols. As we know, Freud believed that his social world had punished him severely, and I have attempted to capture this conviction by characterizing his view of culture as the "cunning of culture." This phrase refers to the ways in which Freud felt forced to conclude that the culture which surrounded him opposed knowledge of the inner world, which he had produced, while at the same time pretending to support such knowledge.

It follows from this that the central theme of the cultural texts is not "totemism," or "monotheism," or "civilization," or "religion." It is not "the universality of the oedipus complex." Rather, it is "the past," and the problems which are always associated with an understanding of the past, especially the ideas of time, history, and mutability. Freud believed that his analytic work had separated the observing ego from its roots in the historical past, in the form of a total break from that past in the service of discovering the developmental past, the "past within." From that break or separation, that fearful sense of total diachrony, follows the injunction to the ego to mourn the cherished lost objects of the historical past, to de-idealize what is "on the outside" (in the common culture) in order to build up structure "on the inside". But a break with the past was only the first of what was essentially a double strategy. The psychoanalytic theory of culture which Freud gradually created in this period also called for a recovery or retrieval of those common symbols which radical psychologization had virtually ablated. In part 3 I refer to this tension between "the pull of the past" and the "drive to the future" as the central contradiction in Freud's theory of culture. Here, however, I am more interested in demonstrating its presence in the texts themselves and in explaining why Freud simply had to formulate his theory of history and culture in this way.

Most of the time, however, Freud did not engage the monumental issue of the past directly but instead addressed it in the form of a series of subthemes, such as death, loss, social and group solidarity, racial hatred, intolerance and anti-Semitism, and even arrogance and righteousness. The master theme of the cultural texts, the loss of the past which psychoanalysis produces, runs beneath these and feeds them like an underground stream. Indeed, as Freud gradually discovered, each increment of psychologization produces an even sharper and precipitous sense of time and of the frightful temporalization of life. This theme surfaced progressively and only gradually as the texts appeared, but it erupted at the end of his life with great force in *Moses and Monotheism.* Throughout that work Freud mourned for *his own* past, in the form of the image of Moses, which also represented the past of Western men and Western culture. But in its closing portion, he realized that the idea of a total break was an illusion. As he came to realize how central was the idea of a lost past, he rose to meet it face-to-face in the final work of his life as he had never quite done before. To trace this progression, let us begin with the effects of the war upon Freud and his movement and with his increasingly strong efforts to insert his psychoanalytic ideas into the world of culture.

Jones stated—mistakenly, it should by now be clear—that Freud took no special interest in political events before 1914. But Jones was also still able to observe that the First World War affected Freud profoundly. He portrayed Freud during these years as moving progressively from an initial period of political idealization and optimistic patriotism to scorn for political leaders and events, and from there to skepticism and mournful disappointment about politics as a whole (Jones 1955, pp. 170–72). At the beginning of the war Freud could say, "All my libido is given to Austro-Hungary" (p. 171). As the war progressed, Freud's family was disrupted, members of the Committee could not visit him or even communicate with each other, and publishing projects came to a standstill. Freud began to experience the war subjectively as a loss of important objects: "What Adler and Jung have left of the movement is being ruined by the strife of nations" (p. 179). He had to renounce his travels to the south, an important source of pleasure and of stimulation for the creation of new thoughts. By 1918 he advised Ferenczi not to trust Hungarian politics: "Disappointment will surely come. . . . So withdraw your libido in good time from your Fatherland and put it at the disposal of psycho-analysis, else you are bound to feel miserable" (p. 200).

The war virtually re-created in a fresh and even more forceful way the earlier isolation of the self-analysis by driving Freud once again inward, into his inner world. But this time he also turned his thoughts outward, toward the surrounding culture. By constructing his theory of culture, Freud was able to articulate his own experiences of his own social world in a language and framework which were not only profoundly meaningful to him in an intimate and personal sense, but which were also at the same time increasingly acceptable in a public sense. As such it facilitated further his separation from his cultural context and his further efforts in self-structuration and individuation.

Jones clearly thought so. The war, he said, "greatly stimulated" Freud's "working powers," producing a "tremendous outburst of productivity," the "final summing up of his life's work"—the famous metaphyschological papers of 1915 (ten essays in twelve weeks [1955, p. 186]). But 1915 was a far richer year than Jones was willing to admit. In 1915 Freud also wrote, in addition to "Mourning and Melancholia," "On Transience," "Thoughts for the Times on War and Death," "The Disillusionment of War," and, only a year later he transposed the 1914 theory of narcissism into the theory of the three blows to Western man ("A Difficulty in the Path of Psychoanalysis"). I call this second group of papers the "protocultural texts" because they body forth the central problems and ideas of the better-known cultural texts which occupied Freud for the remainder of his life.

"On Transience" (1916), for example, contained many of these ideas. Written one year into the war, it opened by reporting a conversation Freud had just before the war, on a summer walk (through "a smiling countryside") with two friends. His friends could not enjoy the beautiful landscape because, they said, time would only destroy it. Freud countered by saying that the transience of "what is beautiful and perfect" and "all this loveliness of Nature and Art" need not spoil one's appreciation of it, and so he questioned his friends' motives ("some powerful emotional factor was at work which was disturbing their judgment . . . a revolt in their minds against mourning"). He reflected, "To psychologists mourning is a great riddle," but he then went on to offer his own theory of mourning which he had developed in "Mourning and Melancholia" several months before. He acknowledged that why "this detachment of libido from its objects should be such a painful process is a mystery to us." He then returned to the present: the war had indeed "robbed the world of its beauties" and its "works of art," and it also "shattered our pride in the achievements of our civilization" and "our hopes of a final triumph over the differences between nations and races." But he did not believe that this loss of cherished cultural objects called for a permanent renunciation. He concluded on an optimistic note. However painful mourning is, it "comes to a spontaneous end. . . . Our libido is once more free . . . we shall build up again." The second and third essays were published as a single piece, and they played out further the theme of disappointment and the sense of loss incurred by the war. I have already discussed the essay on mourning and the centrality of disillusionment for the theory of the three blows. These five pieces are really only extensions of what was in fact the first cultural text, "The Moses of Michelangelo." All six could easily be grouped together under the single title, "the ability to mourn" the loss of cultural objects ("all this loveliness of Nature and Art"), and, through that process, the capacity to find again these esteemed objects "on the other side" of the loss.

The protocultural texts and the metapsychological papers were written under complex circumstances in which Freud's isolation from the social world as a whole and from the movement in particular was central. After the war, these circumstances underwent considerable modification. On the positive side, the curse of isolation lifted, at least for a while, and the movement regained momentum. Psychoanalysis expanded through publications, translations, and the forming of international societies. London replaced Vienna as the new center of psychoanalytic thought and activity. Freud had achieved fame and finally allowed himself to believe that his analytical child would indeed flourish. Furthermore, by the end of the war (he was sixty-two in 1918) Freud thought that he had achieved all that he could scientifically and felt that he no longer needed to suppress the speculative tendencies of his youth, what he called "my fantastic self" (Jones 1955, p. 431). He allowed himself to return to the pleasures of history, philosophy, culture—and, above all, religion—which he had until then rigorously denied himself. These trends culminated in further cultural investigations, chiefly "The Uncanny," *Group Psychology and the Analysis of the Ego*, and *Beyond the Pleasure Principle*. Together these stand as enigmatic intermediaries between the protocultural texts and what are generally referred to as the cultural texts themselves. On the negative side, the curse of isolation soon descended again in the form of more death and mourning: Freud's friend Von Freund; his colleague Abraham; his daughter Sophie; his grandson Heinz; and his own carcinoma.

But the major event of this period was the dissolution of the movement, which was inversely related to the institutionalization of psychoanalysis. That in turn had the paradoxical effect of again isolating Freud and, again, stimulating his creativity. It did so by providing him with a new "envelope" or "container," a new object which would mirror his creativity. The culture at large replaced the supportive function of the movement. This process was triggered in part by Rank's departure in 1924–25. The Committee was dissolved in 1927, and with that the movement, understood as a highly personal group, disbanded. In order to understand how this took place, it is necessary to take up again Jones's theory of psychoanalysis and of the movement and especially his psychology of science, already discussed above, for that psychology linked together his conception of analysis and his conception of the movement as an instrument of the cultural acceptance of analysis.

Rank's departure stimulated Jones to consolidate his understanding of these issues. Jones was convinced that the capacity for psychological self-understanding presupposed "believing in" or "adhering to" a specific set of ideas and that this activity was inconceivable apart from belonging to the movement. As he prepared to pathologize Rank's departure, Jones took it upon himself to state the point: "Adherence to what psychoanalysis revealed signifies the same as retaining one's insight into the workings of the unconscious," and he thought both took place within "the great common bond of devotion to a cause, the pursuit of psychoanalytic knowledge" (1957, p. 45). To think that analytic ideas might simply exist in his current sociocognitive milieu independent of the minds that thought them, as did Darwin's theory of evolution or Newton's theory of gravity, was for Jones an unthinkable thought. But Jones did not "adhere" to Darwin's theory, nor was Darwin captive to any "great common bond." The psychoanalytic ideas of the first analysts were so new, so marginal, and so critical of conventional wisdom that their authors could not trust in their independent existence apart from some sort of group support. But, as analytic ideas became more acceptable generally to the society at large, "adherence"—and also the group—became less necessary.

How this came about can be understood in a descriptive as well as in a sweeping social sense. On the descriptive level it is correct to note that Freud's ideas about the inner world became at this time more and more available to the culture at large. As this took place, the principal purpose of the movement, which was to guard and preserve analytic access in the face of a hostile, antipsychological culture, became redundant and the movement "withered away." Culture itself became the container for analytic ideas, and the movement's containing function was no longer necessary. The institutionalization and bureaucratization of psychoanalysis had begun. I have already noted, in a more sweeping sense, how advancing industrialization and greater social-structural differentiation split up many persons' historic, organic social attachments and forced upon them more autonomous and independent modes of thought and experience. As people became more anomic, liberal, and middle class, their unconscious processes also became more accessible to introspection and reflection. Freud's ideas explained to them what was happening to them. The links between neurosis, an accepting attitude toward psychological modes of thought, and middle-class status are a crucial part of this picture. Gregorio Kohon, a psychoanalyst who belongs to what is now called the British independent group, has observed (1986, p. 48) that those persons among the public at large who have been generally most supportive of psychoanalysis have always been middle-class, educated persons "with some degree of psychological disturbance." These were some of the many social processes which permitted analytic access gradually to become a shared sociological reality, at least among the middle class. As a general rule, upper-class and lower-class persons do not think of themselves as suffering from intrapsychic conflict and do not seek psychotherapeutic assistance.

Jones characterized the time in which Freud wrote *Beyond the Pleasure Principle* and *Group Psychology and the Analysis of the Ego* as the last of his three most creative periods (1918–19): a "truly astonishing fresh outburst of original ideas" occurred, "the bold imaginative visions of the final period" (1957, pp. ii–xii). These two essays were written concurrently at the beginning of the second period, and they anticipate the final one. The underground stream which joins them to the protocultural papers is the fabulous essay "The Uncanny." Its ostensible theme was the shifting psychological experience of the strange and the familiar in the aesthetic experience of artistic objects as these are encountered first "within," in the hidden unconscious recesses of the self, and then "in the other," in social objects which have hidden or unconscious significance. Freud pointed out that these experiences created alternating impressions of first novelty and then repetition. In doing so he probed, in a very preliminary way, the question of whether art, understood as the greatest of mankind's cultural acquisitions, could produce and convey to the developmental ego a genuine sense of fresh historical advance or whether it only appeared to do so, such that art only "really" repeated events and states which had occurred previously.

This preoccupation with the vicissitudes of the familiar and the strange as social experiences was taken up more directly in the two major books of the period, especially the second, and for this reason the two should be taken together. Both restated the central theme of the ego's struggle with the past, although in the seemingly non-historical terms of the tension between the ego and the social other. *Beyond the Pleasure Principle* centered entirely upon the psychological and biological drives of the individual, especially the death instinct, which Freud associated with the individual ego and the tendency of the organism to repeat all earlier experience, so that novelty was in fact an illusion. In contrast, the book on groups centered entirely on the more encompassing life instincts, understood as the source of novelty, and "the great group formations" of mankind. It was as social a book as the other was individual. But in these two books Freud fell into a contradiction of his own making. At first he associated novelty, life, and advance with sociality and community, and repetition and death with the individual. But as he probed this idea, it could also be said that sociality was, in a deeper sense, repetitive and timeless, and only the individual could achieve advance, through deeper psychological self-understanding. In his own life experiences Freud had discovered novelty, life, and advance almost entirely within himself, whereas his social world had offered him only disappointment, decay, repetition, and death. Central to both texts was the thorny and touchy problem of narcissism.

So, in *Beyond the Pleasure Principle* Freud drove his basic inquiry "down and into," so to speak, the individual organism, exploring various forms of repetition and novelty and the key question, How can history happen if the organism is driven entirely by repetition? The leading idea of the book was his new conviction that there was a sector of mental life which was "more primitive and independent" of the pleasure principle, a sector which was "beyond" the pleasure principle. Earlier he had thought of the pleasure principle and the sexual instincts together as the source of novelty, freshness, and therefore of advance and also of attachment (object love), and he had juxtaposed these to the self-preservative or ego instincts. But in the new book he grouped both sexual and self-preservative instincts under the category of Eros, or the life instincts, and decided that these were in the service of death, hate, the individual ego, and repetition. Thus "life," or Eros, "the other," and community were simply activities in which the organism attempted to die in its own way. In all this Freud could not conceive of a form of attachment which was not erotic, nor could he conceive of a form of attachment which could enhance individuality or individuation while at the same time enhancing sociality. Everything was either all individual or all social. In thought as in life, Freud preferred irony and tragedy to paradox. I think that the project or search for something "more primitive and independent" of the pleasure principle was in fact a search for a theory of narcissism, of what contemporary psychoanalytic thought refers to as "the primitive psyche." In this view the ascendant death instinct can be understood as a failure in the transformation of narcissism, and the aggression of the death instinct as the rageful rejection of the social other who inflicts an injury on one's narcissism.

Many of the same ambiguities haunt *Group Psychology and the Analysis of the Ego*. Like its companion piece, this book is also about attachment, the ego's attachment to such "great group formations" as the Catholic church and the army, the historical embodiments of religion and politics, the church and the state. In his book Freud forced the question of continuity over time "up and out," so to speak, dwelling entirely on the sphere of the social rather than the biological, which was "down and in." In order to become a member of a group, the ego evolves sublimated "libidinal (erotic) ties," first with the leader who replaces its ego-ideal, and then with other persons, through an identification with their egos. The price of membership in a group is the surrender of individuality and the potential to individuate. Furthermore, groups only appeared to offer novelty and advance; at bottom the church and the army are timeless, ahistorical structures which are actively hostile to change. Nor did Freud recognize that his preoccupation with the idea of the death instinct actually appeared in his book on groups. It does when one realizes that the army protects the ego from physical death, while the church protects it from spiritual death by annexing the ego to it and through this action offers the ego the promise of immortality. In the book on groups Freud spoke more openly than in any other of narcissism: in forming ties with others the individual "overcomes" his narcissism and becomes a member of the human community.

In what I have called the final period, it became apparent that the public at large was prepared to accept psychoanalysis permanently. Freud became truly world famous. His creation, psychoanalysis, not only would not die; it would prosper indefinitely. But at the same time he himself had become increasingly ill and old, and the earlier social isolation descended with renewed strength in the form of National Socialism and the Catholic church's opposition to psychoanalysis. Both were openly anti-Semitic. Freud retreated into his women, his fame, his illness—and into the writing of the remaining cultural texts. Jones noted that "Anna slept in the adjoining room and acted as a nurse for half the day, his wife and sister-in-law taking turns for the other half" (1957, p. 120). Jones's further and very astute observation of the relationship between Anna and her father captures the depth of

Freud's retreat and in doing so characterizes the emotional qualities of his personal situation, which only intensified as time went
on: "There had grown up in those years a quite peculiarly intimate
relationship between father and daughter. Both were very averse
to anything at all resembling sentimentality and were equally un-
demonstrative in matters of affection. It was a deep silent understanding and sympathy that reigned between them. The mutual
understanding must have been something extraordinary, a silent
communication almost telepathic in quality where the deepest
thoughts and feelings could be conveyed by a faint gesture" (p. 224).
From this point onward, Freud's social world consisted of family and
a few family-like friends, who gave him the strength to meet an
anonymous public. Under these circumstances he continued to reflect on the sweeping historical significance of the culture which
had produced him in order to construct a psychological response to
its oppressions. Increasingly, he turned explicitly to religion and to
its psychological infrastructure. To achieve the inner freedom and
the tolerance—both personal and social—which such freedom conferred, it was necessary, he came to learn, to mourn the past, which
was inscribed in religious ideas.

In its better-known sense, *The Future of an Illusion* (1927) argues
that religious ideas are illusions, a kind of epistemological mistake.
But in a deeper and more submerged sense the book evolved in a
psychological theory of contemporary Western culture, and at the
center of that theory lay the psychology of narcissism and the problem of disillusionment—and not the oedipal theory of *Totem and
Taboo*. For this reason *The Future of an Illusion* should be seen
as a direct continuation of the theory of the three blows to Western
man. As such it makes more explicit the Freudian theory of culture
as a process of mourning in the service of achieving deeper self-
understanding and tolerance, both of oneself and of others, for intolerance of others is only a displacement of one's inability to tolerate
the unconscious conflicts within oneself. Unfortunately, critics of
Freud's thought, especially those who come to it with some sort of
religiously inspired ideal, have centered exclusively upon discredit-
ing the epistemological portions of the essay and have ignored its
concerns with the restoration of community, tolerance, and historical advance.

Although it was a simple one, the leading idea of the treatise was
very powerful. People turned to religious ideas, Freud said, with the
hope of finding in them solace and support for the intense feelings of
helplessness and aloneness which nature and society provoke in per-

sons everywhere. But these promises were, he then pointed out, really illusions, for they offered little actual support. In the face of this Freud nevertheless remained optimistic as he held out to modern Western man the unwelcome but also liberating task of disillusionment as a path to self-knowledge, the only psychologically real and therefore the only true form of consolation. Such thoughts restated, of course, the central theme of Freud's metapsychological epistemology, his intolerance of illusion, which he shared with Jones.

On the surface Freud intellectualized both the problem and its solution. He conceived of religious ideas in an entirely cognitive fashion: as intellectual constructs devoid of any social base. And he offered resignation and renunciation as psychological, but actually also highly cognitive, activities. Through some sort of heroic act of reason, the powerful appeal of religious ideas could be renounced. Beneath this surface argument, however, Freud also addressed the fundamental problem of human community and its enemy, narcissism. The purpose of the renunciation of religious ideals, Freud said, was to oppose "anti-social and anti-cultural tendencies" (p. 7) and "to make communal life possible" (p. 6). The privations of history (fate) and nature produced "a severe injury to his [the individual's] natural narcissism . . . man's self-regard, seriously menaced, calls for consolation" (p. 16). Helplessness, the central issue in the book, owed its origin to "narcissistic needs," for it engaged the mental-developmental sphere of the anaclitic type of object-choice in which the libido attaches itself to the mother (pp. 23–24). Out of this sphere sprang the illusions of religion, the chief one of which was the idea of God and immortality, and for that matter the illusion that one belongs to God's Chosen People," a reference to his own Jewish sense of community (p. 19). Thanks to such illusions, Freud continued, we can "feel at home in the uncanny" (p. 17), for these illusions are "indispensible for man's communal existence" (p. 43).

So, the root of the problem which *The Future of an Illusion* addressed was really a disordered sense of community fractured by man's narcissistic propensities. Religious ideas were "wrong" because they forestalled psychological reflection on this brokenness. But so did Freud's heroic "meta"-psychological reflections. His solution, resignation and renunciation, was a kind of morally toned inner struggle with narcissism, a psychoanalytic version of the religious idea of the bondage of the will. Missing from his constructions, but implicit in all of them, are the psychological processes of de-idealization and mourning. The idealization of religion—its illusions—can undergo, in the face of depth-psychological knowledge, a de-idealization, a "dis-illusionment," and this is the process which Freud in effect called for. Only through this process could the injured ego bring about a rapprochement with society and culture on the basis of tolerance of the inner world, and through that, tolerate the existence of the social other. As an example of an illusion Freud offered "the assertion made by certain nationalities that the Indo-Germanic race is the only one capable of civilization" (pp. 30–31). In such fashion did Freud attempt, yet again, to insert the theory of the three blows into Western culture. He invited his imaginary interlocutor to mourn in order to acquire inner peace—just as he himself was doing. And he knew, of course, how unwelcome such an invitation would be.

Civilization and Its Discontents, written three years later (1930), continued this line of thought but returned to the more structural model of psychological conflict, and, unlike the 1927 piece, its tone was distinctly pessimistic. By this time the political situation had become clearer. Jones said that "the exodus" of analysts to America had begun in earnest in 1931. In this book Freud restated his conviction that a foundational opposition existed between nature or biology (the death instinct and its derivative, aggressiveness) and spirit or culture (the Christian moral idea of love of neighbor, the so-called love commandment), and he prepared a place for psychology as a possible solution to this opposition. He proposed that culture, in the form of Christian ethics, had transformed the aggressive, hate-laden wishes and instincts of men into a symbolic, umbrella-like system of shared unconscious guilt or self-hatred which it had then turned back onto and into the minds of its members. The solution could only be a deeper, more psychological bringing into awareness of the unconscious mechanisms of culture and of their historical prototype, religious experiences, values, and doctrines. As in his other books Freud in effect searched for, but did not find, a psychological theory of structure building or individuation through which persons could reconcile the conflicts of their inner worlds in relation to the principal institutions of modernity, the advancing state and the retreating church, without succumbing to them.

Although this task was always highly personal for Freud, it became even more personalized in the last five years of his life. It was no longer enough to address the predicament of "men" in general or even the men of 1930s European society. With an intensified sense of urgency Freud began to think of *himself* in relation to *his* civilization and culture and *his* discontents. As the political and religious situations went completely out of control, they once again heightened his sense of personal isolation, drove him inward (he was accustomed to that), and reactivated the lifelong tension between his modern, scientific and psychoanalytic self-concept and his childhood and adolescent identity as a Jew embedded in a sense of belonging and heritage. He turned from the problems of groups, institutions, illusions, and cultural oppression in order to give even more emphasis to the group hatred, persecution, and intolerance of his times toward his people and himself. The experience of being hated and persecuted by his surrounding social world probably revived childhood memories of reading the Bible stories and his adult encounter with Michelangelo's Moses. At those times he had sought to individuate from his Jewish past; now, the task was "return" and rapprochement. So he plunged back into the farthest reaches of Western religious tradition to the idea of monotheism, the archetypal "idea" of Jewish faith. This was no abstract search for a psychology of the self—it was a search for *his* self, or "himself"—in time and memory, in history and culture. To carry out this search he reexamined the myth he had once shared with his father, father figures, and forefathers, and at the same time attempted to demythologize that myth once and for all. The attempt was only partially successful.

According to Jones, *Moses and Monotheism* was conceived and for the most part written in 1934, but its ideas "were to engross him for the rest of his life" (1957, p. 192). The first two parts came easily, but the third part was not published until August 1938 (Freud died in September 1939). The ideas were so personal that Freud said to Arnold Zweig of its inspiration, "Now knowing what to do with my leisure time I have been writing something, and against my original intention it so took hold of me that everything else was put aside" (p. 193). Freud felt deeply estranged from the surrounding official Viennese Catholic culture, and this was plainly why the subject "so took hold of" him. As he went on to explain to his friend: "In view of the recent ordinances one asks oneself again how Jews have become what they are, and why they have drawn on to themselves such undying hatred" (p. 193). The essay, Freud said, "brings something new and fundamental for strangers. . . . It is the thought of these strangers that makes me keep the finished essay secret. For we live in an atmosphere of strict Catholic beliefs" (p. 193). The Catholic church was indeed the principal source of his sense of oppression. Only two years later he wrote to Marie Bonaparte: "Our Minister of Education has issued a formal announcement that the days of any scientific work without presuppositions, as in the Liberal era, are over; from now on science must work in unison with the Christian-German *Weltanschauung*" (p. 210).

Freud delayed completion of the essay for several years, partly because of these very realistic fears of persecution and partly because he felt he lacked sufficient historical knowledge to make his case successfully. He called these outer difficulties. But there were inner difficulties as well. As late as April 1938, still in Vienna, he confessed to Jones: "My Moses . . . torments me like a 'ghost not laid.' I wonder if I shall ever complete this third part" (p. 225). Freud finally tore himself away from Vienna in June 1938, when he immigrated to England. Jones said the change "cheered him enormously, and he had moments of great happiness (p. 229). And three weeks later he could tell Arnold Zweig that his mind and inhibitions had completely changed: "I am at present enjoying writing the third part of the Moses" (p. 234). In England the ideas came freely and without anxiety. One of Freud's "greatest wishes" was to die a naturalized British subject (p. 235).

The *Moses* was so hard to write in Vienna and so easy to write in London for two reasons. First, the book was about the psychology of the very political and religious forces in Vienna which sought to destroy him, in an annihilatory fury of persecutory hatred, by destroying the historical essence of the community to which he belonged (the outer difficulty). But the second reason (the inner difficulty) was even more important. Freud's strategy in his book consisted in a kind of ruthless, psychologically grounded truth telling. First, the third part lifted out for all to see the "national pride" of the Jews and gave it a psychological name: shared narcissism. But Freud went even further. He added to this a psychologization of the epitome of Jewish national pride, the figure of Moses. So it was as if Freud were saying to his readers, Jew and gentile alike: "See, through psychoanalysis we Jews can give up our national pride, our shared narcissism, which gives us a sense of separateness, so why can not you other, you 'strangers'—also through psychoanalysis—give up your pride and its religious embodiments, which give you your sense of separateness? In such fashion we both might cease to hate one another and become more tolerant of each other." And so the very act of writing the *Moses* in and of itself virtually deprived Freud of the last remaining form of social support, his sense of belonging, his Jewish sense of community. It reopened his lifelong ambivalence, whether to be a part of, or to part from, his original community of attachment and belonging. The word "transition" describes well the position, both social and psychological, in which Freud found himself.

This ambivalence helps us to understand one of the most elusive facets of Freud's last years, his steadfast refusal to leave Vienna, in spite of the disastrous situation and imploring friends. Jones said that "something deep in his nature had always striven against" the idea of leaving. If it is true that Freud's cultural works were not only "objective" analyses of historical processes but also highly "subjective" responses to these processes, then one work in particular—the most speculative and enigmatic of all to come from his pen—captures and codifies more powerfully than any other his sense of isolation during his last years, *Beyond the Pleasure Principle*. In it Freud concocted, as I have noted, a truly grisly model of the ego's relation to the social realm: the life instincts, located psychologically in the id, draw men into community, whereas the death instincts, located psychologically in the ego, block all efforts in the direction of attachment. And Thanatos is "more primitive and independent" from Eros, so that isolation is more primary than community. We know from Jones that some sort of hideous inertia had seized Freud. As the Nazis descended, he became paralyzed, whereas others around him became mobilized. Perhaps considerations of fright and trauma, which Freud thought of as markers of the compulsion to repeat, also contributed. I have called this paralysis, metaphorically, the curse of isolation, but it could just as easily be given a metapsychological name, the death instinct.

In the end, however, friends (or, to use Freud's word, Eros) prevailed, and with their help he was able to mobilize himself and make the journey to London. He finished the *Moses* in July, and it was published in Holland in the fall. The English translation, by Katherine Jones, came out in March 1939. In the third part Freud inflicted a painful disillusionment upon his fellow Jews and himself and he relentlessly psychologized Jewish national pride and the figure of Moses. But as the argument drew to a close, a strong and unexpected sense of optimistic rapprochement appeared. There we are told that the advance in intellectuality or spirituality and the capacity to sublimate, the cardinal virtues of psychoanalysis, were closely associated with, and supported by, monotheism, the belief in one God. Did this mean that Freud could be a Jew, after all, even though he had also become the first psychoanalyst? One would think so.

Whatever the answer is, the writing of this book clearly served a transitional purpose for its author, for it supported him in the inner world of the self as he journeyed, in the outer world, to a foreign land full of strangers. Might we not also suppose that it supported him in a similar way through the last of life's many transitions? We will never know, but it is clear that Freud thought as much. As he wrote to an old friend, Hans Sachs, one of the original members of the Committee, only months before the end, "The Moses is not an unworthy leavetaking" (p. 242).

9 Final Sociological Reflections: Psychoanalysis, Science, and Society

Charting the vicissitudes of the psychoanalytic movement has shed much light on Freud and his group as they struggled to establish some sort of social space for their work together. It has also had the effect of disclosing the crucial role of science, and in particular of the metapsychology, which is the principal subject of this chapter, in that struggle. The metapsychology came to symbolize the scientific purity of psychoanalysis. To some extent this strategy worked, insofar as the first analysts sought to formulate their clinical observations and clinical theory making by means of it. But they also used the idea of science and the metapsychology to legitimate their attempts to make psychoanalysis acceptable to the culture at large and to implement the evolving psychoanalytic theory of culture. Moreover, they were deeply fearful that analysis would be perceived by others outside the movement, whether they were physicians or intellectuals, "as a religion." This fear forced further insistence upon the scientific status of analysis. Gradually, the validity and legitimacy of psychoanalysis came to be seen as a polarity, really a war, between science, analysis, and the metapsychology, on the one hand, and religion and religious ideas, on the other. Matters were not helped by the fact that, as the movement continued to advance, it actually did take on religiopolitical and scientistic features. This debate or war continues to vex contemporary analytic thought, where analytic thinkers either imitate new developments in physical science or else simply abandon the idea of science entirely and turn to the humanities and one of its key concepts, hermeneutics, which takes its inspiration from traditional, religiously inspired ideas of interpretation and "divining" the meaning of texts.

In some of the preceding discussions I have attempted to break down this tiresome and simplistic polarity by inserting the category of the social in between the psychological and the epistemological. Like the physicalistic investigators upon whose methods Freud modeled his observations, the first analysts also found themselves exploring biologically grounded emotions. But unlike them, the first analysts also had to explore the motives, meanings, subjective states, and intentions of persons within the milieu of their social world, a world which was bordered by attachments to a common culture. The rightful occupants of this border area have always been philosophy, ethics, and religion. By first stereotyping religion as simply a body of ideas and then attacking these on logical grounds, Freud failed to see that his own work and the work of those whose ideas he attacked were both inseparable from the social world. He muddled the issue systematically and definitively when he insisted that, although his identity as a Jew was fundamental to him as a person and as such was therefore inseparable from his scientific identity, the two were in fact completely unrelated as far as knowledge and epistemology were concerned. Analytic biography has dutifully perpetuated this muddle by insisting that in Freud's case "Jewish" was "merely" a social category. Philosophical arguments about science, psychoanalysis, and religion (or hermeneutics) cannot resolve the question of how they are related. If Freud and his followers systematically ignored the social dimension of their work, then only a sociological analysis of his idea of science, which epitomized that work, can shed light on it.

In this chapter I clarify further the metapsychology, which so successfully integrated Freud's life and thought into the movement, by reflecting backward from Freud's time to the social origins of physical science in the West, and forward into the collapse of the metapsychology in interwar London. First I compare and contrast Freud's science with Newton's science in seventeenth-century England, because this was Freud's model of science, not just theoretically but also historically, as is seen in his theory of the three blows, which linked psychoanalysis to physics. To do so, I draw upon Robert Merton's Weberian account of Newton's life and the Royal Society and upon his view that a positive, internal relation existed between Puritanism and physical science, the first generating the second. Then I draw into this discussion the debate about psychoanalysis—Is it "really" scientific or is it "really" religious (Jewish)? Following that I track Freud's model forward into the London of the postwar 1920s and describe the social conditions which facilitated the collapse of the metapsychology in the hands of the theory of object relations. This also enables me to contextualize somewhat my own psychological orientation. I close with some reflections on Max Weber's own "metapsychology," the idea of a value-free social science, by noting its psychogenetic origins in his mourning for the Western religious values which his devoted mother and constant wife so lovingly and unsuccessfully offered to him. This allows me to ally Freud with Weber in significant ways and to show, by way of that alliance, the interesting similarities which exist between psychoanalysis and one kind of social science.

My conclusion is simple: psychoanalysis does and does not share an essential affinity with physical science. From the methods and ethos of physical science it draws its experience-distant approach to its datum, the unconscious inner world, and this separates it from earlier forms of literature, philosophy, and theology, as well from current hermeneutical appropriations of these disciplines. Psychoanalysis is unthinkable apart from a social ethos in which science has been institutionalized. But the unit of analysis in psychoanalysis is the fantasy: the unconscious cannot be grasped directly, but only through its derivatives, especially the dream, which is the prototype of all fantasy. Fantasy is on the one hand grounded neurobiologically in the instincts. But fantasy is also, on the other hand, a "project"— that is to say, a desire-laden attempt to construct and bring about, in the realm of the imagination, a state of affairs which is in all essentials social in character.

Furthermore, the work of analysis takes place entirely in a social field. Therefore, I argue that psychoanalysis is a social as well as a physical science. In this second sense analysis is not a science in the first and strict sense. Like Freud, Weber also incorporated the equivalent of an experience-distant mode into his courageous realization that society and history are arenas in which specifiable forces are at work. There is no reason to think that these modes of thought (Freudian and Weberian) are constitutive for today's appropriation of these disciplines, but there is good reason to want to understand their formation as fully as possible. As this is done, our admiration of them, and our capacity to work in fresh and creative ways with them, grows rather than weakens. As with religious "ideas," so with psychological and sociological ones: as we de-idealize them by understanding their contexts more thoroughly, we come to appreciate them and reappropriate them in new and different ways.

Freud's Metapsychology and the Sociology of Physical Science

The best-known understanding of the origins of physical science in the West links it in an adversarial way to religion: the so-called warfare between science and theology (White 1896). Freud and Jones accepted this metaphor of a war (as did Jung, for a while), which was prominent in their day, and they conceived of the psychoanalytic movement as a kind of "D-Day," the final, decisive victory of the forces of good over those of evil. Robert Merton (1938) thought long and hard about the idea of a war between science and religion, and his now-classic study is one lengthy, learned objection to it. If there had been a war, why then, he asked, was it that the first scientists were also for the most part religious, and Puritan at that? For it is undeniable that these scientists believed deeply in the theological tenets of Puritan Christianity and often felt comfortable with them. Merton decided that the war was in the eye of the beholder, the historian who came later. There had to have been at the time an internal relation between religion (Puritan theology) and physical science in which the former actually supported—paradoxically or ironically—the rise of physical science. Merton concluded that the biblical doctrine of the goodness of creation, a divine imperative, sanctified the motives and researches of the first scientists. Only later, under the impress of secularization, did the more familiar attitude of opposition gradually take shape. Merton assiduously supported his theory with empirical-sociological analyses of the lives and writings of the major figures in the Royal Society.

This position was subsequently attacked by Lewis Feuer (1963), who opposed the internal relation position with a "total break" theory. The men of the Royal Society sought a direct and concrete relation to the natural and bodily processes and endowed their scientific observations of them with a sense of joy and beauty. None of this could possibly have come from the cruel and guilty-centered religion of Protestantism. The Merton-Feuer debate should have a thoroughly familiar ring for all students of the origins of psychoanalysis, for it captures exactly the essential polarity of that question: Freud as Viennese, scientific, humanistic, secular (the psychoanalytic biographers—Jones and Kris, and more recently, Gedo and Wolf); and Freud as Jewish, as "really" or covertly religious, as rabbinic and hermeneutical. Let us examine the two conflicting sociological views of the origins of physical science more closely before turning to the origins of psychoanalysis.

According to Merton, the sociologist "uncovers sentiments crystallized in religious values" (1938, p. 55), and these values or attitudes become the fuel for social forces which, in turn, constellate intellectual and practical activities. In this way a religious ethic (doctrines and values, intertwined) can produce a science: "Puritanism evolved and shaped the sentiments which pervaded every phase of human action" (p. 55) in the Royal Society of seventeenth-century England. In particular, the Christian doctrine of the goodness of creation "furthered a full appreciation of the creator's power" through "the study of Nature" (p. 72). This doctrine was inseparable from the values or attitudes of reason and diligence. Reason "curbed appetites and the master sin, sensuality," produced "disinterested zeal" (p. 80) with regard to nature, and denied "fantasy in favor of fact" (p. 63). Diligence created and energized "unswerving devotion to this activity" (p. 80). In this combination of reason and diligence lies the meaning of Weber's concept of innerworldly or "intramundane" asceticism (*innerweltliche Askese*). Merton synoptically characterized all of this as "the Puritan spur to science" and juxtaposed it to medieval Catholic Christianity, which affirmed the "impermanence and relative worthlessness of matter" and which could find "no purpose to the investigation of natural phenomena."

Feuer also uses the idea of an ethic, but the men of the Royal Society were committed to an "ethics of freedom" (1963, p. 2) composed of hedonistic-libertarian values. This ethic motivated the liberation of human curiosity, which produced satisfaction, joy, and pleasure in the discovery of nature and its beauty. A hedonistic ethic is free from any "sense of primal guilt" (p. 8), such as is found in Calvin's hatred of the body, the senses, and pleasure. It is free from "internalized self-aggression" because what is good can refer only to spontaneous likings and desires. Such an ethic produced "independence of character," and Feuer believes, echoing the theme of isolation, that there is an "asocial element in creative thought": great scientists are those whose thought is not completely socialized (p. 11).

Merton's debt to Weber is clear. As they rationalized and disenchanted the biblical Christian world of spirit, the Puritan scientists turned to nature and matter. These epistemological actions were, in a sweeping historical sense, simply part of the internal logic of Western biblical monotheism. So it would not be inconsistent with Merton's study to add that the idea of science as an Archimedean, entirely objective standpoint from which to view the world of nature and matter derived, "ultimately," from the biblical idea of God as wholly other, as completely transcendent. Just as God in his omniscience and omnipotence transcended his world, so his followers, the Puritans, transcended nature, their world, which was his world as well. They simply engaged in the *"imitatio Dei."* For these further reasons the Puritans had no cause to separate science from divinity, since both partook of the same process.

Because he is a sociologist, Merton can describe the religious ethic which spurred science, but for the same reason he does not and cannot infer the deeper motives, nor does he or can he incorporate into his framework the undeniably hedonistic elements which also characterized the lives and works of members of the Royal Society. And Feuer is completely at a loss to recognize—let alone to explain—the strong ascetic and psychologically conflicted character of these men. Yet the two sociologists each accurately describe real features through their portrayals and analyses of the members of the Royal Society.

A more complete and less split-up sense of the matter is possible— if only as an unsupported speculation—if one inserts into the sociocognitive data the psychological process of disillusionment. The Puritans, such a speculation reads, unconsciously de-idealized the ideal realm of spiritual and divine realities, and, as a result, they were able to turn their minds to natural and material things—at least to some extent. The notion of a warfare between science and theology indulges an idealistic fallacy, the naive view that the Puritans, simply through rational, conscious effort, could just "think their way" from one realm to the other. Merton, and for that matter Weber as well, both make this idealistic assumption, whereas in point of fact the psychological mechanism of de-idealization or its equivalent seems to have been latent or implicit in their theory. On the other hand, Feuer, who makes ample use of psychoanalytic concepts, completely ignores the social context, which was (and here Merton seems the more correct) deeply informed by religious ideas, ideals, and values. The conjecture of an unconscious disappointment lends experiential immediacy to the Weberian historical postulate of disenchantment.

Let us return to the matter at hand, the origins of psychoanalysis. In the sweeping civilizational sense just described psychoanalysis is nothing more nor less than the further carrying out of disenchantment on the infantile unconscious. In the hands of psychoanalysis, spirit becomes psyche and, still further, psyche becomes ego. The ego of psychoanalysis is simply the naturalization of soul. Freud inherited the Copernican and Newtonian, positivistic and mechanistic modes of thought which he employed from Brücke, Fechner, DuBois-Reymond, and others and applied them to the psychoanalytic situations which he encountered in his collaborations with Breuer and, later, to himself and to his "collaboration" with Fliess. In this light Freud's youthful attraction to Franz Brentano, who tried to keep psyche and physics together, and to Ludwig Feuerbach, who broke them apart by replacing spirit (theology) with psychology (anthropology), is more understandable—each embodied one horn of his dilemma. Feuerbach argued that the Hegelian doctrine of Spirit was nothing more than the mind of man projected onto the heavens. The idea of turning Hegel upside down, on his head, which Feuerbach and Marx shared, is simply the conceptual side of the more affective process of de-idealizing. In this way Freud was able to arrive at the idea of the metapsychology, which was first formulated in "The Project," in 1895, and reached its apogee in *The Ego and the Id*, in 1923. He too turned the ideality of the Western religious past "on its head."

How did Freud de-idealize the Western biblical tradition? He did so through his lifelong preoccupation with the figure of Moses. The process began with the idealization of this archetype of Jewish culture, history, and community which he found in the Bible stories of his childhood. Midway in his life, so to speak, there was an intense mixture of admiration for Moses and psychological interpretation of him in Rome in 1914, recorded in "The Moses of Michelangelo," which then inaugurated the turn to culture. And finally, at the end of his life, Freud engaged in his highly ambivalent discussions of what could be called "The Moses of Monotheism." As Freud gradually disenchanted the figure of Moses, understood as representative of a cultural tradition, he withdrew from—it would be better to say, he individuated out of—his Jewish sense of belonging and community. This process of separation was forced upon him by his experience-distant, rational, and scientific approach to his human, emotional needs, which had been shaped by his religious affiliation. But, as we have seen, he only partly abandoned his identity, and so the question can again be asked, and now answered: In what sense was psychoanalysis "really Jewish"?

Psychoanalysis was Jewish (religious) in the same sense that Newtonian science was Protestant (religious). Only recently has it become possible to address this question, for now a small but excellent literature on the subject has gradually offset earlier ideologically motivated prohibitions. David Bakan (1958) opened up the issue by arguing that Freud's psychoanalysis was virtually a latter-day form of Jewish mysticism. Freud, however, dissimulated on this essential point, masking the similarities for complex personal and ideological reasons. While Bakan related Freud's concepts to those of earlier Jewish mystics, he undertook no systematic discussion of Freud's surrounding social or political contexts. Marthe Robert (1976) began her study with a long refutation of Bakan and went on to propose a theory of two cultures: Freud broke with the culture of traditional Judaism in order to realize the central ambition of his life, that of becoming part of German, bourgeois, humanistic culture. The self-analysis served as the crucible in which he worked out this rebellious ambition. John M. Cuddihy (1974) proposed a somewhat similar "social break theory" but emphasized far more than Robert the stress and trauma of adapting to an alien, gentile society (hence the "ordeal" of "civility") and attempted to draw Freud's struggle into a general pattern to which other preeminent intellectual Jews belonged—for example, Marx and Lévi-Strauss. Neither Robert nor Cuddihy offers substantial theoretical formulations, either psychological or sociological, although in this general sense my own view is similar to theirs and I consider these to be excellent studies. At one point in the midst of his elaborate historical discussions Klein (1981) seems to adopt Cuddihy's position, at least as regards the genesis of Freud's key psychological ideas in his self-analysis. During the period 1895–1900, Klein says, "Freud began to shift the focus of his work from the domain of psychopathology . . . to a 'metapsychology' comprehending 'normal behaviour.' Increasingly, from this point on, Freud was engaged in a theoretical and philosophical reconstruction of human behavior . . . he proclaimed that the unconscious must be assumed to be the general basis of psychical life. . . . Psychoanalysis provided Freud with a basis for reinterpreting human behavior, for making sense out of the chaos and divisiveness of his social environment, and for determining the common basis of all human life" (p. 71).

The clearest and most focused version of the psychoanalysis-is-really-Jewish viewpoint comes, however, from Susan Handelman (1982). She says it was "a Jewish Science," a secular version of the Talmud, "an interpretive science" which was "deeply Rabbinic" because it was grounded in a "model of the Jewish psyche." Freud "displaced Rabbinic hermeneutics from the text of the Holy Writ to the text of the dream" (p. 132). The Talmudic or rabbinic mode of thought is "multivocal, indeterminate, rhetorical and poetic." It juxtaposes "deeper meanings" to logical, literalistic approaches. It encourages "opposing opinions" (p. 146) and assumes a "hidden unity behind all disparate phenomena" (p. 150). Thus Freud's method of dream interpretation, with its attention to overdetermination, condensation, displacement, and free association, looks upon the dream as a text which reveals the hidden meanings of the psyche through a seemingly endless variety of guises. All this contrasts sharply with the laws, processes, univocality, linearity, forces, and determinism which are the hallmarks of the science of Freud's day, in which he in fact chose to cast his perceptions and observations.

There is no reason to quarrel with such a view. The rabbinic approach was a central element—I call it the experiential matrix—in Freud's interpretation of his own and others' dreams. As he descended into his self-analysis, he did not descend into some universal, ahistorical, and cultureless psyche, nor into "the Jewish psyche," but into *his* Jewish psyche, with all its historical particularity, uniqueness, and social ambiguity. But Freud also did something else, and that kept him from being simply another in a long line of distinguished rabbis or devout Jews and also kept his patients from simply becoming good Jews. Freud submitted his particularity to the canons of physical science, as he had come to know these, with their experience-distant imperatives. These harsh imperatives alienated him and separated him in a wrenching way from the intimacies of his psyche and allowed him to share, communicate, and verify his introspective probes and gradually accrued sense of analytic access with others from different cultural and epistemological backgrounds and contexts. The science of Freud's day imposed a limitation on his narcissism; it was a "blow," in the very sense in which he himself used the word. Stated psychologically, Freud de-idealized the rabbinic tradition and gradually individuated out of it. But he also continued to cleave to the image of Moses and to the sense of belonging which it promised, as all people do in relation to their cherished cultural objects—and as the child in all of us always does in relation to his or her transitional objects to support, stabilize, and facilitate development or individuation.

This analysis shows that the historical process of secularization in Western culture was integral to the formation of psychoanalysis. Referred to before only in passing, it can now be taken up directly for the first time. There are at bottom two views of secularization. In the first, secularization refers to the transposition of religious meanings into a nonreligious (secular) sphere of activity, wherein not just the shape but the energy as well of the secular continue to derive from the religious. For example, "the idea of progress" has often been understood as a secularization of the Christian theory of redemptive history, or, as it is often said, Marxism is "a secular religion"—it claims to be scientific and nonreligious, but it displays the same charismatic zeal and totalism of the deeply religious person and of religious movements, and so it is "really religious."[1] The second view of secularization can be called the total break theory or the theory of a wholly new beginning. Its best-known instance is the Enlightenment philosophes' views of society. Merton stresses in some ways the first, Feuer the second. Handelman advocates the first in virtually pure form, and Freud himself adopted the second in virtually pure form, as has all analytic biography.

Everything in this study thus far urges that neither of these two views is, in itself, correct. Freud did not simply overturn his past, nor did he simply disguise and repeat it. Psychoanalysis is a secularization of Jewish culture in the sense that, in the very action of discovering the inner world and by making it shareable and communicable, Freud separated himself out from his common culture, although by no means completely. Coming from a very different cultural tradition, Jones and Jung were also able to see similar psychological processes which were "really there" in their own lives, in the lives of their patients, and, upon further retrospective reflection, in their religious traditions as well. They too secularized their religious heritage. The so-called warfare between science and theology should also be understood in the light of this complex process.

Weber and Merton both confronted this more nuanced view of secularization, and they offered their specific explanations of it. They pointed out that Protestants were highly overrepresented in economic (Weber) and scientific (Merton) activities at the time when their activities began. To make this point, they counted people (as I will also do in a moment), and their conclusions are known to all. As time passed, the original pattern of internal relations weakened, such that persons from non-Protestant backgrounds were able to share in these activities. Weber said that the economic-capitalistic activities were "stripped of their religious and ethical meaning" (1904–5, p. 182), and Merton claimed that science "grew away from its religious moorings" (1938, pp. 79, 95). Central to both investigations is the Weberian view that these historical processes were grounded in and authorized by the dynamic, religioethical core of Western biblical monotheism and contrasted sharply with the religions of India and China. I prefer to characterize this dynamic as a "drive to the concrete," a drive away from and down from the spiritual and ideal realms created by biblical religion, which was a religion of transcendence. This view bears some resemblance to Mircea Eliade's (1949) distinction between cyclical and linear time. The latter produces the distinctly modern and Western "terror of history," the terror of being alone and bereft of a past.

Indeed, Freud himself adopted an essentially Weberian perspective on Western cultural and religious history in *Moses and Monotheism*. His word for "material objects" was "libido," and the word he used to frame the idea of "the natural world" was "metapsychology." Freud despiritualized and materialized the rabbinic ethos, the "Jewish psyche." The root word in "dis-en-chant-ment" (*Entzauberung*) is "magic." So it could also be rendered as "de-magic-al-ization." But magic did not mean to Weber the means-end manipulation of either spirits or natural phenomena in the service of an illusory sense of omnipotence and determinism; it referred to the spontaneity by which ritual and ceremony, in the hands of a priest or some such representative person, restored a penitent to the religious community. By evolving naturalistic explanations of mental life, Freud disenchanted his ties to community, both his own and the ties of anyone who chose to accept his ideas. The magic in all this consisted in the unconscious connection between the totalizing, narcissistic ego and the common culture of the religious community, the attachment being cemented and then brought into conscious awareness by the religious symbol—in Freud's case, the figure of Moses. It is this "enchantment" which psychoanalysis disenchants, by shifting the burden of psychological integration (for example, sublimation or the transformation of narcissism) away from the auspices of a common culture and into the mind of the individual, thereby creating the need—and the opportunity—to build psychological structure and individuation.

I now note demographically the affinity which continues to exist between loyalty to a Jewish cultural tradition and the practice of psychoanalysis. Weber and Merton both employed this strategy to their advantage. William Henry (1971) has extensively studied—one could say, exhaustively—the practice of psychotherapy in America during the 1950s. Four major professional groups—psychoanalysts, clinical psychologists, psychiatrists, and psychiatric social workers—together conduct all psychotherapy in the United States (hence, the "fifth profession"). Henry used both depth interviews (four hours in duration) with individual practitioners and a survey. He interviewed 300 subjects in New York City, Chicago, and Los Angeles (100 in each) and sent surveys to all practitioners listed in the respective professional directories (total N, 6,629:1,170 psychoanalysts, 1,584 psychiatrists, 2,183 clinical psychologists, and 1,692 psychiatric social workers, yielding an actual response N of 3,390). During this period the three nonpsychoanalytic groups all made use of broadly conceived psychodynamic principles drawn largely from psychoanalysis, although some psychiatrists were biologically oriented, some psychologists behaviorally oriented, and some social workers community oriented. This pattern continues to exist today. The study centered on five major issues: cultural origins, class, religious apostasy, political beliefs, and life-course circumstances leading to the choice of psychologically oriented psychotherapy as a profession.

Henry's most important conclusion was "a marked congruence between professional identity and cultural traditions" (p. 12), the major component of which was religious attachment: cultural affinity was the crucial factor shaping the personal identity of the psychotherapist. "Our mental health professionals," he said, "came in highly over-represented numbers from Jewish backgrounds, from urban settings, from parental stock with eastern European ethnic ties" (p. 8); "Psychoanalysts are much more likely to be Jewish or to claim no cultural affinity . . . recruitment into psychoanalysis is much more strongly influenced by cultural affiliation than is the case with the other three accepted groups" (p. 12). Second, Henry found that breaking away from a religious tradition was an important biographical aspect of all mental health professionals: 87 percent came from religious family backgrounds, and 36 percent had renounced these (pp. 48–50). Finally, personal psychotherapy was undertaken more readily by those with no religious background and less by those with religious commitments. Lack of religious belief was an important element leading to the decision to undergo a term of personal psychotherapy.

These patterns which Henry's study describes repeat in contemporary demographic and sociological fashion the original historical set of events found to characterize the origins of psychoanalysis: the association of psychoanalysis with a Jewish cultural tradition (the so-called Jewish origins of psychoanalysis), the rebellious repudiation by the psychologically minded person of his family's religious background (Freud's break with his past), and the inverse relationship between religious commitment and the experience of psychotherapy (the self-analysis leading away from a common culture and into access to the inner world). Psychoanalysts and psychotherapists do not simply repudiate their past (the total break theory of secularization), nor are they "really" assimilated by it (the transposition theory); rather, they follow some sort of third or middle path: deprived of social support by advancing social-structural change, upward mobility, and increasing professionalization, they become anomic and alienated and turn in to themselves, there to discover the "inner world" of desires, wishes, fantasies, and infantile objects. Then, with the help of "the other" (their psychoanalyst or psychotherapist), they gradually transform that inner world, building psychological structure, in order to support their separation from, and individuation out of—but also their return to a rapprochement with—their cultural traditions.

To sum up the central issue of this discussion. Drawing upon the lawlike regularities which he observed in his physiological and neurological researches, Freud discerned similar regularities in the socially marginal analytic situation: the patterned interplay between dreams, fantasies, free associations, slips of the tongue, and symptomatic behaviors. He traced these back to the transference and inferred from that, but did not observe, its developmental prototype, the infantile unconscious. It would be more correct to say, however, that Freud's investigations participated in the ethos of his scientific researches and drew it and his observations all together under the idea of a "metapsychology." Before Freud, what we now take for granted as psychological processes were always coded into and represented by social and ethical principles—what Durkheim called the collective consciousness and Schutz, the taken-for-granted world of everyday social life. In this sphere, rational and self-conscious reflection and the freedom of the will reign supreme, and notions such as "psychological determinism" are, to use the historically correct religious designation, "anathema," although today sociologists simply call them unscientific. When the historically grounded idea of science is turned upon the mind of the individual person, it inflicts a blow to the narcissism of the person, for such narcissism "wishes" to see the psyche as a part of the world as a whole, and the social world in particular, as a total and given order of things, of which the individual is but a mere reflection or extension.

But there was more. In a manner which can only be called systematic, Freud failed to recognize that the analytic situation, which he observed in himself and others, was positioned at the margins of the social world and that the rough regularities which he observed there simply could not be replicated outside that situation in the light of social day. For historical reasons, Freud could not understand that what he rightly perceived as "natural" was also—but not only— "cultural." On the shoals of social reality, the bark of psychoanalysis suffered severe damage.

It is now possible to explore the social side of psychoanalysis in yet another way. The metapsychology is the "scientizing" of the mind. It correlates with a distantiated ego, an ego which conceives of itself as no longer organically attached to a social other. When it occurs, authoritarian behavior on the part of the analyst is the social correlate of this methodological formulation. The metapsychology is of course a fiction, a metaphor, an "as-if" construction, a frame with which to order observations, as Freud himself said, although only one part of him believed that. To explain just how fictional it was, I turn to London between the wars. There the metapsychology collapsed, or rather simply withered away, in the face of a new variant of analytic access, a new way of conceptualizing the analytic situation and a new genre of psychoanalytic thought. And, as can now be expected, this occurred in a place and time of great mourning for lost social and religious realities, for that is how psychologies are made, whether they are modern or ancient, Eastern or Western. And it will also become clearer that psychological freedom, which was at bottom the essence of "Freud's truth," is inseparable from political freedom. In London, Freud fulfilled his last and deepest wish, to die in freedom.

1920s London, Object Relations, and the Collapse of the Metapsychology

Psychobiography, it has become clear, always centers upon the uniqueness and novelty of Freud's person and his ideas. Sociology subverts this intention by showing that these achievements were not unique to Freud, that analytic access and all that it implies existed in the lives and works of others, as the careers of Jung, Rank, and Jones suggest. Other psychological virtuosos in other times and places could also have been added. The metapsychology served as a socioepistemological emblem for the cohesiveness of the movement. It was a sign of correct psychological thinking and, along with the idea of the oedipus complex, a password or "shibboleth" for membership in the movement. Freud modeled this concept on the prestigious scientific endeavors of Newton and Darwin. By reflecting backward into the social origins of physical science in the religious milieu of seventeenth-century England, it was possible to illumine the ways in which Freud's concept of science emerged from his Jewish background and to clarify the extent to which it was, and was not, similar to the physicalistic model to which he was so committed.

This short section reflects forward to show in yet another way how social forces shape the emergence of psychological ideas, by examining the rise of the theory of object relations and, intimately related to that, the collapse of the metapsychology in London, England, during the interwar period. Although the historical data supporting this probe are limited, they are sufficient to make the point: the theory of object relations, that is, the analyst's capacity to reflect in a mode of objective thoughtfulness upon the developmental realities of the pre-oedipal mother, required a further advance of industrialization and, as fate also decreed, was simultaneously further supported by shared social mourning. As the psychoanalytic movement gradually dissipated into international societies more and more under local control, the center of creative activity shifted from Vienna to London. There psychologists descended more deeply into their own and others' inner worlds. As they did so, the idea of psychological theory as an Archimedean point of uninvolved, value-free objectivity and the view of the analyst as an observer detached from his patient like a surgeon from his both collapsed, for they were no longer necessary. But the deeper turn inward was also a turn outward, so that the patient as "object" was found more and more to be a social rather than a natural object. The original metapsychology was, it seems, a fortuitous and epoch-specific protection against deeper psychological realities. The capacity to appreciate these psychological realities had to wait for further social-structural change, for there was no way in which Freud could recognize them in his time and place. Once such capacities are codified in a stable community of investigation, however, they can be pursued in social contexts which would otherwise be inimicable to them, provided that the community of investigation in question is given sufficient social support. For those who are interested in it, this turn away from the individualizing metapsychology and toward a psychoanalytic theory of the social other can also be seen as the entrance of psychoanalysis into the postmodern realm of thought and experience.

Let us look more closely at the lead idea. For many complex reasons Freud reflected principally upon the struggles between fathers and sons to possess the oedipal mother, who was the object of their libidinal and instinctual desires. Successful resolution of this struggle required the son's oedipal mortification and consequent instinctual renunciation. Freud of course also reflected on pre-oedipal themes such as orality and anality but always on the model of the drives—he called these component or partial instincts. But he reflected only with great difficulty on the associated issue of narcissism and for the most part not at all on the pre-oedipal mother. As he told Romain Rolland, the oceanic feeling was too vague, too shadowy. And his little grandson's "fort-da" experience, which is today understood as a typical transitional situation in which the experience of maternal loss was mitigated by the creative activity of play, meant to Freud only repetition in the service of mastering an instinctual wish. Such repetitive actions were "beyond the pleasure principle." On the other hand, Rank, Jung, and Jones—all a generation younger than Freud—were deeply concerned with narcissistic issues, the pre-oedipal mother, and the psychology of self. But they could not formulate these issues analytically because the only existing psychological-theoretical frame was the metapsychology, and it excluded them.

There is no place for a theory of early maternal attachment in the metapsychology, despite Kohut's (1971) obedient and heroic attempt.

After the war, however, in the 1920s, when the movement shifted geographically from Vienna to London, it also shifted theoretically from oedipal metapsychology to developmentally earlier problems of attachment. Weinstein and Platt (1969) have proposed that this codification into reflective thought (in contrast to merely idiosyncratic insight) was significantly facilitated by a heritage of advanced industrialization, which occurred principally in England, where the industrial revolution had first begun and had continued to flourish. I have already noted the consequences of this change: a greater sense of social differentiation and personal autonomy, more self-conscious control of inner emotional states, and the abandonment or renunciation of intensive, global (primitive) attachments to representative figures beyond the family. Its principal mechanism was industrialization's drawing fathers out of the family, creating a phase of development over which mothers alone tended to preside. The products and objects of industry and technology have replaced the highly cathected extrafamilial representative persons, who cement community together. It is difficult to form intimate psychological relationships with such objects, although advertising has attempted to reverse this principle. A new sociologically structured developmental situation came into existence.

I am now led to think yet again about this hypothesis, which I explored in relation to the origins of psychoanalysis, but in a very different way, thanks to the careful historical review of two psychologists, Nora Newcombe and Jeffrey Lerner (1981), of psychoanalytic thought and practice in interwar London. This research supports to a remarkable degree the social patterns already discussed in the genesis of Freud's self-analysis and of the psychoanalytic movement, and especially the role of mourning which I introduced into it. After the war, all of England was in a state of social mourning for those who had died in it. But in a more fundamental sense there was also a shared sense of hopelessness in the face of a social fabric severely torn by the war. In addition to this, mourning practices at this time declined, as did the participation of people in church life. The influence of the clergy also weakened. This secularization deprived people of traditional sources of consolation and disturbed their ties to the national, common culture of the day.

As clinicians in London participated in the shared cultural activity of mourning, they began more and more to enter empathically into the inner worlds of their patients, many of whom were shell-shocked soldiers and—an unlikely combination—young children. Although Freud's ideas were by this time well known to these clinicians, they also rejected most of them, especially his views on sexuality, mourning, aggression, and the origins of the neuroses in infantile trauma. The London clinicians instead turned their attention away from object love and to object relations and problems of attachment and their vicissitudes: mourning, loss, separation, even friendship. Newcombe and Lerner think an eclectic British orientation developed alongside the psychoanalytic group, but I think of these men as far more original: they were an emergent native British school with experiences of, and views on, analytic access unique to them and to their historic circumstances. Their views would have emerged even if they had not read Freud; indeed, the presence of his views actually forestalled their reflections in certain ways. In this regard I liken them to the early American functional psychologists, led by William James, and to the recent American self-actualization psychologies, led by Carl Rogers. Both of these psychologies have strong psychodynamic elements, although neither one is psychoanalytic. Moreover, the London psychologists were all Christian in background (so were James and Rogers). Their religiousness was so prominent that their place of work, the Tavistock Clinic, was sometimes called "the parson's clinic." In the midst of these circumstances the metapsychology gradually disappeared from view. Let us look at this situation in more detail.

In Britain during the ten years or so before the war, where Ernest Jones had drifted about, chafing against his medical colleagues and disgusted with his lot before discovering the existence of psychoanalysis, psychiatric treatment in public hospitals was available only to the certifiably insane. Both theory and method "held that the causes of all mental illness were physical." Although there was some limited awareness that loss and bereavement might be possible causes of mental illness, clinicians separated mourning from melancholia, as Freud had done. Freud's ideas, especially his view that infantile sexual trauma was the principal cause of unconscious mental conflict, were looked upon with suspicion "as a foreign and sex-obsessed system" (p. 3). Newcombe and Lerner perceptively note that Freud's famous account of an early case, Anna O., who became hysterical while nursing her dying father at his bedside late at night, completely ignored "elements of grief and anxiety over the severing of inter-personal bonds" (p. 3) in favor of searching out her infantile sexual fixations and repressions. Freud ignored mourning as a psychogenic issue because he thought of it as a conscious process centering upon a recently deceased person.

Concern with grief as a causative factor in the genesis of mental conflict and suffering received an important impetus during the war, chiefly from the treatment of so-called shell-shocked soldiers. At the outset only physical methods, such as elaborate and expensive instruments, were used (for example, cutting of the tendons was thought to heal hysterical contractures). But as the war progressed, "psychological factors began to be investigated as doctors observed their patients more closely, and grief for fallen comrades began to be identified as one possible cause of symptoms" (p. 4). These aperçus and hunches were not, however, pursued at length because at the time "no theoretical understanding of the role of loss in personality functioning" (p. 4) existed. The only systematic theory was Freud's, and investigators were not able to isolate infantile sexual trauma in their patients' histories. This search for the causes of war-induced stress created a movement in British psychiatry which affirmed such processes as repression and unconscious conflict while rejecting their infantile and sexual origins. This movement later consolidated into a "school of British eclectics" centering in the Tavistock Clinic, in which W. H. R. Rivers and Ian Suttie were prominent.

Rivers was a well-known anthropologist who completed training in psychological medicine at the beginning of the war. He was extremely interested in Freud's theories of dreams and repression and applied them to his treatment of disturbed soldiers, although he was never formally associated with the clinic. He thought of repression as a more conscious and voluntary process, and he encouraged his patients to remember their frightening war experiences and to integrate them into their current sense of things. He concluded that the "instinct for self-preservation must be put side-by-side with the sexual instincts" as causes for neurosis, and he believed that it played "a far more important role in the production of the neuroses of civil life" than psychologists then thought (p. 5). Suttie completed medical training in Glasgow in 1914, served in France during the war, and afterward joined the staff of the Tavistock Clinic. His work in the war stimulated a line of thinking which he published only much later, in 1935, in his book *The Origins of Love and Hate.* He rejected Freud's instinct theory in its entirety and believed instead that "the innate need for companionship" and separation anxiety were the primary causes of mental or nervous breakdown. Suttie was deeply religious. He attacked Freud's ideas in his book and offered arguments in favor of a return to Christianity, which he thought of a "a system of psychotherapy" in which matriarchal elements were central.

The ideas of Rivers and Suttie became the basis for "an independent British depth psychology" (p. 6). They were especially attractive to the eclectic doctors who clustered in and about the Tavistock Clinic. These doctors had never been comfortable with Freud's emphasis on sexuality, and they objected that Freud was "insufficiently hopeful" and that he ignored "faith." For example, the founder of the clinic, Hugh Crichton Miller, was the son of a Presbyterian minister and an elder in a London church, and J. A. Hadfield, another Tavistock eclectic, once admonished a bereaved father "to renew his strength by resting his soul in the Everlasting Arms" (p. 5).

The aftermath of the war provided the evolving eclectic British psychology with an even more important stimulus. There was "widespread bereavement" in the general British population. Roughly "three-quarters of a million British men died . . . out of a total population of 38 million . . . about a third of the dead were married, leaving roughly 248,000 widows and 381,000 children . . . there was restlessness and unease about the future" (p. 8). Newcombe and Lerner state that literary evidence, journal articles, and case notes confirm that "pathological mourning or grief-related mental problems" were common (p. 9). Furthermore, war-related industries and tasks eliminated the "elaborate and universally respected funeral and mourning customs" practiced before the war, and these were not subsequently resumed. The war also "accelerated the decline of adherence to the Protestant churches," thereby depriving people of the consolations of the clergy, prayer, "belief in immortality, divine purpose to death and eventual reunion with loved ones" (p. 9). British society at this time presented the observer with a macabre contrast between a stoical mood and a frantic kind of gaiety which served to satisfy the wish that one simply forget it all. In short, hectic immersion in superficial activities of the moment served to mask the deeper inability to mourn.

In all this John Bowlby played a crucial part. His work embodied much of the shared but diffuse psychological feeling in interwar London and codified it into systematic psychological thinking. Bowlby centered his efforts on attachment in the lives of children during their early months and related these patterns to later, adult experiences of separation and mourning. In doing so he contributed in a major way to the formation of object relations theory. Although they remain open to other views of the relation between shared historical experiences and the rise of psychological ideas, Newcombe and

Lerner favor the conclusion that Bowlby and others, such as Rivers and Suttie, "were more sensitive to loss because they lived in a time of widespread separation and death" (p. 11) and that they constructed their theories accordingly. Bowlby finished medical school and made his major observations in the mid-1930s and published his first work on the mother-infant bond in the 1940s. But these ideas about the impact of early separation in children's lives grew out of his experiences working in a school for emotionally disturbed children in 1928–29 (p. 2), and he continued to systematize them over a long period of time. His trilogy, *Attachment and Loss,* some 1,200 pages, was finally completed in 1980. Its titles are instructive: *Attachment* (1969), *Separation: Anxiety and Anger* (1973), and *Loss: Sadness and Depression* (1980). At the outbreak of the Second World War Bowlby wrote about one of the most heartrending (and also thoroughly Dickensian) realities some psychiatrists must at times face, the affectionless thief. They were, he said, "children who were distinguished from the remainder by their remarkable lack of affection or warmth of feeling for anyone" (quoted in Newcombe and Lerner 1982, p. 10). These were children who were unable to mourn the early losses in their lives. They were the prototype of what is popularly referred to as the "hardened" criminal. Like the general population, they too suffered from the inability to mourn.

Melanie Klein's work (1921–45) with children was also very much a part of this scene, at least theoretically. She linked Freud's ideas about sexual trauma in children to depression and pathological mourning in adults, emphasizing that mourning (she preferred the word "pining") was a crucial feature of disturbances in the ecology of internal objects in the early mother-infant relationship. In addition to her manifold and rich clinical observations, Klein created an important and truly psychoanalytic theory of infantile mourning. She succeeded in convincing psychoanalysts that "grief could lead to neurosis" in persons who otherwise seemed normal and that "mourning was, for most people, a difficult and dangerous period" (Newcombe and Lerner 1982, p. 8). Klein supervised Bowlby, and she influenced him a great deal, as did Ian Suttie. Both believed in the link between childhood and adult reactions. But, like Freud, Klein emphasized the elements of unconscious fantasy in these separations, whereas Bowlby, like Rivers and Suttie, was more concerned with real losses and separation. The work of these two investigators was later further elaborated into an explicit object relations theory by H. Guntrip, W. R. D. Fairbairn, and, still later, by D. W. Winnicott, upon whom Melanie Klein also exercised great influence.

Newcombe and Lerner wrote their study in order to put to rest the psychologist's characteristic dread that psychological ideas might come to be seen as "mere" products of their historical, cultural context—that is to say, "culture bound." I on the other hand have the sociological fascination with culture boundedness. It seems clear enough that object relations theory emerged in a context of social loss, grief, and mourning. Another very immediate social stimulus to this situation was the decline of the consolations of ministerial care, the traditional and socially sanctioned resources for the healing of loss. But these declines were part of a far more sweeping decline, the decline of religion itself—that is to say, secularization—which also has its context. Peter Berger (1973) has cogently demonstrated, in a fashion which should be called *"realsoziologie,"* after the fashion of "realpolitik," that industrialization is the most powerful and formidable of the many social forces which has always marginalized religious activity. So, in a more sweeping historical sense, the decline of religion in interwar Britain was produced by the accelerated industrialization of the war itself, which was in turn only the latest in a long heritage of technologically induced social change.

I can now draw these threads together psychologically by pointing out that structural social change weakened people's ties first to the traditional common culture and then, later, to the national common culture, creating a kind of progressive shared desacralization or decathexis of it. The result was an increased, pain-laden mandate for some to introspect into the inner world which had become even more loosened from control-producing internalizations. Faced with these circumstances, and unimpressed by Continental authority, the British clinicians were able to observe new psychological realities, and they codified their own and the painful social experiences of their time into new psychological theories. Mourning in the 1920s in London was difficult because the stoical mood of wartime and the subsequent sense of loss after the war fostered the suppression of grief (a "stiff upper lip") and the desire to forget it all. I think that these social circumstances in the British situation may have stimulated one of Winnicott's most important clinical formulations, his elaboration of Kleinian ideas into "the manic defense" (Winnicott 1935), which includes both the denial of loss and "the inability to be depressed," both of which are varieties of "the inability to mourn."

It is acceptable and perhaps even fitting to end a discussion of industrialization in England on a Marxist note, although I choose to give it a Freudian cast. Had they understood Freud better, the Freudo-Marxists (most of whom are Marxists first and Freudians second) could have realized that to Freud's three blows to Western man Marx in fact added one of his own, which I take as a fourth. The shared social experience of increasingly mechanicalized modes of production always tears self-consciousness out of its traditional modes of connectedness to supportive natural, social, and cosmological worlds and in doing so inflicts a historically specific narcissistic blow to the universal human, spontaneous sense of, and wish for, "the whole." In his magisterial and eloquent compendium of classic sociological thought, Robert Nisbet made the same point far better than I when he attempted to capture the quintessential conceptual leitmotiv of the sociological tradition. Although a sociologist himself, Nisbet (1966) actually formulated this leitmotiv psychologically: the originative sociological thinkers were chiefly concerned with the fate of man's "inmost self" in the face of industrialization: "Loss of community isolates man . . . by fragmenting him into mechanical roles he is forced to play, none of them touching his inmost self but all of them separating man from this self, leaving him, so to speak, existentially missing in action" (p. 265).

Marx had no psychology in his theory of historical materialism, and so when he spoke of the cruel, socially fragmenting effects of industrialization, the revolution of the proletariat, and its final reaggregation into the consummatory community of species being, he spoke of people but not of the person, of society and not personality. Marx did so because there was no psychology in Marx the man. As a person Marx was devoid of any capacity to reflect empathically upon his own or others' unconscious inner worlds in a psychological way, and consequently he could not engage as deeply as he could have the powerful disappointments which the Hegelian dialectic evoked in him. His "transition" from the cruel rigidities of capitalism to the reign of communism remained at the level of morality and rationality. It is difficult to imagine how much Marx must have suffered inwardly as he struggled to think his way rationally out of the injustices he observed, and one can only marvel at the incisiveness he achieved. Clearly, the inability to mourn the loss of a religious past was part of Marx's program, just as it has become a central feature in communist-inspired states everywhere. Nisbet's poignant remarks about the isolated "man" of the nineteenth century may seem sentimental, but they take on reality when it is recognized that they apply as much to the sociologist who is writing the theory as they do to the people he observes, for the sociologist only codifies the experiences he shares with them in his new frames of theoretical understanding.

Of the many such "existential walking wounded" in the sociological tradition, none suffered more or was more introspective, and that in a protopsychological sense, than Max Weber. By charting "the origins of (one) sociology" in the light of issues found in the origins of psychoanalysis, in particular the origins of Weber's ideas of disenchantment (*his* theory of mourning) and value-free social science (*his* metapsychology), we gain even greater insight into the origins of psychoanalysis, for in both their modes of thought and manner of suffering Weber and Freud held much in common. As one's sense of these commonalities deepens, these two remarkable men and the formidable disciplines they founded appear even more luminous and—paradoxically—even more separate than before.

The Struggle to Mourn in the Sociological Tradition: The Case of Max Weber

There is good reason to end a sociological analysis of the origins of psychoanalysis with a psychological discussion of the origins of sociology in the life of one of its greatest architects and practitioners, Max Weber. This reason can be formulated in the two terms central to this study, those of thought and life. Against the psychobiographers and most historians of psychoanalysis, I have argued that Freud's achievements were not unique, as they think, that others, such as Jung and Rank and Jones, achieved similar psychological understanding, and that therefore Freud's activities belonged to the ideal-type. I now extend this view even further, to the case of a sociologist, to show that Freud's mode of thinking was, if only in this ideal-typical sense, not different from Weber's and that Weber trod a personal path very similar to Freud's in order to reach his perspective. This project also has the more general effect of supporting the view that psychoanalysis is in part a social as well as a biological and psychological science.

I think the most significant point of commonality between the Freudian and Weberian perspectives is their shared desire to render into ordinariness the extraordinary qualities which their predecessors assigned to the past. Freud's achievement consisted in bringing into consciousness, for all to see, the inner world of unconscious desires and objects, and he chose to cast his understandings in the scientific frames of the day, his metapsychology. In charting the unconscious dimension of mind and tracing it to society and culture, Freud rendered ordinary the extraordinary world of religiously inspired myths and ideals in which the past is always inscribed. The essential perceptions of Weber's oeuvre closely paralleled Freud's, for Weber also "saw through" the enchanting bonds which bound up persons into communities and created religious systems of thought. Like Freud, Weber also thought that society could be approached in the light of lawlike patterns and that the sociologist could take up a value-free (scientific) or experience-distant perspective in relation to these patterns. Weber too had a metapsychology. And so the sociological perspective shares with the psychoanalytic perspective a similar style of thinking, such that both belong to the same "family" of inquiry, although they have different subject matters and different conclusions.

It is to be expected that a psychoanalyst, and especially the first psychoanalyst, will in his search for psychological truth be powerfully stimulated by his own inner psychological and developmental processes. But that is not expected of a sociologist, who is supposed to reach his truth free of such processes. Nevertheless, Weber was deeply enmeshed in significant psychological events which powerfully shaped his thought, as his very psychologically minded wife's monumental biography (1926) suggests again and again. While Weber's suffering principally involved women and mothers (Freud's, men and fathers), while he lived at the end of the Protestant era (Freud at the end of the Jewish one), and while he fled his developmental realities (as Freud fled his social circumstances), Weber too mourned for lost personal objects and for a waning religious tradition, and as a result achieved his new perspectives on the social world. These parallels and differences allow us to see in a fresh way that psychoanalysis and sociology are not two disciplines which need to be integrated (psychoanalytic sociology), nor is one to be fully overcome by the other; rather, they are to be related to each other by means of a transitional area modeled on the transitional space which always exists between the self and its social world, a space which neither Freud nor Weber chose to recognize, although their work makes such recognition possible. Part 3 explores that possibility.

I think that Weber reached his perspective through a complex series of personal events, among which mourning was a central component. At the conscious and cognitive level there was the biblical Christianity of his own heritage, to which he returned many times in moments of longing, despite his defiant rejection of that heritage. The genetic, unconscious, and affective root for Weber's creativity was his attachment to and merger with, and subsequent separation from, two women, his mother (Helene Weber) and wife (Marianne Weber). Both were deeply religious (his mother more than his wife), both were deeply controlling and impinging upon the autonomy and initiative of others (his mother more than his wife), both were deeply nurturant (his wife more than his mother), and both were remarkably sensitive to psychological processes (his wife more than his mother). Heritage and personal development came together in a decisive way in Weber's tragic but also portentous "nervous breakdown." Before it, he was a relatively happy married man with a promising academic career in a satisfying specialty, economic history—everything seemed settled. Toward the end of the breakdown, however, everything changed. His intellectual curiosity veered sharply toward sociology, the sociology of religion, and he wrote *The Protestant Ethic and the Spirit of Capitalism*; this catalyzed a lifelong fascination with inner-worldly asceticism as a leading issue in comparative cultural studies; he assumed the position, in lonely dignity, of independent scholar; and he began a self-conscious search for his own individuality in association with his remarkable wife, in which he played out in relation to her issues of autonomy and separateness against those of dependency and attachment. Echoing Blake's words we might well say, sociologically, that "he became what he beheld," but from a psychological point of view, he beheld what he had become.

The work of three persons greatly facilitates advancing this point of view and greatly reduces what would otherwise have to be lengthy excursions into the many complex details of Weber's life and thought. The sociologist and Weber scholar Donald Levine has written a concise and rich essay on the remarkable intellectual and psychological parallels between Freud and Weber, and Arthur Mitzman, working as both a psychobiographer and historian of sociological ideas, has opened up and legitimated the use of psychological insights into the genesis and evolution of Weber's thought. Perhaps most important of all, the student of Weber's personality and work has a strong and for the most part unacknowledged ally in Marianne Weber. She not only wrote a long, detailed biography of her husband, but she also regularly employed depth-psychological concepts and sensibilities to enhance her portrait, although not without the ambivalence toward them which she shared with her husband. When I describe her aptitude for psychology, her unusual personality, and her stance toward her husband, it will come as no surprise to the reader that she gave most of her attention to issues of separateness, autonomy, and self-differentiation. I think there is no reason not to take her views seriously. After noting briefly the contributions of Levine and Mitzman, and guided by the cumulative sense of pattern evolved in preceding chapters, I begin as all analytic approaches do, in medias res, with the now-celebrated breakdown, and reflect first backward into Weber's relation to the two key figures in his entire life and then forward into his self-healing in Rome, the writing of *The Protestant Ethic,* and the place which its key ideas occupied in the sweep of his later work as a whole.

Levine (1984) has noted "striking similarities" between Freud and Weber with regard to their personalities, temperaments, the disciplines they founded, and their emotional crises: *personality* (both were born in Central Europe at roughly the same time—Freud in Moravia in 1856, Weber in Thuringia in 1864; both were highly successful university students; both did tours of military duty; both lived as young adults in their parents' homes—Freud until the age of twenty-seven, Weber until the age of twenty-nine; each married, near their thirtieth birthdays, stable and devoted wives); *temperament* (both were serious and stern but also had a lively sense of humor; both enjoyed irony and self-deriding wit; both were distant in personal relationships; both were marginal to institutions; both decried sentimentality and scorned illusions; both were powerfully attracted to interpretations of religion; both possessed a gigantic capacity for work); and *their disciplines* (both psychoanalysis and sociology achieved institutionalization in the period 1895–1915; both produced decisively germinal works on modern society; both led to movements which evoked storms of opposition; both movements claimed an emancipatory potential in the form of enhanced subjective freedom; and both developed only in open, Western societies, each being suppressed by the Nazis and Soviets).

Both men also suffered intense and life-altering emotional crises following the deaths of their fathers, and Mitzman's explanation (1970) of Weber's life centers on this crisis. In the summer of 1897, at the age of thirty-three, Weber was married, financially independent of his parents, and had moved away in order to take up a promising academic position at Heidelberg. By this time the fundamental affective gestalts of his family of origin, as Mitzman understands these, had settled firmly into place. Two central conflicts made up the family's dynamics, the father-mother relation and the father-son relation. Max Weber, Sr., had long since taken up an amiable, comfortable, and servile place in his city's bureaucracy. At home, however, like most men of his position at that time, he played the role of paterfamilias, arrogating to himself the right to control most of his family's activities, especially his wife's. Helene Weber in turn antagonized her husband in three ways. She was unable to enjoy sexual pleasure freely; she was deeply religious and devoted herself to encouraging similar sentiments in her children, especially her eldest son, Max; and she had, the year before, inherited a substantial sum of money, the income from which alone surpassed her husband's salary. He could do nothing about his sexual frustrations, but he openly disparaged her religious activities and insisted upon detailed explanations for her every financial need, including even daily expenditures. Helene Weber accepted all this but turned from him to her children and their religious nurturance as the sole source of satisfaction in her life.

The second, father-son, axis was equally impoverished. Weber bitterly resented his long financial dependence on his family, but he also despised his father's easy compliance with the values of the "power state," and he resented his father's impingements on his mother's autonomy. She shared her misery with her son and he listened attentively. But he also distanced himself unequivocally from her religious solicitations, thereby reluctantly taking up his father's attitude toward his mother in this respect. So the basic family dynamics consisted of a double set of relationships characterized by suppressed, bitter resentments and an overall sense of desperation and sadness.

In 1897, married, financially independent, professionally successful, and in his own house, Weber believed that he had relegated all of this to the past. But in a single, dramatic episode he brought back to the surface this basic family dynamic. Although it was his intention to lay the past to rest once and for all, he in fact actually created his future, and it was not at all the one he had planned.

Helene Weber needed to maintain periodic contact with her children, and in the early summer she planned a visit to Max and Marianne, without her husband. He exercised his prerogatives and insisted on accompanying her. Weber and his wife objected in angry letters, but to no avail. The two parents arrived together. Then, in an uncharacteristic display of filial indignation Weber made his views on the matter known to his father and insisted that he accept them. The father rejected them. Weber ordered him out of his house, and he left. Helene retreated into religiously inspired guilt, remorse, and hope, while her husband simply washed his hands of the affair and went on a trip with a friend. Although in good health at the time, he died suddenly, still in the midst of his journey. The funeral was held in August. Weber did not mourn his father's death, either at the funeral or later in life.

Toward the end of the summer the breakdown began. Marianne described its onset: "irritable and annoyed at minor things—noises

are a torment—nervous exhaustion—feverish and apprehensive—
strong feeling of tension—weeping—sits paralysed for hours, apa-
thizing" (Marianne Weber, 1926, pp. 234–39). But the upshot was
relatively simple: "Everything was too much for him; he could not
read, write, talk, walk, or sleep without torment" (p. 242). Weber
gradually withdrew from the social world into the constant, dedicated, and supportive presence of his wife, where he was to remain for
several years. The worst time was July 1899, when he entered a
sanitorium for a few weeks, the only time he was separated from
Marianne. Gradually and bit by bit there were improvements and he
was able to travel, but only with Marianne. She dated her husband's
recovery to the fall of 1901, during one of a series of Rome visits, but it
was not until the summer of 1903 that he was really able to be with
others, to work, and, at one and the same time, to take care of himself
and to enjoy the capacity to be alone.

Weber's life easily lends itself to psychobiographical study, owing
largely to Marianne Weber's psychological approach to it. Drinking
deeply at the well of Freud's structural psychology, but from Ernest
Jones's study of *Hamlet* and from ego psychology as well, Mitzman
(1970) attempted to reconstruct Weber's inner world along psychoanalytical lines. For years, he thinks, Weber had suppressed and
repressed murderous, patricidal aggressive wishes directed against
his father ("flames of mutiny"), who embodied the personal and political attitudes which he had come to despise, attitudes which he
also came to fear most of all in himself (his father was "the one
German politician whose disposition was etched more vividly in his
memory than any other" [pp. 157–58]). But he also longed for his
mother. Established in his own house, Weber "ordered his father out
of his house to permit his mother and himself the undisturbed enjoyment of one another's company" (p. 152). Noting Freud's observations of the melancholiac in "Mourning and Melancholia"—the
severe self-reproaches, sleeplessness, and general retreat from all the
demands of life—Mitzman concluded that Weber resolved his intense ambivalence toward his father (hatred of him but inability to
accept the loss of his love) by unconsciously constructing within his
own mind a harsh and punishing superego ("the secretion of his father's spirit in his own ego" [p. 159]). Weber's plight was further
exacerbated from the side of his mother, Mitzman thinks, for his ego
was also mutilated "by a superego that still incarnated his mother's
standards of discipline and independence" (p. 159). As further evidence of the fundamentally psychosexual character of Weber's illness, as well of his lifelong intrapsychic conflicts, Mitzman cites

Weber's later acknowledgment that his inability to sleep during the breakdown stemmed from fear of nocturnal emissions (p. 285); his frantic, highly moralistic rejection of psychoanalytic ideas (he feared that they legitimated "free love"); and an extramarital relationship, which he finally had toward the close of his life. Capable at last of tolerating sexual gratification, Weber's ambivalence toward "inner-worldly asceticism" softened, and in middle age he became more interested in eroticism and mysticism.

In his works, Mitzman thinks, Weber universalized his personal dilemma and developed profound insights into social and historical processes. In *The Protestant Ethic* he "was able to gouge out of his superego" its maternal, religious components and to "examine critically the commandment of unceasing labor" (p. 173), the capitalistic spirit. In doing so he performed through intellectual work an act of self-liberation. In his political writings Weber entered into the cultural arena in yet another way and challenged "the mortal hostility of the bourgeois superego for libidinal impulse—the psychological underpinning of the Victorian ethic of transcendence" (p. 304). In all this, Mitzman concludes, Weber sought a vitalistic breakthrough "to all those underground regions of the self which Victorian culture had kept in chains and which were now, in a true return of the repressed, rising painfully to the surface of consciousness—through the Freudian revolution" (p. 251).

Let us look more closely at the "underground regions of the self" which Mitzman says Weber sought but could never engage. I think that Weber's most profound struggle took place precisely in this region but that Mitzman only dimly recognized this, if at all. His loyalty to Freud's metapsychological formulations deflects his attention entirely from Weber's struggle with his attachment to his mother, and from this point on my reading of Weber's inner conflicts breaks away from Mitzman's. I have shown how, in Freud's case, the metapsychology framed his structural psychology and drive theory (the oedipal resolution of the sexual and aggressive instincts) and served to organize his growing political and interpsychical isolation, and also how these served to obscure, in an epoch-specific way, his deeper, unconscious needs for attachment and a maternal presence. The model of the mind as a place-thing in which drive-energy is sent out into objects and then ricochets back into the psyche virtually ablates issues of attachment. This view of the mind's dynamics appears with special clarity in a crucial passage in Freud's paper on melancholia, and this conception is central to Mitzman's account of Weber's breakdown. There Freud notes, but only to pass over, the arousal of the subjective need to mourn and its multiple causes: "In melancholia, the occasions which give rise to the illness extend . . . beyond . . . loss by death, and include all the situations of being slighted, neglected or disappointed" (Freud 1917a, p. 251). Mitzman's commentary on Freud's theory of mourning reads: "The reason for identification, according to Freud, is the inability to accept the loss of the former love object" (p. 159). Loss refers, in Mitzman's mind, to the death of Weber's father. However, as long as one continues to think about a mental apparatus discharging drives and about loss as physical death, one can safely ignore issues of esteem (being slighted, neglected, or disappointed) and of mourning as a subjective response to the loss of objects and their capacity to confer esteem, even though the object has not physically died. This problem of attachment and loss was very strong in Weber's case, and it centered on his mother and her pre-oedipal significance even more intensely than it did on his father and his oedipal significance. Furthermore, the psychology of this attachment explains Weber's well-known "Promethian defiance" (Mitzman 1970, p. 15) and "sovereign self-sufficiency" (Marianne Weber 1926, p. 236), for the emotional intensity behind such personality traits or virtues is mobilized in order to defend against the painful process of mourning. All this becomes clear when we examine the circumstances of the famous breakdown in the light of issues of self and of attachment, alongside the better-known classical (oedipal and metapsychological) formulations.

In his home in 1897 Weber announced that "We demand that Mama should have the right to visit us alone quietly for four or five weeks each year at a time that is convenient for her. As long as this is not done, any family relationships with Papa is meaningless to us and its outward maintenance has no value for us" (Marianne Weber 1926, p. 231). Mitzman read this to mean that Weber primarily sought undisturbed and exclusive oedipal enjoyment of his mother's company (1970, p. 152). Beneath the obvious oedipal coloration of this challenge lay a deeper layer of attachment, conveyed by the words, "us," "we," and "family relationship." The accent of Weber's statement (we have only Marianne Weber's word for it—her husband said "we" and not "I") is on the rearousal of the archaic sociality of his early development. In addition to his struggle with his father, Weber also had an intense, unresolved, and deeply ambivalent psychological merger with his mother, and his unconscious agenda at this time was that of maintaining circumstances which would facilitate self-cohesion, self-differentiation, self-realization, and individuation. Weber's inability to mourn his father's death was linked to this far more primitive agenda. The psychoanalysts Alexander and Margareta Mitscherlich have pointed out in their study of postwar Germans' inability to mourn Hitler's death (1967) that one mourns for what was ugly and hated, even as one mourns for what was beautiful and beloved. Furthermore, at the time of Weber's marriage the deeply religious Helene passed her supportive and nurturant role on to the more psychological and more nurturant Marianne, and the two women together played a crucial part in Weber's self-healing. Most of all, Mitzman entirely ignores Weber's recovery, but a great man's recovery should tell us as much about his life as his "breakdown"—maybe even more.

Much of this is borne out when one reflects backward from the breakdown to Weber's childhood relationship to his mother and understands her religiousness psychologically, for her religious faith was the key to her personality and therefore also the key to her dealings with her son. (In a moment I will reflect forward into the breakdown itself and its role in shaping Weber's creative work.) Marianne said that Helene possessed a "rich and difficult" emotionality and mastered life through "religious resources, ethical passion and selfless kindness" (1926, p. 17). She had an "iron will" and equated "egotism" with the devil himself. She was devoted to her children and to "community consciousness." The "physical aspect of marriage" was "a heavy sacrifice." Marianne Weber repeatedly emphasized Helene's selflessness, dedication, orientation to community, and fear of sexuality throughout her biography. Helene Weber was a woman for whom narcissistic issues, such as grandiosity, self-absorption, and devotion to others, were central, and she understood sexual pleasure as a form of self-indulgence. These features and her exceedingly sharp sense of self were organized entirely by a relationship to the divine which, experienced as the inner voice of her conscience or her ego-ideal, constantly urged her to transform her narcissism (her "selfishness") into devoted object love (her "selflessness"). In this way her religiousness performed two essential psychological functions for her. It conferred upon her empathic access into her inner world, that is, psychological depth, which was wholly lacking in her husband, and it propelled her to care of others. On the other hand, it regularly left her prey to times of shame, guilt, yearning, sadness, and despair whenever she felt unloved by her ego-ideal, and, because her inner world was accessible to her only through the symbolic objectifications of religious symbols, she had to transcend her unconscious narcissistic propensities through acts of will, which she felt God called for, rather than through the work of the imagination. Nor could she become empathic to others if they did not share her religious view of the world, for to do so would have seriously jeopardized and fragmented her self-organization. As a Protestant woman of her time, issues of autonomy and their opposites, attachment and dependence, were, along with sexual pleasures, central for her.

These features of Helene Weber's personality shaped her son's development in a crucial way, and two important episodes in his early life show how that happened. When he was two-and-one-half, Weber's mother and grandmother "were astonished at the early self-sufficiency and playful absorption of the little boy, who did not seem to need anyone." An aunt astutely observed that "He usually plays by himself, but his playthings . . . keep him company in a way that I have seen with no other child. . . . He will play . . . for hours . . ." (pp. 31–33). Mother, grandmother, and aunt all expected far greater dependency and attachment in the little boy, and it was the absence of these that "astonished" them. Weber also loved to play with trains. At the age of four he saw a derailed locomotive lying in a ditch. Some thirty years later he still remembered that sight as "the first 'jolting' experience of my life . . . my first experience of the transitoriness of the great and beautiful on this earth" (p. 32). As a child Weber had "intuitively" come to know about the extremely efficacious role of play and illusion in mitigating separation from early maternal objects; as an adult he could speak of these in an ego-syntonic way as the experience of transience and the ability to mourn.

The second important episode occurred at the time of his confirmation, at fifteen. Weber was a bookish (history and classics were his main interests at the time), intellectually precocious, and introverted boy who also absorbed with pleasure the liberal German politics of his nonreligious father's home. His mother tried to evoke in him "her own religious excitement . . . the world in which she was at home" (p. 57). She even enlisted the services of one of her son's older friends to influence him in adopting her religious feelings. Weber could not accept these solicitations, which centered upon the question of an afterlife, but he could not openly reject them, either. In this case he chose the path of mournful and empty-hearted compliance. As he lamely explained to his older friend, "I really believe that a man who could honestly say he had absolutely no conviction or hope of a hereafter must be an extremely unhappy creature. To wander into life without any hope and in the belief that every step only brings one

closer to utter disintegration, a dissolution that ends existence forever, must truly be a terrible feeling, and deprive a man of all hope of
life." Then he further softened his thoughts, out of respect for his
friend, but especially for his mother: "I believe it is in my nature that
I seldom share my feelings with others . . . I am a bad companion
too" (p. 58). Marianne said that, in the face of these objections,
Weber's mother "had to realize painfully that the fifteen-year-old boy
did not experience any deeper religious excitement and, above all,
that he resisted her maternal influence" (p. 57). Consciously, on the
surface, the issue was the cognitive or epistemic validity of religious
ideals and, in particular, of the belief in immortality, but on a depth-
psychological level Helene Weber had also tried to reforge a primitive, narcissistic bond with her son in the only way she knew how,
and she failed. She responded to his rebuff with guilt. Referring to this
incident a year later, she spoke of "the feeling that I am incapable of
fulfilling and being what I demand of myself. This is especially difficult for me now in the face of my son Max" (p. 39). In Weber's
unconscious mind—and in his mother's—a maternal presence and
the consolations of religion seem to have been fused.

Weber's wife was in important ways a replica of his mother, and
their relationship should be seen in this light. When they married,
Marianne had been living virtually as an adopted daughter in the
Weber, Sr., household. Like her new mother, whom she revered,
Marianne was religious, community minded, maternal, nurturant,
and devoted to others—she was "selfless." She had already suffered a
good deal (there were many illnesses in her earlier family circle,
mostly mental) and she had been shunted about a lot. But she was less
religious, her sense of self was more separate and bounded, and she
was consequently more independent. And she wanted a career for
herself, an unprecedented aspiration for a young woman at this time.
Most important of all for him, she was deeply concerned with her
husband's individuality, and the twin themes of constant devotion
and the realization of individuality are the key to her conception of
her husband's life and of her relationship to him. Weber reciprocated
with genuine concern for her individuality. Therefore, Marianne
played a pivotal role, serving as a kind of holding environment in her
husband's transition from his unconscious, embedded, and paralyz-
ing attachment-loss matrix with his mother to his conscious, adult
self-organization and autonomy. This is seen with special clarity in
his recovery from his illness, which gave shape not only to his adult
life but also to all his originative intellectual achievements.

At the worst time, in the sanatorium, Weber came to the realization that his illness would be "a long siege." But it also forced upon him a greater intensity of introspection and self-definition than he had ever known before. He wrote to his wife: "Such an illness has reopened (for me) the purely human side of living, which Mama always somewhat missed in me. . . . I could say, 'An icy hand has let go of me.' . . . I want, above all, to live a full and personal life with my *Kindele* [baby] . . . earlier I did not even *know how* to live as close together with someone as I have lived with you these past years" (p. 236). At first Marianne wondered whether what she called her husband's "sovereign self-sufficiency" had rendered her superfluous, but she soon realized that he "needed her constant care and presence" (p. 236). Despite his profound psychological needs and vulnerability, and in the midst of his despair, Weber was still pleased that his wife "was living a life of her own" and encouraged her to finish her first book and even "attend a woman's convention" (p. 243). His mother could not understand his "weak will" and recommended "some act of self-transcendence" (p. 240). But the psychologically astute Marianne understood this theological gesture: "Her own heroic will, constantly and mercilessly exerted, had mastered all psychological and physical exertions. Surely her son could do the same" (p. 239). One sees here even more clearly than Weber was able to make it in his book the key unconscious psychological dynamic which implicitly informed his conception of the Protestant ethic. Will power, the voluntary capacity to exercise perfect control over all deep emotionality, was the answer to the Protestant's preoccupation with his favorite doctrine, the bondage of the will. One also sees here the enormous price Weber paid for his insight into it. I can find nothing untoward in Helene's religious orientation; it was common enough at the time.

When Weber recovered enough to travel, he was still far from well. In 1901 the couple made several visits to Rome, the longest during the fall and winter (the very same time of Freud's initial visit to Rome which followed the completion of his self-analysis, when he first became fascinated with the statue of Moses). There healing finally began. He needed, it seems, a period of total dependence. For some time Max and Marianne "lived in complete solitude." Then Weber began "to do a little reading." His mother visited for several weeks, "the most beautiful she ever spent with her children . . . her unselfish love was the dearest part of their homeland" (p. 251). During this visit Weber "began to read a real book again." One volume followed another. The two women "secretly nudged each other: 'Look, he's reading!'" (p. 251). And a bit later: "He even dared to talk" (p.

252). The couple left Rome at Easter 1902. Sufficient psychological structure had been recovered and built up. This long visit to Rome "really marked the beginning" of his recovery, "after three and a half years of illness" (p. 251). Weber had become Weber. And so the question is, How?

In attempting to explain her husband's recovery, Marianne emphasized the confluence of several factors. She spoke of art, Rome, and land: "Weber wanted to submerge his illness and his earthbound self in a sea of powerful impressions" (p. 247). "As he surrendered to this radiant splendor, his equilibrium was restored" (p. 249). "He owed to the sun and to the magnificence of the Eternal City hours impregnated with the past, which had for almost a year made his meager present worth living for. He parted from the south as from a second homeland" (p. 255). Of this stay in Rome Weber himself said, "A historical imagination is the main thing" (p. 257). It is not possible to know to what extent the illness remitted spontaneously. But a constant and devoted maternal presence was surely important. And then there is the illness itself, which, when viewed analytically, was an attempt at self-cure. In short: the supportive, soothing, and unconscious influence of natural, artistic, and maternal objects over a long period of time, that duration determined entirely by "the patient" (sufferer) himself. Winnicott (1960) has observed that some patients whose central pathology is an excessively built-up ego (oversocialized into a too-heavy sense of social role or "false self") need a period of total dependency toward the end of treatment, in order that the "true self," masked but also protected by the false self, can dare to come into existence.

Let us press forward still further, to the work itself. Weber began his book on Protestantism in 1903, coincidental with the beginning of his recovery, and he wrote the crucial methodological essay on the ideal-type in 1904. Marianne noted an intimate relation between *The Protestant Ethic* and her husband's inner life: it was "connected with the deepest roots of his personality and in an undefinable way bears its stamp" (p. 335). But she could not fathom exactly how her husband's personality had stamped itself on his book. As he began to separate and individuate, unconsciously and only in bits and pieces, from the conflict-laden and ambivalent bond to his mother, Weber also began to mourn that attachment and as a result build some psychological structure. He gradually broke up some of his massive internalizations and identifications in relation to her. He always thought he had acquired his driven, compulsive work habits (his false self) from her, and his illness had insisted that he "suddenly" give these up. Nature cried out "Enough!" to spirit. He was able to transform portions of this unconscious psychological agenda by consciously engaging in an analysis of a particular subject matter which would re-present it in forms tolerable to the ego. Without saying why, and probably without knowing why, he turned away from economic history and into the study of Protestantism, the religious tradition or common culture in which he had been formed and which had so decisively shaped his mother's personality and her relationship to him. There he saw historical processes which he chose to call disenchantment and rationalization, in which the spontaneity and immediacy (magic) of communal, religious ritual gave way to a detached inner-worldly asceticism and its psychological substrate, loneliness. That detachment and loneliness permitted the Protestant to forge—but not without the anxiety of loss—a new, creative relationship to the material and economic orders of society.

Weber's theoretical actions were also a further carrying forward of the process of structure building. By detaching himself somewhat from an intimate personal bond and from the traditional values mediated by that bond (the two were one), he had become sufficiently differentiated to see some of the things that were "really there" in his traditions. In one sense he was of course himself in the grip of the forces he was describing ("the icy hand"). But as he separated, he was able to transform some of these forces into a generative matrix within which he could then realize and give expression to his brilliance and genius and form his new vision of the past (the "icy hand has let go of me"). Freud's theory of thinking, although rudimentary, has a certain compelling quality about it and illumines further Weber's intellectual struggle. All genuine thought about the real world, Freud said, can take place only in the wake of the renunciation of emotional gratifications and object loss, which fosters an unavoidable and extremely painful sense of separateness. Whether they are physicists, psychologists, or sociologists, scientists do their best work in moments of struggle in which what Winnicott (1958) called "the capacity to be alone" plays an important part.

This view is borne out further by the unusually intense emotional tone of Weber's book. It is drenched in bitterness, irony and disappointment. Consider these references to the Protestant personality and his ethical ideas: "magnificent consistency . . . colorless deist . . . inner loneliness . . . a renunciation, a departure from an age of full and beautiful humanity . . . fate decreed, the cloak should become an iron cage . . . duty . . . prowls about in our lives like the ghost of dead religious beliefs. . . ." And of course: "Specialists without spirit, sensualists without heart, this nullity. . . ." These are not scholarly flourishes. Weber said he was not religiously "musical," but he was not literarily musical, either. At the center of this melancholy vision was the Protestant's historically shaped subjective-psychological state of loneliness or inner-worldly asceticism. This state characterized not only the ideal-typical Protestant but also the great sociologist who described it, but with one crucial difference. Unlike the Protestant, Weber was free enough to "see through" the surface of ideas and ideals which embodied the religious ethic and glimpse the real historical trends or "forces" which had shaped it. But like his Protestant forbears, Weber too split off the observing ego from its depth-psychological matrix, the self, and its anchorage in the commonalities of religious belonging in order to see clearly what he was looking at.

As one progresses through the works which followed the book on Protestantism, their author draws his reader back again and again into this, his central preoccupation. That is especially so in the case of Weber's sociology of culture and religion. They form the core of his system, insofar as he had one, and he did not really have one. In this sense his studies of religion are elaborate compare-and-contrast exercises around the idea of inner-worldly asceticism and its Protestant and biblical prototypes. In Judaism we see parallels, especially in the lives of the prophets, whom Weber admired greatly. This is quite understandable, for they appeared to him as magnificent, monumental, and highly individualized figures with astounding renunciatory capabilities. On the other hand, India and China—and of course Catholicism as well—fascinated Weber precisely because these traditions lacked an inner-worldly ascetic and renunciatory ethic and emphasized instead the gratification which communal and mystical beliefs and practices confer.

At the end of his life, at the age of fifty-five, one year before he was to die, Weber felt obliged to restate with even more grim clarity the methodological key to sociological theory, the idea of a value-free science of society and of the past, in his lecture "Science as a Vocation" (1919). Again he clothed this seminal idea in the rhetoric of bitterness and disappointment, which suggests that an unconscious struggle to mourn was at work in the self-conscious, rational formulations. But the relationships between the two were subtle and complex and far more intimate than Weber could say. The idea of a value-free science evolved out of—was actually brought into existence by—the precipitous and all-to-rapid unconscious experience of loss of both genetic and cultural objects to which he had been attached.

Weber began by driving a wedge between religion and meaning, on the one hand, and science and value-free sociology, on the other. Separating the two, he said, were the historical forces of disenchantment, rationalization, and intellectualization. He described science as the "link and motive force" to disenchantment: "There are no mysterious and uncalculable forces that come into play" in the work of the sociologist, because the world is disenchanted, "and so one need no longer have recourse to magical means. . . ." The rules of logic and method and "technical means and calculations perform the service" (p. 139). Therefore the historical and cultural sciences (for example, sociology, history, economics, and political science) shared the ethos of the physical sciences, and on the basis of this affinity their task was "to determine . . . the internal structure of cultural values." But it was not their task either to advocate or to discredit the cultural values whose inner structure they discerned (p. 146). It was in exactly this sense that social science is "value free."

Weber linked religion, in contrast to social science, to an open and fervent embrace of value and meaning and to a passionate commitment to "the cultural community" which preferred such value and meaning. But Weber did not accept the facile, theological strategy which claimed at that time—and still claims today—that the idea of "value free" was "really" just another value and therefore was itself an implicit religious affirmation. In such a view science is reduced "upward" into the theological sphere. Such a view would have meant the resacralizing of all feeling and thought, a virtual "reenchantment" of the world. Weber openly admitted that science did of course have its own presuppositions, but these were minimal and in any case not religious. Religion on the other hand was unconditional devotion "to revelation, faith, holy states and possession by the sphere of the holy," whereas science eschewed the unconditional or the extraordinary because it was conditional or ordinary. So he concluded that there was an "unbridgeable tension" between the two. That bridge could only be crossed by "yearning" and "return." In the face of this breach or break, it was best, he said, to go forward in "the dignity of purely human and communal relations" (p. 155).

As Weber once again worked through and set forth his key ideas for his audience, he chose not to suppress the scorn which he felt for those of his academic colleagues who continued to seek some sort of religious consolation in and under the forms of intellectual work. He referred to his opponents in the academy as people "who cannot bear the fate of the times like a man" (p. 155) (which I think can read to mean, "who cannot bear to be independent of a woman"). With mocking and inadvertent psychoanalytic precision he called them "big children." They were "football masters in the vital problems of life" (p. 150). Building upon this latent feminine motif, he noted further that for them "the arms of the old churches are opened widely and compassionately. . . . After all, they do not make it hard" (p. 155). But then, in the final moments of his address, he completely reversed his field, mastered his contempt, set aside his scorn, and quietly stated his own view with courage and dignity. He at least would not make "an intellectual sacrifice in favor of an unconditional religious devotion." In place of that he would obey the "plain duty of intellectual integrity" which required "the courage to clarify one's own ultimate standpoint." In so doing he resisted the temptation of a "religious return" so characteristic of "the many who today tarry for new prophets and saviors." He concluded that "nothing is gained by yearning and tarrying alone, and we shall act differently" (p. 156).

Weber did act differently, but he also did tarry and did yearn, and both were inseparable in his mind from the terrible questions of meaning and dying. In his lecture he expressed how much he himself yearned for the biblical figure of Abraham, who "died 'old and satiated with life' because he stood in the organic cycle of life . . . his life, in terms of its meaning and on the eve of his days, had given him what life had to offer" (p. 140). The biblical figure of Abraham had come to symbolize for Weber an ideal of life from which disenchantment and rationalization had separated him, for these historical processes placed him and his fellow members of the academy "in the midst of a continuous enrichment of culture by ideas, knowledge and problems" (p. 140). For one who is so placed, death comes to be understood as "a meaningless occurrence" and even "civilized life as such is meaningless" (p. 140).

Weber also yearned for the image of the world captured by what he called "the Tolstoyan art." For him the works and religious faith of Tolstoy posed the issue exactly. In Tolstoy's art, Weber asserted, the accent was always upon "true being," "true art," "true happiness," "true God"—but alas, all these had become "illusions" (p. 143). Although there is no evidence that he did or did not read *The Death of Ivan Ilych*, it is no mere guess to surmise that Tolstoy's famous tale captured and bodied forth precisely what Weber felt the historical process of disenchantment had denied to him. Although Ivan Ilych arrogantly and vainly closes himself off from all spontaneous enjoyment of children, wife, friends, community, and faith, he nevertheless dies a meaningful death—and therefore he lived a meaningful life—by coming to appreciate the spontaneous and total human connection with the whole in the mediating presence of the peasant, Gerasim, who transmits this appreciation because he, too, like Abraham, "stood in the organic cycle of life." For Weber "organic cycle" meant "meaning," but meaning meant the inclusion of one's life essence in the transgenerative whole of a communal order. But such meaning in turn further derived, I think, from an unconscious immersion—that is, from an unconscious sense of being a part of, and not of being apart from—the intimate generational cycle of a common culture.

Let us summarize the central intellectual predicament which Weber evolved in his essay by representing it schematically. It consists of two opposing realities structured by the age-old conflict between religion and science. The conflict lines up into two clusters of ideas:

Religion ⟶		*Science*
excited commitment	D	value-free Archimedean point
	I	of view
	S	
surrender to community,	E	individual activity and
brotherhood, standing in the	N	personal dignity
organic cycle of life	C	
	H	
	A	
belief—sphere of the holy	N	thought
	T	
eternal life, meaning	M	death, meaninglessness
	E	
theology	N	sociology
	T	
the past ⟶		the present and the future

Weber said that the historical processes of disenchantment, rationalization, and intellectualization forced this dichotomy into existence and confronted him and those who had the courage to entertain it with an irrevocable choice between the two sets of competing ideas and the two types of personal and social experiences which they embodied. But Weber could not fathom the depth-psychological processes which led from the first to the second.

Psychological reflection, however, suggests that further activity was taking place in Weber's mind beneath the conceptual surface, supporting his intellectual formulations in ways that he could not understand. I think Weber was actually evolving in his essay—and in all his works, but especially in *The Protestant Ethic*—a passage of transition or movement from the one to the other. That is to say, Weber's dichotomy includes a hidden intermediate or transitional activity which, when understood, in fact renders the two highly abstract opposites part of a more complete and inclusive whole. By accepting the renunciatory mandate of physical science, and by studying history and society in the light of it, Weber imposed upon himself a lifelong sense of disappointment. In the face of this disappointment he de-idealized the past, and that in turn stimulated a process of mourning which took place not only in himself but which he thought had also taken place in the past of those whom he studied. As his de-idealization progressed, Weber became a more separate person, more psychologically detached from the collectivities of his own past. In so doing, in effect he authorized the coming into awareness of a conception of the social world the recognition of which, he could only conclude, the religious visions of the past had virtually forestalled.

Weber's perception was of society as "natural." Science meant the capacity to entertain, within self-consciousness, the awareness of sociality as ordinary. On the other hand, religious convictions fostered the view that sociality is extraordinary, and it supports its view by subsuming the activity of thinking under the activity of believing. In the rhetoric of this essay, taking the view that society is extraordinary makes it an object of total unconscious participation. When sociality is viewed as ordinary, however, such unconscious participation breaks down, and that in turn permits to the viewer more psychological separateness, and that in turn yields the viewer up to natural, human curiosity about the social world. The capacity to view sociality as natural and ordinary is, therefore, a step in the direction of individuation. Once Weber achieved this perception toward the end of his illness, it became obvious or self-evident to him; from that point on he sought to help others share his vision with him, provided of course that they too possessed the necessary minimum of internal and external differentiation.

This achievement was purchased, however, at a price. In order to ensure the scientific integrity of the ego and its capacity to observe historical processes "objectively," Weber split that ego (both his own ego and the scientific ego which he commended to his colleagues in sociology) off from the deeper recesses of the self which were inextricably bound up in attachments to the communal, religious past. And so the past became hopelessly lost to him as a living reality. Under such conditions the past could be engaged experientially only by means of the activities of yearning and tarrying. But Weber could only acknowledge, with sad resignation, that "nothing is gained by yearning and tarrying." As he charted the forces of disenchantment, he de-idealized his own past, and he too became a lonely Protestant, even more lonely, for unlike the Protestant he had abandoned all the consolations of belief. But Weber had no choice. To use his own words, "fate decreed" that he had to split ego from self in order to think about society as a construction of human intentions. It was the first step. And here lies the psychological origin of his heroic, defiant "Promethean" self-sufficiency, for defiance is the refusal of someone or something one desires or needs in the service of what one thinks is a greater and more admirable ideal.

But the last word on Weber's achievement should go to Marianne, who understood her husband, Max, better than anyone else, and that included the import of his thought as well as the events in his life. Disenchantment brought the two together. At the end of her book she wrote: "On the basis of his sociological insights Weber calls our attention to the ideal forces that determine action . . . this illusion-free illumination of the various roots of existence may mean a new deprivation for many—for those whose capacity for devotion to a cause is fed by influences that arouse enthusiasm. Others, who do not need such aid, will find that 'the trained relentlessness of vision' for the world as it is will give them greater strength to endure it and be equal to its everyday manifestations" (p. 684).

Conclusion: The Sociological Mechanism Underlying Psychoanalytic Healing, When It Occurs, in the Analytic Situation

To close out this second essay, I propose to show how the striking parallels between the life and work of Freud and of Weber represent concisely my two major conclusions and also generate a fresh set of problems, which are the subject matter of part 3. Before doing that, however, it will be invaluable to make, if only briefly, several sociological observations about psychoanalytic healing, which is sometimes called "the clinical Freud," for it is the process of healing which brings together the social origins of psychoanalysis and the social origins of neurosis, the phenomenon to which Freud and his followers directed their energies. We have seen how social contexts shaped the "self-analysis" or "creative illness" in the lives of these men, and have noted how, in Durkheim's words, "abrupt transitions" and "painful crises" (here defined as social-structural change) subvert society's principal function, the creation of social bonds of attachment, thereby opening up intrapsychic conflict and the possibility of neurosis. And we have even noted how these self-analyses were also attempts at self-healing, and not only efforts to create a new theory of the person and of culture. But healing is what psychoanalytic ideas are all about, and the forces which bring such healing about, when it occurs, are just as social in character as the forces which generated the systematic theory.

This is actually much easier to do than it may at first seem, provided one makes generous use of the concepts which have already been developed, adding at the same time two new ones: role conflict and role hybridization. Psychoanalytic healing has depended upon the advent of the socially constructed role of the psychotherapist. The polarity which has arched over the previous discussions (the tension between a common culture and analytic access), itself an ideal-type, generates in turn two ideal-types of healing: shamanic and psychoanalytic. As Freud himself noted, all cultures use both, although in varying degrees. What Freud did not note was that in traditional and primitive cultures the role of the healer (shaman, priest, magus, etc.) is well established, whereas in modern cultures it is not. As I have emphasized, historical development and social-structural change in the West have worked against the cultural and symbolic organizations upon which traditional healers have depended. Increasing individualization, professionalization, and strain on the personal sector (introspection and fantasy activity) all called for a new approach to healing, but there was no social role in society to support it. Let us look back on all that has been said about the self-analysis and the movement in the light of role conflict, the key to understanding the new situation. The argument is: in his self-analysis, Freud forged a new role in society in order to formulate the conditions for a new kind of healing, and one of the purposes of the movement was to institutionalize that role.

Freud and his patients found themselves engaged in unprecedented introspective activity, which centered on the production and interpretation of fantasy processes. The social context of this activity was, however, medical practice, to which Freud had moved from a career in pure science. But neurology and psychiatry had rejected the psychical (and fantasy) as a legitimate issue in the causation of neurosis (hysteria), while the romantic philosophical and literary traditions, which Freud so often cited as sources which genuinely understood what he was trying to get at, had rejected psychiatry and science as too materialistic and insufficiently humanistic. If we look at this situation in terms of professional roles, it is clear that at this time and place there was no professional role which could structure the symbolic, fantasy-infused processes with which he was working or the kind of healing process he was trying to facilitate. In other words, Freud was in a position of role conflict, and it became incumbent upon him to resolve the situation by devising a new role. In the sociology of science, and in particular in the sociology of psychology, this process of resolution is called "role hybridization." While I think their definition of it is finally too narrow, the work of Ben-David and Collins (1966) provides an invaluable start:

> There are several ways in which new scientific role varieties arise. The present instance (the role of the psychologist) is a case of role-hybridization: the individual moving from one role to another, may be placed at least momentarily in a position of role conflict. This conflict can be resolved by giving up the attitudes and behaviors appropriate to the old role and adopting those of the new role; in this case, identification with the old reference group must be withdrawn. However, the individual may be unwilling to give up his identification with the old reference group, as it may carry higher status (intellectual as well as social) than his new group. In this case, he may attempt to resolve the conflict by innovating, i.e., fitting the methods and techniques of the old role to the materials of the new one, with the deliberate purpose of creating a new role.
>
> Examples of scientific roles created by this process are psychoanalysis, which was created by a man who moved from the prestigious profession of scientific research to the relatively lower-status occupation of German medical practice; Freud attempted to maintain his status by trying to raise medical practice into a form of scientific research, and as a result created psychoanalysis. Similarly, Pasteur gave rise to bacteriology by maintaining his theoretical perspectives after moving into research on wine fermentation, and elaborated his discovery into a new speciality. (Pp. 111–12)

Clearly, Freud did have a major role conflict between pure science (high prestige) and medical-psychiatric practice (low prestige). His attempts to hybridize these roles by applying the "science of his day" to the patient population of his day are yet another explanation of why he repeatedly insisted that psychoanalysis was a science. But neither of these roles was in itself sufficient to accomodate the materials of psychology, that is, fantasy processes and their vicissitudes. The extant social roles which have historically accommodated or "monitored" such fantasy processes—religious practitioners and artists—could not be adapted to the new situation, for their principal strategy was to code them into cultural symbols. The productions of Freud's patients had to be met more directly and with less cultural mediation than either religion or art could provide. So Freud actually "hybridized" four roles rather than two: low-prestige medical practice; high-prestige scientific research; the artist, who he said understood fantasy processes better than anyone else; and, probably, residues from the biblical prophetic tradition, for the prophets (and Moses, the lawgiver, as well) were figures of monumental renunciatory power: in psychoanalysis what "gets renounced" is of course the wishes and desires embodied in fantasy processes. These are best synthesized into the concept of "cultural worker," someone who does the "dirty work" or "dirty laundry" of an age. Erikson has spoken of Luther and Freud as such cultural workers, anguished and creative men who said aloud what everyone else in their time was afraid to think to himself. Freud mixed up and reorganized these roles and transformed them into the professional role of the psychoanalyst. Professionalization is, of course, a form of rationalization (Weber). There is much implicit sociological wisdom in the title of Erikson's seminal paper on the origins of psychoanalysis: "The First Psychoanalyst" (1964). These reflections allow us to link Freud's interpretive work with himself and his patients to the sociological mechanism of psychoanalytic healing, when it occurs.

The link is: the professional role of the psychoanalyst (and, more broadly speaking, of the psychotherapist who uses psychodynamic principles) brought into existence a place in the structures of society for what I call "analytic space," more often referred to as "the analytic situation." This space is inherently social, and without it psychological healing cannot take place. In it fantasy processes can be articulated, shared, discussed, worked over, and even, at times, interpreted—in short, made more conscious, but also more social. Let us now insert this peculiarly modern form of social space into the context of the two ideal-typical forms of healing, already mentioned, and historicize them. The concept of transference in turn links the two forms of healing, illuminating their differences but also their similarities. In this regard it is absolutely crucial to recognize—a point Freud made again and again—that transference is a completely normal and nonpathological phenomenon which occurs within and between all persons in all cultures. It is the psychological "glue" or "cement" of society.

In traditional cultures, the healer gradually draws the sufferer's personal identity and his or her psychological energies into a culturally constituted symbolic center by means of identification with the healer and the use of traditionally sanctioned sacred objects. In other words, the healer works with the transference in a centripetal way. For example, the Indian psychoanalyst Sudhir Kakar (1982) has described the way a Muslim shaman employs a "demonological idiom" for the purposes of healing: by explaining to the sufferer who comes to him how demons work, by showing how demons often make their appearances in dreams and fantasies, and by using devices such as amulets, holy water, and the like. Understandably, this shaman fiercely and proudly rejected Kakar's psychodynamic suggestions to him as "Western" and "scientific." Roman Catholicism has often been referred to as "our India" because its strong emphasis on a universal community, endless varieties of saints (the equivalent to mythological figures), and manifold sacramental objects contrasts sharply with the inner-worldly asceticism and antiritualistic or anti-imagistic thinking of Protestantism and Judaism. Largely through the sacrament of confession, but also through others, such as unction and especially the holy communion, the Catholic priest heals the guilt which separates the penitent from the holy community (the body of Christ) by drawing the penitent's personal identity and psychological energies back into community, reestablishing the broken social bond. So it is no surprise that, like the Indian shaman, Catholicism either rejects or is suspicious of psychoanalysis, for it does not need it. On the other hand, Protestantism, a religion in which the concept of the person is highly individualized, has created the pastoral counseling movement, which attempts to integrate theology and dynamic psychological principles. This is the way healing works in traditional cultures, where the healer's role is clearly defined and understood by both parties.

Like healing in traditional cultures, healing in modern (industrial and postindustrial) cultures also proceeds by means of a definite sociological mechanism, the role of the professional psychologist and psychoanalyst. Although this role works quite differently from its traditional counterpart, the differences are not as radical as Freud and his orthodox followers believed. In modern cultures the transference is managed centrifugally, not centripetally. That is, in the analytic space the psychotherapist "returns" the transference to the patient, in a variety of ways. Infantile and childhood identifications and inter-nalizations are objectified and shared through language and the symbolic medium of dreams and fantasies. These are constantly being broken down and resynthesized as treatment progresses. Great emphasis is placed on the patient's coming to own the products of his mental life, which makes for individualization rather than commu-nalization. This returning of the transference to the patient depends entirely upon the sociologically prior role of the modern healer and the analytic space which that role has institutionalized. For it is this role which permits such a "return" to take place.

This mechanism undergirds the healing process, regardless of which "school" of psychoanalysis is brought forward for considera-tion. Freud's own concept of treatment, which gave central place to insight, renunciation, and sublimation, is closest to the ideal-type of total autonomy from society and from the past. Ego psychology, which adds to these such auxiliary processes as neutralization, is not far behind—maybe even further ahead. When we turn to revisionist psychoanalysis, the situation shifts. Kohut's goal is the transforma-tion of narcissism: greater empathy, wisdom, object love, and a more generous sense of humor. The all-important "classical" goal of in-sight is far less important, for Kohut thinks that, by itself, insight does not heal. So this goal is more social than Freud's, although the "modern break," so to speak, with the common cultures of the past is still present in Kohut's distinction between a cure by understanding and a cure by love. Winnicott's work provides yet another variation. Therapy develops and modifies the true self while keeping the false self intact; the patient is enabled to participate in transitional ac-tivities—the creation of transitional objects, the capacity to dream deeply without a sense of threat, and (most important of all) the capacity to create meaning, which cannot be done without the help of cultural objects.

None of these processes could take place without the prior institu-tionalization of the role of the therapist and the (socially constructed) analytic space which authorizes them. Freud created this space for the first time in his relation to Fliess, where he cast himself in the role of patient and his friend and colleague in the role of doctor in order to understand himself better, first as a person but also as a physician in relation to his patients. However, in the self-analysis this space was not yet a genuinely social one; it had not yet been institutionalized. This is yet another way to think sociologically about the self-analysis and its inherently intersubjective character, which Freud tended to disregard or disavow.

It is also a fresh sociological way to think about the psychoanalytic movement. One of the tasks of the movement, it can now be said, was to resolve role conflict and accomplish a genuine role hybridization. Members sought to understand not only the question *What* is psychoanalysis? but also *Who* is a psychoanalyst in relation to other professional roles? The ambiguities which this question opens up account for much of the pluralism in the movement, which was so disturbing to its leaders. Was psychoanalysis a science (Freud and Jones)? Was it art (Rank)? Or was it a new form of hermeneutics, the correlation (through amplification and interpretation) of depth-psychological experience with the great, monumental symbolic structures of the ancient past (Jung)? In all these cases, the analyst did something radically new with the transference, in contrast to the work of traditional healers. Much of the acrimony which surrounded the question of lay analysis is easier to understand in the light of these considerations.

Finally, the sociological issue of role conflict extends beyond the self-analysis and the movement into the cultural texts. All the originative figures in the movement created a body of cultural texts, and in its present-day form members of the movement continue to do so. And so, of these texts it must be asked, What kind of books are they? To what type of studies can they most easily be likened? Clearly, they are forms of social, historical, and cultural criticism, but, just as clearly, they do not "fit in" with the better-known forms of social criticism, either past or present. These texts make much better sense when it is recognized that they are the productions of a group of men and women who identified with the kind of innovative social role which Freud and his followers created. As such, their task has been to treat both the objects of traditional cultures and those of their own as products of transference, a universal phenomenon, so as to relate these creative activities of culture as a whole to what takes place in the socially constituted space of the analytic situation—that is to say, to an ideal-type of healing experience new to Western culture. In this very important sense, the cultural texts are attempts to heal Western culture.

Let us return to Freud and Weber, for the similarities between them capture in a focal way the burden of this essay and also open up the problems which part 3 addresses.

Both Freud and Weber found themselves torn out of their respective communal past or religious heritages, which had become a torment and a prison for both and others like them, and each struggled creatively to transform that break or rupture by demarcating a space in the mind in which thought itself, in the form of natural, human curiosity, could move freely and unimprisoned, as it never had before. In Freud's case this space was the inner world of unconscious, subjective wishes, desires, and objects; in Weber's, it was the capacity to perceive the outer, social world of persons' intersubjective intentions, aims, and goals. Each man modeled his conception of this space after the natural science of his day, and the harsh schooling of this science forced upon each the renunciation of the gratifications and consolations which the religious past had offered. In Freud's case this schooling led to the formation of the metapsychology, in Weber's to the value-free stance of the scientific sociologist. In the course of creating their new epistemological spaces, both men also split the observing ego off from the deeper recesses of the self and its unconscious communal attachments. As a result of this splitting, the new constructed space became a new kind of prison. Although Weber used the term "iron cage" (translated better, probably, as "steel-hardened housing") to characterize the social and psychical legacy of the Protestant ethic, it is no facile gesture to say that he found himself in the iron cage of lonely defiance, in which his only company was the rational, mechanical-like forces of society and culture. In Freud's case the metapsychology became a prison, a walled-in area of isolation which protected him from the forbidding and punishing world of surrounding social circumstance. Furthermore, each man could make his discoveries only by actively and totally denying validity to the arena in which the other worked. In full flight from the politics and religion of his social world, Freud reduced history to the purified timeless, synchronic, seamless, and artfully simple unconscious oedipal struggle, while Weber fled the dreaded spirits of unconscious intrapsychic conflict through repression, denial, disavowal, splitting, and moralistic repudiations of psychoanalysis.

And finally, although both men sought to extricate themselves and the many others for whom each worked and wrote from the prisons of the past through their prodigious and creative labors, each man failed to recognize that the key or way out of the new prison he had subsequently created for himself (in Freud's case the metapsychology, in Weber's the value-free society) lay—ironically—in the prison of the other. But here the overworked metaphor of the prison or cage breaks down. There is only one key, and it unlocks both doors. The idea for which I am reaching is, of course, the surprising and paradoxical process of individuation, through which the inner world of psychoanalysis and the social world of Weberian sociology, in the very act of being drawn together, finally break apart and, in so doing, constitute the self, the intersubjective reality which undergirds "the psychological ego" and "the sociological actor" alike and which, for that reason, makes a reappropriation of the past possible.

That is the conviction which drives the following essay forward. It seeks to begin to sketch a fresh psychoanalytic theory of culture by situating it within the context of more recent social theory and contemporary cultural criticism. A corrolary of this basic conviction is a second, namely, that the psychology of the inner world, if properly recast, is a most powerful instrument for understanding the contemporary cultural situation and, even, for making that situation not only bearable but also enjoyable and meaningful. The red thread which runs through this project-in-the-making is easy to describe but difficult to grasp: yes, mourning does lead to resignation, but it is double-faced. It also opens out into the transitional space of social and cultural experience, within which individuation and the creation of meaning take place. The monument is the social complement to mourning, missing in Freud's formulations: it is to the structure of culture what the dream is to the structure of the mind. Mourning and monuments link the past to the present.

The elements of this argument, how it should proceed, the paths it must and must not follow, and the sources which best support it are explained in detail in the opening pages of part 3.

III Mourning, Individuation, and the Creation of Meaning in Today's Psychological Society

10   Framing the Argument with Freud's "Little Discourse" on Mourning and Monuments

> Ladies and Gentlemen. If I may be allowed to general-
> ize . . . I should like to formulate what we have learned so
> far as follows: *our patients suffer from reminiscences.*
> Their symptoms are residues and mnemic symbols of par-
> ticular (traumatic) experiences. We may perhaps obtain a
> deeper understanding of this kind of symbolism if we com-
> pare them with other mnemic symbols in other fields. The
> monuments and memorials with which large cities are
> adorned are also mnemic symbols. . . . These monuments,
> then, resemble hysterical symptoms in being mnemic sym-
> bols . . . every single hysteric and neurotic . . . remem-
> ber[s] painful experiences of the remote past, but they
> cannot get free of the past and for its sake they neglect what
> is real and immediate. Her [Anna O.'s] traumas . . . and . . .
> symptoms can only be regarded as mnemic signs of his [her
> father's] illness and death. Thus they correspond to a dis-
> play of mourning.
>
> Freud, *Five Lectures on Psychoanalysis*

Freud announced this striking parallel between mourning, an internal or inner psychological conflict, and monuments, rudimen-tary structures underlying many cultural activities, only moments after he had stepped forth onto the platform at Clark University in Worcester, Massachusetts, in September 1909, to address for the first time an American audience on the subject of his psychoanalysis. This striking remark was accompanied by an equally unusual con-flict within himself. Reflecting many years later on this moment, he described it as "the realization of some incredible day-dream: psy-choanalysis was no longer the product of delusion, it had become a valuable part of reality" (1925, p. 52). It is not difficult to understand Freud's disturbance of his reality sense (it was in fact somewhat

261

similar to the famous "disturbance of memory on the Acropolis" five years earlier). His large audience included not only his two rugged lieutenants, Ernest Jones, who had traveled south from Toronto for the occasion, and Carl Jung, who had made the ocean crossing with him; also present were G. Stanley Hall and William James, the founders of American psychology, and many eminent American physicians and neurologists, all curious to learn more about the new mode of mental healing. Freud clearly thought of his lectures as a once-in-a-lifetime opportunity to expand the psychoanalytic movement and, through that, to insert his ideas, which were so intimately linked to his own inner world, into contemporary culture at large—to memorialize and monumentalize both, as it were.

This "little discourse" on mourning and monuments was not, however, merely one more of Freud's many brilliant aperçus. Rather, when properly understood and correctly elaborated, it expresses in a rapid and condensed way the deepest and most central conceptual leitmotiv in his entire (psychoanalytic) theory of culture, and, as such it reflects all the richness as well as the poverty of that theory. For this reason it also forms the basis and starting point—but by no means the goal—of this third essay, which draws together the many loose ends and incomplete thoughts and arguments of the previous two (a kind of summary and integration) and then outlines, critiques, and reconstructs the beginnings of a psychoanalytic theory of culture in the context of the contemporary psychological society which, I will also suggest, must be understood as the "heir" to the psychoanalytic movement.

I propose accomplishing this task by pursuing three separate lines of thought, in extremely close proximity to each other. First, to deepen my previous analysis of the overarching central theme of Freud's theory of culture, his wholesale repudiation of the past, which I now call its central contradiction. Second, to draw this contradiction into several leading clusters of thought in contemporary society in order to demonstrate its continued relevance as well as to specify its extraordinary limitations. And third, to begin to sketch a revisionist psychological theory of culture which will be responsive to the criticism which I have made of it. To do all this I introduce a master concept, the process of individuation. But it is also one which is far from new. The previous two essays frequently alluded to it, but only in passing, nowhere explaining it in any detail. Historical allusions referred to Freud's heroic attempts to break away from the ideas, ideals, and values of the world of social circumstance in which he found himself embedded (in other words, how he and psychoanalysis "individuated" out of these), and methodological references associated it with that link or space which exists between a common culture and analytic access, although no effort was made to characterize that space. The process of individuation is one that Freud missed, although it was everywhere present in, within, and around his efforts to give birth to the psychoanalytic project. It is also a process which the social theory I have used has missed, although it is nonetheless everywhere present there as well. In the very act of putting forth their formidable sociological systems, Weber, Durkheim, and Marx found it necessary to separate themselves in a highly personal way from the very social contexts which they were then able to interpret anew. In doing so they brought about profound internal conflicts within themselves, and through that they became the highly individualized and virtually monumental figures which they have become for us.

Although it may at first seem so, individuation is not at all a facile third term which simply joins two grandiose abstractions (self and society), although its essential characteristic is very much one of mediation. The process of individuation acquires clarity and concreteness when it is understood in relation to the twin realities of mourning and monuments—the one psychological, the other social structural. It is the creative outcome of mourning, and the outcome of individuation is in turn the creation of meaning, a building up of new structures of appreciation born of loss. Despite their complexity, these intrapsychical processes are easier to understand than their most elemental sociological referent, which I suggest is the monument. But this is so only because neither Freud nor the psychoanalytic movement (both past and present) could or can generate a theory of culture commensurate in depth and complexity with its theory of the mind. Like the seemingly simple and obvious dream, which Freud elaborated into a systematic theory of mental and social life, the monument is also a rudimentary but fundamental structure which, although a social one, can lead to fresh and unexpected understandings of social reality, if it is carefully attended.

To clarify further the form and direction of this argument, I first dissolve the central contradiction in Freud's theory of culture into its three elemental components and then go on to explain why, in order both to comprehend fully and to begin to transform the psychoanalytic theory of culture, it is necessary to draw these ideas into clusters of thought created by such diverse men as Claude Lévi-Strauss, Paul Ricoeur, and Hans Blumenberg, for these clusters can at first glance only grate on the reader's sensibilities and seem not worth the effort, despite the contention that they provide the best materials for the task at hand. With this overview in mind I pick up where I left off on Freud's little discourse on mourning and monuments, explain his theory of the relationship between the two in detail, and then, building upon that, evolve a sketch or first approximation of the process of individuation. So let us begin: What is Freud's central contradiction, what are its elements, and how can reflection upon mourning, monuments, and individuation transform them?

Three Contradictions in Freud's Theory of Culture

Earlier discussions of Freud's life, movement, and thought strained to reach the most comprehensive understanding possible of his cultural texts. At the end of part 2 I cut beneath a variety of his particular—and, it will now seem, distracting—analyses (the ego-eroding forces of groups, the crushing severity of the cultural super-ego, religion as illusion) to reveal his powerful resistance to and repudiation of the past. This resistance was predicated upon his fear that the warm and affectionate embrace of the past would smother his newly born "analytical child," the introspecting, historically advancing, and individualizing ego of analytic access. And I pointed out that his theory of culture, like his theory of the mind, was born of mourning in the face of his personal, historical, and social-structural circumstances. So the central contradiction is: the ego can gather strength only by cutting itself away from the common cultures of its past, but as it does so, it becomes inceasingly unsupported by and deracinated from its social and historical surround. Homelessness is the price of self-possession. Alas, it is not humanly possible to possess oneself without retaining some active sense of having been "at home." This contradiction contains all the power and all the limits of Freud's vision of culture. Its power lies in the capacity Freud conferred on the ego to penetrate into the disguised latticework of cultural symbols so that persons could relate the uniqueness and specificity of their inner worlds to the mysterious, cryptic, and coded objects of culture, to what congeries of predecessors (to use Alfred Schutz's term) have considered worth idealizing—one might say, worth memorializing and monumentalizing. This "psychology of culture" put the ego in some sort of contact with the very minds of these predecessors. The limits of this vision lie, as I have said, in Freud's fear that the past would again, as it had always done before, colonize and depotentiate the ego, if permitted to do so. Stimulated by his discoveries into the psychodynamics of personal life and by their portentous bearing on collective behavior, Freud "saw through" the mechanisms of culture. What he saw there was oppression and deceit, and this vision convinced him to rid himself and his fellow man of the cunning of culture, to become free once and for all from the clenched hand of the past. So Freud created a problem for himself, and for us: he could find no way to relate the great cultural objects of the past to the ego in a manner that would confer depth and dignity upon both and that would also, at the same time, permit a certain and crucial amount of separateness or space to exist between them within which the ego could create transactions with the past without being engulfed by it and, in so doing, create meaning.

Social theory (especially the anthropology and sociology which I have used) has supported this contradiction by simply inverting it, limiting psychological self-understanding to the inner world of the individual ego and splitting that off from the moral, conscious collective representations of society and culture. Moreover, this contradiction is not merely academic; Freud's contradiction has become ours—or vice versa—in the sense that psychodynamic understandings of persons and life have become so firmly welded to the contemporary liberal-democratic ethos that the two have together created the psychological society of psychological man. Elites in our contemporary life make lavish use of psychodynamic ideas, principles, and assumptions, even when they do not recognize their sources—even when they do not recognize the psychological nature of their ideas at all—and these ideas have made any substantive appropriation (one should say, reappropriation) of the past acutely problematic. While this psychological orientation has recently been challenged (MacIntyre 1981; Bellah 1985), the solutions to it which have been offered are collectivistic and antipsychological, such that the splitting so characteristic of Freud's central contradiction nonetheless persists unabated; it is just that the other side of the split is idealized.

Three closely related themes which take the form of tensions compose Freud's central contradiction: that between an ancient, original humanity, understood globally and sweepingly as "primitivity," and what he took to be "civilized" or "modern"; that between the contemporary individualizing ego or self and its ever-widening and collectivizing sociohistorical surround; and that between religion and science, the so-called warfare between theology and science. In Freud's mind each was an instance of the others: he juxtaposed primitivity, society, and religion to modernity, the individual self, and science, and he depreciated the first set in order to enhance the second. The first cluster composed "the past," the second the advancing historical ego which psychoanalysis had discovered and which it augments. But the form of the texts, their underlying and unifying pattern, was, as I have pointed out, the activity of mourning for the past, understood as a series or latticework of monuments. Although all three tensions appear with varying emphases in all his cultural works, the first dominates in *Totem and Taboo* and *Moses and Monotheism*, the second in *Group Psychology and the Analysis of the Ego, Beyond the Pleasure Principle,* and *Civilization and Its Discontents*, and the third in *The Future of an Illusion*.[1]

To illumine and reformulate the tension between primitive and civilized, and especially Freud's specious yoking of "child," "savage," and "neurotic" and his narrow and uninformed analyses of totemism, I turn to the most brilliant and articulate defense of the idea of a common culture which I have been able to find in the cultural sciences: Claude Lévi-Strauss's theory of the origins of humanity and world culture in the social life of primitive peoples, his theory of totemism and of savage thought, and his view that these cultures are primarily synchronic or timeless because they fiercely resist the historicization of their lives. This also allows me to place in a sweeping, civilizational context the theme of time or transience, so central to Freud's thought about culture and so ignored by the regnant wisdom of the psychoanalytic community. To capture and evolve the "civilized" and "modern" side of the polarity, I turn to Lévi-Strauss's acrimonious assault on Jean-Paul Sartre, whose thought represents philosophically so well the plight of Freud's historical ego shorn of the past, of analytic access bereft of a common culture. In Sartre's existential phenomenology the ego, understood as a "project," is virtually "pure" diachrony. It is very important to add that the thought of both of these men is inconceivable without psychoanalysis. Lévi-Strauss avers that Freud's work was one of the three most important formative influences on him (the other two were Marxism and geology). Did he not say that totemism was a kind of hysteria? And Sartre has repeatedly tried to psychoanalyze himself and his literary-biographical subjects.

Into the unbridgeable gap which Lévi-Strauss and Sartre represent between the synchronic, timeless realm of primitive life and the modern diachronic ego I introduce the transitional idea of mourning over the lost past, for a heightened consciousness of the passage of time or temporalization of life is synonymous with the psychologization of life, Freud's central project. So Lévi-Strauss's constructions provide me with a cross-cultural, possibly even an ontological, frame within which to consider mourning and individuation as philosophical principles. Indeed, Lévi-Strauss is himself a great mourner for the lost collectivities of the past; his autobiography, *Tristes Tropiques,* displays throughout a strong elegiac tone. (The French words *"triste"* and *"tristesse"* are often translated as "mournful" and "mourning.") I hope to show that in this he is hardly alone.

The debate between Lévi-Strauss and Sartre, however, wholly ignores the impact of psychoanalysis upon contemporary social life, the way in which psychoanalytic ideas, of which the psychoanalytic movement was the first principal carrier, have filtered into the very fabric of the liberal, democratic, scientistic, and individualistic worldview of the emerging middle classes to constitute their central value of privacy. Philip Rieff was the first to see that Freud's thought was not only clinical but also moral and historical, and he thinks that psychoanalytic ideas have broken members of contemporary society away from their Western, Christian common culture (an "organizing symbolic"), creating a new social type ("psychological man"), who defines himself and his society by means of a kind of psychoanalytic ideology. Paul Ricoeur has, on the other hand, attempted to reverse or invert this trend by integrating the individualizing thrust of psychoanalysis "back" into an historical, Christian-communal conception of the person. It is no accident that Rieff and Ricoeur have together produced the two most powerful and learned interpretations of the import and significance of Freud's work for the understanding of contemporary culture, for they engage directly and massively Freud's second contradiction, situate it firmly in its Western, Christian context, and elaborate its implications and complexities in ways that Freud and his followers have not even been able to dream of.

Precisely because they capture so well the refractory character of the contemporary self (torn between breaking from the past and returning to it), thereby exacerbating the contradiction, these two "readings" of Freud also render more urgent the importance of mediating between them, which I call individuation, but, further, they provide important elements for a deeper understanding of this process, although that is not their intention. Rieff opens up the manifold ironies of a society built up on a psychological ideology which has as its principal purpose the breaking down of solidarity. Ricoeur's most significant contribution to Freud studies is his cogent point that the fundamental element in the analytic situation is fantasy and that it is not a behavioral-scientific process. It calls for interpretation as well as explanation, and mourning is central for the work of interpretation, as Ricoeur understood this.

With these ideas in mind, I propose that the psychological society is not at all composed, at its deepest ideological level, of psychological ideas but that it is really a "culture of fantasy" inaugurated by a further advance in industrialization which I call the technologizing of fantasy. Therefore, I argue that the interpretation of shared fantasy is a central element in any philosophy of contemporary culture and also another aspect of the work of individuation. Only the interpretation of the culture of fantasy can reappropriate the past, for it is this culture which both separates us from but also mediates it for us, if only our interpretive nets are so designed as to bring this about. Mourning is central to all this, but at this point I note only that neither Rieff nor Ricoeur is a stranger to mourning. Ricoeur was the first to point out the centrality of mourning for Freud's work as a whole, and mourning is a crucial stage in the phenomenologist's passage to a philosophy of reflection. And Rieff thinks that modern culture is, at bottom, nothing less than a kind of mourning for the Christian past. His writings on Freud, drenched as they are in irony, display bitterness, sadness, and not a little despair. But irony is the trope of mourning or, rather, of the inability to mourn.

Freud bequeathed to us a third contradiction, that between religion and science, and his constructions on this point were even more opaque and confused than his other two. To begin untying this knot, I reintroduce the historical process of secularization, whereby religion gradually gives way to science. Freud mistakenly thought that he could simply replace—after the fashion of a replaceable part—Western man's historic body of religious ideas with scientific, analytic ones. For a variety of complex reasons it could not occur to him that the relations between religion and science were easily as historical as they were cognitive, that they were more intimate, more subtle, more complex, more internal. He could not imagine that physical science, and especially his own science of psychoanalysis, evolved gradually and organically—that they precipitated out of—a theological matrix, through a series of renunciations of that matrix. My earlier discussions of Robert Merton's work on the linkage between Protestantism and physical science in seventeenth-century England began to advance this point of view, but these formulations need to be filled out and in some ways corrected.

Hans Blumenberg has illumined the complex historical relations between religion, science, and psychoanalysis in a way that no one

else has. He identifies the essence of Western science as "the enjoyment of theoretical curiosity" about the natural world, and he
associates it with the emergence of a new method, with the idea of
progress in knowledge, with a community of investigators dedicated
to this ideal, and—this is most interesting—with the disintegration
of the religious ideal of immortality. Blumenberg traces the origin of
this cluster of activities and ideals back to the debates in medieval
theology about the omnipotence of God (theological absolutism) and
to a disappointment with that ideal which led to renunciation and
resignation of it and from there to an epistemological recovery in the
form of curiosity about the natural world. Blumenberg thinks the
final consolidation of this sweeping process was brought about by
Ludwig Feuerbach, who was able to see the hidden relations between
the religious ideal of immortality and human curiosity: curiosity was
simply immortality which had finally come to understand itself. It
remained for Freud only to generalize or transfer this ideal (curiosity
about natural objects) to curiosity about psychological objects—that
is, objects in the inner world. In chapter 13 I draw selected central
features of Freud's life, work, movement, and cultural reflections
into this conception of secularization. And by now the reader will
understand why I find it necessary to add to the moral and epistemological actions of renunciation and resignation of the
omnipotence of God the psychological process of mourning for this
loved and lost historical object, why I also think of secularization as a
process of individuation, and why I take religion as the primary or
archetypal monument which constitutes and undergirds Western
culture.

These considerations open out into the final problem of my essay,
the way mourning and individuation inaugurate the central task of
the postmodern self, the creation of meaning. The creation of meaning is a process which breaks radically with the past and yet also
reappropriates that very past. To understand why and how this is so
requires a revision of Freud's theory of unconscious fantasy (the unit
of analysis in psychoanalysis) at both the cultural and the clinical
levels. Unconscious fantasy and its interpretation is not, I argue, only
a retreat from social life, as Freud claimed. Rather, it can also fill the
intermediate space between persons with objects which are simultaneously both made (fantasized by the individual) and given (by his
cultural surround). This process is located in a global social sense in
the midst of the contemporary culture of fantasy, and it mediates
between the past and the present. In such fashion does paradox lie and
hide in and within contradiction. But to reach this point it is first

necessary to go back and reflect further upon Freud's striking remark about mourning and monuments, for in putting the two together in the way that he did he too was trying to explain how meaning is created—or, rather, how sometimes people fail to do this.

Mourning, Monuments, and Individuation: A First Approximation

Let us begin to explore the complex relationships which might exist between mourning and monuments by understanding as clearly as possible exactly what Freud had in mind when he first connected the two. Freud gave his lectures from memory, without notes, in German, and wrote them out only when asked to after returning to Vienna. He virtually began the American presentation with a summary of Breuer's case, the famous Anna O.: her dying father, her lonely and fear-laden vigil, the consequent symptom formation, and Breuer's subsequent hypnosis and cathartic "cure." Then he backed away and launched into the digression cited above: hysterical symptoms are like monuments.

To explain the point the Viennese physician invited his American audience to take an imaginary walk with him through the streets of London. In front of the great railway terminal, he said, they would together look upon "a richly carved Gothic column—Charing Cross. One of the old Plantagenet kings of the thirteenth century ordered the body of his beloved Queen Eleanor to be carried to Westminster, and at every stage at which the coffin rested he erected a Gothic cross. Charing Cross is the last of the monuments that commemorate the funeral cortège." Jones told him later that the name "Charing" was derived from "chère reine." As a second example he offered the memorial of the Great Fire of 1666, known simply as "The Monument." Then he drove home his point: "What should we think of a Londoner," he asked his American audience, "who paused today in deep melancholy before the memorial of Queen Eleanor's funeral instead of going about his business in the hurry that modern working conditions demand?" And, "What should we think of a Londoner who shed tears before the Monument," when his city "has long since risen again in far greater brilliance?" Yet every single hysteric and neurotic, he concluded, "behaves like these two impractical Londoners." They cling to painful experiences "of the remote past," and they "neglect what is real and immediate." And so did Anna O. Her symptoms derived, he also concluded, from the time when she was nursing her sick father, and they were "mnemic signs of his illness and death. Thus they correspond to a display of mourning" (1910*a*, pp. 16–17).

Then Freud abandoned his aperçu in favor of the intricacies of clinical exposition, which occupied him throughout the remainder of the five lectures. Let us explore the aperçu in more detail. In saying that an hysterical symptom was a "mnemic symbol" (*Erinnerungsymbole*—really, a memorializing symbol) of a personal experience, Freud meant that a sort of compromise formation appears in the mind by means of which the ego can remain engaged with the past (the traumatic event—Anna O.'s disruptive thoughts and feelings at the bedside of her dying father, which presaged an unbearable experience of loss) while at the same time forcing back the painful affects and thoughts which the loss aroused, thereby producing "a display of mourning." Earlier in his work he had spoken of a mnemic symbol as a kind of "foreign body" in the mind which represents the forgotten memory, although it is not recognized as such. At this earlier time Freud also thought that hypnosis and cathartic therapy could deconstruct ("abreact") the foreign body and dissolve it, so that the patient need no longer "suffer from reminiscences."

So too, he thought, with culture and one of its privileged objects, the monument. Monuments contain a psychological core: they are also mnemic symbols. Experienced unconsciously as objects, the monument is a sort of compromise formation by means of which a group can unconsciously immerse itself in an experience of loss (loss of persons, ideas, ideals, or a lost "reality," such as when a traumatic disaster destroys many members of the group) but not directly feel the full force of the pain which the loss arouses. The group is thereby enabled to immerse itself in the past (the loss itself), move on into the present (the construction of the monument), and from there to release into the future (the ability to mourn and return to, or create a rapprochement with, the great necessities of life). Symptoms and monuments both begin with loss, and both seek to soften the loss by building structures within the context of the activity of mourning.

But there is a difference, too. In what I have called Freud's little discourse on mourning and monuments the individual person's symptoms are deconstructed so that the ego (of course Freud spoke of the ego only much later) gradually comes to accept the "historical" events which it has denied to awareness and memory. This process is best understood along the lines of his later ego-psychological model found in *The Ego and the Id* (1923): "The character of the ego is a precipitate of abandoned object-cathexes and . . . it contains the history of these object-choices" (p. 29), and the superego is "a memorial of the former weakness and dependence of the ego" (p. 48). Something of the lost person and the lost past is "taken in" (introjected and internalized). Much psychoanalytic therapy seeks to mitigate and partially deconstruct the unwholesome force of the superego, to "de-monumentalize" it, so to speak. In the case of monuments, however, something very different happens. The shared mnemic symbols which structure the collective memory are not deconstructed. Instead, the group makes an enormous collective effort to construct them, maintain them, and preserve them. Nothing is more offensive to a group than the destruction of its monuments, whether they are, literally, statues, or whether they are sacred texts or even representative persons. Still, the memorial or monument is also decathected in the sense that, once established, it is "just there" and taken-for-granted as such—unless, of course, one is like Freud's two "impractical Londoners," who weep in front of an impersonal and anonymous object.

But Freud was not quite right on this, and it is here that I part from him. Who would deny that powerful, complex, confused, troubling, but also solace-conferring, affects and thoughts overtake him unaware, from time to time, in moments of contemplation and reflection, as he stands in the presence of a shrine or monument? In such moments the mourning process is reopened. But does it activate only the unconscious infantile losses, the unconscious images and our primal dread of their possible instability? Or does it also stimulate the uncanny feeling, which can at times intensify to the point of irrefutable conviction, that we are, in some mysterious and disturbingly inexplicable way, "a part of all that," and further, that apart from "all that" we might not be at all? Do not such experiences also suggest that in some way or other our essence is constituted as much by "all that out there" as it is by "all this in here"; it is only that we did not understand this very well, before we had this experience?

Let us call Freud's little discourse what it really is, a parody of culture and of its principal purpose, the re-presentation to the conscious ego of the collective past or collective memory. So once again we stumble into the central contradiction in the psychoanalytic theory of culture, its power and limits. But now I draw this contradiction into the idea and process of individuation, which has two poles, one individualizing, the other collectivizing, retaining Freud's unsurpassed analyses of the former while beginning to repair his ablation of the latter. The individualizing component is, of course, the drive to analytic access, the introspecting and self-observing ego. The collectivizing component is the drive to the other or the others who compose a common culture. It includes identification (the drive to be like others) and typification (in Schutz's sense) and the soul (in theological terms), the common, transindividual, and eternal element of the person. Just as the ego is the hithermost structure of individualization, the monument is the thithermost structure of collectivization, of culture. Individuation (not individualization) is the capacity to mourn the loss of collective structures (the "parting from") without losing touch with them (the "being a part of"). So its key term is the self and not the ego and not the soul. Without some sort of real and stable sociological referent, which in this formulation is represented by the monument, the psyche and all Freud said of it rapidly dissolve into solipsism, which is simply the time-honored philosophical term for narcissism. Freud's theory of culture is drenched in irony because, in breaking so precipitously with the communities of his past, the wholly cut-off ego which he both experienced and observed could only reconform to a new collectivity, the culture of science, rationality, and positivism. So his past had its revenge on him, after all. Monotheism and positivism are but mirror images of each other: when applied to the mind, both are forms of absolutism; the first spiritual, the second material. In sum, I wish to fathom the currents of paradox which flow beneath this irony, but the way to do this is to become more, not less, psychological; that will permit us to become more, not less, sociological. And so I begin with, but do not end with, the psychologist par excellence of paradox.

Winnicott opened his now-famous essay "The Location of Cultural Experience" (1967) with the observation that "Freud did not have a place in his topography of the mind for the experience of things cultural." He did give new value to "inner psychic reality" (what I have called the inner world of analytic access) and to "things that are actual and truly external," but even the process of sublimation did not "point the way to a place where cultural experience is meaningful . . . to . . . where in the mind cultural experience is" (p. 112). In other words Winnicott sought to undercut the subject-object dichotomy upon which Freud built his metapsychology, which split up the life world into "inner psychical" and "external material" reality, into "inside" and "outside." To do so he introduced a third reality which he believed he had observed in his clinical work with infants and children, the concept of transitional space. It existed between inner and outer and was occupied by transitional objects—specifically, by the objects and activities of play and symbol formation. The transitional object was, he said, "the child's first use of a symbol and the first experience of play" (p. 113).

Although it is intrinsically psychological, the transitional object is also social, for it mediates between the infant and its mother. As the infant's omnipotent illusion of oneness with its mother is gradually broken down or disillusioned, the passage to reality slowly takes its place. This "reality" is that of Freud's reality principle and of Hartmann's average expectable environment, and its model is the view of the world offered by physical science. Transitional objects are constructed by the child to facilitate this passage, which would otherwise be unthinkable and unbearable. So the child's first experience of culture (in the sense of "the experience of things cultural") is located in the transitional space between mother and infant and takes the form of play, symbol making, and the creation of meaning. Because the objects of play are given to him—that is, not fantasized or made by him—they are culturally constituted. The passage from illusion to reality is also a passage from nature to culture. The worst thing an adult can do in this context is to challenge the child's activity: Did you make this (the transitional object), or was it given to you? If it is ever asked, this question is the first persecutory gesture. As growth continues, these objects (at first toys, teddy bears, etc.) are gradually put to one side. They are decathected but not mourned in the sense in which Freud spoke of mourning (the abandonment and renunciation of a tie to a lost, deceased person). Rather, such objects and the psychological processes which support them are continuous with the more sophisticated cultural objects usually referred to by parents, teachers, and professors as "culture."

At this point we would do well to refocus the crucial difference between Freud's and Winnicott's theories of the mind. Winnicott accepts Freud's characterization of reality as that which is shorn of projections, that is, as intrinsically ungratifying and therefore a constant source of frustration. In the face of this state of affairs Freud counseled renunciation and went on to note the way in which unconscious fantasy arose to provide substitute gratifications. But Winnicott adds to these formulations a developmentally earlier, more archaic layer of mental activity. In the face of the ungratifying character of reality, the mind responds by developing a creative relationship to it, and not only by retreating from it, although this also happens. The mind blends fantasy and the social elements of the cultural surround. It is the socially shared character of transitional objects which prevents them from being classified as simply defensive mechanisms or substitutions. These objects are a third reality between the inner world of fantasy and the outer world of reality.

In adult life, according to Winnicott, the infantile "experience of things cultural" persists but takes on new forms and new significance. The adult experience of things cultural is essential for the establishment by the individual of a sense of meaningfulness: "the question of what life is all about," the capacity "to feel that life is real, to find life worth living." Such questions of meaningfulness are, he said, "phenomena of life and death." These are not, however, philosophical or theological statements but rather psychological ones. Winnicott is also very clear that these issues of life and death are grounded in psychotic rather than neurotic experience. Psychotic rather than neurotic processes "appear in our cultural experiences." Cultural experience is a historical and not a psychogenetic category. It refers to "the inherited tradition . . . something that is in the common pool of humanity, into which individuals and groups may contribute and from which we may all draw, *if we have somewhere to put what we find.*" Cultural experiences "provide the continuity in the human race that transcends personal existence." They are composed of "myth" derived from "the oral tradition," and they are "in direct continuity with play." In sum, cultural experiences are the foundation for the well-established capacity in the adult for "total experience." This capacity is related to the original paradox of separation and union, which is both individual and social, for "when one speaks of a man one speaks of him *along with* the summation of his cultural experiences. The whole forms a unit" (pp. 116–18).

So Winnicott did indeed devise a place in the mind for cultural experiences, and this is a crucial advance over Freud. But what has already been said of Freud must now be said of Winnicott as well: he too had no place in culture for the psychological experiences of the individual ego or mind. If one begins by approaching the problem psychologically, one must necessarily view culture as a series of displacements of inner, psychical reality into the outer and external realm of "fact." This was Freud's approach. On the other hand, if one begins by approaching the problem sociologically, one sees inner psychical reality as a series of internalizations of prior social rules, codes, and symbols. In this second sense both the form and content of the mother-infant dyad take their shapes primarily from culture. This dyad is the first group, the first successful attempt at classificatory activity, and the first interpretive community. This was Durkheim's approach. Winnicott's observations and formulations show that this polarity is too simple, because there is a space or interface between the two, and this space is equal in dignity to the inner and outer realms. So the next question may now be asked, although Winnicott did not himself pose it: Where in culture do the psychological experiences of mind appear? At no point in his work did Winnicott choose to think of culture in terms of social structure. His conception of the intermediate space is purely formal, synchronic, and spatial. For example, presumably some cultural objects would facilitate separation, others forestall it. But Winnicott was not interested in such questions.

At this point what has been suggested in a general and abstract way above about mourning, monuments, and individuation begins to take on much-needed concrete significance. The monument, I now wish to suggest, is the place in culture for the mind. Mourning is intimately related both to it and to the central internal processes of psychological growth. Individuation is the activity whereby the various conflicts which beset all persons—losses which are intrapsychical, interpsychical, and sociohistorical—are worked over, broken down, and built up. The result is the formation of new psychological structure and a new entity, the unique self of each separate and individual person. Let us place alongside these more familiar psychological processes at least one complementary social structure.

Conventional wisdom makes a number of time-honored distinctions regarding mourning and monuments. While these are in their own way correct and should be preserved, it is also necessary to go beneath them, even to the point of undercutting some. One usually distinguishes personal mourning over the loss of a deceased person with whom one has been intimate from forms of mourning which involve social and impersonal figures and events. One also ordinarily thinks of monuments as entirely public and not at all personal objects, although the ordinary person's humble gravestone and cemeteries are personal monuments. And it is generally assumed that neither mourning nor monuments alter in any positive way the inner world of individuals or (especially) the shared inner world of a group.

These assumptions can—and ordinarily do—forestall awareness of deeper and more complex relations or "cross-overs" between these activities and objects—for example, continuity between personal mourning and the mourning process which undergirds the formation of monuments; continuity between public monuments and monumentalization as an inner, psychological process; and, most of all, the complex things which can happen when these deeper relations are engaged, which inaugurates individuation. Let us begin with the formation, structure, and function of monuments, turn to their role in personal life, and then locate the individuation process in the space between the two.

Monuments are rudimentary prototypes of all cultural symbols, and, as Durkheim noted, they embody aspects of the sacred. Their formation derives from the efforts of men to grapple with a shared episode of social loss. The sectors of the social order to which these efforts are usually assigned are religion and politics. Myths are notable examples, for they are structures which re-present events thought to be lost or buried in the past. In the West at least, the holy communion (the mass) is a preeminent example: the Gospels tell us that Jesus commanded Christians to eat and drink the bread and wine (his body and his blood) in order to unite themselves to his death and resurrection (Do this in remembrance of me) and, through that, to one another and to God the Father. Public monuments are usually memorials of wars, terrible struggles and disasters in which members of the body politic, especially great leaders, have perished. Monuments take shape in society in response to mourning—mourning done together.

The structure of monuments presents one of the most interesting and perplexing problems for any theory of groups and the symbolic forms which support them because, whereas individuals have bodies, groups do not. The individual ego is rooted in bodily processes, some of which are unconscious, and the body also materially binds and individualizes the person. As Freud was fond of saying, the ego is always a bodily ego. But while groups also have a psychology and an unconscious, they have no body. In addition to being eminently social, however, monuments are also entirely material: they are to the group what the body is to the ego—the material soul of the group, as it were. It is simply impossible for any single person to make a monument to himself. Any attempt to do so would be like laughing at one's own joke or granting deference to oneself—deference comes from others because only they can give it. Even when monuments take immaterial forms—for example, in the study and recitation of sacred texts—the human drive is to render them tangible and material, usually in the form of ritual objects.

The function of monuments is best characterized along the lines of re-presenting and mediating, although the more precise terminology would be union/separation. Monuments engage the immediate, conscious experience of an aggregate of egos by re-presenting and mediating to them the lost cultural experiences of the past: the experiences of individuals, groups, their ideas and ideals, which coalesce into what can be called a collective memory. In this the monument is a symbol of union because it brings together the particular psychological circumstances of many individuals' life courses and the universals of their otherwise lost historical past within the context of their current or contemporary social processes and structures. But monuments are symbols of separation as well. They not only draw individuals and groups into society and the past; they also free and liberate them from that past, in what seems to be a kind of double action. In doing so they release persons into the present, into what Freud referred to as the "business" and the "hurry" that "modern working conditions demand." In this sense monuments are also a kind of shared transitional object, facilitating a passage or separation from an imagined lost union with the past, a transition which people are always making together.

Monuments obviously bear an important, complex relation to the personal experience of mourning. Mourning is the mental and individual counterpart of the material and social character of monuments. Both are responses to loss. But in the case of the individual, the experience of loss which finding oneself in the presence of a monument can catalyze activates unconscious memories of earlier losses endured over the life course, most especially the original loss of union with the mother, and calls for a reorganization of them. The positive outcome of such a process is the building up of psychological structure and an enhancing of the sense of "being a self," which might be referred to as "the monument within," but which can also be called the framework for individuation. I have already noted Freud's view of the ego's structure as "the precipitate of abandoned object cathexes" and of the superego as a "memorial" to the ego's developmentally earlier dependence on social objects. Important too is the fact that more than any other typical, primary human experience, mourning temporarily neutralizes aggression, the death instinct, and narcissism. Even more important, mourning renders with great intensity and force what is perhaps the most fundamental of all human paradoxes:it is a heightened individualizing and interiorizing experience which is also accompanied by a profound—if only transient—sense of unity between oneself and all mankind. In such experiences the strife and power of love and hate (which are forms of becoming) are transcended and replaced by a sad sense of peace (a form of being). In this sense mourning is the mirror opposite of being in love and of domination, and the birth of a child is the mirror opposite of the monument. For these reasons even the child's teddy bear can be thought of as a monument building of sorts. When understood in the context of monuments, the ability to mourn foreshadows the advent of individuation because it is, in its simplest sense, the capacity to support oneself internally while recognizing in full conscious awareness both the collectivizing and individualizing realities within which one inevitably exists.

No two things would seem more different than the sight of children at play and monuments. The first portrays aliveness and the future and is usually considered to be the essence of what is profane, whereas monuments are deadly serious and are assumed to exude an aura of the sacred. But it seems that society knows better. It has constructed a more complex relation between the two which I refer to metaphorically as "the statue in the park." At least in public places such as parks, monuments and playing are both closely related (union) and carefully kept apart (separation). There, statues and playing exist side by side, as if to testify to the social fact that a double unconscious relation to the past is necessary to support playing, a nonaggressive and nonloving social activity in the present. Much the same can be said of museums, in which a kind of playing with the past takes place in the presence of art objects, which take on a monument-like character. The desacralizing effects of commerce have often been noted and recall the emphasis given above to the crucial role of industrialization in tearing persons out of the past. Freud unconsciously recognized this point in his lecture on symptom formation (1916–17). After discussing primal fantasies and primeval experiences and times, he observed that "the creation of the mental realm of phantasy finds a perfect parallel in the establishment of 'reservations' or 'nature reserves' in places where the requirements of . . . communications and industry threaten to bring about changes in the original face of the earth. . . . The mental realm of phantasy is just such a reservation withdrawn from the reality principle" (p. 372). The limitations of Freud's theory of fantasy and its relation to the creation of meaning are discussed in the last section of this essay.

There is another way to make clearer the distinction between mourning and monuments without abandoning their commonalities. The mechanisms which produce monuments are not identical with those of the individual psyche as those have been described by Freud and his more orthodox followers. In psychoanalysis unconscious fantasy (the focal unit of analysis) is the phenomenon which mediates—or re-presents—instinctual processes to the ego as these pass through the grids or filters of social norms and rules. The mechanisms of mediation are the familiar ones of condensation, displacement, representability, and symbolism. In so saying, Freud recognized that both conscious and unconscious symbolic-cultural processes authorized, instantiated, and valorized the form and the content of the individual's mind. Monuments and all that they imply also mediate and re-present, although their subject matter is the shared typical experiences of groups, and their mechanisms are therefore different. In the case of collective activities, generally psychotic or psychotic-like processes are the principal ones. Collective behavior tends to employ dissociation, disavowal, splitting, and projective identification, rather than repression, regression, defense, sublimation, and so forth. There is, in other words, in the case of cultural objects and processes far less distortion of content and far more inhibition of narcissistic affect. Myths provide the best example of this distinction, for they are, as I have said, monuments or structures which re-present events thought to be lost or buried in the past. Clearly, myths do disguise and distort, but their deceptions are far more easily discerned than are those in dreams. While interpretation can often dissolve an individual's dream symbolism into its instinctual and interpersonal substrates relatively easily, myths powerfully resist this process. They can be understood analytically, but the force and power of their claim upon the imagination is far greater than that of dreams, even when their psychological dynamics are understood. To put the matter metaphorically, the veil of myth is more transparent than that of neurotic distortion, but its texture is deceptively thick: power is less clothed than desire. Psychoanalysis has no theory of power—it is a theory of love and of love's twisted and tragic relations to reason and will.

The best empirical example I can offer of this distinction between personal-individual and collective psychological dynamics is, of course, the psychoanalytic movement itself. There I portrayed men coming together who possessed to an extraordinary degree depth-psychological self-understanding. Yet, once they had assembled and formed a group, they engaged in all the characteristic unconscious mechanisms of collective behavior, in particular, splitting of objects into wholly good and wholly bad, the creation of an absolutistic, idealized leader through projective identification, and the disavowal of the primitive sector which enjoined these operations. These processes persist in the analytic societies of today, which, despite their members' unusually deep personal self-understanding, display all the customary maneuvers of those groups and movements which are not at all concerned with psychology—political, artistic, military, and religious. Sherry Turkle (1978) has called attention to the "Protestant" character of organized psychoanalysis, by which she means its endless propensity to split off new sects out of old ones.

This example draws our attention back into the role of monuments in social behavior, for the analytic societies have attempted to make Freud himself into a monument, and the only real argument is,

Who has rightful possession of this historical object? There seems to be no way to have the monument and let go of it at the same time, an action which requires first mourning and then individuation. Moreover, at this point an ironic sense of self-consistency makes an unexpected appearance when I point out that it was also Freud's deepest wish that his work, so intimately connected to his inner world, become a monument. During his self-analysis, while he was detaching himself psychologically from his cultural surround and filling the empty space with his theory of dreams, which was inseparable from many of his best insights into the oneiric dimensions of art, literature, groups, and religion, he also deeply wished that these efforts be honored by society with an appropriate memorial. "Do you suppose," he asked Fliess in the midst of his inner struggle, "that some day a marble tablet which will be placed on the house [where he was staying when he wrote out his first dream analysis], inscribed with these words:

> In this house on July 24, 1895,
> the Secret of Dreams was revealed
> to Dr. Sigmund Freud

At the moment I see little prospect for it" (Freud 1954, p. 322). That the English-language reader should see Freud's "memorial" surrounded by a black border was the idea of Ernst Kris, one of the editors of the Freud-Fliess letters. There is no border in the more recent translation and edition of these letters by Jeffrey Masson (1985). I include the border here because I think that it expresses Kris's wish, which he shared with Freud, that his master's discovery be memorialized, and his conviction that in so doing he spoke for all of Freud's followers. The black border represents the followers' unconscious identification with their leader's inner world—so that even today the movement is organized at its deepest and most fundamental level by an unconscious, shared idealized object.

Freud's wish was, of course, fulfilled. The house in London to which he fled and in which he died has been converted into "The Freud Museum." There one can see his books, his furniture, his collection of objets d'art, and, especially, the couch on which his patients lay, some now famous simply for having lain there. Nor does it occur to us, when we visit this museum, to wonder whether it is "the real couch." All we ask is that it be shown to us.

To summarize and move on. Freud's little discourse on mourning and monuments captures the central contradiction in his theory of culture, the tension between the ever-advancing, individualizing, and historical ego of modernity and the retrograde collectivites of the past. Mourning captures the first, the monument the second. But Freud's method was that of the forced choice, one or the other, and he did not hesitate. With the help of Winnicott I was able to show that between these two there is in fact a third area, a piece of transitional space. I now wish to learn more about this space, within which I think the activity of individuation takes place. To do so I need the help of others and begin by rethinking the first of Freud's three great contradictions, the tension between the primitive and the civilized in humankind, which also has at its center the problem of time, in relation to the work of Lévi-Strauss.

11 The Fate of the Ego in "Primitive" and "Civilized" Cultures: First Contradiction

The twofold construct of a common culture and its juxtaposition to depth-psychological self-understanding or analytic access have become increasingly central to this project. Now the time has come to strengthen this formulation by taking it out of its modern, Western context and giving it both universality and contemporaneity. The richest understanding of what a common culture really is lies in Claude Lévi-Strauss's rendition of the "primitive" or savage mind. He has devoted all his work to preserving the dignity of savage thought and society, which he associates with the synchronic and timeless, and to attacking its opponents—for example, Compte, Levy-Bruhl, and Sartre—who, he thinks, have privileged diachrony and history at the expense of primitivity and synchrony. Lévi-Strauss's depiction of savage thought allows me to reexamine Freud's concept of the primitive (the Freudian equation based on stage theory: savage = children = neurotics) and his views of totemism and phylogeny, and to deepen my understanding of the cultural significance of time, so central to Freud's whole project. Even more than Sartrean existentialism, psychoanalysis is committed to diachrony and splits the ego off from synchrony. This discussion also allows me to reflect on the wider, contemporary significance of primitivity as it has come to be understood in revisionist psychoanalysis, where it is closely allied to narcissism, such that the two have together become its virtual trope for the human problematic. This is an area of mental life which Freud missed. Finally, these Lévi-Straussian reflections provide me with a cross-cultural and even, possibly, with a more or less ontological frame for understanding mourning and individuation. At the close of this chapter I suggest that the "passage" from timelessness to timefulness, from synchrony to diachrony, and from myth to history had to have included such activities as mourning and the construction of monuments. It is essential to remember in this regard that Freud thought of the unconscious as timeless and that

Winnicott considered transitional phenomena in a spatial rather than a temporal manner, for he believed that contiguity rather than continuity was their most basic characteristic.

In *The Savage Mind* (1962a) Lévi-Strauss brought together major strands of his work in order to communicate it to a lay audience and to mount, for everyone to see, his defense of primitive modes of life. Toward the end of his book he marshaled all his forces on a plain of battle under the banner of "timelessness" and challenged his arch-enemy, Jean-Paul Sartre, who he believed had made a true and real myth of "time-fullness" and history—and, along with that, of psychology. Then the anthropologist-philosopher proceeded to demolish the philosopher-psychologist. I make no attempt to summarize these ideas (which many have rightfully said is impossible) but only draw upon those several of his most powerful concepts which are directly related to the task at hand. What, then, does "primitive" really mean? Why is it the exact opposite of history and psychology? And, how can one move beyond this contradiction which Freud has given us and which Lévi-Strauss thinks he has resolved?

"The characteristic feature of the savage mind is its timelessness" (p. 263), the way in which it embodies synchrony, an atemporal sense of self-awareness. Mythic thought has the effect of annulling any sense of transience. But the agency of synchrony is totemism, wherein the natural order (plants and animals, especially) provide the basis for explaining and interpreting the social order (the relations among men). Such primitive thinking is, however, a genuine form of thought, not grounded in affectivity or need, and so it is a science, albeit of the concrete, equal in dignity to science itself, abstract science. Ritual and rite draw all things together and, along with mythic thinking, forestall the emergence of diachrony and historical thinking—and, one must add, psychology of the psychoanalytic sort.

Diachrony is Lévi-Strauss's term for societies which think about themselves historically, in particular, modern Western societies. But his book is also deeply concerned with the view of primitives entertained by such modern Western writers as Compte, Levy-Bruhl, and Sartre. They think that primitives occupy a stage of history which is simply earlier and less developed than their own. These moderns are so engulfed, so to speak, by time that they cannot even imagine timelessness. To these three villains I add a fourth, Freud, whose cultural texts sought, ironically, to annul timelessness, a kind of negation of a negation. More than any other form of modern thought, psychoanalysis ushers in the full-scale temporalization of life. Psychologization and temporalization are virtually one and the same.

Let us look at these ideas more closely, especially the tension between synchrony and diachrony, and let Lévi-Strauss speak for himself.

"There are," he says, "two distinct modes of scientific thought" (p. 15), a science of the abstract ("our" science: physics, chemistry, and biology) and a science of the concrete ("their" science). As examples of the latter he offers the elaborate systems of classification which natives use to order the natural world of plants, insects, and animals and, from there, to organize the social world of their kinship relationships, marriage rules, and customs. These modes of ordering are "steps towards rational ordering" because "any classification is superior to chaos" (p. 15). Such thought is not based on "practical purposes" and "meets intellectual requirements rather than . . . satisfying needs" (p. 9).

The practitioner of concrete science is the *bricoleur*. This French term is roughly translatable as "handyman" or "jack-of-all-trades." The best contemporary example is the bourgeois householder who fixes the leak in the pipe under his kitchen sink by making use of a few tools and supplies acquired from the local hardware store. Such a task requires thoughtfulness, and the job has to be done properly. In a similar fashion the primitive organizes perceptions of the inorganic, organic, and social worlds (which Lévi-Strauss calls "events") into classificatory, mythic, and ritualized wholes (which he calls "structures"). Both (householder and savage) "subordinate" all materials and plans "for the purpose of the project" (p. 17). Unlike them, however, the engineer (and the abstract scientist) thinks in terms of breaking down existing materials, plans, and projects in order to create a wholly new design or blueprint. The *bricoleur* lacks distance from the objects in his world and cannot think abstractly (as does the chemist, for example). Focal attention consumes all his mental efforts, and he works midway between percepts and concepts, with images. The *bricoleur* is always making events (images which are derived from percepts of the inorganic, organic, and social orders) into structures, whereas the abstract scientist breaks structures (existing theories) down into events (new theories or designs). Most psychoanalytic technique is, I will in a moment point out, bricolage.

The practical matrix of all this—the context in which it is lived from day to day—is totemism. In totemism "concrete logic" proceeds chiefly by means of the activity of identification. Lévi-Strauss means by this that primitive thought is concerned with beings that are seen as "exhibiting a certain affinity with men . . . the feeling of identification is stronger than the sense of difference" (p. 37). To make this point Lévi-Strauss cites ethnographic evidence: "A Hawaiian's oneness with the living aspect of native phenomena . . . with spirit and God and with other persons and souls is not correctly described by such words as . . . empathy . . . or neurotic, or mystical. . . . It is just a part of natural consciousness for the normal Hawaiian" (p. 37). A longer citation from a second source, which contrasts primitive and abstract science, focuses the point about identification even more directly: primitives say that

> We know what the animals do, what are the needs of the beaver, the bear, the salmon, and other creatures, because long ago men married them and acquired this knowledge from their animal wives. Today the priests say we lie, but we know better. The white man has been only a short time in this country and knows very little about animals; we have lived here thousands of years and were taught long ago by the animals themselves. The white man writes everything down in a book so that it will not be forgotten; but our ancestors married the animals, learned all their ways, and passed on the knowledge from one generation to another.
> (Quoted from Jenness, Lévi-Strauss 1962a, p. 37)

And so does Strehlow's work on the Northern Aranda's "passionate love of the soil":

> Mountains and creeks and springs and water-holes are, to him . . . the handiwork of ancestors from whom he himself has descended. He sees recorded in the surrounding landscape the ancient story of the lives and deeds of the immortal beings whom he reveres; beings who for a brief space may take on human shape once more; beings, many of whom he has known in his own experience as his fathers and grandfathers and brothers, and as his mothers and sisters. The whole countryside is his living, age-old family tree. [It is] the story of his own doings at the beginning of time, at the dim dawn of life, when the world as he knows it now was being shaped and moulded by all-powerful hands. . . . (P. 243)

If totemism is at the heart of the synchronic, the *churinga* (revered stones or carved pieces of wood deposited in sacred spaces for the purposes of care, concern, and worship) are at the heart of totemism. But identification is also central here. The *churinga* are a kind of monument to social solidarity and a vista into timelessness: "The churinga furnishes the tangible proof that the ancestor and his living descendant are of one flesh" (p. 241). The function of the *churinga* is "to offset the correlative impoverishment of the diachronic dimension. They are the past materially present and they provide the means of reconciling empirical individuation and mythical confusion" (p. 238). These two magnificent sentences compress and convey the fashion in which "the synchronic structures of . . . totemic systems" (p. 67) annul and ward off a sense of history. Ritual practices and objects neutralize time and convey an aura of timelessness which might otherwise be eroded by "demographic changes" (p. 67) and "demographic evolution" (p. 68). These are, of course, simply Lévi-Strauss's terms for what I have called "social-structural change."

Beneath or within all this ethnography and philosophizing lies a simple and breathtaking point: to become human, Lévi-Strauss tells us, the modern must be able to imagine the living and thinking of the primitive in its own rightful fullness through an imaginative action in which the compulsions of historical reason are suspended. From Lévi-Strauss one derives a rich sense of what a common culture really is: it is primitive, synchronic, concrete, and structure conferring. Most of all, it is not just a precursor, something rudimentary and half real, which betrays the real, civilized culture by way of the absence of the latter. A common culture is "the past," and the social exceeds and therefore precedes the historical, the individual, and therefore also the psychological. Let us now reconsider the conception of primitivity which Freud held, in the light of this understanding of a common culture.

Freud did, I think, actually reach for this very same view, or for something close to it, but he failed utterly to grasp it. This failure was not due to some kind of "inability to introspect" or to "anxiety," although such explanations have been offered in hindsight. Rather, Freud's conception of the primitive was forced upon him by structural factors of two sorts—sociological (social-structural change) and epistemological (the conceptions of science of his day). The prevailing social conditions and models of science did not permit the sort of reflection Lévi-Strauss has made available to us. Rather than point to any so-called failure on Freud's part, I want instead to note the way in which he reached, in a psychological way, for this dimension in human life. "The Uncanny" is a paper which is absolutely crucial in this regard. There Freud spoke of a dimension in human life which had been, he said, "surmounted and overcome." Such processes were real and identifiable but not necessarily analyzable. I think Freud here touched upon what revisionist psychoanalysis has come to call primitive states, the primitive psyche, and primitive personalities. If this is so, then it may be the case that psychological and anthropological primitivities are not entirely different, and the psychologically primitive portions of modern society are not so different from the constitutional bases of primitive society. While I cannot resolve these issues here, I can track Freud's pursuit of them.

The first psychoanalyst's interest in primitivity and in its correlate, the idea of a common culture (and in the potential ubiquity of both), did not have its origin in the so-called first period of his life and work, the time of the self-analysis, or in the writing of *The Interpretation of Dreams*, or in the work which directly followed these. Rather, this twofold interest owed its inception entirely to the second or middle period of 1906–14, and in particular to Freud's involvement with Jung and in the psychoanalytic movement. It really emerged only after the Jung episode—or better, in the act of breaking off from Jung—and it is coincident with the turn to culture. This trend increased and reached its better-known high point in the later cultural texts. The double concern first surfaced in *Totem and Taboo* (1912–13), conceived when the relationship with Jung was both intensely affectionate and competitive. Jung realized that their new knowledge of the inner world led inexorably to a reunderstanding and revisioning of the history of culture, and it was he who put Freud onto this problem. Freud then attacked it with his key ideas of the omnipotence of thought and magical thinking, in the context of a primal group or horde. These ideas came together in his psychological conception of totemism, and its principal feature, primal fantasies. But *Totem and Taboo* also contained the "first draft," so to speak, of the theory of narcissism (the quintessence of primitivity from the psychological point of view), and neither one (the theory of totemism or the theory of narcissism) should be separated from the epochal paper on narcissism, from the study of "The Moses of Michelangelo" (where Freud encountered his own primitivity and his own narcissism at the foundations of his own common culture, his Judaic heritage), or from the essay on the psychanalytic movement. The purpose of the movement was, in Freud's eyes, to overcome the residues of primitivity in modern, civilized culture. The protocultural texts followed, with their intense dwelling upon the problems of time and transience, provoked as these in turn were by the loss of the central values and idealized objects of European civilization, which the Great War foreshadowed. Then came "The Uncanny," which also presaged what I would call "the terror of repetition," an idea which reached its zenith in *Beyond the Pleasure Principle* but was softened somewhat by such concepts as Eros and community in *Group Psychology and the Analysis of the Ego*.

Taken all together, these many texts captured a melee of ideas: a lost common culture, the structure of a common culture (for example, primitive society, the Catholic church, and the army), narcissism (the ego's retreat from culture), and the problem of the ego's continuity over time and its eventual death. But the principal issue underlying these various particular concerns was the way in which the advancing diachronic, historical ego might offset continuity, timelessness, and the cultural supports for them.

It would be an understatement to say that Freud did not take readily to the idea or the reality of either a common culture or its principal feature, primitivity. He could not, for he was overwhelmed by diachrony. Obsessed with time, transience, and loss, he was unable to reflect fully upon what, in fact, had actually been lost. So acute was his sense of this loss that he had to subvert the past by showing the way in which a common culture was "really" only protopsychological, that the primitive people who participated in it were simply "backward" and therefore could not "see" the psychological mechanisms at work in their social worlds. Neither Freud nor his followers could grasp the "otherness" of primitivity. The common cultures of Catholicism, of the dying liberal state, and especially of his own Jewish sense of belonging were the major sources of primitivity which he denied in the immediate sense. This denial in turn forestalled Freud's ability to mourn and his further individuation. The scientific models with which he worked further hampered his formal investigations. These models pervaded the ethnographies of his time, which he read and cited. They too conceived of the primitive as only an earlier stage of a later and "more" real state of affairs. In sum, for several reasons, Freud simply took for granted that primitivity had been surmounted and overcome by an ever-forward-marching civilization, its methods, and leading minds. It is worth noting at this point that this assumption alone is the deepest root of Freud's atheism, for atheism is simply the refusal, at the level of belief, to be socially incorporated in a relatively undifferentiated way into a primitive group or common culture.

Freud and Lévi-Strauss also have a strange—because it is inverse—affinity with each other. Each affirms exactly what the other negates, within the frame of a common polarity. Both split life into the same opposed dimensions. For Lévi-Strauss the fundamental reality is synchrony and savage thought. Everything that follows (diachrony, demographic or social-structural change, history, timefulness) is of but slight interest to him. Freud reverses all this. In his thought everything is time, diachrony, advance, and—enhancing them all—psychology. That which is prior to these is of no interest to him, and none of it has any ontological reality. But if one presses this opposition further, it opens out into a fresh line of thinking which moves toward overcoming the opposition.

Lévi-Strauss has observed that "Totemism is like hysteria" (1962b, p. 1). By this he means that the investigator regards "the other" (whether the primitive or the hysteric) as alien to his own moral universe, thereby "protecting the attachments felt" in himself toward that moral universe. Perhaps Freud's most striking insight into the mental life of the hysteric was his proposal that there is no qualitative difference between the hysteric and the so-called normal person. Hence his proposition that in effect "we are all in some way or other ill," that everyone's mental life is in principle no different from the neurotic's or the hysteric's, that there is a psychopathology of everyday life. For this reason one can and should speak of Freud's own neurosis and, for that matter, of every analyst's neurosis, which drives him into psychoanalysis in the first place. Lévi-Strauss not only accepts this insight of Freud's; he extends it from hysteria to the primitive and to totemism. He wishes in effect to say, "We are all in some way or other primitive," wherein primitive refers to a synchronic sense of oneself, to feeling part of a common culture, and to employing concrete as well as abstract modes of reasoning and thinking. So Lévi-Strauss is understandably fond of pointing out to his readers that "there are still," in their modern society, "zones in which savage thought, like savage species, is relatively protected" (1962a, p. 219), such as art, politics, parks, and mass culture in general. In a moment I will suggest that another such zone is the monument, which, as in the psychoanalytical concept of overdeterminism, at once reminds one of the terror of the past (here Eliade's term, "the terror of history," is useful) and yet assures and consoles because it is, quite simply, "there" and, moreover, "there for us."

This affinity between totemism and hysteria can bring about a deeper understanding of the proper relations between a common culture and psychological self-understanding, between the social world and the inner world, between "culture" and "psychology." The pathway this effort must take is clear enough. It touches on revisionist psychoanalytic work on primitive states, groups, and movements. But it also includes a theory in which social-structural change has forced back primitivity from its original social ubiquity in the history of Western culture, first into the family, from there into the mother-infant dyad, and from there into the individual—all already alluded to at length in earlier sociological discussions. But this step is best begun by first engaging directly Lévi-Strauss's disturbing acrimony for psychology, which he has fastened upon Jean-Paul Sartre. As he says, "He who begins by steeping himself in the allegedly self-evident truths of introspection never emerges from them" (1962*a*, p. 249), and "it is vain to go to historical consciousness for the truest meaning" (p. 254). Does this mean that timefulness so distorts the past and therefore contemporary self-understanding that no knowledge of the present can be had (Sartre's fatal mistake)?

The answer to this question lies not in the wrongheadedness of such methods as introspection and psychology, but rather in the assertion "He who begins by steeping himself" in these. What is wrong, in other words, is beginning with, rather than ending with, psychology. This mistake produces an incremental series of distortions which Lévi-Strauss finds, virtually "in pure culture," in Sartre's ablation of synchrony from the human situation. His own account of the emergence of diachrony is most revealing. He states that European civilization displays a "totemic void" because its people "have elected to explain themselves by history" (p. 232). Primitives explain themselves totemically by erecting a series of botanical and zoological species alongside human groups and cultures. They then insist that the former preceded and engendered the latter. Lévi-Strauss calls the former "the original species." But "when a society sides with history," when demographic or social-structural change occurs, then the original series disintegrates and "the human order" is no longer "a fixed projection" of "the natural order." The result is a resolute "internalizing" of the historical process which eventually leads to domesticated thought, historical knowledge, and analytical reason. To the last belong science and also Lévi-Strauss's own theory of culture: a symbolic series of unconscious binary oppositions, derived by anthropological science. Most of all, science demonstrates that birth and death, the two most sacred realities of primitive life and thought, are really biological and chemical processes. In such fashion are science, diachrony, and the destruction of the idea of immortality all of a piece. The "internalization" of the historical processes, which is a key to Lévi-Strauss's explanation of the emergence of diachrony—and of psychology—is better understood, I will in a moment point out, as individuation, a kind of principle of change at the cross-cultural or philosophical level.

Sartre has, however, produced an enormity by raising diachrony to the *n*th degree. Like the bourgeois Victorian who could acknowledge the existence of hysteria only in another person but never in himself (that is, only in the form of what Harry Stack Sullivan has called a "not-me" construction), Sartre could see primitivity only in the other, in the primitive, but not in himself or in those inhabiting his own civilization. So it would have to follow that for him primitives are simply not capable of analytic reason. The prestige of analytic reason is reserved for moderns. In so saying, Sartre has fallen into his own subjectivity and interiority (he has begun with "the truths of introspection") and made a myth of history and diachrony. Gazing on all this, Lévi-Strauss can only sardonically observe that every civilization in human history "has claimed that it contains the essence of all meaning and dignity of which human society is capable. . . . [There is in this] a good deal of egocentricity and naivete" (p. 249). Analytically informed thinkers will recognize an important linkage between this claim and narcissistic processes and will also realize that it has hardly been, in Freud's words, "surmounted and overcome." Unable to comprehend savage thought, Sartre too (Lévi-Strauss believes) thinks like a savage.

And so, it would seem, did Freud. Sartre's entire oeuvre is steeped from beginning (the early existential psychoanalysis of *Being and Nothingness*) to end (his "psychoanalyses" of Genet, Flaubert, himself, and even of Freud) in psychoanalysis. For good reasons analysts do not accept his integration of psychoanalysis into the existential "project," but the clinical status of Sartre's psychoanalytic perceptions and assertions is not at issue here. For that matter, some of his psychological observations are no cruder than are those of some of the analysts who criticize him. In any case existentialism (and not analytic philosophy and not philosophical phenomenology) is the correct philosophical idiom for psychoanalysis, because only existentialism dares to engage and comprehend the modern thinker's loss of culturally shared, idealized objects (God, "essences" which precede "existences," idealized or a priori categories of thought, etc.). In fact, it is ideality itself—religious or secular—for which existentialism is a de-idealization, for to say that "existence precedes essence" is to de-idealize essence. Everyone knows that Sartre said that "existentialism is a humanism," but this doctrine of man is a poor one indeed unless it is also recognized that "existentialism is a mourning" for the lost idealities of the past. For Freud as well as for Sartre the individual ego, temporality, duration, and science absorb everything that is ideal, permanent, and eternal. Neither one could grasp in philosophic or psychologic imagination the impressive reality of culture for the ego. Instead, both began with the fiction of an ego separated a priori from culture. They could not tolerate a conception of the ego embedded in a social context, such that it was "a part of" its cultural surround as much as it was "apart from" that surround.

In the face of these reflections it is reasonable to ask, What might the relation between a common culture and analytic access look like, were one to avoid the fatal Sartre-Freud error, beginning with the truths of introspection and psychology, from which Lévi-Strauss offers protection, and instead end with them? Lévi-Strauss has never taken this step. He has steadfastly refused to occupy himself with contemporary culture, except as it has served as a foil for his principal interest, savage thought and society. He has, in other words, no way of accounting for the transition from synchrony to diachrony. So, in his works the savage mind stands as a kind of lofty monument to human dignity, in fatal contrast to the follies of modern societies, not unlike the timeless beauty of the figures on Keats's Grecian urn. Since in all great men life and thought are rarely wholly separate, his autobiography, *Tristes Tropiques* (1955), is understandably drenched in a sense of elegiac sadness over the loss of this dignity and beauty. This observation itself suggests what the next line of thought must be.

Mediating between synchrony and diachrony, between timelessness and an inexorable sense of transience and flow, between myth and history, and between structure and event, there exists, I wish to suggest, a kind of world-historical principle which I would characterize as the double activity of monument making and mourning and their "dialectics" of retreat into the past and advance out of it. These activities are grounded in the intermediate space or nexus between "self" and "society," of which psychoanalysis and sociology have become the respective contemporary reifications. In this space symbols are born or created as a result of shared unconscious experience, for synchrony and diachrony are not absolute states. In the former case (retreat into the past), individuation, symbol formation, and structure building take place "on the outside," which is to say, in myths, rituals, and doctrines; in the latter case (advance into the future), the same activities occur through dreams, introspective probes, and distance-conferring insights into depth-psychological self-understanding. This intermediate space is both the location of cultural experience in the mind and the location of personal experiences in culture. Surprisingly, it is possible to be a bit more specific about this transition from synchrony to diachrony.

I refer to Lévi-Strauss's observations on mourning in primitive societies when they are contrasted with mourning activities in advanced industrial societies. The contrast yields what can be called a structural displacement of mourning, from the personal to the social. According to Lévi-Strauss, primitive societies are rich in rites of two sorts, commemorative rites and mourning rites in the strict sense (1962*a*, p. 237). The former are "historical" in that they draw the past (what he calls "the dream age") into the present; the latter draw the present into the past. But both are, for our purposes, forms of mourning. In primitive societies there is little mourning in a collective sense over a lost past because members of these societies are in constant contact with their beginnings through myth and ritual, which together annul the threat which diachrony (and the mourning which diachrony instigates) poses to the culture as a whole. In these societies time stands still.

In modern societies, on the other hand, where ever-advancing industrialization remains the central feature, the reverse would appear to be the case, in the following way. In these societies there has been a decline of mourning rites, for many reasons, one of which is surely the decline in a spiritual understanding of birth and death and of a belief in the Christian idea of the immortality of the soul. And in these societies demographic change is everywhere. Therefore, there has to have been a displacement of mourning from the personal to the social in heavily diachronic societies, and the construction of monuments can be understood as an attempt, on the collective level, to mitigate this shared social problematic. But even in these modern societies the need for mourning of both sorts is rigorously denied or disavowed, in favor of the new realities which will replace older ones, presumably making mourning unnecessary. So I think that it is right to infer that in these societies—of which America is the outstanding instance—some sort of unconscious mourning is constantly taking place at the social level, although it is constantly being denied and disavowed at the individual level. Just as one unconsciously shares and affirms symbols with others, people can also unconsciously share the disavowal of them as well. Moreover, in advanced industrial societies little attention is given to monuments and, more important, to the sentiments they ordinarily evoke. Advanced societies have little time for monuments, and they also take up too much space. Nor is there much time or space for their "cognates": art, parks, religious buildings, and ceremonies of many sorts—all of these of course exist, but they are constantly being driven to the periphery. So here, diachrony is all; here time is ever on the move.

Psychoanalysis is, of course, very much a part of modern Western societies and their inherent instability, which derives from "the special prestige" they accord to "the temporal dimension" (p. 256). Some have even argued that psychoanalysis is a kind of psychological ideology which has actually induced this instability. I turn to this question, that of the so-called psychological culture, in the next section, to examine this argument in detail. Before doing that, I conclude this review by noting briefly the epistemological status of psychoanalysis in the light of Lévi-Strauss's concepts of concrete and abstract science. Proponents of analysis insist that their discipline is an exact or abstract science (something Lévi-Strauss has never accepted); opponents, that it is, in one way or another, really religious, ideological, and so forth—in other words, a science of the concrete, which is to say, it is bricolage. I think it is in the strict sense neither, but that both of these categorizations help explain what it really is.

In one sense a psychoanalytic institute is much more like a ballet company than a scientific organization. There are right and wrong ways to do things, and candidates must learn the right ones. The choreographer says to his dancer, Put your foot here, not there; lean to the left more when you make this turn; and so forth. And the supervising analyst tells his candidate, With her you should interpret less; with him try waiting until the end of the hour before you speak; the best interpretations are made when . . . and so forth. All of this is bricolage. But analysts also study the biology and physiology of dreaming and the ethology of social attachments, and in this sense they strive to construct an abstract science.

Both of these arguments, however, miss the most important point, which is, as Lacan has pointed out, that although psychoanalysis is not in any sense an exact science, it is also simply unthinkable apart from a culture in which science and industrialization are the principal elements and that it is completely structured by these elements. At this point Lévi-Strauss's distinction between structure and event performs an important clarifying function in relation to Lacan's observation. Myths, it will be recalled, form structures out of events and then repeat these structures; science begins with structures (scientific theories) and creates events out of them. Emerging as it did from the disintegration of a common culture (which can be called a set of structures), psychoanalysis sought to create a new series of events, psychological theory, epitomized by the metapsychology. The psychoanalyst seeks to repeat or recapitulate this process in the life of his patient, facilitating his emergence from his common culture, which is represented by the excessive unconscious force of the id and the superego on the ego. When the venture is successful, the "event" is the birth of the self in the life of the patient—in other words, the "event" of individuation. When the venture is unsuccessful, the patient simply becomes a reincarnation or a new version of the old structure. But in the best of circumstances there is some event and some structure. This is because psychoanalysis is both concrete and abstract, both art and science, because it is itself a form of understanding which is "in transition" from a science of the concrete (drawing the individual back into his common culture by allowing the transference to come into being and flourish) to a science of the abstract (through interpretation the transference becomes an instrument for self-understanding and the building blocks of psychological structure). In the first case psychoanalysis resembles traditional spiritual healing practices; in the second, a science of healing mental disorders. Because it is a form of understanding which is constantly "in transition" from an old to a new culture, its attempts to comprehend transitional processes seem unexceptional.

12 The Plight of the Modern Ego Cut Off from Its Christian, Communal Past: Second Contradiction

Lévi-Strauss left us in the lurch when he told us that modern societies are wholly diachronic and thereby miss the quintessential human trait of primitivity but told us nothing more about these historical societies. But he has also pointed the way. He shows us where to look and what to look for. We must look deeper into our own contemporary cultural situation without, however, abandoning our analytical tools. And we must seek out in that situation not only the grim fatality of diachrony but also the possible but unrecognized persistence of synchrony, primitivity, and a common culture. And we must evolve out of these searches fresh ideas and approaches for understanding this culture. There is no better way to begin such a search than to plunge into what Philip Rieff has called the contemporary psychological society. In doing so we reencounter the psychoanalytic movement, the original carrier of psychoanalytic ideas and the mediator of these ideas to the contemporary psychological society, and the most salient features of both: avowed psychological rationality (the commitment to diachrony) and disavowed primitivity (the unconscious group self, etc.). It is not difficult to show that this path has already been carefully cleared for us: the two most brilliant interpretations of Freud's significance for contemporary culture center upon this, Freud's (and our) second contradiction.

Freud confessed openly several times to an irrational need for always thinking in twos (ego instincts/sexual instincts, life instincts/death instincts, etc.). With characteristic psychoanalytic aplomb he traced this tendency back to an early infantile rivalry in his own childhood. This duality, which certainly is central and crucial to both his life and his thought, can also be traced to the social context of psychoanalysis, which forced Freud to cut the ego off from its surrounding social and historical circumstances. The interpretations of

Freud's thought offered by Rieff and Ricoeur engage precisely this issue, although in opposite ways. For Rieff, Freud's psychological-scientific investigations into the unconscious components of the mind and culture have had the effect of permanently separating moderns from the supports of their surrounding social order and from the anchorage of these supports in the Western, Christian past. After Freud, there is no way back, no return to such supports. For Ricoeur, on the other hand, Freud did indeed accomplish such a "break." But the philosopher (who also describes himself as "a listener to the Christian message" [Spiegelberg 1965, p. 568]) has proposed a deeper or higher reading of Freud's works which draws them back into the Western-Christian past by means of the interpretive work of a philosophy of reflection. Each of these two opposing points of view seeks to reconcile the alienation of the diachronic psychological ego from its Western, Christian past. And we could, if we wanted to, trace back to these two views most of the lesser-known works which interpret Freud's impact upon contemporary culture and their varying epistemological and sociological estimates of it.

Although I think that both Rieff and Ricoeur presuppose an essentially individualistic conception of the ego which forestalls any solution to the problem each has so astutely identified and so thoroughly analyzed, either by cutting it off from society and the past (Rieff) or by resubsuming it under the past (Ricoeur), I also think that their opposing positions on Freud's significance for contemporary culture generate deeper, richer, and more wholesome understandings of the contemporary self and its social contexts. So, after breaking down and analyzing their clashing arguments, I draw out elements from both and use these to redefine the parameters of a psychoanalytically informed theory of contemporary culture. From Rieff I draw out the idea that contemporary society is really a culture of fantasy; from Ricoeur I draw out the idea that a hermeneutics of fantasy should be a central component in any philosophy of contemporary culture. Both themes are intimately related in the thought of the two men to the—by now—central concept of mourning and, I will also add, to my own evolving understanding of individuation. Finally, harking back to the previous chapter, I will also plead for a more generous view of primitivity as it makes its inevitable appearances in both contemporary society and in the Christian past.

The student of Rieff's work (1959, 1966) must at the outset separate firmly its style from its contents. The style is rich in nuance and ambiguity, the content is lean, simple, and parsimonious. With Rieff style overrides content, and the powerful effect of his work lies in his capacity to drench the reader's awareness with metaphor, irony, parody, inversions, wit, sarcasm, and bitterness. Through his style Rieff conveys to the reader what he thinks "it feels like," psychologically, to be cut off from the past, the "existential" condition which he insists Freud has forced upon the unsuspecting modern. Although the effect is highly aesthetic, it also produces an overall sense of mourning, which Rieff makes no attempt to disguise. His opening sentence sets the tone for all that follows: "Literature and sociology have long supplied eloquent and knowing professional mourners at the wake for Christian culture . . . much modern poetry constitutes an elegiac farewell . . . to the religious culture of the West" (1966, p. 1). There is no point in trying to summarize Rieff's style; one might just as well try to summarize a poem or (more to the point) a confession. It is best to stay with the conceptual structure, which, though simple, is unusually powerful.

Rieff's is a three-step theory of Freud's impact upon contemporary culture. He thinks that traditional culture, by which he means Western, Christian culture, remained basically intact (though badly eroded) until the end of the nineteenth century. That culture provided an "organizing symbolic," which balanced commitment to its moral imperatives with patterns of release from them but always tipping the balance in favor of the first. The organizing symbolic is "a moral demand system" energized by "primary group moral passion." It is completely and unabashedly authoritarian and is identical to Freud's concept of the unconscious cultural superego. This is the Durkheimian component in Rieff's social analysis, his version of what I have referred to again and again as a common culture.

The second step, "deconversion," is Weberian. As Freud's theories of the way cultural forces have unconsciously coerced individuals (what I call the "cunning of culture") became better and better known to the educated public and to the liberal elites whom this public trusted, these ideas forced upon both more and more psychological skepticism toward the moral demands of their culture and the past. The term "deconversion" is an ironic parody of the Christian experience of conversion into a sociologically grounded, anxiety-reducing system of religious ideas and practices, symbolized beautifully by the religious idea of "the peace of God which passeth all understanding." This is the inner peace which social solidarity confers. Deconversion refers to the break or rupturing of the bond with the organizing symbolic, a Weberian "breakthrough" to a new social ethos stimulated by seminal (which is to say, psychoanalytic) ideas. Just as the Protestant broke from medieval Catholic culture and turned to economic-material reality, so has the post-Protestant broken from Protestantism and turned to the material-libidinal realities of psychology ("the spirit," so to speak, "of psychoanalysis").

The result (third step) is "the triumph of the therapeutic." This phrase is also deeply ironic because the so-called victory does not lead to a new or better organizing symbolic but instead to a virtually permanent (for the time being) state of inner emptiness and despair brought about by the new conviction that what was formerly always assumed to be a solution for despair (commitment to an organizing symbolic) has in fact become the problem. This triumph in effect legitimates the death of culture, for once culture has been "seen through," its capacity to bind the energies of individuals together into a communal whole and thereby reduce intrapsychic conflict is lost. The void is then filled with more and more psychological ideas: the therapeutic is egocentric, prudentially hedonistic, favoring newfound pleasures of release over against all injunctions to submit to primary-group moral passion. The final result is a hideous and bottomless spiral inward in which each new "insight" produces a deeper sense of alienation from the common culture. This ideal-type of contemporary man and culture has been elaborated politically by Christopher Lasch (*The Culture of Narcissism*, 1978), quantitatively by Veroff et al. (*The Inner American*, 1981), who think that Americans are actually less anxious and more psychological than they were twenty years ago, and has been attacked by antipsychological, neoreligious collectivist thinkers, such as Alisdair MacIntyre (1981) and Robert Bellah (1985), who advocate a return to a religious and moral heritage without, however, retaining any psychological self-understanding. Let us move from exposition to analysis.

Just as Weber noted the psychology of the ideal-typical Protestant (his inner loneliness, his anxiety or guilt or low self-esteem, and his methodical-compulsive work habits), so it is also possible to note the psychological features of the therapeutic, which is also an ideal-type. This leads to ironies far deeper than any imagined by Rieff. Outstanding among these is the inability to mourn, which persists beneath the pervasive psychological rhetoric. Broken off from the past, the therapeutic does not allow himself to come in touch with the deeper psychological processes—and the objects associated with these processes—such as, for example, the experiences of cultural loss and the subsequent spontaneous fantasies which loss and breaking away inaugurate. In lieu of these activities psychological man erects a system of ideas and builds up psychological structure "on the outside," in the form of a kind of total psychological belief system which resembles a set of religious doctrines. Such an activity does have the effect of forestalling any engagement with the narcissistic potential which the breakdown of a common culture almost always stirs up in individuals so affected. This state of affairs is more ironic than the ironic triumph of the therapeutic because it means that psychological man is not psychological at all. Instead, he perpetuates the ideology of the psychoanalytic movement, its metapsychology. As Ernest Jones noted of the "tenets" of psychoanalysis, one must believe in them.

The mistake in all this is Freud's truly fantastic assumption that the common cultures of the past could be vanquished by means of analytic reason. This criticism is not, however, a historical or sociological or moral one; it is psychological. The breaking up of a common culture produces more, not less, psychological activity. As the emergence of psychoanalysis itself testifies, such breaking up also produces an opportunity to appreciate, in an even deeper fashion than Freud and his followers thought, the primitivity which lies both within and around the person and these social circumstances. And, we also know, Freud and his followers negotiated this break or transition ambiguously. On one hand they did indeed engage the experiences of loss and transformed these into psychological theory; on the other hand, they split off major portions of the deeper primitivity in their lives and settled for a group solution to it, thereby disavowing the collectivist character of their efforts. So the psychological culture is not composed, at its deepest levels, primarily of a network of psychological ideas, as Freud hoped and as Rieff has said, but of a network of shared psychological processes which are much more primitive and far more deeply unconscious than those described by Freud's classical theory of neurosis. I prefer to characterize this deeper dimension of the psychological culture as a "fantasy culture" or as a "culture of fantasy," and I think that it calls for a fresh theory of interpretation. Whatever shortcomings Rieff's analysis may or may not have, it points us in precisely this direction: to explore more deeply the idea that contemporary culture is composed of shared fantasy processes and not only ideational-cognitive ones and that these processes motivate the actors in this culture in a major and fundamental way which has yet to be understood.

Before turning to this task, however, one might well wonder, if a total break with the past has such deleterious consequences, whether perhaps the reverse, a return to the past, is the more correct psychological and culturological strategy. Such an approach is of course already firmly in place in the work of Paul Ricoeur. While I think that, by drawing the contemporary ego as forcefully and totally back into the past as Rieff drove it forward into the future, Ricoeur forestalls in his way, just as Rieff did in his, the kind of analysis which will reduce this contradiction, Ricoeur's work is also invaluable for my project. For he has shown that the proper object of psychoanalytic inquiry—what stands as "a fact" in psychoanalysis—is not experimentally observable behavior but rather fantasy activity. From this he concludes that psychoanalysis is not an observational science at all but is instead a theory of interpretation of cultural symbols, albeit a mixed one which resides midway between force and meaning (between science and hermeneutics). Ricoeur also thinks that, without including in it the ability to mourn, the philosopher's work of cultural interpretation cannot take place at all. With these thoughts he liberates psychoanalysis from the bondage of experimentalism, positivism, and scientism, although I prefer to characterize this new freedom as a psychoanalytically informed humanistic social science rather than as a philosophy of reflection. Exploring the culture of fantasy (what Rieff has taught us must be done) requires a hermeneutic of fantasy (what Ricoeur tells us must be done). Furthermore, in this coming together of what is to be interpreted and how that is to be accomplished I think that Freud's cultural investigations in his cultural texts—which are but continuations of the clinical writings, and vice versa—find their true and proper object in our own social world, which is but a continuation of his.

Ricoeur is, of course, a preeminent philosopher with extraordinarily wide-ranging interests and commitments. As his work has proceeded, the inevitable summaries and criticisms have appeared to discuss and evaluate each new advance. It is difficult to see how his studies of Freud's theory and therapy are constitutive of this work. These studies actually occupy a middle point—perhaps even a transition point—between his early phenomenological and existential investigations and his more recent, and in a basic sense definitive, work on the humanization of time by means of narrative. In fact, I suspect that his work on Freud, conducted in the middle of his career, freed him from the static idealities of the earlier studies and permitted his most creative current work to take shape. However that may be, Ricoeur's contributions to psychoanalysis remain seminal for it if not for him. They are contained in his enormous, complex, highly poetic, and difficult book, *Freud and Philosophy* (1970), which originally appeared as *De l'interpretation: essai sur Freud* in 1965. Fortunately for us, he has performed a service of great value by reducing its major themes into two short but very compressed discussions in which serious students of the former will recognize all its essentials. After presenting three central ideas drawn from the first (1974) and two additional concepts found in the second (1977), I return to the culture of fantasy and propose that the theory of the interpretation of culture which has been brought forth is all of a piece with the work of individuation, for individuation is a form of psychological work which has an interpretive dimension, and this work must take place in direct relation to the person's cultural ethos, which is the culture of fantasy.

These two papers show how closely wedded is Ricoeur's philosophical interpretation of Freud's theory of culture to what I have called his characteristic "drive to the past": his desire to insert Freud's work into the Christian-philosophical past, to transform that past through psychoanalysis, and then to transform psychoanalysis in the light of that past. The argument moves in three steps. First, a "decentering" or "dispossession" of earlier philosophical understandings of consciousness at the hands of Freud's theory of unconscious fantasy, a theory which Ricoeur refers to as an "archaeology." Second, a "passage" (in the mind of the philosopher) from this archaeology to teleology, which is in effect an overcoming of the reign of primary process in mental life, an overcoming or a mourning which releases the person for living in the present and the future. And third, the fruition of the teleology, the achievement of "Spirit" or "self-consciousness," which might also be called, to keep in the foreground as well the sense of Rieff's work, a "triumph" of the philosophical. But there is no irony here: this is a real victory. These three steps constitute a philosophic interpretation of Freud, which is to say that they refer to processes which take place, at least initially, in the sphere of reflective thought and not in the shared consciousness of society at large. Because this interpretation draws Freud back into the Western philosophical and theological tradition, transforms that tradition, and then transforms psychoanalysis on the basis of that tradition, we can say that in Ricoeur's hands the total break theory which Rieff (and Freud) so adamantly set forth, is totally broken. Let us look at the argument in more detail.

Ricoeur begins with the great Western philosophies of reflection created by Descartes and Husserl, which place a premium on the conscious, reflecting subject or ego or self (the "cogito," the "I think"). Psychoanalysis decenters or dispossesses this cogito by pointing out to the philosopher, who engages in it, that beneath his conscious conviction of the validity of his thinking there lies a dimension of unconscious fantasy, of which he is unaware. Like Copernicus and Darwin (Ricoeur accepts Freud's theory of the three blows), Freud too "decentered the world and life with respect to the claims of consciousness," thereby inflicting "a wound and humiliation to narcissism" (1974, p. 179). So, as a result of Freud's investigations, "one can no longer establish the philosophy of the subject as a philosophy of consciousness" (p. 179). To this must be added Ricoeur's perception that what constitutes a fact in the analytic situation is not an observable, behavioral datum (as in experimental and academic psychology); the only "facts" in psychoanalysis are fantasies, or, more correctly, reports of fantasies. The analyst does not observe fantasy, even when it is reported. Therefore, psychoanalysis is not a behavioral science, although its findings have validity comparable to that of science. Ricoeur also refers to the decentering which psychoanalysis brings about as a "hermeneutic of suspicion": Freud is rightly "suspicious" of the claim of the philosopher's ego to omniscience.

The source of psychoanalysis's power to decenter the philosopher's ego derives from analytic observations of the primary process in the transference, to which the philosopher has no access, and Ricoeur calls this primary process "an archaeology." It is his way of referring to the genetic premise of psychoanalysis, the premise that unconscious infantile conflict lies at the core of all human being. Hence "the restrained archaeology of instincts and narcissism, the generalized archaeology of the superego and idols, the hyperbolic archaeology of the war of the giants Eros and Thanatos" (1974, p. 181). But exactly here the plot thickens and a reversal is inaugurated. Reflective thought also requires that "only a subject which has an *arche* has a *telos.*" Ricoeur believes that it is intrinsic to the life of any and all human subjects that they (or we) "appropriate meaning consolidated prior" to it, so that even the subject who makes use of analytic knowledge in the service of self-knowledge is also "drawn ahead of itself by a succession of 'figures' . . . figures of the spirit" (p. 181). These figures lure the self out of its infantile past by giving "philosophical sense to all psychological maturation and to man's growth out of childhood" (p. 181). They do this by providing the self with "a certain meaningful itinerary" grounded in "a certain number of cultural configurations" (p. 181). These figures and all that they do constitute the teleological side of the dialectic between archaeology and teleology. The (Hegelian) figures of the spirit bring about self-consciousness, Self, Spirit, and history. And so one asks, What are these figures?

They are, quite simply, "culture": "the symbols of art, the ethics of religion," the drives to "economic possession" and to "political power" (p. 182). As Ricoeur is fond of saying, "the symbol gives rise to

thought." He characterizes this movement of thought from archaeology (unconscious infantile forces) to teleology (conscious self-
reflection) as a "passage." This passage, which is a movement within
the sphere of philosophical reflection, is also the dynamic center of
Ricoeur's reading of Freud, and at the center of this center is the
process of mourning, the ability to mourn. In this passage Freud's
theory of culture, which decentered the philosopher's illusion of omniscience, "passes" back into the modes of reflection which it had
wounded and is then reembraced, as it were (one might even say, in a
spirit of respect which recognizes this philosopher's Christian loyalties, "forgiven"). These modes of reflection, which belong to the
Christian past, incorporate the timeless Freudian unconscious and,
having done so, move the human enterprise forward into history,
timefullness, and the future. But only the activity of mourning
makes possible this "passage" from the philosopher's wounded consciousness (his "object loss" of his idealized philosophical ideas) to
its healing by the figures of the spirit: "In this terrible battle for
meaning" (this phrase refers to the famous Ricoeurian "conflict of
interpretations"), he concludes, "nothing and no one comes out un-
scathed. The 'timid' hope must cross the desert of the path of
mourning" (p. 182).

I now wish to lift out several points from Ricoeur's analysis and
put the rest aside, for these points structure and support my attempt
to reformulate the proper object and method of a psychologically
informed approach to contemporary culture and especially the place
of individuation in it. In order that individuation take place, thinking
about the symbols of culture is essential, although that thinking is
not by any means always conscious. But first a criticism. Yes, the
Hegelian teleology is too spiritual: in Ricoeur's construction its "figures" somehow lose contact with their fantasy substrates, the
realities which Freud discovered. So the self is removed—although
this is not the philosopher's intention—from its immediate social
context and from the primitivity which swarms about and within
that context in the form of shared social fantasy. Ricoeur's "pull"
back into the spiritualities of the Christian past (his and our common
culture) has the unintended effect of actually ablating its primitivity.
So the Ricoeurian self is, ironically, as egological, as individualistic,
and as diachronic as Freud's—and Rieff's. When juxtaposed to one
another, they tear the ego to pieces. And indeed these two interpretations of Freud frame on an intellectual level the contemporary ego's
social and psychological condition. Individuation is the work
through which a healing of this rupture can at least begin to take
place.

Ricoeur's studies of Freud make a threefold contribution to the psychology of contemporary culture and of individuation. First, the heart of psychoanalysis, the analytic situation, is (he tells us) constituted around fantasy. Fantasy is psychical, which is to say that it is neither experimental-observational nor spiritual. It is "between" them. This perception can be extended without loss to socially shared fantasy as it makes its manifold appearances in the social contexts of both the present and the past. Second, the appropriation of fantasy activity for the criticism of culture is firmly anchored in the processes of mourning and its consequent, associated process of structure building. Earlier I pointed out that the entire psychoanalytic theory of personal development can be understood as a process of unconscious mourning for the deeply desired but lost objects of the infantile life. Later I proposed that this dynamic pertained as well to lost social objects in historical situations—cherished ideas, ideals, and principles. But only Ricoeur has had the wisdom and the courage to point out that this very same dynamic characterizes the innermost activities of the philosopher's work of reflection, activities which are to some considerable extent psychological in nature. For the journey from the archaeology to the teleology, which he asks the philosopher to make, must "cross the desert of the path of mourning." In sum: the child in all of us struggling with his own growth processes, and the great originative figure struggling with the terrors of his changing historical situation, and the philosopher who attempts to comprehend both—all share a bond, the "bond" of mourning.

So the sequence would seem to be: loss → mourning → structure building, these together constituting individuation. But this is still not right, for something is missing. It is loss (object loss) which produces fantasy activity (understood in Freud's sense as "imagination"—*Phantasieren*), it is interpretation (of fantasy) which yields up mourning, it is the consolidation of interpretation which facilitates structure building, and it is these together which produce the inner conviction that one is, in the course of such actions, becoming an imperishable, unique, and single self, which is to say, individuating. In all this, contact with the ubiquitous commonalities of the cultural surround is not lost. Rather, inner and outer come together in the realization that both are genuinely made or created by the individual and also given to him by his cultural heritage—they were "there" all the time; it is just that before he did not see them. How this combination of "made" and "given" comes about is explored in more detail in the closing chapter under the topic "the creation of meaning."

So the sequence should read: loss → fantasy → interpretation/ mourning → structure building on the inside, these together constituting individuation. It is a bad mistake to restrict the activity of interpretation to the work of the philosopher, or to the work of the psychoanalyst, or to the work of the social critic. For the growing child also interprets, albeit unconsciously, and so does the originative cultural worker who derives new modes of self-understanding in order to revision his own and his fellow man's world. All are "hermeneuts," for all say (consciously and unconsciously), "I interpret, and therefore I am." The mourning/interpretation/individuation "dialectic" (the term can now be used) is the red thread that links together, despite their manifold differences, the psychological, the sociohistorical, and the philosophical. But this dialectic must be grounded in the ego's immediate and also intermediate social space, for when I interpret I always interpret someone, or something which someone has made, and that something is always a part of that someone, and my interpretation is always to some extent a part of myself. A preliminary and necessarily brief probe can now be ventured, in which one moves out of the sphere of philosophical reflection and into the arena of contemporary cultural symbolic structures.

The so-called psychological society does not consist primarily of an aggregate of unattached individuals invested in and making sense of the world through psychological ideas. It is, rather, a mass society or a mass culture, the principal element of which is its unique and peculiar kind of instability: it is constantly breaking itself down and building itself up, virtually before our very eyes. This instability owes its origin in part to the prior breaking up of the common cultures of the Western past, and in this sense this instability is unprecedented. Despite its novelty, this mass or psychological society is not as completely unstable and chaotic as moralists (Rieff, Lasch, MacIntyre, Bellah) are fond of pointing out, for it also has a structure, although this structure differs from the sociological realities which conferred structure upon earlier social periods. Neither the usual explanations of its instability (urbanization, industrialization, technology, and the mass media) nor the usual explanations of its stability (autonomy, rationality, differentiation, division of labor, bureaucracy) go deep enough.

What accounts for both the instability and the stability of modern mass society is its fantasy structure. To clarify this point, let us go back to the origins of psychoanalysis. McGrath (1986, pp. 314–16) has called attention to Schorske's extraordinarily apt phrase, "the politics of fantasy." It refers to the way political leaders in fin-de-siècle Vienna composed what he called "ideological collages" or "ideological mosaics" which gave substance to the observation of the poet Hugo Hofmannsthal: "Politics is magic. He who knows how to summon the forces from the deep, him will they follow" (Schorske 1973, pp. 120, 134). Here Schorske has called attention to the political leader's unconscious but also devastatingly accurate inner perception and conviction that his power lies precisely in his capacity to engage—by means of displaced and coded or disguised ideas and ideals—the unconscious fears, wishes, and inner objects of citizens and then to draw these in upon himself. Schorske thinks that turn-of-the-century Vienna (and not postwar Europe and America) was the real birthplace of "psychological man" and the psychological society. Hofmannsthal and Schnitzler "both affirmed as fact the emergence of psychological man from the wreckage of the old culture" (p. 22). But psychoanalysis, which embodies exactly the inverse of the dictum that "politics is magic," also emerged from the same wreckage. It is an irony of considerable—and generally unacknowledged—magnitude that a politics of fantasy and a fantasy-centered psychology of politics (which is to say, psychoanalysis) both appeared and existed side by side in the same place and at the same time. I attempt to account for this irony in the closing chapter.

Perhaps it is even more ironic—it is certainly also of great significance—that both forms of consciousness migrated into (or that the same twin social mechanisms repeated themselves in) current Western societies and that both have expanded their activities there. For contemporary Western societies are now no longer composed of only a politics of fantasy. They contain different orders or subuniverses of fantasy and also a burgeoning of different types of psychoanalysis. For example, we now have an "economics of fantasy." Fantasy is bodily, and groups unconsciously construct shared social fantasy formations by taking the human body as a template for their imaginative activities. Persons unconsciously construct stock markets along the lines of the human body, through the mechanism of projective identification: so we are told that the market is "sluggish" (constipated); it has "panics"; it is "healthy" or else it is "feverish"; it is "falling" or "rising"; it is, in some strange sense, a "mystical body." Advertising conflates fantasy processes with objects drawn from physical, social, and economic orders and in doing so constructs human social situations in which all doubt, anxiety, and even thought itself are either highly typical or eliminated. There is, too, an "aesthetics of fantasy": the figures and gestures of mass entertainment build up fantasy patterns, while the plays and novels of "high culture" attempt to transform these fantasy typifications of shared social experience back into the more individualized recesses of the solitary reader's searching mind. Together these various sectors of fantasy activity make up an entire symbolic system which derives its structure from the special characteristics of shared fantasy, which has become institutionalized.

Moralists of every sort of course know all this. But it is also a rule of public discourse that all participants in the fantasy-grounded symbolic system must disavow, in the course of public discussion, any direct consideration of its deeper dynamics: fantasy is recognized, but only as "mere" fantasy. Like the dreamer who, upon waking, says "It's only a dream," and like the joke maker who, after expressing unconsciously a consciously unacceptable social perception, says, "It's only a joke," the culture of fantasy has no meaningful status in public discourse. A serious, thoughtful and introspectively sensitive discussion of socially shared fantasy is just not possible within the sphere of public communications. What is important there is ideas, not fantasy. This rule is continuous with the "high culture" approach to contemporary culture. In the minds of literary elites the culture of fantasy is of no significance because they do not choose to see a relationship between it and real culture, which is to say, their culture, the great works of the past. Let us take this discussion one step further.

It is also possible to characterize the culture of fantasy as primitive, both in the sense in which Lévi-Strauss has used this term (the savage mind, synchrony, mythic thought, etc.) and in the depth-psychological sense (unconscious, prestructural group processes), as previous discussions have already suggested. I have used both views of primitivity to interpret major features of the psychoanalytic movement. Many of the themes and ideas contained in and expressed by the culture of fantasy are mythic in the sense just mentioned. In this regard they are meaningful, which is to say that they have a structure and that this structural property confers some stability on society as a whole. Furthermore, the structures and contents of the culture of fantasy are by no means wholly discontinuous from the past (although those who produce it deny this), a past which is in all major respects the Christian past. This past is also primitive—something which the curators and producers of Christian culture always deny. Just as socially shared fantasy structures (the culture of fantasy) have mythic components, so do socially shared mythic structures (the "cultures" of Christianity) have fantasy components. Liberal-modern Christian philosophers and theologians who could be referred to as "the religious Left," have valiantly attempted to overcome the primitivity of their own religious past. The most eminent of these, the German theologian Rudolph Bultmann, called this project of overcoming "demythologization," but that can also be called "de-primitiv-ization." One of Bultmann's best-known collections on the subject is entitled *Primitive Christianity in Its Contemporary Setting* (1956). The disavowal of the generative force of fantasy in both modern and ancient social settings betrays a contempt for a sense of continuity over time and a frantic attempt to maintain the idea of the new, which is now of course an old idea.

Although these remarks do not purport to evolve a theory of the culture of fantasy, a crucial observation on the sociological mechanism of its origins is hardly inappropriate. Industrialization is cited often enough as a key engendering factor, but it alone (or any of the others mentioned above) could never have produced an entire culture of fantasy. For that, the confluence of two unrelated factors, one social, the other technical, was necessary. Decentered by industrialization, the integrating functions of the common cultures of the West weakened, and persons' fantasy processes no longer had the advantage of a shared symbolic container. At precisely this point the technologizing of these very fantasy processes, released by social-structural change, began through the inventions of the motion-picture camera and projector and, later, of television. The fundamentally human capacity for fantasy became "transferred" into a technological medium, such that the inner worlds of individual persons' minds have come to be represented, again and again, first in mechanical and then later in electronic forms. Transposing Walter Benjamin's well-known title, one must now think anew of "the work of fantasy" as it takes place in "an age of 'electronic' reproduction."

The relatively recent technologizing of fantasy has produced a new site for what I have repeatedly referred to as "the intermediate space," in which both the ego and the social other are embedded and within which fantasy and symbol are generated. I refer of course to "the screen." Today one cannot simply refer to the film screen; one must also include the television screen, the pictorial magazine screen, the photographic screen, and so forth. One perceptive critic has referred to "the dream screen" (Eberwein 1984) and has suggested (correctly, I think) that the film screen is an extension or a kind of psychical prosthesis of the invisible, intrapsychical, but also phenomenologically all-too-real "screen" on which each of us, alone and late at night, projects his own dreams, their "manifest content."

Taken in its broadest and most inclusive sense, it is this socially shared screen which today has come to mediate between the contents of the individual person's unconscious inner world and the myriad productions of the various social orders of modern society, for these productions are more and more likely to reach individuals in the form of fantasy structures, of which the "politics of fantasy" was but the first and only the most rudimentary. The screen is, in this sense, the generative source of a new "common culture." The step from this fundamental structure of contemporary culture to individuation is much shorter than might at first seem.

If this culture of fantasy is the social context within which the ego is embedded, and if this culture is mediated to the ego by way of the screen, upon which culture constructs its figures, typical situations, and ideals, then individuation, when it occurs, can take place only in relation to and within this context, and it is to this context that interpretation, which individuation stimulates and which in turn advances the creation of meaning, must be directed. Such activity provides the only finally reliable stability for that instability which is the culture of fantasy. It is through interpretation that the ego separates itself from, but also reappropriates, the collective contents of the cultural surround. For the most part, our shared self-understanding has restricted both (interpretation/individuation) to the products of high culture. But the line between these two is now no longer clearly drawn. The fundamental feature of the culture of fantasy is its recombinant or intermixed character. The figures of culture (ideas, ideals, images of representative persons) together move in and out of both spheres (high and mass cultures), often existing side by side. Furthermore, only the analysis of this culture can lead to a reappropriation of the past, for it is this culture which stands between present and past. The culture of fantasy is so thick and so ubiquitous that only interpretation can see through it and make contact with what came before it. Its utter novelty has been badly overestimated. And so, in the context of this culture an analytically informed philosophy of reflection upon contemporary cultural forms can be built up. In sum, I think that in the culture of fantasy Freud's investigations of culture, the cultural texts, which always sought the fantasy infrastructures beneath the cognitive and ideological superstructures of what he called *Kultur*, find their most appropriate objects.

The question now arises, What attitude is the interpreter of culture to take up in relation to his objects? In other words, Is there an epistemology of fantasy? To answer this question I once again engage in the strategy of a detour, going back to the historical emergence of science in the West. But now I refer to that emergence as the development of "the enjoyment of theoretical curiosity"—except that this time the concern is not with the origins of curiosity about the world of natural objects but how the enjoyment of theoretical curiosity about the inner world and especially about its social manifestations became a historical reality. This quest draws me back, once again, into the heart of Christian theology. The ideal of enjoying theoretical curiosity precipitated—or as I will say, "individuated"—out of that theology. That development, that "individuation," reached its fruition, in the West at least, in the appearance of Freud's psychology.

13 The Conflict between Religious Absolutism and Curiosity about the Inner World: Third Contradiction

The process of secularization is almost always omitted entirely from authoritative accounts of the origins of psychoanalysis, but as this study has proceeded it has loomed larger and larger. It appeared in Freud's unconscious struggle to separate himself from his Jewish sense of belonging; he actually used a version of it in his theory of the three blows to Western man's narcissism; Merton's work on the origins of science in the Puritan Royal Society touched on it; and Lévi-Strauss, Rieff, and Ricoeur all offered versions of it in one way or another. These discussions have all been either sweepingly synchronic (Durkheim, Lévi-Strauss) or extremely local (historical studies of disenchantment in turn-of-the-century Vienna or in the contemporary psychological society). Helpful as they may have been, none has provided a precise sense of the term or of those historical processes in Western culture to which it repeatedly refers. But a theory of secularization which is at once far-reaching, concise, and specific is essential for a more complete understanding of the origins of psychoanalysis, because only it fully recognizes and then explains the riddle or mystery of how a scientific view of the world, upon which psychoanalysis is predicated, could and did emerge from a religious one. As such it clarifies and corrects Freud's simplistic and ahistorical account of the origins of his entire project. For he believed that he need only substitute psychological ideas for religious ones. He could in no way fathom the intimate, internal, and processive relations which actually existed between religion and science, and between religion and his own science—hence what I have called his third contradiction. A good case can be made for the view that this tension is the deepest and most pervasive of all three.

Evolving a more precise understanding of secularization has a second advantage, related directly to the subproject of this third essay:

that of acquiring a broader and more historical understanding of the roots of individuation. I have already suggested in a general way that the breakdown of persons' unconscious, undifferentiated ties or attachments to a common culture stimulates mourning, individuation, and structure building. Now I want to build upon this formulation by proposing that the nature of individuation is further clarified when it is understood historically as a response to secularization. Although it is a phenomenon found in all cultures, the conception of it which I wish to evolve here—the depth-psychological conception—is best understood as a response to the secularization of the Western, Christian religious tradition. In this sense, individuation *is* secularization but "out of" and "away from" a set of common cultures with a unique and very specific historical shape. Mourning is but the first half of individuation, its backward-looking dimension; if that is successful, the forward-looking component—I will here suggest—makes its appearance and takes the form of enjoyable curiosity about the inner, psychological world and—I hasten to add—about its social surround. Such enjoyment is also the proper epistemological stance of the modern person, for the "social surround" is none other than the culture of fantasy, already described above. In the final chapter, I attempt to formulate a revisionist conception of fantasy activity which actually facilitates a bringing together of the past and the present through the creation of meaning, the central and most elusive psychological action of individuation, for in it curiosity, the past, the individual's propensity for fantasy constructions, and meaning all support—rather than oppose—each other.

Both of these concerns (Freud's with the clash between religion and science, mine with individuation) meet in the work of the brilliant German philosopher of history Hans Blumenberg (1966). Blumenberg's is the most learned and extensive historical review in contemporary scholarship of the process of secularization in the West. He traces the idea from early gnostic speculations into the several periods of medieval Catholic theology, from there into the scientific, philosophical, and theological controversies of the seventeenth century, from there into the Enlightenment, Romanticism, and modern philosophies of history, and from there (at last) into the works of Ludwig Feuerbach and Freud, which he thinks together constituted a final integration of the secularization process into modern Western thought. Out of this sweep I draw out a small cluster of closely related ideas which I think constitute the core process of secularization and situate within it leading moments of Freud's life, work, and movement.

The crucial issue in the process of secularization is the emergence, within a religious context, of three closely linked ideas: theoretical curiosity about the natural order, the social organization of that curiosity into a community of men who called themselves scientists, and their wholehearted commitment to the idea and ideal of progress. But the process of this emergence is just as important as the product. The medieval Christian-theological view of the world foreclosed such curiosity because it presented the world to man as given by God, who, because he had made the world, already understood the world fully and completely. So his knowledge of the world was such that man's curiosity could take the form only of theological curiosity—curiosity about the divine mystery of creation. Blumenberg refers to this given cosmic ordering of things as the reign of "theological absolutism." At a particular time and place, however, men turned away from this absolutism, although the liberation of theoretical curiosity (about the natural world) from it inaugurated a centuries-long debate about it: the "trial" of theoretical curiosity. It is a legal metaphor. Curiosity was "on trial": Was it legitimate or illegitimate? Was this secularization a transposition of theological curiosity, or was it a wholly new kind of inquiry which broke away entirely from the old? If the former, then it had to be returned to its origin; if the latter, it needed to be exposed as such and discredited. The trial lasted a long time and did not end until the most cunning lawyer of all for the defense, Ludwig Feuerbach, pointed out and exposed a hidden relation between Christianity, theology, and the belief in immortality, on the one hand, and the omnipresence of temporality, curiosity, and psychology, on the other hand. It only remained for Freud to generalize or pluralize theoretical curiosity from the natural world into "the inner world" by repeating, on a new set of materials, the pattern of secularization which Feuerbach had mediated to him from the theological absolutism of the Western past.

And so there are three phases in the trial of theoretical curiosity in the West which are of central interest to the student of psychoanalysis: its late medieval inception, its Feuerbachian replication, and its Freudian explication and conclusion. But of even greater interest in all this is the question, How could theoretical curiosity have emerged from within the highly theological matrix which was so inimicable to it? The answer lies not so much in the nature of theological absolutism, or in the character of science and progress, as in the nature of the shift itself from the first to the second, which consisted in "resignation" and "renunciation." Let us look at the process of secularization in more detail.

Late medieval Christianity provided Western society with a religious view of the world: "an ordered structure of the world oriented to man" (Blumenberg 1966, p. 139). This structure promised "that the world has a particular quality for man that in effect prescribes his basic mode of behavior" (p. 143). This quality consisted in "the belief that one is confronted throughout reality with what is already finished, that all one can do is either adapt oneself to this order or violate it" (pp. 214–15). Doubt in the existence of this order, however, produced "a new concept of human freedom . . . responsibility for the condition of the world as a challenge relating to the future . . . an existential program" in which "man posits his existence in a historical situation and indicates to himself how he is going to deal with the reality surrounding him" (p. 138). This "modern will to knowledge" was linked to "the elementary concern for self-assertion" (p. 182). So secularization consisted in a transition from the religious sense of the world as "what is already finished" to a view of the world understood as unknown but also capable of being known by men through their own efforts. Through these efforts men actualized "the primeval right to self-assertion" (p. 196).

The agent of this transition was the theologian William of Ockham (1300–49). Ockham challenged the religious view, redirected reason to the idea of an orderly nature to be understood by method, and in doing so also inaugurated the experience of time as the (from then on) principal human problematic. Blumenberg explains:

> Raising theology to its maximum pretension over against reason had the unintended result of reducing theology's role in explaining the world to a minimum, and thus preparing the competence of reason as the organ for a new kind of science that would liberate itself from tradition. . . . [It] included . . . the continual revisability of its results . . . [and] explaining the phenomenon by means of hypotheses. (P. 347)

> . . . the God whose activity does not allow us to assume immanent laws . . . Who places no constraints on Himself . . . makes time into a dimension of utter uncertainty . . . the human spirit's "temporality," its being in time, becomes the cruel handicap. (Pp. 161–62)

Blumenberg's account of the "mechanism" of this transition makes repeated use of the words "renunciation," "resignation," and "disappointment": "What still had to happen between the fourteenth and the seventeenth centuries in order to lay the foundation for the formation of the modern age . . . looks like a very decisive renunciation, a resignation" of the tendency "to measure oneself (in one's theoretical relation to nature) against the norm of knowing the Creation from the angle of vision and with the categories of the Creator" (p. 352).

This shift, begun by Ockham, gradually consolidated at the time of Descartes into the ideals of method and progress, a "methodically regulated theory" which was "a coherent entity" and which evolved "independently of individuals and generations" (p. 30). Men began to commit themselves to generating a body of knowledge whose results they knew would not be realized within the duration of their own life courses. Hence, "the necessary disappointment of each individual . . . doing work in his particular situation for a future whose enjoyment he cannot inherit" (p. 35). In this shift we see the emergence of a new model of knowledge, one very different from the old theological approach, in which time, science, and the problem of personal mortality become fused. All of this, taken together, is secularization, the trial of theoretical curiosity.

It was this model of knowledge which Freud acquired as a young man through his studies at the University of Vienna before he decided upon a medical practice. It was mediated to him in important ways by his reading of Ludwig Feuerbach, who thought there were crucial relations between the idea of Christian immortality, temporality, curiosity, theology (belief in God), and psychology. Before turning to that, I wish to add one psychological observation to this historical-philosophical understanding of secularization. I have already referred to it as a "transition" and have noted Blumenberg's use of such terms as disappointment, resignation, and renunciation. In addition to these conscious, moral, epistemological, and cognitive responses, I think that any shift of this magnitude in a world outlook had to have included unconscious components as well—which is of course to say that mourning (both conscious and unconscious) accompanied renunciation and resignation. The history of theology shows us that its representative persons (theologians and priests) deeply love their God. After all, Christianity is a religion of love. And so, when they turn away from him, any such turning has to have at its center the unconscious experience of object loss and its disturbing consequences.

Principal among these consequences was the attempt to replace a lost structure (the omniscient, eternal God) with a new kind of structure, and it also has to have followed that the new creation would bear traces of the old. Deprived of participation in the life of a divine, all-knowing object who conferred immortality upon his creatures, these men underwent loss and built up a new structure: a trans-generational community of investigators dedicated to forms of knowledge the final features of which they knew they would never have the opportunity to know. For them, as for Freud, the idea of progress was "the only regulative principle which can make history humanly bearable" (p. 35). The new model was not a mere repetition of the old under a new guise. It was not "the transposition of authentically theological contents into secularized alienation from their origins" (p. 65). Nor was it a total break with these contents, although it was consciously experienced as such. While it is true that in the process of mourning the object is truly lost, it is also true that the object "lives on" in the person's life—although deprived of its original forms of influence—in a modality which to some extent transforms the earlier mental organization. It is in this double and eminently psychological sense that the idea of progress can be rightly understood as a "secularization" of the Christian theology of history. The psychologist does have this to say to the historian of philosophy, but he comes to his realization of what he has to say only after the historian has spoken.

Blumenberg observes that the trial of theoretical curiosity, begun by Ockham, and found in almost pure form in the works of Copernicus, and consolidated philosophically in Descartes's theory of method, received its final integration into modern Western "philosophical," not "social," anthropology in the works of Feuerbach and Freud. In fact, this integration proved that the trial had really been won after all. While it initially "concentrated, in terms of its objects, on nature," this trial was diffused "to other realms"—there arose a "pluralism of curiosity" (p. 437). So "other possible ways of going beyond boundaries" set by theology emerged (p. 440). Feuerbach thought that the Platonic and Christian philosophies contained the premise that man has a knowledge drive "by which . . . his immortality is guaranteed and given meaning" (p. 441). But Feuerbach also proposed that theology was "the true, the objective, the manifest, the complete psychology" (p. 441). By this he meant that the religious ideas of God and immortality embodied the essence of man but in externalized and disguised form. This externalization was not, however, "defensive" in the psychological sense, but creative. By externalizing and disguising, men could begin to know themselves anew. Only the correct translation "back" was required. The translation which Feuerbach offered was, however, truly devastating: "The idea of immortality is curiosity that does not yet understand itself in its rational economy; it is the negation of history." Immortality is "the uncomprehended aspect of temporality" (p. 442). But this shift from immortality to temporality was not a secularization, it was "the retraction of a projection" (p. 443). Feuerbach's conception of the knowledge drive (curiosity) was very similar to Descartes's idea of method: "In the progress of knowledge, individuals are only functionaries. They do not partake of the totality of knowledge. Not immortality but the finality of death is the real catalyst of curiosity" (p. 444).[1]

Obviously, it is but a short step from these reflections and their historical roots in the emergence of Western science to the life and work of Freud. But when we finally get to it, Blumenberg's discussion of Freud is surprisingly sparse. Fortunately, however, only one of his few key observations is needed to send us on our own way. In introducing his reader to *Beyond the Pleasure Principle*, Freud understandably felt the need to hedge a bit: "What follows is speculation . . . it is . . . an attempt to follow out an idea consistently, out of curiosity to see where it will lead . . . it is surely possible to throw oneself into a line of thought and to follow it wherever it leads out of simple, scientific curiosity" (p. 448). It is of great interest to observe that this, the most direct and explicit of Freud's statements linking science and curiosity, occurs in the context of the most speculative of all his books, one which even most analysts wholly reject.

When secularization is understood in Blumenberg's sense, most of what we know about the life and work of Freud appears to be a product of it. Were not the self-analysis and the writing of *The Interpretation of Dreams* expressions of Freud's deep curiosity to know, and to form a theory about, the inner world? And did he not derive great enjoyment from this work, in which he permitted the inner world of his fantasies and dreams to reveal themselves to him, while he took up toward them an attitude which was one of both "free-floating attention" and objective scrutiny? That world had in former times been the sacrosanct precinct of religion and politics—of theological absolutism and its heir, political absolutism. The model of investigation was the dream, which, in a fashion virtually identical with the Feuerbachian dialectic, objectifies (projects) and codes the inner essence of man and, as such, calls for the tactic of retracting the projection and returning it to its natural origins and context. Here "natural" refers less to objective laws and forces and more to a subjective sense of "letting be" or a "letting go." What seems at first extraordinary and mysterious—that is, given to man as an order of experience which is "already finished" and to which he must either adapt or violate (Freud did neither)—becomes ordinary, human, and therefore in principle comprehensible by virtue of the reason of men. What was first experienced phenomenologically to have been "on the outside" (cosmology and myth) was returned to its proper or natural place "on the inside" (psychology).

Freud had to call these researches science because he clearly conceived of himself and his work as in some real sense the culmination of the trial of theoretical curiosity in the history of Western culture. The theory of the three blows was his own personal version of the final winning of this trial. This theory was, in effect, his way of saying, It is I who have finally won this trial and put it to rest. Hence too the generous references in his works to Copernicus, for both men enjoyed theoretical curiosity about the natural order. The reality alone of this enjoyment precedes all disputes about the existence of physicalistic laws of the mind (the metapsychology). For this reason too Freud found no difficulty in admiring da Vinci as much as he did Copernicus. That artist-scientist had, in a way Freud thought exemplary, dared to interest himself "in what is remote, out of the way, unexamined, or traditionally prohibited . . . in what was deep in the sea and distant in time"—in other words, he was curious about things which "had hitherto remained invisible to the onlooker at the world spectacle" (p. 363).

This formulation of the secularization process also sheds some much-needed additional light on the shape of the psychoanalytic movement. It embodied in its own way much that was constitutive of Descartes's method. For similar reasons Freud had to see his little group as transgenerational, and for the same reasons he claimed truth and authority for his findings and theories. The movement was, after all, a community of investigators, none of whom (but chiefly Freud himself, for most of his followers were a generation younger) would ever know what others with whom they or he worked (his followers) would eventually come to understand. The chilling finality of death, so subtly linked to the capacity for curiosity, generated a commitment to an ideal of human progress, but it also constituted the only major consolation of the movement. So too with Freud's "death anxiety." I have already noted some of its psychological and sociological components, but it had this virtually ontological dimension as well. So Freud struggled against his longings for immortality by consoling himself with curiosity. He fought against the all-too-human preference to dream rather than think, by thinking about dreaming. And then he mourned for himself and what he had done and for the future of his work. We have here before us a very special kind of courage.

And so too, the cultural texts, their inception in the theory of the three blows and the primacy it accorded to Copernicus. The cultural texts were but the coming to completion of their precursors, the self-analysis and the dynamics of movement. But the rhetoric of secularization permits us to speak, now, of the origins of all three in terms of "absolutism." The historical emergence of psychoanalysis was but a much, much later version of Ockham's disillusionment with religious reality. His God, the God of theological absolutism, was the cosmological instauration of medieval, Christian men's shared propensity to totalize and constellate their grandiose, narcissistic potential around and within a socially agreed-upon idealized object. In his cultural texts Freud generalized and pluralized yet again the theoretical curiosity about the inner world which he had satisfied earlier in the self-analysis, and this time directed that capacity to the shared unconscious components of the social world. To accomplish this goal he simply had to return again and again in text after text to the psychological dynamics of Western religion, even more than to philosophy, for he intuitively understood that his own work bore an internal relation to this tradition. It was just that he was unable to comprehend the complexities of how such an intricate relation could exist—he did not understand "the mechanism" of secularization. Hence his third contradiction.

It would no doubt be hazardous and probably foolish as well to speak of "Darwin's razor," but there is little risk in speaking of "Freud's razor." "Ockham's razor" claimed that entities must not be multiplied beyond necessity; Freud said, projections must not be multiplied beyond necessity. Freud's razor slashed away at the projections of first theological and then political absolutism. Alas, to these two absolutisms we have had to add a third, psychological absolutism, especially as it is found in the activities of the psychoanalytic movement. But the disappointment and mourning which this realization calls forth in those who idealize Freud and psychoanalysis are softened, at least a little, by the recognition that psychoanalysis—at least in the form of its key, central tool, the transference in the analytic situation—also contains within it the context and "method" whereby absolutism of every stripe can be reduced, at least in principle, through a depth-psychological understanding of its relation to unconscious developmental and sociological conflict.

And now the centrality that psychoanalysis accords to the agony of temporality and its impatience with the past, which more than a few times bordered on a hatred of culture, appear even less mysterious than before. If time and temporality did indeed explode into Western forms of historical thought through Ockham's and others' resigned disenchantment with their deity's timeless eternity, then it reexploded into the deeper recesses of contemporary consciousness in the form of Freud's psychological investigations. In them the impact of the revolution begun by Copernicus struck not just the conscious minds but also the hearts of men. The unconscious, Freud thought, was timelessness itself, and so, under the aegis of the psychoanalytic project (the imperative "to make the unconscious conscious") the mind becomes increasingly historical and temporal. Freud was so captured by this dynamic that he could not envisage a return to, or a retrieval of, or a rapprochement with, the past. There would be no friendship, not even a treaty, with such a past. But this simplistic splitting has not held up. There is now some evidence that the id itself contains diachronic components or strains, a thought which Freud himself clumsily reached for when he attempted to fathom the problems of transgenerational psychological inheritance. And, as I have been at some pains to point out, the ego is not nearly as diachronic, individual, and historical as Freud makes it out to be. There is a subterranean echo in Freud's cultural texts which signals a profound and anguished yearning for—indeed, a true love of—the past, as his passion for antiquity and its memorials clearly indicates.

This invaluable understanding of secularization and its leading elements poses once again, this time in the most direct way possible, the central contradiction of Freud's theory of culture, the problem of the ego's relation to its historical past, and these considerations bear directly on the theory of individuation. Just as psychoanalysis belongs, in an extraordinarily intimate sense, to the secularization of the West, so does individuation: individuation *is* secularization. In the words of Ricoeur, once one has crossed "the desert of the path of mourning" (1974, p. 182), one is not only able to engage in more authentic forms of philosophical reflection; one is also able to become curious about the inner world, to enjoy that curiosity and—this is most important—to recognize that the very objects of that world are deeply implicated in the social order from which they have in fact sprung. So individuation is also a form of reflexivity in which the self can recognize the social contexts of its becoming (the "soulish" part of the person) even as it is becoming within these contexts (the egological parts of the person). Individuation is not just the gradual emergence of a personal center out of an unconscious familial matrix; it is also the emergence of that matrix out of the social and historical matrices of which the family matrix is itself but an emergent part.

But this construction of the secularization/individuation dynamic also differs in an important way from Blumenberg's or Freud's sense of the process. The inclusion of mourning in this construction distinguishes individuation from Blumenberg's ideal of theoretical curiosity and from Freud's ideal of the identity between adult ego formation and a scientific view of the world (science was, for Freud, the prototype of the ego's capacity to test reality). These views of curiosity are excessively individualistic and positivistic because they do not allow the ego to become implicated in a depth-psychological way in the kind of mourning process I have described, a process which has a powerful social component. In such mourning nothing is ever completely given up; something of what has been lost is always retained, albeit in transmuted form. Because the modern ego has individuated out of the social-historical and collective structures of the past, through a mourning instigated by science, the imprint of that past, which is in its primary sense fundamentally religious, is never entirely erased. So a creative relation to the past (which I have referred to at times as return, as retrieval, as rapprochement or, more simply, as "friendship") is always possible. To some extent one always remains a part of what one has parted from. The idea of individuation which I am evolving here retains the individualistic thrust of Blumenberg and Freud but also includes the deeper components of the mind already alluded to in the history and sociology of psychoanalysis: the primacy of prestructural aspects of attachment, of narcissistic processes, of the group self and the group illusion. Individuation is indeed the actualization of the primeval right to human self-assertion and theoretical curiosity, to be enjoyed by men together, but these are predicated upon a "historical a priori" of mourning.

In short, the emergence of natural science was indeed accompanied by a renunciation of shared, cherished divine objects and by resignation to this state of affairs. But its emergence also required a repression of those deeper self-processes just alluded to. In recent times these processes have "returned" in a variety of social and existential forms: revisionist psychoanalysis, the contemporary culture of fantasy, the revival of religion, and, more generally, in the shift from modern to postmodern thought in a number of disciplines. This observation formulates in a far better way, I think, the famous Freudian dictum "the return of the repressed" because its essential characteristic, in both its repressed and remanifesting forms, is primitivity, and this forcing back of self-processes has been a crucial ingredient in claims to total objectivity, especially in psychoanalysis and the social sciences.

The actualization of curiosity which is individuation can be conceptualized by the psychological activity of structure building, which I think of metaphorically as taking place both "on the outside" and "on the inside" and which has both cognitive and affective dimensions. As secularization has proceeded, there has been, one can say, a shift from what men thought to be real "on the outside" (beliefs in myth, doctrine, and religious ethics) to a sensing that what is real is "on the inside": a realization of enhanced autonomy and self-structure through a gradual owning of the capacity to think and reflect without the aid of an already "finished" divine perspective. The curiosity about the natural order which Ockham's theology made historically possible took place "on the inside" in the sense that the evolving Western ego's knowledge experience gradually became autonomous from divine authority. What was once thought to be given as finished was later thought to be unfinished but in principle finishable by men. But in the more strict psychological sense this knowledge was still "on the outside" because in its earliest forms it did not include a direct and socially unmediated encounter with the contents of the inner world. Nonetheless, the initial emergence of theoretical curiosity provided the social ethos and epistemological frame for the subsequent acquisition of genuinely "inner" knowledge. It is in this sense that the early forms of curiosity and self-assertion were also authentic instances of structure building, understood as an important aspect or component of individuation, and these forms made the eventual emergence of psychoanalysis possible.

Let us put the same point in a sociological rather than a historical way. From within a social perspective individuation is a process in which the ego's sense of self-consciousness separates itself from an undifferentiated—because it is unconscious—union or attachment to the central elements of its common culture. The early episodes in the trial of theoretical curiosity brought about or "won" this separation in what were largely cognitive and perceptual ways. Men separated themselves at the level of conscious, rational thought from a social matrix organized by Christian theological formulations of what was right, true, and permissible. On the other hand, affective separation—the realization of unconscious attachments—from the same matrix came about more gradually and much later, though it would be a mistake to distinguish too sharply between these two forms of separation. In both cases there was "a retraction of a projection." This retraction produced, first, the capacity for theoretical curiosity about what is "on the outside" (natural science) and, later, about what is "on the inside" (psychology).

These reflections on secularization open up the possibility of reappropriating the past in a fresh and new way. According to Blumenberg and (we may now say) Freud, the direction of secularization is always into the future. So too for at least the diachronic "half" of Lévi-Strauss, all of Sartre, and most of Rieff. Understandably, these post-Freudian instances of the total break theory also offered their readers a message of despair which contrasts dramatically with the consoling nostalgias of Ricoeur, of the synchronic "half" of Lévi-Strauss, and, within psychoanalysis itself for example, of Jung's theory of the archetypes "in" the collective unconscious. I now wish to explore the psychological actions which make possible such a rapprochement with the past. To do this I reopen the problem of the ego's relation to the social other, understood as the intermediate space between the two, because I think that, whenever the ego relinks itself with the past, it does so within this space and through the medium of its structures. However, in order to understand these processes, I become more and not less psychological than Freud. To do that I introduce the idea of "the creation of meaning." The product of mourning, it is a double movement of return (mourning) and release. The creation of meaning unifies the two components of this movement because meaning is, paradoxically, a product of what the person makes (his unique developmental experience, both conscious and unconscious) and of what is given to him by his past, the collective memory, his cultural heritage. Fantasy activity, the prototype of symbol formation, holds the two together. But the revised theory of fantasy activity to which I now turn is not limited by Freud's duality of "inner" and "outer" or by Winnicott's understandable lack of interest in the cultural location of mind (Where, in culture, is the mind when mind is understood psychodynamically?).

14 Toward a Rapprochement with the Past: Mourning, Individuation, and the Creation of Meaning

Let us restate as briefly and concisely as possible the problem to which we now seek a solution. Freud's theory of history and of the ego's development are always in the direction of separation from the social order, from the past and from the unconscious moral mandates of both, and toward internalization, structure building, and the depth-psychological self-understanding which all three facilitate. In all this one moves from what is "on the outside" to what is "on the inside" and to the capacity to enjoy curiosity about the inner world. Any movement "back" into the social other, into history and tradition and into a cosmological point of view, is a mistake because it is a retreat which forestalls these achievements. Freud's sense of these things, however, consciously omitted—although it unconsciously included—the process of mourning. So do those who side with him (the total break theorists), and so do his opponents (the theorists of transposition and return).

I now wish to undercut both viewpoints and explore what they ignore. The path of mourning and individuation leads into fresh territory, the experience of creating meaning. Freud was convinced that analytically informed interpretations of the symbols of the past propelled the ego forward and that this action gave it meaning. His opponents say that the ego can find a meaningful life only by reattaching itself to the symbolic structures of the past and community. These dualities must be reformulated. I think that people neither simply repudiate nor simply reappropriate meanings but instead create meanings in an arena of social space which lies midway between the past and the future, and I propose the following explanation of this process, the elucidation of which constitutes the burden of this chapter. A certain amount of technical, psychological discussion is unavoidable.

326

The key to this process of reappropriation lies in the psychology of fantasy activity and in understanding that activity in terms of the construction and perception of movement, which is in turn related to the human propensity to narrate. These three elements (fantasy activity, movement, and narrative) provide the means whereby the ego is enabled to link itself to structures of meaning which it creates but which are also, paradoxically, given to it. One must call this creation of meaning "cultural activity" because it cannot be accomplished without the aid of symbols which reside in the intermediate space between the self and the social other. These symbols are both invented anew and received from the past, understood in the sense of a collective memory. This is the nuclear process which undergirds all the many forms of rapprochement which modern society has, in its wisdom, devised. I think of this cultural activity as common to both the ordinary person and the representative person (priest, politician, artist, philosopher) because the creation of a meaningful life and the creation of a shared, esteemed cultural object both make use of the same materials and processes. Naturally, I find in the creation of meaning the wellspring of individuation, which is captured best, if only in a simple and preliminary way, by the common-enough phrases "having a life of one's own" or "having a mind of one's own." But this is of course not as simple or as easy to understand as it sounds. Let us begin with the concept of meaning and its origins in fantasy as Freud formulated these and move on from there to a social theory of fantasy activity and to the part that fantasy plays in narrative building and in the formation of cultural symbols.

Freud's clearest and most explicit statement about "the meaning of meaning"—which is to say, about the creation of meaning—occurs in the early chapters of *The Introductory Lectures*, where his sole purpose is to show the reader that errors or slips, dreams, and symptoms have meaning, sense. At first seemingly arbitrary, they do make sense: "By 'sense' we understand 'meaning,' 'intention,' 'purpose' and position in a continuous psychical context" (1916–17, p. 61). A symbolic structure (utterance, dream figure, symptomatic action, transference response) becomes meaningful when its creator recognizes (at first with dismay but later with bemused curiosity) its unconscious purpose or intention and assimilates that into the already existing flow of everyday mental and social life. When the analyst-interpreter or the patient-person does this, the opaque symbolic structure "becomes meaningful." But the medium or material on which the ego performs this operation is not a drive (affective desire) or a concept (cognitive), it is a fantasy (image) which represents a wish. The "great group formations of mankind," the symbolisms of religion and politics, of church and state, also become meaningful in the same way as do the products of the analytic situation.

In Freud's formulations conscious but mainly unconscious fantasy activity is the unit of analysis and as such the core or essence of psychoanalysis. It is also the key to his and my evolving conception of the creation of meaning. However, as I have also repeatedly noted—and must now justify with some direct observational evidence—Freud's conception of fantasy was excessively and unrealistically individualistic or intrapsychical. The historical root of this excess was the total break mentality, which overloads diachrony and temporality and thereby creates a barrier between the inner and the social worlds of the person. On the other hand, the conception of meaning which I now wish to propose is an interpsychical one in which the products of one's own subjectivity (unconscious fantasies) are synthesized with the world's products of objectivity in a fresh and unique way. Meaning consists in inserting the unconscious products of subjectivity into the space between the self and the social other. As this occurs, the inner world of the self and the outer, coded, and opaque world of social and historical circumstance gradually become to some extent transparent to each other. But this conception depends on a view of fantasy activity which is quite different from Freud's.

So the issue really is the fundamental character or structure of fantasy activity. Is it inherently individualizing, such that recognition of it brings about only a retreat from the social world? And, Does its interpretation reduce the products of the mind to an imageless and value-free reality principle? Through this formulation Freud rationalized—in the Weberian sense of the word—the infantile unconscious. Or, Is fantasy inherently social, does its recognition require some sort of rapprochement with the social world, and does its interpretation actually draw the individual back into that world? My choice of this second, fresh, and different understanding of fantasy activity is based upon clinical-empirical investigations derived from Herman Rorschach's psychology.

This psychology has been badly misunderstood by both clinical psychologists and the public at large. The first have attempted to scientize it, which it to say, metapsychologize it by integrating it into Freud's theory of fantasy. The second have converted it into an ideological weapon. When one wants to discredit a political opponent, one need only point out that the latter views the controversial political issue under discussion "like a Rorschach"—that is, he simply "has fantasies" about it which bear no direct relation to the reality at hand. This is a repetition of the "it's-only-a-dream" or the "it's-only-a-joke" mentality. All such strategies remove, through the process of disavowal, the dread and anxiety which ensue whenever one is confronted with the obligation to own one's fantasy activity and to think about it, rather than to displace it onto another. So I ask the reader's indulgence, but only for a moment or two, as I correct these two misunderstandings.

It was Herman Rorschach's genius to provide the means for demonstrating that the structure of fantasy activity is grounded in the phenomenologically or experientially observable perception and construction of movement. This innovation produces an understanding of fantasy as inherently social and symbolic, both before and after interpretation. Furthermore, such a "psychology of movement" is the correct and more developed psychology of what I have repeatedly referred to—and also left unclarified—as "the intermediate space." In part 1 I made use of the psychology of movement in the form of a historical tool in order to understand more deeply and clearly Freud's inner life while he was studying Michelangelo's statue of Moses in Rome in 1913–14. At that time (in "the first" cultural text, "The Moses of Michelangelo") Freud was able to relate his own unconscious fantasy activity to selected symbolic structures embedded in the Western religious tradition. Only by allowing himself to participate in the illusion that the statue of Moses was "really" moving could Freud arrive at his theory of its meaning. Hence his felicitous phrasing, "in imagination we complete the scene of which this movement is a part." Through his interpretive work Freud also came to understand better both the personal and the historical meaning of what he himself had been doing all along, the meaning of creating psychoanalysis, for he put together the personal and the historical. By interpreting the statue, he created some meaning and individuated out of his past. He attempted to deepen this work in the final years of his life by writing *Moses and Monotheism*. Now I take up this same psychology of fantasy and movement as a resource for understanding something crucial about a theory of creating meaning and its relation to individuation.

It is not difficult to review concisely those features of the psychology of movement which are essential for the present discussion. In the test situation the subject (*S*) and the examiner (*E*) face each other across a bare table. The atmosphere is a relaxed one in which *E* is curious only about *S*'s forms of fantasy activity, thinking and imagining (that is to say, knowledge will not lead to action), and *S* is agreeable to *E*'s procedures (*S* too is curious about these things, but in a far less explicit way, and is grateful not to have to think about them directly—*E* will do that). So *E* presents *S* with a plate or card (ten in all), one at a time, each about the size of an open book, upon which a blot of ink has been spread out in a random manner to form a bilateral pattern. These blots or plates are referred to as "unstructured stimuli" precisely because they are not meaningful: in and of themselves they make no sense. Nonetheless, *E* asks *S* in effect, with regard to each plate under consideration, What might this be? And, as everyone knows, *S* "sees" all sorts of things in each blot and so informs *E*. When each of the ten cards has been examined separately and discussed at length, the test is over. Scoring is complex, but three major determinants are of special significance. In some cases, the form (*F* response) of the blot determines *S*'s response. For example, "It is a butterfly because it is shaped like one." In other cases color (*C* response): "It is a lake because it is blue." In still others, movement (*M* response) is the determinant: "I see two little girls doing a dance together; I say this because they are moving about in the manner of a dance."

One may now ask, What is the psychological significance of perceiving movement in and upon that which is "in reality" only a screen filled with random and bizarre contents? For *S* does indeed "see" people "doing things"—*S* constructs situations—within the context of a framed, intermediate space which exists between him and *E*, in which nothing is, in fact, happening at all. For, according to Freud's reality principle, to *E*'s question, What might this be? *S* would simply have to say, This is an inkblot, as anyone—with the apparent exception of you, a psychologist—can plainly see. Unconscious fantasy works, psychologically, in the subjunctive and not in the indicative mood: when we become interested in "what might be," in contrast to "what really is," we have moved from reality to fantasy. Or rather, we have moved away from what is "in" *S* and from what is "in" *E*, from the polarity of inner and outer, and to what is "between" *S* and *E*. Fantasy is an intersubjective transitional form of mental activity.

According to depth-psychological theory, movement responses indicate four closely related components in *S*'s psychological makeup (Schachtel 1966): (1) deep bodily feelings (this evokes Freud's observation that the ego is always a bodily ego, that the perception of self and other is rooted in bodily states and somatic processes), (2) issues of narcissism and self-esteem, (3) the capacity for empathy, which is (paradoxically) grounded in narcissism but which is also an overcoming of narcissism, and (4) the capacity or readiness to engage in fantasy activity. In so telling us about the unique role and structure of fantasy activity in S's personality, M responses register S's deepest, innermost mental activities. They bring into being the core or essence of S's personality. There is an unintended but also extremely illuminating pun in the phrase, "movement response (M)," in the sense that the perception of movement tells us what "moves" or emotionally stirs S. Movement indicates what is "moving" in the physical sense of motion in space "on the outside," but also in the psychological sense of what is deeply affecting of S "on the inside." A second, even worse, but even more illuminating pun is found in the colloquial reference to films or shows as "movies"—movies also "move" in these two senses. These two puns are illuminating because they signal a continuity between the processes at work in Rorschach's little experiment and many of the processes which are also at work in what I have called the culture of fantasy. The framed inkblot and the public screen have something of great importance in common. The movies "which move" and "which move us" are constructed in the social space of the blank film and television screen, and this space mediates between and integrates individual psychodynamics and the shared unconscious components of the social order. Each needs the other, but both need a screen or frame for the purposes of objectification and representability.

These notations allow me to draw the psychology of fantasy, so understood, into the main arena of concern, the creation of meaning. It is now possible to say what Freud could not say, and what Rorschach himself and his orthodox (Freudian) followers did not say, namely, that S's perceptions of "figures doing things" are inherently social. In order to produce and complete the work of fantasy which the Rorschach test task demands of him, S must draw upon what Alfred Schutz has called the typifications of the social world. To understand another person, Schutz says, "I rely upon my stock of knowledge, which contains typifications of fellow-men. . . . In projecting my own action I take account of my fellow-men by fancying . . ." (1932, p. 32). The furniture or contents of S's movement responses are entirely social, drawn from his "stock of knowledge" of typical or representative situations. But the form of S's projections is also social or interpsychical because they occur to him only in the presence of E. Even if S attempts the test alone, an invisible social other is nonetheless present. As Khan has pointed out, a person can observe himself only through the medium of another's presence (1970, p. 109). It is not our fault that Schutz's debt to the rationalistic biases of Husserl and Weber and his lack of familiarity with psychology prevented him from recognizing not just the depth-psychological but also the depth-sociological character of his key constructs, "fancying," "projecting," and "stock of knowledge."

There is a second and even more important point. Movement responses, which are fantasies that are essentially social, also display an incipiently narrative character, and this second feature is all of a piece with what has already been said about the social origins of psychoanalysis. In these responses we see, *in nuce,* as if taking place before our very eyes, what I have called the essential tension in the social and historical origins of a psychological point of view, the tension between a common culture and the drive to achieve analytic access. But we also see in them the beginnings of what I have called rapprochement. Faced with an ambiguous and unstructured stimulus, which is the equivalent—in the research situation—of a common culture, of which E is a representative person, S turns in to himself and engages in the work of fantasy activity. These circumstances facilitate the incipiently narrative character of movement responses. That is to say, S responds to the unconscious sense of loss which the test situation imposes by beginning to tell a story, for the figures which he perceives are always "doing things." Responses of M are "plotlike"—they reach out for the construction of plots, the essential element in narrative, although they never really achieve that. And S takes recourse to plot in order, in Shakespeare's well-known phrase, "to give airy nothing a habitation and a name." However misguided one may think the narratological accent in contemporary psychoanalysis (Schafer 1980; Spence 1982) is, one must also agree that it has a very legitimate grounding. Its weakness lies not in its non- or antiscientific mood but in its ablation of the inherently social character of the analytic situation and of the psychical generally— what can be called, in other words, the familiar sociophobic standpoint of all psychoanalytic theory, of whatever stripe. However, the clinical research character of the test situation forestalls, as it should, S's unconscious propensities for further fantasy building and the construction of narrative. These propensities have been explored in other ways by means of the thematic apperception test (TAT), in which S is actually encouraged by E to tell stories in response to ambiguously structured stimuli (standardized pictures of representative or typical social situations).

In sum, the psychology of the perception and construction of movement asks that one link together the phenomenon of fantasy activity, the environing world of social force and form, and the work of narrative building. When taken together in this way, these processes constitute the nucleus of the creation of meaning. Through the medium of narrative building, S relates the contents of his own unconscious inner world to the unconsciously perceived social order. This activity or work might also be called the construction of symbols. Furthermore, in the perception of movement S is playing, in the strictly Winnicottian sense of play, and in such playing he is creating and building up a meaningful structure. Put in yet another way, in constructing movement, S is creating a meaningful illusion.

These observations on the psychology of movement belong to the wider processes of mourning and individuation, already set forth. Individuation has two components, return and release. In the first, there is the loss of symbols or meaningful structures, the response to which is mourning; in the second, a movement forward into consequent structure building and the creation of meaning, of new structures of appreciation. The response to loss opens up the transitional space, which is both social and historical, and in this space persons construct a bridge of symbols between inner and social worlds through fantasy activity and its implicitly narrative character. This activity can also be called, drawing upon Gombrich's investigations into the psychology of art, "making and matching." In this I do not abandon Freud's psychology of fantasy but rather retain his sense of its essential structure—that fantasy activity is a response to object loss. But I add to it a second component, the way in which fantasy activity also facilitates the activity of what can be called "object gain"—the formation of new structures of appreciation.

Freud missed this second component in the structure of fantasy for two reasons. Because he thought of fantasy activity as a retreat from the frustrating and ungratifying character of reality, he could not grasp the way in which fantasy activity could also be an attempt to return to that reality by constructing a creative relation to it without necessarily denying the ungratifying character of reality, the point which Freud rightly emphasized. Freud's conception of fantasy was also rooted in a sociologically shaped "a priori": the assumption that pre-oedipal, narcissistic issues and especially their correlate, more primitive processes of attachment and what I have called the intermediate space, had all been "surmounted and overcome" by the development of Western civilization and especially Western science. Therefore they could not be investigated psychologically. This conviction was in turn based, in a very particular sense, upon his terrible dread of unconscious, shared social fantasy in the religious and political spheres of his personal and social experience. In response to these life-historical circumstances, Freud cut the ego out of the historical past like a surgeon, and the knife he used was the psychology of fantasy. We see here too an unbroken line of continuity between his theory of fantasy and the contradictions in his theory of culture, and we are also placed in a position to recognize that the "clinical" and the "cultural" Freud are all of a piece because the very heart of "the clinical Freud" is its psychology of fantasy.

In contrast to Freud's individualizing and scientistic conception of fantasy, the creation of meaning also includes elements of interdependence and the possibility of an appreciative understanding of illusion. Whenever the mourning process is allowed to deepen, one becomes more and more conscious of how profoundly attached one has been to the objects of the past. As a result of this, the ego's capacity to become separate from the past—its independence— is enhanced. But because this activity takes place in an intermediate space, which is already filled, by definition, with symbolic structures, a new and actually ego-enhancing pattern of dependence upon the social world and upon the past can also come into being. In such cases, the ego is both more independent from the past and more dependent upon it than it thought, before the process of individuation began. The reality and recognition of interdependence is the point at which a structure within the organism deeper than the ego begins to take shape. It is best to call this structure the self.

Any such deepening of interdependence between the ego and the realm of cultural symbols is predicated upon an understanding of illusion as a creative as well as a destructive force in development. Whenever a person comes to recognize how psychological are his attachments to the common cultures of his past, he will also come to realize how psychological all culture is. Through this recognition he can then come to "own" in a more conscious way the character of his participation in culture and his commitments to its imperatives and consolations. But this is not the end or death of culture, as some have said. It is, rather, its beginning or—to be still more precise—a new beginning of cultural activity. The creation of meaning need not always be unconscious and absolutistic in order to be effective and life enhancing. We know that meaning is formed in the transitional space, the area of play and illusion and of playing with symbols, and that these are both made and already given. The symbols which culture provides are "just there" and can be appropriated if one will but allow them to exist for him instead of always interpreting them. In the first instance, the products of culture are experienced unconsciously in an undifferentiated and identificatory way, and one is inclined simply to believe in them or—as the case may be—reject them entirely. In the second instance, when psychological understanding prevails, the products of culture do not "die" simply because their psychological significance is known; rather, they "return" to the person in the form of powerful illusions which the ego-self then uses as the raw material for the construction of new meanings and of a new relationship to the past. However, this psychological recovery of the products of one's cultural past does rob them of their absolutistic power, although not entirely. The former absolutism continues to persist and is experienced as necessary, but it is also recognized as illusory. Such products are, in other words, "necessary illusions." This shift accounts for the "instinctive" distrust by representative persons (priests and politicians) of the psychological approach to things, because psychology does indeed relativize the absolute (theological absolutism and political absolutism). For the ordinary person, however, what psychology has apparently stolen is actually given back: the absolutistic claims of culture return in the form of necessary illusions with which the mind must actively grapple and which the mind badly needs.

The activity of creating meaning is also intimately related to two of modernity's most vexing problems, already discussed, those of narcissism and time. Meaning can mitigate the force of both. As Schachtel has pointed out, movement responses express the deepest and unique aspects of the self (issues of self-esteem and self-love), which is to say, issues of narcissism. Because such responses are also incipiently narrative-like in character, it is worth asking, What might the relationship be between narcissism and narrative? It seems reasonable to suppose that the work of narrative building transforms some bits and pieces of the self's original, archaic narcissism (Kohut) and its residual, unconscious memories of maternal and infantile omnipotence (Winnicott) into a conversation with the social order. This supposition is grounded in the social character of all narrative, on the one hand, and its roots in depth-psychological personal experience, on the other hand. The most common examples are the keeping of a diary, the reading or writing of an autobiography or novel, and the viewing (or writing) of a play or a movie. Complex as such experiences are, all of them include a fundamental transaction or interchange between individual, unconscious fantasy processes and socially and historically grounded and shaped events and figures which play out human relations, situations, and predicaments over a set time span. In imaginatively entertaining such experiences, persons work out and over and build up relations between their inner worlds and the world of shared collective meaning and memory. As old meanings are sorted out and discarded and new ones entertained and formed, the distance between the ego and the social order at first lessens but then later also deepens. Such activities facilitate transformations in persons' narcissistic organization.

In his most recent studies Ricoeur (1983) has suggested that narrative has the effect of humanizing time. Although the philosophical basis for this point cannot be pursued here, it is not difficult to see that it makes sound psychological sense, although the philosopher may not agree with this assertion. Hovering in and around the psychoanalytic movement and its heir, the contemporary psychological society or culture of fantasy, is the specter of virtually total diachrony, transience, and an agonizing sense of passage which has lost all sense of "from what" and "to what." Such circumstances understandably produce intense anxiety, which attempts to heal itself in the form of a deep yearning or nostalgia for a condition of timelessness or synchrony. Narrative humanizes this anxiety by drawing the ego out of its unbearable diachronic misery. It creates a small though temporary bit of space for synchrony—the "world" of fiction and myth. Within that world time does indeed "fly," but in the reader/viewer's total world the sense of transience decelerates appreciably. A life-giving world of illusion and play has been created. Narrative accomplishes this by objectifying the unthinkable into patterns—sometimes even into models—of states, relationships, situations, statuses, and orders. But narrative without psychology is just as alienating as psychology without narrative. The capacity for psychological self-understanding also humanizes narrative by establishing a new intimacy between the depths of personal consciousness and the impersonality of the text. It draws the fictive and mythic representations of narrative back into the inner world of the experiencing subject's developmental and historical flow. Within this "to and fro" the unbearable complexities of transience are softened and made tolerable as the text becomes meaningful.

I now wish to close this discussion of creating meaning by first directing the reader's attention once again to the most terrible of all the historical ironies which the psychoanalytic movement as a whole presents to us: the fact that analytic access and its associated capacity to tolerate the chaos of the inner world—and through that to tolerate the chaos of the social world—emerged historically directly alongside its moral and psychological opposite, the rise of National Socialism (the politics of fantasy). There is a similarity between the two as well. What links these two "movements"—and both were indeed movements—is not so much the opposition which they represent between the psychology of fantasy, which Freud and his followers directed against politics and religion, and the politics of fantasy, which the church and the state directed against empathic psychological immersion in the inner world, as what the two had in common. They were both responses to the same historical challenge or social-structural change: the first responded to this loss with the ability to mourn; the second, with the inability to mourn. This contrast and similarity allow me to make the final suggestion, namely, that the ability to mourn the lost common cultures of the Western past has been instrumental in making possible not only psychoanalysis but also major components of sociological thought.

Robert Lifton (1986) has cut through much of the flood of psychoanalytic literature on the Holocaust (mass psychoses, psychotic leaders, etc.) by proposing in his recent study of the Nazi doctors the concept of "doubling." It is the capacity of all persons have to live in two antithetical mental worlds at the same time without consciously experiencing any anxiety about the way they differ. Lifton thinks that doubling explains how these doctors were at once Nazis and also good, decent, ordinary people, for indeed they were both. In reviewing this psychological approach, Ravitch (1987) suggested what he thinks is a more historical one, although I find in it yet another restatement of the transposition theory. He emphasized "the radical secularization of German society in the late nineteenth century . . . which undermined the hold of traditional religion, particularly among Protestants, favored materialistic views of man" and "substituted the rules of the physical, material universe for those of the moral universe." This "scientific or positivistic pride . . . substituted for the Judeo-Christian view of man . . . the Faustian urge to divine power" (pp. 9–10). In this way the Nazis were, Ravitch thinks, able to view Jews as infrahuman, biological organisms upon which they could conduct experiments ordinarily performed on animals without feelings of guilt. Alexander Mitscherlich (1967), a psychoanalyst who remained under house arrest for the duration of the war and who, after it, became a member of the German Medical Commission to the American Military Tribunal at Nuremberg, proposed the concept of "the inability to mourn" to explain postwar Germany's political confusions. Germans as a whole, he proposed, unconsciously loved and idealized Hitler, and, when the war's end forced them to give up this love by confronting them with (making them conscious of) the evil they had been a part of, they warded off intense shared feelings of mourning over what was loved and lost by massive denial of mourning and depression. This in turn inhibited their capacity for responsible reconstructive action in the present and future.

Suppose we push Mitscherlich's brilliant observations back into the prewar decade (the origins rather than the effects of Nazism), put it in the context of Ravitch's historical point about secularization, and insert into both Lifton's concept of doubling. The speculation would then read: both psychoanalysis and Nazism were confronted with the same rapid social-structural change, the same experience of being uprooted precipitously from a religiously informed common culture and from the moral (self-control) and psychological (self-esteem) supports which such a culture invariably confers. In the face of this, psychoanalysis went one way (the ability to mourn), National Socialism another (the inability to mourn). Because they were capable of mourning the loss of the past, Freud and his followers were subsequently able to transform a devastating historical situation into an instrument for its investigation and into a mode of self-understanding which made possible the tolerance of the chaos, both inner and outer, which was in and around them. On the other hand, by denying the painful psychological consequences of the social and historical changes that were taking place—in other words, by refusing to mourn—the German Nazis became intolerant of chaos. Instead, they sought to reinvent with great rapidity and astonishing creativity a total common culture in which a sacred symbolic structure overcame time, the sense of transience and diachrony, as Leni Riefenstahl's brilliant and cynical film documentary of the Nuremberg rally (*Triumph of the Will*) has devastatingly portrayed. For them, the manic defense and persecutory activity successfully energized a new cosmology which abolished the ability to mourn and what I would also call "the capacity to be depressed." It was as if they had said, There has been no loss at all. This analysis of the rise to dominance of political absolutism out of the ashes of religious absolutism is, I think, a better way to conceptualize Freud's famous concept "the return of the repressed" because it is a historical rather than an evolutionary observation.

Let us summarize and conclude by returning to the ability to mourn in the Freud-Weber confluence, already noted at the end of part 2, which called forth these many reflections on individuation. That will clarify further what the disciplines which they founded do and do not share with the religious and scientific traditions out of which they both emerged. There I proposed that, as the secularization process continued, each man was confronted with the loss of his attachments to the religiously inspired common cultures of his past and that, through painful inner struggle and mourning, each reached a new and original perspective on that past and cast that perspective in the physicalistic, scientific language of his day. In so doing both the first psychoanalyst and the first *"verstehen"* sociologist recognized the disturbing fact that the religioethical realities which their predecessors had taken for granted could also be understood as unconscious fantasy activity (Freud) or as enchanting and charismatic (Weber). What men had theretofore experienced as extraordinary, mysterious, sacred, and transcendent was, for these two originative thinkers, in fact ordinary and in that sense "natural" and immanent. The sacred is, we know, that which cannot be touched, either by the hand (a point Durkheim made) or by the head (as Eliade has shown)—it is, that is to say, both untouchable and unthinkable. However, in the minds of these two men the unthinkable became thinkable: they thought unthinkable thoughts about unthinkable things. In the light of their perspectives, the sacred became an object for the enjoyment of theoretical curiosity, and as their work proceeded they achieved an entirely new mode of consciousness, the gift they left to Western culture. But the phenomenologically irrefutable facticity of their achievement preceded its scientific formulation and codification. Psychoanalysis and "understanding sociology" were creative responses to social-structural change: that change called for mourning and individuation, and these two activities resulted in the creation of new systems of meaning.

This anteriority of the phenomenological in the work of Freud and Weber clarifies further the scientific status of psychoanalysis and at least one major tradition in social theory. Ever since their inception, some critics have repeatedly observed (correctly, I think) that the approaches and works of both are simply qualitatively different from those of physical science: the psychologist and the sociologist participate in their chosen objects of study in a way that the physical scientist does not, and this participation invalidates their methodological claims. Therefore, Freud and Weber and others like them were wrong, it is said, in claiming metapsychological and value-free status for their observations and theories. More recently, this conviction has produced the desire to abandon such claims entirely and, instead, to insert psychoanalysis and interpretive social science back into philosophy and hermeneutics. Since it is not physical science, such an argument reads, it simply "has to be," it "really" is, some sort of philosophy. But it is possible to accept fully the thrust of this point without, however, framing psychoanalysis within either philosophical or scientific-positivistic modes of investigation.

The foundation for such a possibility does not lie in some yet-to-be-written, all-inclusive, and systematic philosophy of social science but rather in the answer to the question, In what way, exactly, do the psychologist and the "understanding" social scientist participate in their objects? The answer lies in the psychology of fantasy activity, an activity which underlies all forms of investigation. In the already-cited words of Schutz, the social scientist "fancies" about his objects and about those objects' "fancies" about the world. Schutz's concept of "fancying" is just the colloquial and as such excessively idealistic word for fantasy activity. The conventional rationale for the social scientist's participation in his objects—empathic or experience-near involvement (*verstehen*) and then detached or experience-distant reflection on that involvement—need not be abandoned, only deepened. Such deepening consists in the realization that the medium of both moments (participation and observation) is fantasy activity (both conscious and unconscious) and that the research situation into which the psychoanalyst and sociologist alike enter is none other than the intermediate space, with its characteristic structure and dynamics. It is probably true that physical scientists do experience intense psychological mergers with the objects of their investigations and that this participation stimulates fantasies and feelings about these objects, both conscious and unconscious, but it is also probably just as true that these objects do not (as far as we know) "fancy" in return about their observers or about the objects adjacent to them. The psychology of the intermediate space and its principal elements (fantasy activity, the construction of movement, and incipient narrative building) provides the investigating psychologist and social scientist with an invaluable tool for understanding the deeper underlying structure and dynamics of the conventional and time-honored participant-observer model, wherein the conscious ego and its contents are the sole arbiters.

The crux of this matter devolves finally to the cultural location of the unconscious, and once again Lévi-Strauss points the way to further clarity. Human life is, he has repeatedly told us, a constant series of symbolic transformations which take place along a continuum between nature and culture, the twin foundational polarities of society. Although he does not discuss the individual person's life course, which is of interest chiefly to psychology, there is no trouble in realizing that it begins in nature (at birth) and goes on through to culture by means of its gradual inclusion in a series of social formations, until the person is formed as a kind of "culturalized nature." At the close of the life course (at death), the self recedes from its social formations and dissolves in a return to nature, but, unlike the individual organism and like God, culture lives on beyond the limits of every individual person's life course. We already know that the phenomenological-experiential reality of fantasy activity, which is the proper object of psychoanalytic study, exists between biology (instinct) or nature and the collective representations of society (the superego). Therefore so does the psyche or the psychical, which is to say, "the psychological," especially its deeper aspects. For these reasons it makes good sense to think that the unconscious is that universal intermediate area of human life experience which has its existence and reality midway between nature and culture. It cannot be reduced to either one, and neither one can be reduced to it. So understood, the unconscious is the anvil or template upon which and within which the "passage" from nature to culture is forged and worked out by each developing individual within his group context. Hence, the following three generalizations: psychoanalysis is like and unlike the physical sciences, which study natural processes apart from their cultural instantiations; like and unlike the humanities, which are dedicated to appropriating the uniqueness of cultural forms for the purpose of enriching personal inwardness, apart from their relationship to nature; and most like the human or cultural sciences, which are concerned with the interplay between nature and culture, and only then with the structures and processes of either one (nature) or the other (culture) in and of themselves.

Let us press this argument further by moving away from the idea of a structural, timeless, and original or primary humanity and into diachrony's privileged site, the dynamic-historical, highly temporal, and ever-secularizing modern West. When this is done, we see something new but also something old. Here the relations between science and religion have been, and continue to be, primary. But they are also simply the distinctively Western words for nature and culture. Moreover, we see right away, even more clearly than was possible before, why Freud repeatedly chose to locate and define his psychoanalysis primarily in terms of religion and science, and why this essay has had to do the same. Lévi-Strauss continues to point the way, but only if we do not forget all that has been learned about "transitions" and "the intermediate." Psychoanalysis, we are now permitted to claim, is that discipline which lies between—no, it is better to say, which is bounded by—religion and science.

The essence of religion, we have come to understand, lies in its capacity to mold events into structures by means of myth and ritual, whereas science makes structures into events by means of abstract thinking. Both work with the same materials, but each does so in different ways. The event for which religious myth and ritual is the structure is the passage from nature to culture, the birth of the human species, the appearance of the human scene or world spectacle (or, as the cliché has it, "the dawn of mankind"). In this sense religion must be recognized as the essence of humanity, the oldest form of being fully and truly human. It is the first, original, primary, and most exemplary prototype of all later human monuments. But religion weaves its tapestries in symbolic, coded ways and not, for example, in terms of evolutionary theory. Religion always resurgently remythologizes the nature side of the polarity. So, in totemism plant and animal life is constantly mythologized, such that biology, zoology, or, for that matter, anthropology is rendered superfluous. And in Western monotheism human communities, their leadership, and their social, psychical, and instinctual infrastructures are constantly mythologized into the divine drama of God's creative and redemptive actions or interventions in man's ever-changing historical vicissitudes. But science not only emerged in the West; it emerged in the very midst of Western religion, and the two together have come to compose its fundamental intellectual and social axes, its fundamental socioepistemological structure. I prefer to call these axes or structures "spaces." These two spaces (science and religion) provide the key to the social and cognitive location of psychoanalysis, in the modern West, insofar as all three are considered historically.

Robert Merton attempted to explain how physical science emerged in the West out of a religious ethos in his study of the Protestant scientists in the Royal Society in seventeenth-century England. Hans Blumenberg advanced a somewhat similar argument with regard to theology's renunciation of the omniscience and omnipotence of God and the consequent rise of science. These de-idealizations were relatively complete because the objects under investigation were natural rather than social, and it is psychologically easier to adopt an experience-distant posture toward natural objects and more difficult to become distant with respect to social objects. In the case of psychoanalysis, on the other hand, the objects of investigation were and continue to remain social ones, and the sociality of the investigator is always part of the equation. While the early scientists passed through the transitional space on their way "down" from religious idealities to their new objects and theories about them, once the existence of these objects was established, the theories took shape outside the transitional area—they were not psychological. And while the theologian and priest may well pass through the same transitional space on their way "up" in order to create their spiritual, idealized cultural objects, once they have been constructed, they retain an aura of permanence which is difficult, although not impossible, to penetrate psychologically. In the strict sense, then, neither science nor religion resides in any permanent way in this third or transitional space. Although each may at times visit, each in its own way primarily bounds this space. On the other hand, the principal activities of transitional space—psychological and sociological study and psychotherapy—are bounded on either side by science and religion. These disciplines do not visit this space; they reside in it permanently. They do so because they are always participating and always observing, whereas the priest loves most of all to participate, while his counterpart, the scientist, prefers to observe.

Psychoanalysis and the "understanding" forms of social science not only owe their origins to science and religion, but they are always also breaking away from both. For this reason their structures and processes have had to be forged anew, eschewing both simple imitation of science and simple repetition of religion. Freud and Weber both imitated science, and this style has failed. Transposing their work back into philosophy and religion will also fail. Learning about the origins of psychoanalysis has taught us something important about its structure: the way it individuated out of both science and religion. Of the two fixed spaces or spheres the religious one seems the more important, at least for the present moment, but only because it is far less recognized by those who study psychoanalysis and psychology. The best guarantee of the uniqueness, irreducibility, and autonomy of psychoanalysis, both as a form of investigation and as a profession, and the best assurance that it will not continue in its now-customary splendid isolation from the communities of knowledge which surround it, lie, paradoxically, in recognizing its complex, double relation to its religious and social contexts—how it began as "a part of" these and how it came to "part from" them.

Epilogue: When the Mourning Is Over: Prospero's Speech at the End of *The Tempest* as a Model of Individuation

When psychoanalytic writers have exhausted their efforts to express and explain their ideas in the usual way, they have invariably turned to art, for only through art can they, finally and truly, complete their task. This is no optional strategy but seems to be internal to the psychoanalytic project itself. All the originative writers in the psychoanalytic movement, starting with Freud, have chosen this path. Analytic writers do so because they see their work—and themselves, for the two cannot be separated—more clearly in art than in their theories. And just as invariably, it is to Shakespeare that they most often turn, and almost always to the tragedies and not to the comedies, histories, or romances. Shakespeare would seem to be—if we are to believe the analysts—the poet par excellence of the unconscious.

The following notations do the same, but with three exceptions. I have chosen *The Tempest* (and not the tragedies) because I think it is the most psychological of all Shakespeare's plays and that it (perhaps for this very reason) depicts the beginning of the individuation process most explicitly, whereas the tragedies seem to say that individuation is not a possibility. *The Tempest* does this by making central to its structure the tension between the inner, unconscious fantasy-filled psychological world of the individual person and the nonpsychological common culture of social fact and reality. And it proposes at its end a new, more flexible relation between these two, between the familiar polarity of inner and outer which we have inherited, at least in psychology, from Freud. In so doing, it depicts in a most artful way the phenomenon of transitional space, which cannot be reduced to inner fantasy or outer social reality and in which the starting up of individuation takes place.

Shakespeare accomplished this depiction by creating a play found-

344

ed upon three levels of interacting tensions: physical, sociomoral, and psychological. There is first the sheer physicality of the geographical separateness of the island and the mainland. Within that, there are opposed Prospero's conflicts with people in Milan (forgotten wife, usurping brother, and that brother's ally, the king of Naples) and his presocial and prepolitical world of the island, composed of an idealized relation to his innocent daughter, Miranda. Psychologically his omnipotent control of nature and others' minds through his magic and Ariel's obedience and his total subjugation of brute instinct (Caliban) contrasts with his ineptitude, introverted bookishness, and virtual helplessness and dependence on the mainland. Each level is in the other. The island is indeed only a piece of land, but it is also a society of one family and therefore no society at all, for there can be no society without intermarriage between families (men exchanging women), as Lévi-Strauss has pointed out, and it is the arena in which the unconscious is avowed and unleashed. The mainland is a real culture where men exchange women and seek to dominate each other through politics and murder and where the existence and power of the unconscious is disavowed. The action of the play juxtaposes these tensions and seeks to resolve them. Prospero has left the mainland and has encountered the unconscious on the island in the form of magic and omnipotent thoughts. Having done so, he can become whole and return, but how can he remain whole in a land where the unconscious, which he has come to accept, is not allowed to exist? Not the renunciation and reconciliation of the play's conclusion, but only the epilogue provides the answer, and in doing so portrays artistically the psychological phenomenon we seek to understand.

As most readers will recall, the narrative falls nicely into six single frames. In the first, the tempest brings the occupants of the mainland to the island, against their wishes; the second (a kind of prologue) fills in the background: Prospero's ejection from Milan years before, his current idealized unconscious merger with Miranda on the island, his relations to Ariel and Caliban, and his reason for bringing about the tempest (to punish his enemies and force their repentance); in the third frame (which might be called "The Enchantment") Prospero avenges himself upon his enemies by terrorizing them (that is, making them mad or insane) with apparitions and spirits (delusions and hallucinations). At the same time Miranda and Ferdinand (the son of his enemy) fall in love (here mainland and island intertwine), and as his separation from Miranda increases, Prospero's magic decreases, so much so that at the end of the betrothal masque (frame 4) which he has created for them he momentarily fears for his sanity.[1] In the resolution (frame 5), as only our own conscious, everyday sense of things could expect, Prospero renounces his magic (releases Ariel and admits that Caliban is "my own"), his enemies repent, and he becomes reconciled to leaving the island and returning to the mainland with them, where the marriage ceremony between Miranda and Ferdinand will take place. Thanks to Prospero, it would seem, everyone gets what he wants.

Time-honored, conventional readings of *The Tempest* accept this formulation of the conclusion as Shakespeare's true intent: the play is about the renunciation of magic and about social reconciliation, so that the bringing about of both constitutes a decisive and unambiguous ending of the story. However, as Stephen Orgel (1987) has pointed out in his review of recent literary and psychoanalytic work on *The Tempest* (pp. 50–56), the conventional readings are rife with "comfortable assumptions" which fail to recognize an entire set of darker ambiguities: "Neat as the conclusion is . . . 'The Tempest' in its final moments opens outwards . . . there will always be a great deal of unfinished business," and this ambiguity "is finally the life of the play." Principal among these ambiguities is the psychological one: Prospero promises to give up his magic but never actually does. So "Prospero's is a story for which Shakespeare provides no ending" (Orgel 1987, p. 56). Furthermore (a point Orgel does not make) Prospero is in despair: he says that after he has witnessed his daughter's marriage he will return to Milan, "where every third thought shall be my grave." Everything is resolved, with the exception of the main problem of the play: Prospero's future. His despair and his return are closely related: without politics (why he left the mainland in the first place) and without magic (why he left the island), how can he find a meaningful life? How is he to live on the mainland without magic, in a land where the terrors of the unconscious are either not acknowledged at all or are allowed to exist only in the twisted forms of politics and religion? It is the epilogue, and most of all its structure and not only its contents, which provides an answer, for it speaks of the conditions of possibility for what I call the starting up of individuation. Let us look at these closing lines carefully.

Immediately following what Orgel calls the "comfortable resolution" and Prospero's despairing thoughts, all the figures of the play withdraw (exeunt all), and Prospero steps forward and addresses the audience directly ("Please you draw near"—i.e., come in). Shakespeare creates here an event of extraordinary intimacy between audience and actor. In having Prospero do this, Shakespeare strains to its uttermost limit the aesthetic illusion upon which all art depends, for he invites the audience (a social fact) to participate directly in Prospero's despair (a fantasized situation), as if the latter were "real." On one hand, Prospero really has given up his magic ("Now my charms are all o'erthrown") and he is whole, although for that very reason limited ("what strength I have's my own, which is most faint"). But his renunciation is only a displacement: he has transferred his magic to the audience/us, and he asks that they/we assist him in his return to the common culture of the mainland. Some sort of inner transformation has to take place for him to do this:

> ... Now 'tis true
> I must be here confined by you,
> or sent to Naples. Let me not,
> Since I have my dukedom got,
> and pardoned the deceivers, dwell
> In this bare island by your spell,
> but release me from my bands
> with the help of your good hands.

The next and final two lines of the play explain how the audience/we can facilitate Prospero's release: "As you from crimes would pardoned be / Let your indulgence set me free." The epilogue strains the aesthetic illusion to its limits because in it Shakespeare momentarily identifies the common culture within the play (Milan, the dukedom, etc.) with the common culture of his day (the audience watching the play). Watching a play is a social fact or activity into which illusory fantasy activity is temporarily inserted—although the polarity of inner and outer remains foundational. But Shakespeare momentarily puts pressure on the stage frame which contains illusions and associates the audience with them.

In doing so I think that he is here calling upon his audience/us to adopt a more flexible relationship between illusion and reality in which the irreality of the inner world of fantasy is not simply or rigidly polarized over against the outer (nonpsychological) reality of social fact. Put in another way, Shakespeare is asking the audience/us (the mainland) to accept the existence of the unconscious (the island) by calling attention in a dramatic way to the transitional space between them. Only under such conditions can a common culture, which, by definition, does not allow the unconscious to be recognized, become tolerable for those who do recognize it. Moreover, only under such conditions can a common culture become enjoyable as well, and beyond that, meaningful, which is to say, one in which despairing can be supported. Freud was certainly right to divide the world into inner, psychical reality (fantasy) and social fact—it is indeed good to know the difference between a dream and reality. In this sense, when the stage lights go down and the house lights go up, the play is really over and the illusion is really broken. But Prospero's closing gesture suggests that something of the illusion persists and that it is also "real"—that, in the idiom of this essay, culture does indeed locate itself in the mind, and the mind does find itself in culture, and we can learn how to understand the ways both of these actions are performed. Such knowledge does not destroy these actions, nor does it dissolve the dichotomy between what is inner and what is outer; rather, it illumines the first and reconciles the second.

Because the inner-outer polarity is fundamental, Prospero could not go to Shakespeare's play, but for the same reason we can. When we do, that polarity is weakened and new psychological work is done. When the play is over and its joy has passed, there is sadness and disillusionment—but there is also relief and gratitude. Prospero's closing words express gratitude to the audience/us and rightly so, for although the play ends before we see him reach Milan, we know, "deep down," that his arrival need not produce despair. His individuation has begun, but that is also open-ended.

This is the right way and the right place to end a book which is really all about islands and mainlands but especially about the transitions between them—be they Freud's, or Weber's, or Prospero's, or those of the ordinary person who, in studying theirs, may be more able to realize his.

Endnotes

Chapter 1

1. This approach to the relation between psychological and historical events owes something to, but also departs from, the well-known efforts of Erik Erikson to create "psychohistory." Central to all of Erikson's efforts—though rarely recognized as such—is his crucial distinction between "psychological reality" and "historical actuality." "Reality," Erikson says, "is the world of phenomenal experience perceived with a minimum of distortion and with a maximum of customary validation agreed upon in a given state of technology and culture, while *actuality* is the world of participation, shared with other participants" (Erikson 1964*b*). Here Erikson links psychological reality with Freud's idea of the reality principle and historical actuality with his own concept of ego identity, which he thinks is lacking in Freud's theory.

Like Erikson, I too attempt to decenter the timeless and mechanical ego of Freud's reality principle (and of Hartmann's average expectable environment), but unlike Erikson I conceptualize the historical "world of shared participation" in terms of self psychology and the relation of the self to actual objects. In what follows, the achievement of historical actuality by Freud is understood as a transformation of narcissism.

Chapter 2

1. In order to emphasize the epistolary nature of the Freud-Jung relationship, I cite their letters by number (no.) rather than by page.

2. Further examples of this double merger are available: in the case of Freud, see Gedo (1983); in the case of Jung, see Homans (1979*b*).

3. Since the editors of the Freud-Abraham correspondence did not number the letters, I refer to them by page number.

4. Lou Andreas-Salomé continued to play the part of a "mirroring other" to Freud as he separated psychologically from Jung, and in this she seems to have taken her place beside Karl Abraham. As late as 1917 she sent Freud a long analysis of her own on what it now seems clear to have been a favorite subject of hers—and Freud's—the psychology of narcissism. Freud's reply confirmed once again the centrality of the libido theory for his break with Jung, and he also told her, with disarming directness, how he had come to respond to people whose ideas and personal presence stimulated him: "I shall do what I have always done with your comments: enjoy them and let them

349

have their effect on me. It is quite evident from them how you anticipate and complement me each time, how you strive prophetically to unite my fragments into a structural whole. Without this, I feel, you too might have slipped away from me to the system-builders, to Jung or even more to Adler. But by way of the ego-libido you have observed how I work, step by step, without the inner need for completion, continually under the pressure of the problem immediately at hand and taking infinite pains not to be diverted from the path. It seems that in this way I have gained your confidence" (Pfeiffer 1972, pp. 60–61).

5. Jung chose to blend, for his mentor and father-figure, his own excited and affectionate appreciation of one of the most important events in the child's—and a man's—life with evidence that he was thinking psychoanalytically every time he had the chance:

> Contributions by my 4-year-old Agathli: The evening before Franzli's birth I asked her what she would say if the stork brought her a little brother? "Then I shall kill it," she said quick as lightning and with an embarrassed, sly expression, and would not let herself be pinned down to this theme. The baby was born during the night. Early next morning I carried her to my wife's bedside; she was tense and gazed in alarm at the rather wan-looking mother, without showing any joy; found nothing to say about the situation. The same morning, when Mama was alone, the little one suddenly ran to her, flung her arms round her neck and asked anxiously: "But, Mama, you don't have to die, do you?" This was the first adequate affect. Her pleasure over the baby was rather "put on." Up till now the problems had always been: Why is Granny so old? What happens to old people anyway? "They must die and will go to heaven."—"Then they become children again," added the little one. So somebody has to die in order to make a child. (No. 126)

6. The thoughts about Honegger which Jung decided to share with Freud were:

> This blow struck home. How wasteful children are, even with their own, precious, irreplaceable lives! Not to speak of friendship and the distress of other people! When I contemplate his fate I cannot but admit that suicide is a thousand times better than sacrificing the most brilliant gifts of the mind in all their abundance to the Moloch of neurosis and psychosis. If only he had left off quarrelling with the order of the world and instead quietly submitted to its necessities! It was his first act of self-sacrifice, and alas it had to be suicide. (No. 252)
>
> I am now beginning to see what I did not see with Honegger. It seems that in Dem. praec. you have at all costs to bring to light the inner world produced by the introversion

of libido, which in paranoiacs suddenly appears in distorted form as a delusional system [*Schreber*], as I have apparently succeeded in doing in the present case but failed to do with Honegger because I had no inkling of it. I tell myself that this lack of knowledge of mine led to his death. What if this view should be confirmed? I have the feeling that I am practicing vivisection on human beings with intense inner resistance. It seems that introversion leads not only, as in hysteria, to a recrudescence of infantile memories but also to a loosening up of the historical layers of the unconscious, thus giving rise to perilous formations which come to light only in exceptional cases. (No. 259)

7. The following citations are offered as evidence for the view that the tension between art and science, and their juxtaposition to religion, form an important theme in Freud's paper on Leonardo. In his introductory remarks, Freud noted (1910*b*): "In an age which was beginning to replace the authority of the Church by that of antiquity and which was not yet familiar with any form of research not based on presuppositions, Leonardo—the forerunner and by no means unworthy rival of Bacon and Copernicus—was necessarily isolated" (p. 65). Then, toward the end of his essay, Freud observed: "When anyone has, like Leonardo, escaped being intimidated by his father during his earliest childhood, and has in his researches cast away the fetters of authority, it would be in the sharpest contradiction to our expectation if we found that he had remained a believer and had been unable to escape from dogmatic religion" (p. 123). This was followed by a restatement of his views at the time on the psychological meanings of religion and a discussion of Leonardo's critical attitude toward Christianity. There then ensued this grim conclusion: "The reflections in which he [Leonardo] has recorded the deep wisdom of his last years of life breathe the resignation of the human being who subjects himself to 'Ananke,' to the laws of nature, and who expects no alleviation from the goodness or grace of God" (p. 124–25). In later portions of my essay and explicitly at its end, I discuss an issue in Freud's life which is only hinted at in these thoughts about Leonardo: an intimate, unconscious connection between a son's ambivalent, mournful feelings toward a nurturant maternal presence, a preoccupation with dying, and a positivistic and resigned approach to knowledge in the realm of nature.

8. This psychological analysis of the social significance of the Catholic priest is supported by, and partly drawn from, Ann Parsons's psychoanalytic anthropology of contemporary southern Italian society, which is organized by Catholic religious imagery (A. Parsons 1964). Parsons proposed "a simple global complex which can be perceived simultaneously either as intrapsychic or collective" (p. 310). In the case of the male, the central axis of this society is an internal object which is feminine and which Parsons characterizes as "a matriarchal rather than a patriarchal 'superego' " (p. 312) derived from the idealized figure of the Madonna. The psychological function of the man's matriarchal superego is to preserve a maternal figure or presence as the

central element in his unconscious mental life. Catholic mothers responding to the Mother-Son card of the TAT singled out the theme of "the penitent son who is returning to the mother" (p. 309).

Chapter 3

1. This usage of the word "typification" derives from the work of Alfred Schutz, although I introduce a psychoanalytic aspect into it (Schutz 1932). By "typification" Schutz refers to the activity in which an "I" comes to know a social other, transforming an anonymous contemporary into an intimate fellow-man: "I rely on my stock of knowledge, which contains typifications of fellow-men. . . . In projecting my own action I take account of my fellow-men by fancying—that is to say, rehearsing—likely courses of his future conduct" (p. 32). By creating typifications, one constructs and thereby comes to know the social reality of another person. As Freud, Jung, Jones, Abraham, and others came together, they struggled to form a coherent "social world" and employed the social mechanism of typification. Because of their intense and historically innovative preoccupation with the *inner* world, the first analysts were unwilling, or unable, to reflect upon the *social* world which they were all the while attempting to create.

However, this unwillingness should not be allowed to obscure a far more important point, namely, that the psychoanalytic movement served Freud as a social structure by means of which he could introduce his discovery of the unconscious mental life of man into the broader *cultural* world which surrounded the movement. In order to understand this historical process, a rapprochement is needed—on the level of theory—between the phenomenology of the social world and the psychoanalytic understanding of the inner world. Part 2 takes up this problem.

2. Freud's book on group psychology engages both issues of the ego and issues of the self, thereby embodying a confusion which has continued to vex contemporary discussions of theory. This portrayal of the psychoanalytic movement as a group suggests that socialization antecedes the oedipal and adolescent periods, which are usually referred to as primary and secondary socialization. Therefore, in addition to the ten defense mechanisms of the ego which Anna Freud described (A. Freud 1946), an eleventh defense should be added: attachment to a group.

3. Justin Miller has observed that intellectual and biographical commentary on Freud can be broken down into three periods: mid-1920s to 1950s, emphasizing Viennese influences and deemphasizing Jewishness; 1950s to 1960s, reversing the first; and 1960s to mid-1970s, emphasizing the historical emergence of psychoanalysis as a compromise formation between secular/scientific/German trends and Jewish/religious/traditional trends (Miller 1981).

Chapter 4

1. I am indebted to William Parsons (1984) for pointing out that Romain Rolland was far more important to Freud than analytic biographers have thought and that Freud's deep interest in Rolland and his ideas stemmed from

Freud's preoccupation with a psychoanalytic theory of religion. Parsons thinks that the principal form of religion in which Freud was interested, throughout his works, was mysticism.

2. Freud's experience of something that was for him "too good to be true" was not, however, restricted to his visit to the Acropolis. Writing in 1925 about his trip to America in 1909, Freud recalled that he had felt despised in Europe, whereas "over there" he felt treated "as an equal": "As I stepped on the platform at Worcester to deliver my Five Lectures on Psycho-Analysis it seemed like the realization of some incredible day-dream: psycho-analysis was no longer a product of delusion, it had become a valuable part of reality" (1925, p. 52). This passage supports the view that one of Freud's deepest, unconscious wishes was the wish to historicize his psychoanalytic theories—his words for "history" were "valuable part of reality." In the most creative period, psychoanalysis was still but a product of Freud's mind ("a product of delusion"). In 1909, when his friendship with Jung was at its height, his hopes for historicization were high, and attached to Jung. By 1925 the Committee had lost its usefulness. It was roughly at this time that Freud began his idealization of Rolland.

Chapter 6

1. I take the three theories upon which I draw in the following discussion to be representative of the sociology of knowledge, and I go on to note the way in which they capture essential elements found in the classic sociological tradition. But the reader deserves some further explanation why the works of these specific authors are the best current representatives for the task at hand.

Mannheim was the first to consolidate key elements of the sociological tradition with the sociology of knowledge. Berger represents a contemporary and far more readable version. Although Weinstein and Platt draw chiefly upon the work of Talcott Parsons and Erik Erikson, their style of thinking is very similar to that of the sociology of knowledge, and they also extend that to include detailed discussions of psychoanalysis. But this is not the only reason for these choices.

Merton (1957) has pointed out that the sociology of knowledge has taken two forms, or "species"—European and American. Both are concerned with the social bases of ideas, the interplay between ideas and social structure, but the American version has centered upon popular opinion and belief, in the form of mass-communications research (sometimes called mass society, sometimes popular culture) and is far more behavioral, operational, and quantitative. I have chosen the European version because of its more direct affinity with classic sociological theory, because it is more inclusive (but also more speculative), and because it centers upon knowledge rather than upon popular or mass opinion or information. Although psychoanalysis is clearly a form of popular opinion, at least in America, it is also considered a form of knowledge and a source of truth. For a more general and introductory discussion of the sociological approach to the rise of psychological ideas, see Homans (1979*a*).

A still more fundamental reason for my choice, however, lies in the compatibility or parallelism which exists between the sociology of knowledge and psychoanalytic theory: both recognize that the products of mental life originate in human depths or infrastructures and make their way to self-consciousness through the processes of projection, objectification, and construction. In this sense I think of psychoanalytic theory as a kind of "psychology of knowledge," although I do not explore that line of thinking, and I continually situate my psychological observations within the context of nonpsychological structural social change. Historical support for the social understanding of the origins of psychological thought can also be found in the following footnote.

2. Two well-known and highly regarded studies, those of Marcel Mauss (1938) and Karl Weintraub (1975), seek to understand—one from an anthropological, the other from a historical perspective—the emergence of the category of the "self," with its introspective and individualizing features, in the modern Western world. When these studies are read carefully, it becomes clear that they both presuppose—and therefore lend considerable support to—the central concept I am advancing in this section, that persons' introspective tendencies and capacities always emerge when they find themselves on the margins of their common culture.

Inserting reviews of these studies into the text at this point would only be distracting. On the other hand, this theoretical sketch needs as much substance as possible, and the sociologically uninformed reader is entitled to more than a well-rounded hypothesis. To remedy this situation, I have appended below an optional "excursus" which summarizes these two studies in some detail. At the end I briefly note their limitations as well.

Following the lead of his teacher and uncle, Emile Durkheim, Mauss has created a comparative social history of "the notion of the person," understood as "a category of the human mind," from primitive to modern times. He begins by announcing that all cultures, in all times and in all places, have always had some version of the person as a being separate from the collective ("There has never been a human being without the sense not only of his body, but also of his simultaneously mental and physical individuality" [p. 61]). Having said that, however (and having thereby rejected Freud's theory that primitives have an incompletely developed ego), he goes on to show that the category of the person "was slowly born and grew through many centuries and many vicissitudes" (p. 59) in the direction of what many have called—including Durkheim—individuation.

Beginning with primitive groups ("that sort of museum of facts . . . presented to us by ethnography" [p. 62]) such as the Pueblo Indians, tribes of the American Northwest, and clans in Australia (e.g., the Arunta), Mauss notes that their roles and names confer self-definition almost entirely through social position in the group. Self-definition apart from the group is extremely weak ("The category of the mind is weakly implanted" [p. 75]). India and China are the oldest civilizations "to have had the notion of the individual, of his consciousness . . . of the self," but they dissolved it almost as quickly as they created it. In Roman law, however, through the ideas of persona and citizenship, the category of the person came into being and into history for the first time (there "the 'person' is more than an organizational fact, more than a name or the right to a role and a ritual mask; it is a fundamental fact of law" [p. 78]). The Greek concept of face (*prosopon*) supported this development further. But "it was the Christians who made the moral person a metaphysical entity" (p. 85). St. Paul's reduction of Jew and Greek, slave and freeman, and male and female to "one person in Christ Jesus" and the trinitarian controversies (God is one person in two natures) consolidated the view that "the person is a rational, indivisible substance" (pp. 85–86). Western philosophy then gradually further transformed the notion of the person by creating "the category of the self, psychological consciousness," through its meditations on the nature of the soul, as these are found, for example, in the writing of Descartes, Spinoza, and Leibnitz. But Christian sectarian movements, especially the Pietists, were even more influential in this development, for they "established the notion that the Person = self, the self = the consciousness. . . ." Finally, Kant (who was also a Pietist) "posed the question as to whether the self, *das Ich* (the ego), is a category," and Fichte "made the category for the 'ego' the precondition of consciousness and science" (pp. 88–89).

Weintraub concerns himself with the same problem which vexed Mauss, but his perspective is entirely different. He too wishes to understand the historical development of the capacity for self-awareness and self-consciousness, but he approaches this issue through autobiography, a distinctly modern and Western genre of writing, in contrast to the diaries, confessions, memoirs, annals, and chronicles of earlier times. Before 1800 in the West, there was virtually no autobiography (and therefore virtually no way to represent directly persons' experiences of the self), but, since 1800, autobiography has become a major form of literary expression, itself the product of historicist thinking.

All autobiography is concerned with the inner experience of a socially isolated self ("the essential subject of all autobiographic writing is concretely *experienced* reality and not the realm of brute external fact. External reality is embedded in experience, but it is viewed from within the modification of inward life forming our experience" [p. 823]). The experience of the self (character, personality, self-conception) is best understood as "a weave of self-consciousness and inter-related experience, an aware self aware of its relations to its experiences" (p. 824). The great autobiographers were men like Petrarch, Montaigne, Rousseau, and Goethe, the most exemplary of all (Goethe was, along with Shakespeare, the writer whom Freud most admired).

But how did this increasing capacity of the person to appreciate and register culturally his individuality and inwardness take place? Weintraub thinks that in tribal societies, "where kinship ties have extraordinary strength, where the individual is firmly embedded in the enveloping social realities, where only a very limited degree of functional differentiation prevails, the personality conception tends to be but a prolongation of fairly pervasive social realities" (p. 835). He cites Hellenic and Roman civilization as his principal examples. In these cultures a socially grounded model dominated all self-conception (the great hero, the paterfamilias, the polis, the cycle of training, etc.). In medieval Christianity, the model became the *Imitatio Christi*, which prescribed "the essential contours of life and personality" (p. 837). The model or ideal for the Renaissance, however, was the actual rejection of all such previously valid models, as these had been proffered by the social order. In place of such models, the writers of the Rennaissance sought out "refinement in sensitivity, in registering the subtlest details of inner stirrings" (p. 843), such that Goethe could later proclaim that the individual was ineffable and, in so saying, usher in the view that a man's "very self represents one unique and unrepeatable form of being human" (p. 839).

Both Mauss and Weintraub each track in different ways the gradual emergence into modern, Western industrialized culture the self, self-consciousness, psychological being, "the self aware of its awareness of itself"—in short, what Freud took for granted when he spoke of *"das Ich."* But neither one of these two authors has chosen to make the final step or transition from this state of things to the emergence of psychology and psychoanalysis. This is surprising since Mauss published his essay in 1938, a year before Freud died, and by then his writings had become well known throughout European intellectual circles, and Weintraub ended his survey by cautioning the reader against "blindly staring within ourselves" (p. 848). For good or for ill, Freud did just that: he stared into "the self," but not blindly, in order to write *The Interpretation of Dreams*, and in his case histories he helped his patients write, or rather rewrite, their autobiographies.

And so, in order to understand the shift from religious and philosophical knowledge of *das Ich*, from Christian personalism and pietism (Kant and Fichte), from the self aware of itself through its autobiographical reflections ("conscious psychological being"), to psychoanalysis, we must turn elsewhere. But it is of great help to know that the category of the self emerged gradually in the history of cultures, and in particular in the history of Western culture, and that the so-called modern ideal of the science of personality is of recent origin and has had a complex and lengthy historical foreshadowing.

3. Valuable support for this point of view comes from empirical studies of the attitudes persons entertained toward representative persons before industrialization.

For example, MacDonald (1981) studied the medical practice notes of the early seventeenth-century English astrological physician Richard Napier. MacDonald examined 2,000 descriptions of insane or troubled persons treated by Napier. Napier was not, however, a "professional family physician" such as is found in today's medical practice; he was, rather, "a magus," that is to say, a practitioner of prophetic and healing magic who drew upon alchemy, medicine, and religion. But Napier was also famous: tens of thousands of people came to him for help. He was a representative person who healed through a variety of means, one of which was his extraordinary (in Weber's sense, which is to say, charismatic) stature.

Working from an anthropological rather than an historical perspective, Levine (1973, pp. 257–69) studied witchcraft beliefs and accusations (which were "frequent"), also in seventeenth-century England. Such accusations arose when a person refused charity to a poor woman and then underwent misfortune. Levine thinks unconscious guilt over the refusal of charity (the refusal was experienced unconsciously as a hostile action) set in motion a projective process in which the unfortunate person inferred malevolent wishes on the part of the rejected person, and these inferred wishes "explained" the misfortune: the misfortune occurred because "she is a witch." But Levine situates this psychological explanation in a sociological context. Such accusations were due, in a deeper sense, to a clash between the "demand of old communal values" and a "new ideology of individualism." The old values, he says, consisted in the villager's view of himself as "mystically interdependent on his neighbors." As long as such interdependence remained the dominant social value, charity would not be denied. Witchcraft accusations declined, however, as persons' views of themselves became "less symbiotic, or individuated."

These two studies suggest—but do not prove—that in seventeenth-century England, at least before industrialization, people invested representative persons outside the nuclear family with intense unconscious affect, affect which is today found more and more within the family. As the modernization process continued, opportunity for these investments was gradually denied to persons: the social world of representative persons was desacralized.

4. I realize that this formulation of Weber's conception of the ideal-type introduces into it a psychological dimension which is missing from Weber's own usage. But I do not think that this violates his intentions; in fact, I think it supplements them, for two reasons. First, Weber himself stated that his sociological approach lacked a psychological dimension, and he often deplored his inability to create one. Second, my conception of psychological discovery—Freud's or anyone else's—draws upon Winnicott's formulation of transitional space. Winnicott thought of this space as "the place in the mind for culture" (1967). In it, elements of personal uniqueness (developmental experiences) and elements of culture meet. These cultural elements are sociologically shared and are therefore properly described as "typical," although Winnicott was as innocent sociologically as Weber was psychologically.

In the analysis which follows I am interested only in the ideal-typical aspects of depth-psychological self-understanding. To introduce at this point the complex and confusing questions of understanding psychologically how elements of culture are appropriated by persons or the parallel question of "where, in culture, is the mind (that is, a person's developmental processes) located?" would only be distracting and frustrating. However, these questions are taken up in detail in part 3 (chap. 10), which builds upon a careful exposition and interpretation of Freud's psychology of culture in chap. 8 of the present essay.

5. These psychological and sociological discussions of the self and the other could be improved by including philosophical and theological views, but that would also be distracting. Still, two such theories deserve at least brief mention because they resemble my own (at least on the surface), they are psychologically sensitive, and they are the work of men strongly influenced by the Jewish tradition, as was Freud. They also illustrate the limitations of the philosophical approach.

Martin Buber's conception of the I-Thou and the I-It relationships (1937) and David Bakan's theory of agency and communion (1966) are both concerned with the fate of the individual I's personal interiority in the face of an encroaching realm of impersonal social collectivity, but both finally sacrifice the sociological dimension of the self or I either to philosophy (Buber) or to psychology (Bakan) in order to preserve for the I or ego such attributes as depth, relation, and intimacy. For example, Buber set up the I-Thou relationship, characterized by "the personal" and "relation," in sharp contrast to the realm of social institutions, which comprise the realm of I-It, of social conformity, of "seeming," and of roles. Although his conception of the I is in one sense very psychological, it is finally philosophical, for it is composed entirely of conscious self-reflection, decision, and willing. On the other hand, Bakan's concept of agency (his term for the individual) is a depth-psychological one which includes the dynamic unconscious, but his concept of communion (his term for the social other) is so depth-psychological in character that it contains virtually no sociological base.

Both authors have deep personal commitments to Jewish mysticism, which shape their view of Freud's thought. Buber's Hasidic background forced him to reject Freud's concept of the unconscious, whereas Bakan thinks Freud's psychology was a disguised fulfillment of the Jewish mystical tradition. Freud's Jewish identity is a central issue in the following discussion, and I allude to it frequently—but always in sociological context—and take it up (and also Bakan's theory) in detail in chap. 9.

Chapter 7

1. Khan's interpretation of Freud's self-analysis (his "epistemology of self-experience") is heavily sociological and historical and as such contrasts sharply with the individualistic and intrapsychical view of traditional, psychoanalytically oriented psychobiography. Khan seeks the precursors of Freud's psychology in the lives and works of thinkers in the Western philosophical tradition and finds Montaigne a key figure. Khan sees social factors everywhere—in a personal sense, in Montaigne's friendships, and, in a cultural sense, in his experience of the absence of the presence of God (the historical process of secularization), and he thinks the latter was the crucial factor which stimulated Montaigne's capacity to explore his inner world through psychological self-understanding.

Understood as a key instigating factor in the origins of psychoanalysis, secularization receives greater and greater emphasis as this essay proceeds. But Khan's exposition of this linkage is so lucid and informative that it deserves fuller exposition. He begins by noting that, in the sixteenth century, "the process of the absence of the presence of God in man's consciousness had started in a definitive and irreversible way in European cultures" (p. 99). The presence of God had always provided Western man with "a unique instrument both of relating to himself and objectifying his own nature." The secularization of this self-experience brought about a new state of affairs: "Crucial friendship with the other became exigent only when there was a gap left by the absence of God's presence . . . the first example of this is Montaigne's relation to LaBoétie. . . . It was not necessary for St. Augustine to involve himself in a human relationship in order to write his *Confessions*. God was a sufficient witness and object for him to achieve that end" (p. 100). Montaigne "internalized" his relationship to his friend LaBoétie "and idealized it into a private presence that was to guide him for the rest of his life." The absence of God's presence, Khan implies, was also directly related to the inability to believe in a life after death and to an attitude of resignation in the face of this. Montaigne called *Les Essais* "an honest book," by which he meant that "I intended it solely for the pleasure of my relations and friends, so that, when they have lost me—which they soon must—they may recover some features of my character and disposition, and thus keep the memory they have of me more completely and vividly alive" (quoted in Khan, pp. 102–3).

Montaigne's essays captured his experience of his self, and, Khan thinks, this type of experience anticipated Freud's own version of the epistemology of self-experience: "Montaigne had asked the question: What do I know? (*Que sais-je?*); and Rousseau: Who am I? (*Qui suis-je?*); and Freud added the third dimension: How am I what I am, and how can I know it? The answer he arrived at was that it is not possible to know oneself through one's introspection alone. One needs another to know oneself with" (p. 108).

It is instructive to note that a recent psychobiographical approach (Gedo and Wolff 1976) also finds the precursor of Freud's self-analysis in the works of Montaigne. But these authors think that Montaigne and Freud came to know themselves largely through introspection alone. There is little concern in their study with LaBoétie (friendship) or with the absence of the presence of God (historical change). Instead, they think of Freud's inner world as a self-contained entity without sociocultural referents. So they simply list twenty psychoanalytic concepts which they think Montaigne anticipated (psychic apparatus, trauma, defensive functions, etc.). Their concern is with "a scientific introspective psychology" (p. 16).

The crucial role of secularization in the origins of psychoanalysis is taken up for the first time in detail in chap. 9 below, which discusses the role Protestantism played in producing physical science and then the role of Freud's Jewish identity in producing psychology, and in the lengthy excursus (chap 9 n. 1) on the simplistic notion that psychoanalysis is "a secular religion." Part 3 (chap. 13) reviews the entire issue thoroughly and sweepingly.

2. Such terms as "freely subjectifying" and "objectivity" and their classic psychoanalytic counterparts ("free association" and "scientific") capture

welt the essential ambiguity of the psychoanalytic claim to science, as do their revisionist formulations (experience-near and experience-distant). Freud virtually grounded his theory of psychic determinism on this distinction. As this essay proceeds, I progressively attempt to clarify this point, but it is only at the end, in chapter 9, that I discuss the issue in detail. However, some deeper understanding of it can come at this point by noting, if only briefly, what it was, exactly, that Freud himself meant with regard to the interplay between free association and objective or scientific knowledge. The distinction is, I think, grounded as much—maybe even more—in shifting senses of social reality as it is in alternate epistemological connotations.

Freud confronted this issue head-on in an important passage in *The Interpretation of Dreams* (1900, pp. 101–2), where he made a crucial distinction between "reflection" and "observation." Ordinarily, one thinks of observation as scientific and reflection as a more immediate, subjective, and introspective form of thought, but Freud reversed this common assumption. Speaking of the analyst's efforts to help his patients free associate, he said that "some psychological preparation" has to be made. "We must aim," he explained, "at bringing about two changes in him: an increase in the attention he pays to his own psychical perceptions and the elimination of the criticism by which he normally sifts the thoughts that occur to him." Freud called this attitude self-observation and contrasted it with reflection. In psychoanalytic work, "the whole frame of mind of a man who is reflecting is totally different from that of a man who is observing his own psychical processes. In reflection [*Nachdenken*] there is one more psychical activity at work than in the most attentive self-observation [*Selbstbeobachtung*] and this is shown . . . by the tense looks and wrinkled forehead of a person pursuing his reflection as compared with the restful expression of a self-observer." Freud concluded that observation very gradually transformed involuntary or unconscious ideas into voluntary or conscious ideas or thoughts. So, the question is, Which of the two attitudes (self-observation or reflection) is the scientific one? For Freud also thought that self-observation consisted in "a completely impartial attitude" toward the productions of one's mind.

I think that the answer to this question is more complex than the question itself allows. There are two senses in which the idea of "scientific" seems to be valid in this case, and they are distinguished as much by social as they are by epistemological factors. In an immediate and directly experiential sense, free association is a highly subjective activity (hence my phrase, subjectifying freely); but free association also contains an objective element, and that distinguishes it from, say, "wool-gathering" or "brown study." This objective element is provided, first of all by the diminished and all but virtually *absent* sociality of the analytic situation, because "reflection" refers to the activity of the censorship, which is social in character, and, second, by the unique *presence* of "the other" (the analyst, or in Freud's case, Fliess). This other is very much a social other, but, unlike the other social others, who are deliberately excluded, he does not interfere (does not take action, is not an agent of socialization). Still, he is a presence nonetheless, and it is this unique presence which provides the necessary psychological space within which self-observation can proceed and become real.

None of this guarantees, however, that the products of one's freely subjectified imagination become knowledge, and therefore it is necessary to think of self-observation (or self-analysis or analytic access) in a second and more conventional sense. Freud drew upon the scientific paradigms of his day in order to frame the products of his imagination, his fantasies, and that frame gave him the necessary further psychological and epistemological capacity to view them "objectively" and to infer relations between them and early childhood experiences, on the one hand, and cultural symbols, on the other. At this point "reflection" does become operative and also necessary, but it is effective only because self-observation (the restful and relaxed attitude of openness to the inner flow of what is not at the moment entirely conscious) has preceded it. The term experience-distant belongs to this second sense, and experience-near to the first.

Chapter 8

1. It is highly instructive to pursue in greater psychological detail Rank's de-idealization of the Hebrew Decalogue, because the depth and structure of the de-idealization process is especially clear when it is seen in relation to cultural objects and not only in intimate personal relationships. This understanding can be achieved by placing Rank's "commentary" on the Decalogue next to Friedrich Nietzsche's three-line commentary on the biblical myth of creation because Rank's attack on his religious tradition was virtually identical with Nietzsche's, and Nietzsche's is even more psychologically transparent than Rank's. This comparison also illumines further Rank's great debt to Nietzsche, for it was through the philosopher that he came to Freud, and both Nietzsche and Freud de-idealized the same religious tradition (biblical monotheism)—except that Nietzsche's was precipitous, rage filled, and therefore incomplete, whereas Freud's was gradual, gentler, more thoughtful, and never fully accomplished.

Nietzsche's commentary (1908), which must be savored to be fully appreciated, reads as follows: "Theologically speaking—listen closely, for I rarely speak as a theologian—it was God himself who at the end of his day's work lay down as a serpent under the tree of knowledge: thus he recuperated from being God. —He had made everything too beautiful.—The devil is merely the leisure of God on that seventh day" (p. 311). These lines read like a dream, in the sense that they condense and displace a wealth of latent meaning, and, because that meaning is by no means self-evident, the passage itself calls for commentary. I know of no better exposition of Nietzsche's intent than that of Hans Blumenberg (1979). According to Blumenberg, Nietzsche means that God himself is bored with being God—bored, that is, with his perfection and with the cloying satiety which he has created. Therefore, he needs to recuperate from being God. So he makes himself into a snake (the principle of evil) and lies down to rest under the tree of knowledge:

The God who is recuperating from being himself sees, in the paradisiac state of his creation, temptation itself. It is the temptation of stationary finality and completeness. The self-enjoyment of the seventh day turns into satiety with the good that he has made, because he sees that it cannot have any future, any history.

... God's true secret is that the good bores him, even the good that he himself is. His day of leisure is his simulation of his absence (simulated, since he does after all lie under the tree of knowledge as a snake), as a means of driving man, by means of prohibition and promise ... into his world history.

Paradise is the negation of history, the epitome of God's boredom: thus God becomes the devil, in order to propel his work toward, not the pleasant outcome of paradisiac harmlessness, but the dramatic catastrophe of world history: "He had made everything too beautiful ... The devil is merely the leisure of God on that seventh day." ... It is evident that the "theological" attitude is meant ironically. (P. 177)

Blumenberg then goes on to explain how Nietzsche's lines condense all the central concepts of his complex philosophy, as only myth itself can do. The purified ideality which the biblical myth objectifies brings about "the metaphysical tyranny that can only be escaped by one who makes good and evil and true and false matters of absolute indifference for himself—the tyranny that demands the superman, because only the superman can escape it" (p. 178). Nietzsche could create his own thought, it seems clear, only in the form of a countermyth. His own myth could emerge only in relation to the biblical one, which represented the cultural heritage in which he lived. So it is appropriate to ask, What mental process made it possible for him to move from the first to the second? What mechanism, so to speak, lay "between" the transition from the biblical myth to the myth of God's boredom and the superman?

Like Rank's, Nietzsche's reading of the biblical myth of creation expresses the breakdown of the capacity to idealize an esteemed cultural object, and it is therefore properly understood as a symbolic elaboration of disillusionment. Nietzsche's myth embodied his own personal and intimate relation to his own religious past, and his works consisted in his attempt to reconstitute both himself and the historical changes which separated his age from the past. His works are highly creative efforts to recover from—one might say, to individuate out of—the epoch-specific impact of de-idealization. So secularization and disillusionment are intimately related processes. Although we did not seek it, we are also here offered nonetheless a glimpse into the psychology of *"ressentiment"* (and also of what is sometimes called "nihilism"), the most uncanny and unwelcome of all guests in the household of religious ideality.

Chapter 9

1. The claim that Marxism is a secular religion is of great importance to this discussion because it is just as often said that psychoanalysis is a secular religion. Both claims are so commonplace among the public at large, the press, and even learned men and women that any discussion of psychoanalysis and secularization simply has to address it. But this claim is also of recent origin and was not part of the historical situation under discussion in this chapter. Therefore, I append here an excursus or subtext which first analyzes it and then draws it into the general argument of this second essay as a whole.

In both cases the observation is a gross oversimplification of the complex terms "secular" and "religious" which forestalls any further thought about the deeper issues and ambiguities which the existence of Marxism and psychoanalysis calls forth. Both claims evince a dismissive, sloganlike and maximlike tone which calls to mind the familiar rationalizations, "it's only a dream" or "it's only a joke," which we all utter when we no longer wish to think about something which is more important to us than we care to realize. As long as one can say that Marxism or psychoanalysis is a secular religion, one can avoid the pain involved in thinking more deeply about historical change and the difference it produces among peoples over time.

Anthony Wallace's analysis of revitalization movements (1956) continues to be one of the best discussions of the "secular religion" issue. Wallace thinks that Marxism is best understood as a revitalization movement rather than as a secular religion, and his observations can be extended to the psychoanalytic movement as well. All revitalization movements, he thinks, pass through the same phases, whether they are sweeping (like the Protestant Reformation) or narrow (like John Wesley's revivalism), or whether they appeal to supernatural activities or to naturalistic forces. These phases are an initial period of increasing socially shared stress, due to increasingly unsatisfying and anxiety-inducing social-structural change; the reformulation of existing social arrangements and of taken-for-granted understandings of the social order, in the form of a powerful and benevolent leader's visions, fantasies, and dreams of an ideal state of affairs; that leader's capacity to communicate his personal revelations and make them compelling to a controlling in-group through the promise of reducing stress; the formulation of new programs for the reduction of stress and the appeal of such programs to a widening circle of persons; and, finally, cultural transformation, routinization, and a new steady state, relatively free of the former stress.

Wallace takes Marxism as a paradigm for revitalization:

> A few "purely" political movements like . . . the Russian communist movement and its derivatives have been officially atheistic, but the quality of doctrine and of leader-follower relationships is so similar, at least on superficial inspection, to religious doctrine and human-supernatural relations, that one wonders whether it is not a distinction

without a difference. Communist movements are commonly asserted to have the quality of religious movements, despite their failure to appeal to a supernatural community, and such things as the development of a Marxist gospel with elaborate exegesis, the embalming of Lenin, and the concern with conversion, confession, and moral purity (as defined by the movement) have the earmarks of religion. The Communist Revolution of 1917 in Russia was almost typical in structure of religious revitalization movements: there was a very sick society, prophets appealed to a revered authority (Marx), apocalyptic and Utopian fantasies were preached, and missionary fervor animated the leaders. Furthermore, many social and political reform movements, while not atheistic, act through secular rather than religious means and invoke religious sanction only in a perfunctory way. (P. 277)

But Wallace also notes that the stimulus to revitalization, what sets the entire process into motion, is the experience of disillusionment: "The revitalization movement as a general type of event occurs under two conditions: high stress for individual members of society, and disillusionment with a distorted cultural *Gestalt*" (p. 279). The revitalizing leader's visions function "almost as a funeral ritual: the 'dead' way of life is recognized as dead. Interest shifts to a god, the community, in a new way" (p. 270).

Let us reflect upon Wallace's analysis, first in the light of the concerns of this essay, and then, on the basis of that, upon psychoanalysis. Although he does not agree or disagree, I think that what distinguished the Russian case from earlier forms of religious revitalization was its disillusionment, not only with earlier ways, but also with religious revitalization itself, that is, with traditional appeals to supernatural means for bringing about relief— cognitive, affective, and symbolic. In this case one could suppose that under the impact of extraordinarily rapid mass disillusionment with the Orthodox church and the monarchy and the political and economic arrangements which they authorized, a wholly new mode of social change had to be devised, one which would not be simply a new variation on the old religion. In contrast to this, the Protestant situation was a far more gradual one. While it is certainly true that, disillusioned with Catholic spiritual practices, Martin Luther revitalized medieval Catholic Christianity, the Protestantism which resulted modified the religious framework without, however, totally abandoning it. Later, within the support of that framework, Protestant culture gradually generated over a long period of time capitalism, science, and industrialization and the new naturalistic and materialistic framework which encompassed them. In both cases (the Eastern Catholic and the Western Protestant) a shared ideal world of religious symbols was desacralized in the direction of an increasingly naturalistic orientation. But in the first case, the modification was rapid and precipitous and as such did not allow for comfortable inner adaptation over a time span of many generations to the new, despiritualized realities. Because this disillusionment process was incomplete, the old ideality (the idealization of supernatural symbols) persisted, although it was transferred to a new set of naturalistic symbols (modes of production and so forth). In this context "supernatural" simply refers to persons' symbolically constituted unconscious shared sense of belonging together.

It is in this sense that the revolution of the proletariat (Marxism) looks "like a religion" to Westerners, who have had the benefit of a gradual and adaptive disillusionment. And in this sense the revolution looked "scientific" to those who participated in its work, for they genuinely experienced themselves as having withdrawn their attachments to the religious communities of the past. Communism is "really a religion" in the sense that it shares with religious organizations the same "socio-cultural processes and psychodynamics" (Wallace 1956, p. 277), the activity of revitalization. But it is not religious (that is, it is really secular) in the sense that members have genuinely broken away from and de-idealized the religious past. The formulaic charge of "secular religion" has the function of protecting Westerners (who alone make the charge) from thinking clearly and deeply—which is to say, psychologically—about their own heritage and the ambiguities which surround their own disillusionments.

But there is another sense in which the Russian case shares something important with its religious predecessor, the Catholic church, and this is an entirely psychodynamic commonality and not at all a commonality with regard to "sociocultural processes." The Russian case shares with the Catholic church a reluctance to allow the disillusionment process, or the de-idealization of a religiously informed common culture, to run its course and thereby produce introspective psychological self-understanding. In Marxism, the driving, ever-present call to action in the outer world preempts the turn inward, which disillusionment prompts, in the form of massive, undifferentiated attachments to the common culture, the scientific-materialist order. In Catholicism disillusionment is completely forestalled by a powerful, religiously inspired sense of social solidarity. In both cases, the inability to turn inward—the inability to mourn—also sets the stage for the release of persecutory anxiety and behavior, the unwelcome side of the threat of disillusionment. So it is no surprise that the two constantly persecute each other and both scornfully denigrate psychoanalysis, as well as any social theory which calls for introspection. Stalin was indeed correct when he said, in explaining his purge of psychoanalysis, that it was "an unscientific idealist concept" (Fischer and Fischer 1982, p. 701). For psychoanalysis eschews the material or economic order (in that sense it is unscientific) in favor of the inner world of unconscious wishes (which Stalin and all communists call "idealistic").

To return to the question at hand. These considerations permit some further clarification of the view that the psychoanalytic movement was also a secular religion or a revitalization movement. Elements of revitalization were certainly present—that was one of the central points in part 1 of this

study—especially in Ernest Jones's prepsychoanalytic years of deep dissatisfaction with "existing social arrangements." This restlessness energized his
turn to the movement, which provided him with a fresh and more convincing
theory of the social order than he had been able to find in any of his earlier
studies. Such elements were also present in the early phases of the movement
as well, as I have also shown, and the cultural texts were Freud's attempt to
transform or revitalize the traditional but antagonistic world of social and
cultural circumstance which surrounded him.

But here the revitalization or secular religion argument breaks down,
because the thrust or logic of psychoanalysis is finally against revitalization,
secular or religious. Like revitalization, psychoanalysis had its origins in
profound disillusionments and dissatisfactions with the social world, but,
unlike revitalization (unlike religious movements and unlike Marxism as
well), it turns a person's attention inward in order to reflect upon the depth-
psychological forces which impel individuals to transform their disillusionments with the social world by taking totalistic or revolutionary action in
that social world. Instead, it seeks the origins of the desire for power (what
Weber called *Herrshaft,* or domination) in the infantile unconscious of both
the self-analyzer and of the political or religious reformer, and it attempts to
bring these forces into awareness, thereby making them more tolerable. This
point takes on poignant historical actuality when one reflects for a moment
backward to what Freud called his "revolutionary dream" of 1898, dreamt
the night after he experienced a renewed sense of disillusionment with German political liberalism at the hands of the arrogant and aristocratic Count
Thun on the railroad platform (see part 1, chap. 4).

Furthermore, psychoanalysis does not even revitalize the inner world, as
do certain mystical states of consciousness or political-revolutionary states
of consciousness. Both of these provide a totally convincing sense of inner
cohesion and rightness, predicated upon psychological structure which is
built up "on the outside," in the world of cultural symbols; instead, psychoanalysis attempts to build up psychological structure "on the inside" and
thereby permit some freedom from excited mystical or revolutionary activity.

In these several ways sociological and psychological reflection discloses a
much deeper and far more complex set of forces which lie hidden beneath the
simplistic and sloganlike conception of a "secular religion." But they do
more than that. The ideal of building up psychological structure "on the
inside" is no happy ending, as most analysts seem to think, but rather a sad,
tragic, and even ironic one. For Freud's search for a solution to the "discontents" of culture drives the ego into virtually pure diachrony and cuts it off
permanently from the past. So the deepest question of all, masked by the idea
of a secular religion, emerges: How can the ever-forward-moving ego of modernity recover a living relation to the past without abandoning its hard-won
separation from it? In part 3 I take up this question, which I call the central
contradiction in Freud's thought as a whole, and attempt to resolve it.

Chapter 10

1. These contradictions in Freud's theory of culture must eventually be discussed in a way which is more systematic, treatise-like, or monographic. But that cannot be done here. It is first necessary to indicate their grounding in Freud's thought as a whole and the way they become the three central unsolved problems of any contemporary psychology of culture. As such, they provide the psychoanalytic and culturological thinker with some continuity with Freud's work while at the same time constituting an advance away from that. In the final chapter I propose a loosely framed resolution to them, in the full recognition that this is no resolution at all but only an approximation. On the other hand, it is certainly easy enough to note the fresh formulations which these contradictions lead to, in an expository and systematic way.

They are (1) the problem of a collective or socially shared unconscious, which Freud and Jung divided up between them (Freud taking the personal unconscious and Jung the collective), thereby together collaborating to ablate what I call the transitional space or area and a collective memory, (2) the problem of individual fantasy activity, which is a principal source of personal uniqueness, and its relations to the typicality of social life; this could be called the problem of "type, archetype, and stereotype," to which I adduce the processes of typification and the interpretation of fantasy, and (3) the problem of illusion—are illusions necessary for wholesome living or are they destructive of living well?—which is of course the problem of the socially constituted cultural symbol and the types of meaning which emerge from its inner or personal appropriation. Discussing these problems comprehensively in relation to existing (and conflicting) bodies of scholarly literature would be the next step. In a rough and inexact sense, the triad of mourning, individuation, and the creation of meaning is an effort in this direction because they correspond, respectively, to the three contradictions and our attempts to reconcile them.

Chapter 13

1. Even the most serious students of Freud's thought may not realize how strongly he believed that a sense of immortality instigated curiosity about psychological matters and how closely his own thinking resembled Feuerbach's on this point. In the spring of 1915, only months after the outbreak of the Great War, Freud (1915) wrote a long essay, "Thoughts for the Times on War and Death," which he broke down into two parts: "The Disillusionment of War" and "Our Attitude towards Death." Before publishing it, he read the second part to the B'nai B'rith, which Strachey described as a "Jewish club" (see Freud 1915, p. 274). Strachey's use of the word "club" helped him deflect attention away from Freud's Jewish identity and to dissociate psychoanalysis from "Jewishness," for the B'nai B'rith was not a club; it was a religious group or society formed in order to provide support and esteem for the maintenance of its members' Jewish pride and identity in the face of anti-Semitism.

In the second part Freud attempted a psychology of death—of the origins of man's fear of his own death and of his desire to kill others ("murders of peoples"). It attempted to apply to present-day circumstances lines of thought and speculation recently developed in *Totem and Taboo*, and so it spoke in phylogenetic and evolutionary terms of "primaeval history" and "primaeval man." It centered on men's experience of seeing those they loved die, the central experience in war for both civilians and soldiers. Freud thought that this experience forced men into painful recognition of their own deaths, and at this point his thinking repeated Feuerbach's earlier linking up of immortality and curiosity: "Philosophers have declared that the intellectual enigma presented to primaeval man by the picture of death forced him to reflection, and this became the starting point of all speculation. I believe that here the philosophers are thinking too philosophically. . . . In my view . . . what released the spirit of inquiry in man was . . . the conflict of feeling at the death of loved yet alien and hated persons. Of this conflict of feeling psychology was the first offspring. . . . It was beside the dead body of someone he loved that he invented spirits. . . . His persisting memory of the dead became the basis for assuming other forms of existence and gave him the conception of a life continuing after apparent death" (Freud 1915, pp. 293–94). Freud nowhere says who these "philosophers" were, but it seems likely that he had in mind his study of Feuerbach during his years as a student at the University of Vienna. In any case, his view of the origins of psychology is most interesting, for it recalls the linkage he himself made many years earlier between his experience of his father's death, his self-analysis, and the writing of *The Interpretation of Dreams*.

Epilogue

1. Prospero's fear for his sanity is also a moment of disenchantment and mourning. Although the words themselves are not mentioned, we can read them "between the lines." As he explains to Ferdinand:

> Our revels now are ended. These our actors,
> As I foretold you, were all spirits, and
> Are melted into air, into thin air,
> And, like the baseless fabric of this vision,
> The cloud-capped towers, the gorgeous palaces,
> The solemn temples, the great globe itself,
> Yea, all which it inherit, shall dissolve,
> And, like this insubstantial pageant faded,
> Leave not a rack behind. We are such stuff
> As dreams are made on, and our little life
> Is rounded with a sleep. Sir, I am vexed,
> Bear with my weakness, my old brain is troubled.

References

Abraham, H. C., and E. L. Freud. eds. 1965. *A Psychoanalytic Dialogue: The Letters of Sigmund Freud and Karl Abraham, 1907–1926.* Translated by Bernard Marsh and Hilda C. Abraham. New York: Basic Books.

Anzieu, D. 1984. *The Group and the Unconscious.* London: Routledge and Kegan Paul.

Bakan, D. 1958. *Sigmund Freud and the Jewish Mystical Tradition.* Princeton: Van Nostrand.

———. 1966. *The Duality of Human Existence.* Chicago: Rand McNally.

Beck, S., et al. 1961. *Rorschach's Test.* Vol 1, *Basic Processes.* New York: Grune and Stratton.

Bellah, R., et al. 1985. *Habits of the Heart.* Berkeley: University of California Press.

Ben-David, J. and R. Collins 1966. "Social Factors in the Origins of a New Science: The Case of Psychology." In *Historical Perspectives in Psychology: Readings,* edited by Virginia S. Sexton. Belmont, Calif.: Brooks-Cole, 1971.

Berger, P. 1965. "Toward a Sociological Understanding of Psychoanalysis." *Social Research* 32:26–41.

———. 1967. *The Sacred Canopy.* New York: Doubleday.

———. 1973. *The Homeless Mind.* New York: Random House.

Bibring, E. 1914. "The Development and Problems of the Theory of Instincts." *International Journal of Psycho-Analysis* 22:102–31.

Binswanger, L. 1957. *Sigmund Freud: Reminiscences of a Friendship.* New York: Grune and Stratton.

Blumenberg, H. 1966. *The Legitimacy of the Modern Age.* Translated by Robert M. Wallace. Cambridge: MIT Press, 1983.

———. 1979. *Work on Myth.* Translated by Robert M. Wallace. Cambridge: MIT Press, 1985.

Bowlby, J. 1969. *Attachment and Loss.* Vol. 1, *Attachment.* New York: Basic Books.

———. 1973. *Attachment and Loss.* Vol. 2, *Separation: Anxiety and Anger.* New York: Basic Books.

———. 1980. *Attachment and Loss.* Vol. 3, *Loss: Sadness and Depression.* New York: Basic Books.

Brome, V. 1983. *Ernest Jones: Freud's Alter Ego.* New York: W. W. Norton.

Buber, M. 1937. *I and Thou.* Edinburgh: T. and T. Clark.

Bultmann, R. 1956. *Primitive Christianity in Its Contemporary Setting.* New York: Meridian Books.

Clark, R. W. 1982. *Freud: The Man and the Cause.* London: Granada Publishing.

Cuddihy, J. M. 1974. *The Ordeal of Civility.* New York: Basic Books.

Davies, T. G. 1979. *Ernest Jones.* Cardiff: University of Wales Press.

Durkheim, E. 1897. *Suicide: A Study in Sociology.* New York: Free Press, 1951.

Eberwein, R. 1984. *Film and the Dream Screen: A Sleep and a Forgetting.* Princeton: Princeton University Press.

Eliade, M. 1949. *The Myth of the Eternal Return.* New York: Pantheon Books, 1954.

Ellenberger, H. 1970. *The Discovery of the Unconscious.* New York: Basic Books.

Erikson, E. H. 1958. *Young Man Luther: A Study in Psychology and History.* New York: W. W. Norton.

———. 1964a. "The First Psychoanalyst." In *Insight and Responsibility.* New York: W. W. Norton.

———. 1964b. "Psychological Reality and Historical Actuality." In *Insight and Responsibility.* New York: W. W. Norton.

———. 1980. "Themes of Adulthood in the Freud-Jung Correspondence." In *Themes of Work and Love in Adulthood,* edited by N. J. Smelser and E. H. Erikson. Cambridge: Harvard University Press.

Feuer, L. 1963. *The Psychological and Sociological Origins of Modern Science.* New York: Basic Books.

Fischer, R., and E. Fischer. 1982. "*Psychoanalyse in Russland.*" In *Tiefen Psychologie: Neue Wege der Psychoanalyse,* edited by Dieter Ficke. Weinheim and Basel: Beltz Verlag.

Freud, A. 1946. *The Ego and the Mechanisms of Defense.* New York: International Universities Press.

Freud, E. L., ed. 1964. *The Letters of Sigmund Freud.* Translated by Tania and James Stern. New York: McGraw-Hill.

Freud, S. 1900. *The Interpretation of Dreams. Standard Edition* 4–5. London: Hogarth Press, 1953.

———. 1909. "Family Romances." *Standard Edition* 9:235–41. London: Hogarth Press, 1959.

———. 1910a. "Five Lectures on Psychoanalysis." *Standard Edition* 11:9–55. London: Hogarth Press, 1957.

———. 1910b. "Leonardo da Vinci and a Memory of His Childhood." *Standard Edition* 11:59–138. London: Hogarth Press, 1957.

———. 1912–13. *Totem and Taboo. Standard Edition* 13:1–164. London: Hogarth Press, 1955.

———. 1914a. "The Moses of Michelangelo." *Standard Edition* 13:210–38. London: Hogarth Press, 1953.

———. 1914b. "On Narcissism: An Introduction." *Standard Edition* 14:73–102. London: Hogarth Press, 1957.

———. 1914c. "On the History of the Psychoanalytic Movement." *Standard Edition* 14:3–66. London: Hogarth Press, 1957.

———. 1915. "Thoughts for the Times on War and Death." *Standard Edition* 14:274–301. London: Hogarth Press, 1957.

———. 1916. "On Transience." *Standard Edition* 14:305–7. London: Hogarth Press, 1957.

———. 1916–17. *Introductory Lectures on Psychoanalysis. Standard Edition* 15–16. London: Hogarth Press, 1963.

———. 1917a. "Mourning and Melancholia." *Standard Edition* 14:243–60. London, Hogarth Press, 1957.

———. 1917b. "A Difficulty in the Path of Psychoanalysis." *Standard Edition* 17:137–44. London: Hogarth Press, 1955.

———. 1919. "The Uncanny." *Standard Edition* 17:217–56. London: Hogarth Press, 1955.

———. 1920. *Beyond the Pleasure Principle. Standard Edition* 18:3–66. London: Hogarth Press, 1955.

———. 1921. *Group Psychology and the Analysis of the Ego. Standard Edition* 18:67–144. London: Hogarth Press, 1955.

———. 1923. "The Ego and the Id." *Standard Edition* 19:3–67. London: Hogarth Press, 1961.

———. 1925. *An Autobiographical Study. Standard Edition* 20:7–74. London: Hogarth Press, 1959.

———. 1926. "Address to the Society of B'nai B'rith." *Standard Edition* 20:273–4. London: Hogarth Press, 1959.

———. 1927. "The Future of an Illusion." *Standard Edition* 21:3–57. London: Hogarth Press, 1961.

———. 1930. *Civilization and Its Discontents. Standard Edition* 21:64–145. London: Hogarth Press, 1961.

———. 1933. *New Introductory Lectures on Psychoanalysis. Standard Edition* 22:33–183. London: Hogarth Press, 1964.

———. 1936. "A Disturbance of Memory on the Acropolis." *Standard Edition* 22:238–49. London: Hogarth Press, 1964.

———. 1939. *Moses and Monotheism. Standard Edition* 23:3–139. London: Hogarth Press, 1964.

———. 1954. *The Origins of Psychoanalysis: Letters to Wilhelm Fliess, Drafts and Notes, 1887–1902,* edited by Marie Bonaparte, Anna Freud, and Ernst Kris. New York: Basic Books.

Fromm, E. 1955. *The Sane Society.* New York: Holt, Rinehart, and Winston.

Gedo, J. E. 1968. "Freud's Self-Analysis and His Scientific Ideas." In *Freud: The Fusion of Science and Humanism: The Intellectual History of Psychoanalysis,* edited by John E. Gedo and George H. Pollock. New York: International Universities Press, 1976.

———. 1983. *Portraits of the Artist: Psychoanalysis of Creativity and Its Vicissitudes.* New York: Guilford Press.

Gedo, J., and E. Wolf. 1976. "From the History of Introspective Psychology: The Humanist Strain." In *Freud: The Fusion of Science and Human-*

ism: The Intellectual History of Psychoanalysis, edited by John E. Gedo and George H. Pollock. New York: International Universities Press.

Gombrich, E. H. 1961. *Art and Illusion: A Study of the Psychology of Pictorial Representation.* New York: Pantheon Books.

Handelman, S. 1982. *The Slayers of Moses.* Albany: State University of New York Press.

Henry, W. E., J. H. Sims, and S. L. Spray. 1971. *The Fifth Profession: Becoming a Psychotherapist.* San Francisco: Jossey-Bass.

Homans, P. 1979a. "The Case of Freud and Carl Rogers." In *Psychology in Social Context,* edited by Allen R. Buss. New York: Irvington Publishers.

————. 1979b. *Jung in Context: Modernity and the Making of a Psychology.* Chicago: University of Chicago Press.

James, W. 1907. "Pragmatism's Conception of Truth." In *Pragmatism.* New York: Meridian Books, 1955.

Jones, E. 1953. *The Life and Work of Sigmund Freud,* vol. 1. New York: Basic Books.

————. 1955. *The Life and Work of Sigmund Freud,* vol. 2. New York: Basic Books.

————. 1957. *The Life and Work of Sigmund Freud,* vol. 3. New York: Basic Books.

————. 1959. *Free Associations: Memories of a Psychoanalyst.* New York: Basic Books.

Joseph, E., and D. Widloecher. 1983. *The Identity of the Psychoanalyst.* International Psychoanalytic Association Monograph no. 2. New York: International Universities Press.

Jung, C. G. 1961. *Memories, Dreams, Reflections.* New York: Random House.

Kakar, S. 1982. *Shamans, Mystics and Doctors: A Psychological Inquiry into India and Its Healing Traditions.* New York: Alfred A. Knopf.

Khan, M. 1970. "Montaigne, Rousseau and Freud." In *The Privacy of the Self: Papers on Psychoanalytic Theory and Technique.* New York: International Universities Press, 1974.

Klein, D. B. 1981. *Jewish Origins of the Psychoanalytic Movement.* New York: Praeger Publishers.

Klein, M. 1921–45. *Love, Guilt, and Reparation and Other Works, 1921–45.* New York: Free Press, 1975.

————. 1940. "Mourning and Its Relation to Manic-Depressive States." In *Love, Guilt, and Reparation and Other Works.* New York: Free Press, 1975.

————. 1959. "Our Adult World and Its Roots in Infancy." In *Envy and Gratitude and Other Works, 1946–1963.* New York: Free Press, 1975.

Kohon, G. 1986. *The British School of Psychoanalysis: The Independent Tradition.* New Haven: Yale University Press.

Kohut, H. 1966. "Forms and Transformations of Narcissism." In *The Search for the Self: Selected Writings of Heinz Kohut, 1950–1978,* edited by

Paul H. Onnstein. 2 vols. New York: International Universities Press, 1978.

——. 1971. *The Analysis of the Self: A Systematic Approach to the Psychoanalytic Treatment of Narcissistic Personality Disorders.* New York: International Universities Press.

——. 1973a. "The Future of Psychoanalysis." In *The Search for the Self: Selected Writings of Heinz Kohut, 1950–1978.* New York: International Universities Press, 1978.

——. 1973b. "Psychoanalysis in a Troubled World." In *The Search for the Self: Selected Writings of Heinz Kohut, 1950–1978.* New York: International Universities Press, 1978.

——. 1976. "Creativeness, Charisma and Group Psychology: Reflections on the Self-Analysis of Freud." In *The Search for the Self: Selected Writings of Heinz Kohut, 1950–1978.* New York: International Universities Press, 1978.

Kris, E. 1954. Introduction to *The Origins of Psychoanalysis: Letters to Wilhelm Fliess,* by S. Freud. New York: Basic Books.

Lasch, C. 1978. *The Culture of Narcissism: American Life in an Age of Diminishing Expectations.* New York: W. W. Norton.

Leavy, S. A., ed. 1964. *The Freud Journal of Lou Andreas-Salomé.* New York: Basic Books.

Levine, D. 1984. "Freud, Weber and Modern Rationales of Conscience." In *Psychoanalysis: The Vital Issues.* Vol. 1, *Psychoanalysis as an Intellectual Discipline,* edited by John E. Gedo and George H. Pollock. New York: International Universities Press.

Levine, R. 1973. *Culture, Behavior and Personality.* Chicago: Aldine.

Lévi-Strauss, C. 1955. *Tristes Tropiques.* Translated by John and Doreen Weightman. New York: Washington Square Press, 1977.

——. 1962a. *The Savage Mind.* Chicago: University of Chicago Press, 1966.

——. 1962b. *Totemism.* Translated by Rodney Needham. Boston: Beacon Press, 1963.

Lieberman, E. 1985. *Acts of Will: The Life and Work of Otto Rank.* New York: Free Press.

Lifton, R. 1986. *The Nazi Doctors: Medical Killing and the Psychology of Genocide.* New York: Basic Books.

Lopez Pinero, J. 1983. *Historical Origins of the Concept of Neurosis.* New York: Cambridge University Press.

MacDonald, M. 1981. *Mystical Bedlam: Madness, Anxiety and Healing in Seventeenth Century England.* Cambridge: Cambridge University Press.

MacIntyre, A. 1981. *After Virtue: A Study in Moral Theory.* Notre Dame, Ind.: University of Notre Dame Press.

Mannheim, K. 1936. *Ideology and Utopia: An Introduction to the Sociology of Knowledge.* Translated by Louis Wirth and Edward Shils. New York: Harcourt, Brace, and World.

Marx, K. 1927. "Economic and Philosophical Manuscripts of 1844." In *The*

Marx-Engels Reader, edited by Robert C. Tucker. New York: W. W. Norton, 1978.

Masson, J. 1980. *The Oceanic Feeling: The Origins of the Religious Sentiment in Ancient India*. Dordrecht: D. Reidel.

Masson, J., ed. 1985. *The Complete Letters of Sigmund Freud to Wilhelm Fliess, 1887–1904*. Translated by Jeffrey Moussaieff Masson. Cambridge: Harvard University Press, Belknap Press.

Mauss, M. 1938. "A Category of the Human Mind: The Notion of Person, the Notion of Self." In *Sociology and Psychology: Essays by Marcel Mauss*. Translated by Ben Brewster. London: Routledge and Kegan Paul, 1979.

McGrath, W. 1986. *Freud's Discovery of Psychoanalysis: The Politics of Hysteria*. Ithaca, N.Y.: Cornell University Press.

McGuire, W., ed. 1974. *The Freud-Jung Letters*. Princeton: Princeton University Press.

Menaker, E. 1982. *Otto Rank: A Rediscovered Legacy*. New York: Columbia University Press.

Merton, R. 1938. *Science, Technology and Society in Seventeenth Century England*. New York: Harper and Row, 1970.

———. 1957. "The Sociology of Knowledge and Mass Communications." In *Social Theory and Social Structure*. New York: Free Press.

Miller, J. 1981. "Interpretations of Freud's Jewishness, 1924–1974." *Journal of the History of the Behavioral Sciences* 17:357–74.

Milner, M. 1955. "The Role of Illusion in Symbol Formation." In *New Directions in Psychoanalysis: The Significance of Infant Conflict in the Pattern of Adult Behavior*, edited by Melanie Klein, Paula Heimann, and R. E. Money-Kryle. London: Tavistock Publishers.

Mitscherlich, A., and M. Mitscherlich. 1967. *The Inability to Mourn: Principles of Collective Behavior*. New York: Grove Press, 1975.

Mitterauer, M., and R. Sieder 1982. *The European Family: Patriarchy to Partnership from the Middle Ages to the Present*. Chicago: University of Chicago Press.

Mitzman, A. 1970. *The Iron Cage: An Historical Interpretation of Max Weber*. New Brunswick, N.J.: Transaction Books, 1985.

Newcombe, N., and J. Lerner. 1981. "Britain between the Wars: The Historical Context of Bowlby's Theory of Attachment." *Psychiatry* Vol. 44, no. 1 (February).

Nietzsche, F. 1908. *Ecce Homo*. In *On the Genealogy of Morals and Ecce Homo*. Translated and edited by Walter Kaufmann. New York: Vintage Books, 1967.

Nisbet, R. 1966. *The Sociological Tradition*. New York: Basic Books.

Orgel, S. 1987. Introduction to *The Tempest*. Oxford: Oxford University Press.

Parsons, A. 1964. "Is the Oedipus Complex Universal? The Jones-Malinowski Debate Revisited and a South Italian 'Nuclear Complex.'" In *The Psychoanalytic Study of Society*, vol. 2. New York: International Universities Press.

Parsons, T. 1964. "The Superego and the Theory of Social Systems." In *Social Structure and Personality*. New York: Free Press.

Parsons, W. 1984. "Psychoanalysis and Mysticism: The Freud-Rolland Correspondence." Manuscript.

Pfeiffer, E., ed. 1972. *Sigmund Freud and Lou Andreas-Salomé: Letters.* Translated by William and Elaine Robson-Scott. New York: Harcourt, Brace Jovanovich.

Rank, O. 1903–5. *Tagebücher.* 5 vols. Translated by Dennis Klein. Otto Rank Collection, Columbia University, January 1, 1903–August 21, 1905. (Courtesy of Dennis Klein.)

———. 1905. "The Essence of Judaism." Translated by Dennis Klein. In D. Klein, *Jewish Origins of the Psychoanalytic Movement*. New York: Praeger Publishers, 1981.

———. 1907. "Der Künstler" (The artist). Translated by Eva Salomon and E. Jones Lieberman. *Journal of the Otto Rank Association* Vol. 15, no. 1 (1980).

———. 1924. *The Trauma of Birth*. New York: Robert Brenner, 1952.

———. 1929. "Truth and Reality." In *Will Therapy and Truth and Reality*. Translated by Jessie Taft. New York: Alfred A. Knopf, 1964.

———. 1931. "Will Therapy." In *Will Therapy and Truth and Reality*. Translated by Jessie Taft. New York: Alfred A. Knopf, 1964.

———. 1932. *Art and Artist*. Translated by Charles F. Atkinson. New York: Alfred A. Knopf.

Ravitch, N. 1987. "Reflections on Robert Jay Lifton's *The Nazi Doctors*." *Psychohistorical Review: Studies of Motivation in History and Culture* 16 (1):3–14.

Ricoeur, P. 1970. *Freud and Philosophy*. New Haven: Yale University Press.

———. 1974. "A Philosophical Interpretation of Freud." In *The Philosophy of Paul Ricoeur*, edited by Charles E. Reagan and David Stewart. Boston: Beacon Press, 1978.

———. 1977. "The Question of Proof in Freud's Psychoanalytic Writings." In *The Philosophy of Paul Ricoeur*, edited by Charles E. Reagan and David Stewart. Boston: Beacon Press, 1978.

———. 1983. *Time and Narrative*, vol. 1. Chicago: University of Chicago Press, 1984.

Rieff, P. 1959. *Freud: The Mind of the Moralist*. New York: Viking Press.

———. 1966. *The Triumph of the Therapeutic*. New York: Harpers.

Roazen, P. 1975. *Freud and His Followers*. New York: Alfred A. Knopf.

Robert, M. 1976. *From Oedipus to Moses: Freud's Jewish Identity*. New York: Doubleday Anchor.

Rozenblit, M. 1983. *The Jews of Vienna, 1867–1914: Assimilation and Identity*. Albany: State University of New York Press.

Schactel, E. G. 1966. *Experiential Foundations of Rorschach's Test*. New York: Basic Books.

Schafer, R. 1980. "Narration in the Psychoanalytic Dialogue." *Critical Inquiry* 7 (1):29–54.

Schorske, C. E. 1973. "Politics and Patricide in Freud's 'Interpretation of

Dreams.' " In *Fin de Siècle Vienna: Politics and Culture.* New York: Vintage Books, 1981.

Schur, M. 1969. "The Background of Freud's 'Disturbance' on the Acropolis." *American Imago* 26:303–23.

———. 1972. *Freud: Living and Dying.* New York: International Universities Press.

Schutz, A. 1932. "The Dimensions of the Social World." In *Collected Papers.* Vol. 2, *Studies in Social Theory.* The Hague: Martin Nijhoff, 1964.

Slochower, H. 1970. "Freud's 'Deja Vu' on the Acropolis: A Symbolic Relic of 'Mater Nuda.' " *Psychoanalytic Quarterly* 39:90–101.

Spence, D. 1982. *Narrative Truth and Historical Truth: Meaning and Interpretation in Psychoanalysis.* New York: W. W. Norton.

Spiegelberg, H. 1965. *The Phenomenological Movement: A Historical Introduction,* vol. 2. The Hague: Martin Nijhoff.

Stolorow, R., and G. Atwood. 1976. "An Ego-Psychological Analysis of the Work and Life of Otto Rank in the Light of Modern Conceptions of Narcissism." *International Review of Psychoanalysis* 3 (pt. 4): 441–59.

———. 1979. *Faces in a Cloud: Subjectivity in Personality Theory.* New York: Jason Aronson.

Stolorow, R. D., and F. M. Lachmann. 1980. *Psychoanalysis of Developmental Arrests: Theory and Treatment.* New York: International Universities Press.

Sulloway, F. J. 1979. *Freud, Biologist of the Mind: Beyond the Psychoanalytic Legend.* New York: Basic Books.

Suttie, I. 1935. *The Origins of Love and Hate.* London: Kegan Paul.

Taft, J. 1958. *Otto Rank: A Biographical Study Based on Notebooks, Letters, Collected Writings, Therapeutic Achievements and Personal Associations.* New York: Julian Press.

Trotter, W. 1916. *Instincts of the Herd in Peace and War.* New York: Macmillan, 1947.

Turkle, S. 1978. *Psychoanalytic Politics: Freud's French Revolution.* New York: Basic Books.

Veroff, J., et al. 1981. *The Inner American: A Self-Portrait from 1957 to 1976.* New York: Basic Books.

Wallace, A. 1956. "Revitalization Movements." *American Anthropologist* 58:264–81.

Weber, Marianne. 1926. *Max Weber: A Biography.* Translated and edited by Harry Zohn. New York: John Wiley and Sons, 1975.

Weber, Max. 1904. "Objectivity in Social Science and Social Policy." In *Max Weber: The Methodology of the Social Sciences.* Translated and edited by E. Shils and H. Finch. New York: Free Press, 1949.

———. 1904–5. *The Protestant Ethic and the Spirit of Capitalism.* New York: Charles Scribners Sons, 1958.

———. 1919. "Science as a Vocation." In *From Max Weber: Essays in Sociology.* Translated and edited by H. H. Gerth and C. W. Mills. New York: Oxford University Press, 1958.

Weinstein, F., and G. Platt. 1969. *The Wish To Be Free: Society, Psyche and Value-Change.* Berkeley: University of California Press.

———. 1973. *Psychoanalytic Sociology: An Essay on the Interpretation of Historical Data and the Phenomena of Collective Behavior.* Baltimore: Johns Hopkins University Press.

Weintraub, K. 1975. "Autobiography and Historical Consciousness." *Critical Inquiry*, Vol. 1, no. 4 (June).

White, A. D. 1896. *History of the Warfare of Science with Theology in Christendom.* New York: Dover Publications, 1980.

Winnicott, D. 1935. "The Manic Defence." In *Through Pediatrics to Psychoanalysis.* New York: Basic Books, 1975.

———. 1950. "Some Thoughts on the Meaning of the Word Democracy." In *Family and Individual Development.* London: Tavistock Publications, 1965.

———. 1951. "Transitional Objects and Transitional Phenomena." In *Playing and Reality.* Harmondsworth: Penguin, 1980.

———. 1958. "The Capacity To Be Alone." In *The Maturational Processes and the Facilitating Environment: Studies in the Theory of Emotional Development.* New York: International Universities Press, 1965.

———. 1960. "Ego Distortion in Terms of True and False Self." In *The Maturational Processes and the Facilitating Environment: Studies in the Theory of Emotional Development.* New York: International Universities Press, 1965.

———. 1967. "The Location of Cultural Experience." In *Playing and Reality.* Harmondsworth: Penguin, 1980.

Wolf, E. 1971. "Saxa Loquunter: Artistic Aspects of Freud's 'Etiology of Hysteria.'" In *Freud: The Fusion of Science and Humanism*, edited by John E. Gedo and George H. Pollock. New York: International Universities Press, 1976.

Index

Abraham (biblical figure), 247
Abraham, Karl; and Freud, 29, 35–40, 44, 51, 63, 65; and Judaism, 72, 140; and Jung, 35–36, 63; and psycho-analytic movement, 143
Acropolis: Freud and, 53, 88, 89, 93–94, 353 n. 2
Adler, Alfred, 38, 63, 164, 195
Aesthetics of fantasy, 308
Aggression and mourning, 278
America, Freud's trip to, 37, 62, 148, 261, 270–71, 353 n. 2
Analytic access: defined, 5, 127; Freud's, 133–39; and individuation, 202, 272; as ideal-type, 112, 116, 122–28; Jones's, 7, 183, 186–87, 189; Jung's, 7, 145, 151; and neurosis, 138; object relations and, 222, 225; past and, 264; Rank's, 7; sociohistorical context of, 123, 138, 199, 336–37; tension between common culture and, 5, 111, 114, 122–28, 134, 150, 263, 266, 293; too-rapidly acquired, 142
Analytical psychology, 150
Analytic situation: and analytic access, 116; fantasy in, 267; and healing, 250–58; and meaning, 328; and soci-ety, 135, 221
Analytic space, 253–57
Andreas-Salomé, Lou, 29, 34–35, 40, 43, 87, 349 n. 4
Anna O. (case of), 225, 270
Anomie, 109, 112
Anthropology, 193, 214, 265, 291, 342, 351 n. 8
Anti-Semitism: and Catholicism, 74; and Freud, 69, 91, 131, 192, 194; and

psychoanalysis, 201; and Rank, 166. See also National Socialism
Anzieu, Didier, 25, 60, 63, 64, 73
Archetypes, 150–52, 325
Art: fantasy and, 253; in Jung's theory, 151; novelty and, 199; psychoanalysis and, 2, 48–50, 58; psychoanalysis as, 137, 152–71, 256, 296; as primitive, 290; in Rank's theory, 162; science and, 51–52, 137; as symbol of culture, 304; in Weber's theory, 243, 247–48
Artistic objects and social objects, 199
Attachment: and the creation of mean-ing, 103, 334–35; in Freud, 110, 114, 200; to group, 111, 352 n. 2; in Jones, 177, 188–90; and object relations the-ory, 225–28; in Weber, 232–33, 238–40. See also Idealization; Loss; Merger
Atwood, George, 16, 22, 54, 150, 153
Autobiography, 355–56
Average expectable environment (Hartmann), 274, 349 n. 1 (chap. 1)

B'nai B'rith, Freud and, 71–72, 130, 133, 149, 367 n. 1 (chap. 13)
Bakan, David, 68, 215, 358 n. 5
Beck, Samuel, 49
Bellah, Robert, 300
Berger, Peter, 116–18, 229, 353 n. 1
Bernays, Martha, 52, 54, 130, 201
Bernays, Minna, 38, 56
Bibring, 41
Binswanger, Ludwig, 62, 72
Bleuler, Eugen, 150
Blumenberg, Hans, 10: on culture, 263; on curiosity, 323; on Nietzsche, 361–

Blumenberg, Hans (*continued*)
62; on science, 342; on secularization, 314–19; on Western society, 268–70
Bowlby, John, 227–28
Brentano, Franz, 131, 214
Breuer, Josef, 54, 69–70, 95, 99, 133, 149
Buber, Martin, 358 n. 5

Catholicism: Freud and, 52, 54–56, 73–75, 205; healing and, 254; maternal presence and, 54–56, 351 n. 8; as primitivity, 289; psychoanalysis and, 54, 201; Rolland and, 91; Weber on, 245
Christian Humanism: Jung and, 59; Rolland and, 88, 93, 94
Christianity: Freud and, 51, 68, 91, 103, 351 n. 7; Jones and, 172; Jung and, 46; Moses and, 50; object relations and, 225; self and, 355; as sociohistorical stage, 116–17; Suttie and, 227; Weber and, 232
Christian past, modern ego and, 6, 297–312
Churinga, 286–87
Circle, psychoanalytic movement as, 17, 64, 139, 182
Collective memory, 121, 277
Collectivization, 272–73
Committee, The: functions of, 38, 62, 65–67, 78; history of, 182, 185, 188, 192, 195, 198
Common culture: the creation of meaning and, 248, 334–35; defined, 5, 287–88; individuation and, 295, 324; introspection as marginal to, 119, 126, 219, 300, 354 n. 2; Jung on, 152; Lévi-Strauss on, 266, 283–96; loss of, 8, 136–37, 224–25, 229, 289, 300–301, 337; psychoanalytic movement and, 140–43, 194, 197; religion and, 112, 114, 126; Rorschach test and, 332; Sartre on, 266; and shared psychic formations, 37; tension between analytic access and, 5, 111, 114, 116, 122–28, 134, 150, 263, 266, 293, 344–47; transitional space and, 120, 263, 293; Weber and, 244, 256

Community: and healing, 254; and narcissism, 201–3; psychoanalytic movement as scientific, 223, 320; and Weber, 246–50
Copernicus, 76, 80, 303, 318–22
Count Thun, Freud and, 82–87, 95, 366
Creation of meaning: attachment and, 103; child's, 274; cultural objects and, 255; and ego and the past, 265, 269; and individuation, 9–11, 262–63, 270–82, 306, 311, 326–43; interpretation and, 311; and loss, 1; and perception of movement, 333; and mourning, 325; transitional space as locus of, 258, 326, 329, 334–35. *See also* Meaning
Creative illness, 21; Freud's and Weber's, 251; Jung's, 150; Rank's, 161
Creativity, transference of (Kohut): discussed, 21, 43; Freud's, 21, 66, 72
Creativity: analytic access and, 4, 88, 112, 143; Freud's, 29, 33, 41–45, 70–71, 85, 93, 136–38, 191–208; mourning and, 4, 7; psychogenesis of, 43; Rank's, 155, 159, 161; secularization and, 317–19; transitional space as locus of, 5, 121; Weber's, 232, 241
Cuddihy, John Murray, 68, 216
Cultural forces, in Freud's life, 30, 58, 64, 68–81
Cultural objects: archetypes as lost, 150; and the creation of meaning, 255, 327; Freud and, 41, 46, 49, 57, 96, 265; ideals as, 25, 119, 223; monuments as, 276; narcissism and, 80, 280. *See also* Social objects
Cultural texts: analytic access and, 17, 112, 256; culture of fantasy and, 311; discussed, 191–208, 288–89; Freud's de-idealizations and, 30, 68, 91, 101–2; "The Moses of Michelangelo," as first, 7, 46, 51, 197; as mourning, 113; psychoanalytic movement and, 8, 113, 366; religious values and, 81; role conflict and, 256; secularization and, 321; social world and, 193, 302
Culture: analytic access and, 124; death of, and "triumph of therapeutic," (Rieff), 300–301; ego split off from,

265, 292; Freud and Weber on, 115; Freud on, 27, 96, 98, 102; integrative functions of, 11; Lévi-Strauss on, 291; psychology and, 290; Rank on, 162–70; religion and, 3; Ricoeur on, 303, 305; self and, 81; transitional objects and, 274; Weber on, 245

Culture, psychoanalytic theory of, 141, 194; and fantasy, 334; and Freud's mourning, 104, 262, 264; and loss of common culture, 6, 27; and science, 209; summary of contradictions in, 10, 264–70, 272, 367 n. 1 (chap. 10)

Culture, psychological. *See* Modern culture; Psychological society

Culture of narcissism (Lasch), 122

"Cunning of Culture" (Freud), 191, 194, 265

Curiosity about the inner world, 313–25

Darwin, Charles, 76, 80, 159, 178, 198, 222, 303

De-idealization: of common culture by psychoanalysis, 77, 102, 140, 142; and creativity, 71; defined, 23–28, 132; disenchantment and, 7; existentialism as, 292; Freud's life, as theme in, 20, 29–57, 67, 82, 95–96, 100, 144; Freud's of Judaism, 70–71; Freud's of Jung, 38, 40, 29–57, 73; Freud's of religion, 92–95, 203, 215, 217; Freud's political, 82–86, 132, 194–95; at group level, 102; Jones's incomplete, 184; Jung's, 144, 149; Kohut on, 28; maternal presence and, 96; mourning and, 26, 103; as narcissistic issue, 18–19; as task of psychoanalysis, 80, 125, 132; Rank's, 157, 166–67; self-esteem and, 24, 26, 133; structure-building and, 86, 194; too rapid, 79–81, 143–44, 149, 157, 166–67, 246, 249; "trial identification" and, 101; Weber's, 246, 249. *See also* Idealization

Death: ego and, 289; Freud on, 367 n. 1 (chap. 13); Freud's, 102–5, 191; in cultural texts, 194; Jones and, 187–89; primitivity and, 291; Rank on, 156; science and, 317; Weber and,

234–35, 239, 247–48; World War I and, 227

Death anxiety, Freud's, 51, 60–61, 64, 93, 96–100, 192, 320

Death instinct, 200–201, 207, 278

Democracy, 86–87, 126, 265, 267

Descartes, René, 317–20

Deutsch, Felix, 97

Diachrony, 283–96, 336

Disappointment: analytic access and, 126; as historical process, 28; Jones's, 177–78; Rank's, 166; secularization and, 317–24; Weber's, 245, 249. *See also* De-idealization; Disillusionment; Mourning

Disenchantment: de-idealization and, 7, 26; etymology of, 219; Freud's, 74, 82, 112, 149; as historical process, 27–28, 82, 110, 113; Jung's, 148; psychoanalysis as response to, 27, 104; in psychoanalytic movement, 141; psychological discovery and, 143–208; science and, 80, 113, 214; in *The Tempest*, 368 n. 1; Weber on, 76, 115, 231, 244, 246–48, 250

Disillusionment: disenchantment and, 7; Freud's, 33, 63, 83, 95, 121, 131–32, 202; in Freud-Jung relationship, 41, 67; as historical process, 27–28, 214, 362; infants', 28, 136, 274; Jones's, 176–78, 180; Jung's, 150–52; psychology of, 80; Rank's, 153; revitalization and, 364–66; self-psychology and, 125; in *The Tempest*, 348; transition and, 131. *See also* De-idealization; Disenchantment; Illusion; Mourning

"Double allegiance" (Jones), 172

Dreams: fantasy and, 124, 211, 309; Freud's self-analysis and, 131, 134, 138; Jung and, 145, 151; monuments and, 263; in Rank's work, 156, 162, 170; secularization and, 319; the social and, 125; as text, 216

Durkheim, Emile, 4, 76, 109–11, 118, 126, 221, 263

Ego: illusion and, 186; individualizing vs. sociohistorical context of, 264–68; in primitive and modern cultures,

Ego (*continued*)
1, 283–96; self and, 145, 245, 257, 273, 334, 352 n. 2 (chap. 1); social objects and, 111, 119–20, 207, 325; social order and, 180–83; split off from its past, 9, 199, 264–65, 292, 297–312, 322, 326
Ego identity: reality principle and, 349 n. 1 (chap. 1)
Ego psychology, 81, 119, 125, 255
Eitingon, Max, 65
Eliade, Mircea, 218, 290
Ellenberger, Henri, 21, 41, 150
Empathy: Freud's, 45–46, 48, 168; healing and, 125, 255; Jones's, 187; movement as, 49, 330; primitive thought and, 286; social science and, 340
Erikson, Erik: applied psychoanalysis, 2; on "cultural workers," 253; on Freud, 21, 53; on identity formation, 161; on psychoanalytic movement, 16; on psychohistory, 349 n. 1 (chap. 1); on sociology of knowledge, 353 n. 1, 119
Ethnocentrism, common culture and, 126
Existentialism, psychoanalysis and, 292

Fairbairn, W. R. D., 228
Family: industrialization and, 174–75, 224; social change and, 118, 120–21, 322. *See also* Fathers; Mothers
Fantasy: aesthetics of, 308; analytic access and, 127, 267; artists and, 253; as attempt to mourn, 182; the creation of meaning and, 325–43; economics of, 308; Freud and, 132, 134, 137, 333; healing and, 251, 253; hermeneutics of, 10, 298, 302; individuation and, 306–7; as intermediate space, 124, 269, 279; in Jones's life, 182; in Jung's life, 145, 151; Klein on, 228; narrative and, 327, 332–33, 335; past and, 309; perception of movement and, 327, 329–33; politics of, 337; psychoanalysis and, 124, 211, 269, 302–6; psychological man's inability to experience, 300; as social, 306, 328–33; structure building and,

306, 333; technologization of, 268, 310–11; in *The Tempest*, 347; transitional objects and, 274; *verstehen* and, 340
Fantasy, culture of: individuation and, 303, 314; interpretation and, 311; modern society as, 268, 298, 301–2, 307–12
Fantasy structure of mass culture, 307–9
Fathers: Freud's, 83, 98–99, 131, 133; in oedipal theory, 223; Jones's, 172, 173–75; Rank's, 158–59, 161; Weber's, 235, 239. *See also* Family
Ferenczi, Salvador: Freud's correspondence with, 33, 39, 42, 56, 65, 195; in Freud's life, 52, 62, 98; at 1910 meetings, 61
Feuer, Lewis, "total break" theory, 212–13, 217
Feuerbach, Ludwig, 131, 214, 269, 314–19, 368
Fliess, Wilhelm: Freud's correspondence with, 52, 171; Freud's deidealization of, 20–22, 46, 63, 95, 133; Freud's idealization of, 16, 20–22, 53, 66, 99, 149
Foulkes, D. W., 189
Freud Museum, 281
Freud, Alexander, 52, 94
Freud, Amalia, 97–100
Freud, Anna, 56, 98, 201, 352 n. 2
Freud, Jacob, 99, 131, 133
Freud, Julius, 53
Freud, Sigmund: Abraham and, 35–40; as historical context for psychoanalysis, 100–102; as monument, 280–82; compared to Jones, 189–91; compared to Jung, 144; compared to Lévi-Strauss, 283, 287–90; compared to Weber, 114–15, 211, 231–34, 250–51, 256–58, 338–39, 343; compared to Winnicott, 274–75; Count Thun and, 82–87; early life, 130–34; in England, 206–8; isolation and, 192–208; on the primitive, 283, 287–89; Rank and, 153, 165, 168; Rolland and, 88–95; Rome and, 51–57; self-analysis, psychological context of, 2, 33, 52, 149, 281; self-analysis, social context

of, 6, 69–70, 104, 129–42, 192, 319.
See also Freud-Jung relationship
—works: "The Anatomy of the Mental
Personality," 81; *Beyond the Pleasure Principle,* 197–201, 207, 266,
288, 319; *Civilization and Its Discontents,* 91, 192, 204–5, 266; "A
Difficulty in the Path of Psychoanalysis," 75–76, 196; "The Disillusionment of War," 196; *The Ego and
the Id,* 81, 150, 215, 271; "Family
Romances," 168; *Five Lectures on
Psychoanalysis,* 261; *The Future of
an Illusion,* 89, 90, 92, 202–4, 266;
*Group Psychology and the Analysis
of the Ego,* 67, 75, 89, 90, 109, 199–
201, 266, 288; *The Interpretation of
Dreams,* 21, 70, 74, 82–83, 98, 133,
136, 138, 171, 288, 319, 356, 360;
The Introductory Lectures, 75, 327;
Moses and Monotheism, 93, 149,
192, 195, 205–6, 218, 266, 329; "The
Moses of Michelangelo," 30, 36, 46–
51, 54, 91, 197, 215, 288, 329;
"Mourning and Melancholia," 30,
189, 196, 237; "On Narcissism," 18,
30, 35, 39–46, 52, 54, 67; "On the
History of the Psychoanalytic Movement," 33, 39, 42, 67; "The Project,"
70, 215; "Thoughts for the Times on
War and Death," 196, 367 n. 1 (chap.
13); *Totem and Taboo,* 74, 76, 266,
288; "On Transience," 196; "The
Uncanny," 75, 197, 199, 287
Freud-Jung relationship: break in, 17–
18, 33–35, 38–47, 53–57, 91, 192,
288; de-idealization in, 29–57, 195;
formation of, 148–50; Freud's work
and, 42, 74–75, 288; Jung as maternal
presence in, 56, 62, 96; Jung's idealization of Freud, 29–33; psychoanalytic movement and, 6, 59–65, 73,
96; religious differences in, 35–36,
51, 140
Fromm, Erich, 164

Gedo, John, 16, 29, 53, 150
German political liberalism; Freud and,
18, 27, 68–69, 82–86, 95, 132, 366; as

historical force, 110; Weber and,
240–41
Gombrich, E. H., 49, 333
Graff, Max, 78
Grief: Jones on, 188; and mental illness, 226, 228
Group: attachments to, 96, 201; Catholic Church as, 75, 201; common
culture and, 111, 141; Jones and, 190;
monuments and, 271, 277; narcissism and, 44, 75; psychoanalytic
movement as, 59–67, 79, 103, 139–
42, 163, 280, 352 n. 2; primitivity
and, 290, 297; as transitional objects,
7, 63. *See also* Psychoanalytic
movement
Group formations: Freud's de-idealizations of, 110, 133; individuation and,
200–201, 323; meaning and, 328; object relations and, 119, 126; origin of,
102, 109
Guntrip, Harry, 228

Hadfield, J. A., 227
Hall, G. Stanley, 262
Hammerschlag, Samuel, 69–70, 99,
133, 149
Handelman, Susan, 216–17
Hartmann, Heinz, 80, 119, 274
Healing, 8, 250–58, 305
Henry, William, 219
Hermeneutics: of fantasy, 298, 302;
psychoanalysis as, 144–52, 209, 216,
256, 302; social science and, 339–40
History: Freud on, 22, 31, 102, 192,
200, 326; as loss of illusions, 28, 76;
mourning and, 194, 293, 305; psycho-
analysis and, 19, 84, 96–97, 100–104,
192, 321–22; Rome and, for Freud,
52, 57; time and, 283–96; Weber on,
245
Hitler, Adolf, 239, 337
Homans, Peter, 16
Honegger, Johan, 45–46, 350 n. 6
Humor, sense of, 23, 67, 255
Hysteria, 270–71, 290

Idealization: of cultural symbols, 25,
46, 264–65; of Freud by Jones, 33,
102–5, 148; of Freud by others, 19,

Idealization (*continued*)
23, 29–33, 58, 281; of Freud by Rank, 153, 162–63, 167; Freud's of Jung, 29–33, 61–67, 73; Freud's of others, 22, 52, 70, 72, 88–95; groups and, 60, 64; Jones's of others, 172, 177, 181; maternal presence and, 22, 96, 100. *See also* De-idealization

Ideal-type: analytic access as, 112, 116, 122–28, 143–208; definition of, 122–23; healing as, 251–56; therapeutic as, 300; Weber as, 231

Illusion: analytic access and, 127; as creative, 333–36; Freud and, 95, 184, 202–4; group and, 60; individualizing ego and, 10, 76, 186, 200; Jones's intolerance of, 181–84; religion and, 202–4; in *The Tempest*, 346–47; transference as, 124–25, 135; Weber and, 247. *See also* Disillusionment

Individualization: healing and, 254–55; industrialization and, 117; religion and, 52; tension between sociality and, 58, 102, 125, 200–201, 328

Individuation: creation of meaning and, 258, 269, 311, 326–43; defined, 9, 257, 262–63, 276, 306–7, 324; as mediating between ego and common culture, 267–73, 305; fantasy and, 303, 305, 311; Freud's, 97, 194–95, 217, 289; healing and, 305; historicization and, 97, 291; Jung and, 151, 171; mourning and, 258, 262–63, 270–82, 326–43; psychoanalysis and, 124, 219, 257, 295, 324, 333, 343; secularization and, 313, 322–24; in *The Tempest*, 344–48; Weber and, 238, 241, 243, 249

Industrialization: changes in family structure and, 118, 174–75, 225, 356–57; fantasy and, 268, 310–11; loss of social solidarity and, 112, 117–21, 356 n. 2; mourning and, 294; object relations theory as requiring, 222, 224, 229; psychoanalysis and, 174, 199, 295; sociology of, 230, 307. *See also* Secularization; Social change

Intellectualization: Freud's, 203; Jones's, 185–86; Weber on, 246–48

Intermediate space: as locus of creation

of meaning, 269, 307, 325–34; fantasy and, 269, 310–11, 340–41; Winnicott on, 275. *See also* Transitional space

Interpretation: creation of meaning and, 306–7, 311, 334; of fantasy, 268, 311, 328–29; psychoanalysis as, 101, 302

James, William, 44, 225, 262

Jokes, function of, 63, 185, 309. *See also* Humor, sense of

Jones, Alfred Ernest. *See* Jones, Ernest

Jones, Ernest: as example of analytic access, 171–91; compared to Freud, 112, 190–91, 218; on Freud's life, 33–34, 37, 52, 72, 195–96; on Freud's work, 21, 41, 46–47, 74, 85; idealization of Freud, 15–16, 23, 33, 102–5, 262; compared to Jung and Rank, 140, 143–44, 172, 182, 185, 191, 223; Jung's meeting of, 175, 182; biographical details, 172–82; in psychoanalytic movement, 140, 143, 366; on psychoanalytic movement, 17, 61–62, 64, 68, 72, 182, 198; religion-science conflict and, 172, 176, 181; as social revolutionary, 172, 176, 181–82; Weber and, 175, 236

Jones, Gwyneth, 174, 183, 187–89

Jones, Morfydd Owen, 174, 183, 187–89

Judaism: Freud's ambivalence towards, 93, 110–11, 206, 289; 313, Freud's, and Rolland, 89; Freud's, and Abraham, 35–37, 140; Freud's de-idealization of, 18, 27, 51, 70–71, 95; Freud's identification with, 6, 38, 46–47, 68–70, 72, 99, 129–33, 149, 217, 358 n. 5; healing and, 254; Moses as symbol of, 123; psychoanalysis and, 54, 59, 61, 70, 114, 139–40, 219–20; Rank and, 154–57, 165–67; Weber on, 245

Jung, Carl: and Abraham, rivalry with, 35–36; in America, 62, 262; as example of analytic access, 144–52; as Christian, 46, 51, 59, 73, 140; compared to Freud, 32, 112, 144, 149; as symbol for Freud, 30, 56, 62–63; biographical details, 144–52; in psychoanalytic movement, 61–65, 143; compared to Rank, 143–44, 152–54; religious common culture and, 218;

own "Rome neurosis," 57; works: *Collected Works*, 152; *Memories, Dreams, Reflections*, 57, 171; *Symbols of Transformation*, 150. *See also* Freud-Jung relationship

Khan, Masud, 134–35, 192, 358 n. 1
Klein, Dennis, 23, 69, 72, 216
Klein, Melanie: on mourning, 25; as object relations theorist, 189, 228–29; on pining, 4, 28, 228
Kohon, Gregorio, 199
Kohut, Heinz: as applied to Jones, 179; on de-idealization, 4, 24, 28; on Freud, 19, 21, 45, 54; on groups, 44, 59, 60, 62; on neurosis, 138; on problem of illusion, 186; on psychoanalytic healing, 255; on transference of creativity, 21, 43
Kris, Ernst, 2, 21, 281

Lasch, Christopher, 122, 300
Leonardo da Vinci, Freud on, 51–52, 320, 351 n. 7
Lerner, Jeffrey, 224–25, 228–29
Lévi-Strauss, Claude: compared to Freud, 283, 287–90; on primitivity and common culture, 10, 83, 266, 283–96; on Sartre, 266–67
Levine, Donald, 233–34
Lifton, Robert, 337
Loss: creation of meaning as response to, 3–4, 263, 306–7, 333; cultural texts as response to, 27, 47, 194; in Freud's life, 47, 110, 192, 197; modernization and, 119–20; monuments as response to, 271, 277; mourning as response to, 3–4, 238, 271; psychological man's inability to experience, 300–301. *See also* Attachment; Object loss
Loss of illusions: narcissistic processes and, 76
Lüger, Karl, 132

MacIntyre, Alisdair, 300
Mannheim, Karl, 116–18, 126, 353 n. 1
Marx, Karl, 77, 215, 229–30, 263, 266
Marxism: inability of, to mourn, 230;

and Jones, 181–82; as secular religion, 79, 363–66
Mass communication, 310–11, 331, 353 n. 1
Mass culture, 290, 307–9
Masson, Jeffrey, 90, 281
Maternal presence: in Catholicism, 351 n. 8; Freud as, in psychoanalytic movement, 61, 103; in Freud-Jung relationship, 56; in Freud-Rolland relationship, 91–93; Freud's ambivalence towards, 22, 51–52, 96–100, 136, 351 n. 7; groups as, 60, 63; Rome as, for Freud, 52–56; in Weber's life, 241, 243
Mauss, Marcel, 354–56
McGrath, William, 129–32
Meaning: defined, 328; in *The Tempest*, 347; interpretation and, 305; Weber on, 246. *See also* Creation of meaning
Merger, psychological: creativity and, 41, 43; Freud's with followers, 29–31, 35, 38, 66, 70; Freud's with Moses, 49; Freud's with mother, 97; in groups, 60, 62; Jones and, 103; Rank and, 153; Weber and, 238. *See also* Idealization
Merton, Robert, 8, 114, 210, 212–14, 217–19, 268, 342
Metapsychology: authoritarianism and, 221; collapse of, 210, 221–31; context of creation of, 192, 196; as defense, 54, 114, 183–84, 237, 301; as emblem of psychoanalytic movement, 222, 295; and psychoanalysis as science, 7, 81, 193, 113–14, 209–22; as transitional object for Freud, 136; value-free social science as, 115, 210; Winnicott's critique of, 273
Miller, Hugh Chrichton, 227
Miller, Justin, 352 n. 3
Milner, Marion, 137, 186
Mitscherlich, Alexander, 239, 337
Mitzman, Arthur, 233–37
Modern culture: ego in, 283–96; healing in, 254; hermeneutics of fantasy and, 298, 302; new theory of, 298, 305–12; contrasted with primitivity, 265–67. *See also* Industrialization; Psychological society

Monument: defined, 276; Freud as, 58, 280–82; Freud on, 261–63; individuation and, 263, 270–82; intermediate space and, 293–94; mourning and, 258, 271, 277–80; primitivity and, 286–87, 290; religion as, 342

Moses: Freud's de-idealization of, 50; Freud's self-analysis and, 135; as self-object for Freud, 46–50, 66, 74, 131, 192; as symbol of Judaism, 51, 74, 123, 205–6, 215. *See also* Freud, works: "The Moses of Michelangelo," *Moses and Monotheism*

Mother: Jones's, 172, 173–75; in oedipal theory, 223; priest as, 54; Rank's, 156, 158; relationship to infant as prototype for common culture, 136, 273–74. *See also* Family; Maternal presence; and under person of interest's name

Mourn, inability to: Catholicism's, 365; crime and, 228; Freud's, 97, 289; Germans', Hitler, 239, 337; irony and, 268; Marxism's, 230, 365; psychological society's, 300, 302; sociology's struggle to, 231–50; Weber's, 235, 238–40, 245; following World War I, 227, 229, 338

Mourning: creation of meaning and, 7, 262–63, 269, 306–7, 326–43; of Freud, 103; Freud on, 25, 26, 44, 189, 196; in Freud's life, 40, 97, 104, 195, 320; in Freud's work, 113, 197, 203; individuation and, 7–11, 262–63, 268–82, 306–7, 314, 323, 326–33; intermediate space and, 258, 293, 334; Jones's, 177, 183, 187–88; Klein on, 25, 28; Lévi-Strauss's, 267; of lost historical objects, 150, 194, 292; monuments and, 262, 278–80; object relations theory and, 114, 222–31; as past-present link, 258, 266; as origin of psychoanalysis, 4, 104; Rieff on, 299; Ricoeur on, 303, 305; secularization and, 3, 268, 293–94, 317, 323; in *The Tempest*, 368 n. 1; as enabling transition, 27, 104, 305; Weber's, 115, 210, 232, 238, 249–50. *See also* De-idealization; Disillusionment; Loss

Movement (perception of): fantasy, narrative, intermediate space and, 327, 329–33, 335; Freud's theory of, 48–49; and social science method, 340

Movement, psychoanalytic. *See* Psychoanalytic movement; Group

Movies. *See* Mass communication

Munich meeting (1913), 33–34, 37–38, 47–48, 51

Myth: culture of fantasy and, 309; as monument, 276, 280, 293; religion and, 320, 342; structure and, 295; as annulling transience, 284, 294, 336

Narcissism: as antithetical to community, 201, 203, 289; cosmic (Kohut), 91; creation of meaning and, 33, 335; loss of cultural objects and, 37, 80, 301; Freud on, 7, 41–46, 75, 94, 200–203, 206, 288, 304, 349 n. 4; Freud-Jung relationship and, 18, 31, 34–35, 39–40, 45, 74; Freud's failure to consider, 95, 223, 333; in Freud's life, 54 63, 85, 99; in Jones's life and work, 171, 179, 182, 184, 185, 188; in Jung's life, 146, 150; mourning and, 278, 323; "oceanic feeling" and, 88, 91; perception of movement, 330; in Rank's life and work, 153, 167, 168; science as blow to, 217, 221

Narcissism, culture of (Lasch), 122

Narcissistic rage: de-idealization and, 24, 26; death instinct and, 201; Freud-Jung break and, 33, 39, 42; Jones's, 177; Moses', 47; Rank's, 168

Narrative, 327, 332–33, 335–36

National Socialism, psychoanalysis and, 201, 336–38. *See also* Anti-Semitism; Hitler, Adolf

Neurosis: as cultural category, 74, 199; Freud's self-analysis and, 133, 138–39; Rank on, 154, 165; social causes of, 109, 226, 228, 250

Newcombe, Nora, 224–25, 228–29

Newton, Isaac, and Freud, 210, 222

Nietzsche, Friedrich: on Christianity, 81, 361–62; influence on Jones, 180; influence on Jung, 143–44, 146–47;

influence on Rank, 143–44, 154, 159, 160, 162–65
Nisbet, Robert, 230

Object loss: common culture and, 119, 136–37; de-idealization and, 24–25, 28; mourning and, 3, 305; structure building and, 43, 126, 306. *See also* De-idealization; Disillusionment; Loss; Mourning
Object relations theory, 189, 210, 222–31
"Oceanic feeling" (Rolland), 90–93
Ockham, William of, 316–17, 321–24
Orgel, Stephen, 346

Parapraxis, 99, 132–33
Parsons, Ann, 351 n. 8
Parsons, Talcott, 111, 119, 353 n. 1
Parsons, William, 352 n. 1 (chap. 4)
Past: as theme of cultural texts, 115, 194, 199, 265; Christian communal, ego as cut off from, 297–312; Freud and Weber on, 231, 256; Freud's relationship with, 202, 262, 264, 322; mourning and, 141, 258, 269; reappropriation of, 258, 325; Weber's de-idealization of, 231, 249, 256. *See also* History
Persecutory anxiety, 66, 87, 126, 365
Platt, Gerald, 80, 117, 224, 353 n. 1
Politics: as cultural symbol, 201, 277, 290, 304, 328; of fantasy, 132, 307–8, 337; Freud and, 68–87, 111, 131–32, 195, 319; psychoanalysis and, 58, 85, 86–87, 102, 123, 132; Weber and, 236, 237. *See also* Democracy; German political liberalism; National Socialism
Postmodernism, 223, 269, 323
Primitivity: Christian past and, 299, 305; contemporary culture and, 5, 265–67, 283–97, 309, 323; Freud on, 75, 287–89; Lévi-Strauss on, 37, 284–86; self in, 354–55
Protocultural texts, 40, 67, 192, 196–97, 288–89
Psychoanalysis: as art, 136–37, 152–71, 256, 296; as bricolage, 285, 295; as

disenchantment, 27, 104, 214, 219; as de-idealization, 77, 102, 132, 195, 292; fantasy and, 124, 211, 269, 302–8; as Freud's child, 62, 63, 65, 136, 193, 201; healing and, 250–58; as hermeneutics, 144–52, 256, 302; history, relationship to, 19, 74, 84, 96–97, 100–105, 142, 303; humanities and, 341; industrialization as prerequisite for, 118, 174, 217, 294–95; institutionalization of, 94, 193, 197, 201, 262, 294; Judaism and, 114, 215–22; politics and, 85–87, 126, 308; psychological structure building as goal of, 4, 104, 124; tension between religion and, 37, 52, 74, 77–81, 95, 313–25; as intermediate between religion and science, 71, 113–14, 209–22, 296, 341–43; as science, 37, 171–91, 211, 253, 256, 360; as intermediate between science and art, 136–37, 296, 302; social origins of, 1, 97, 105, 115–22, 220, 332; as social science, 115, 211, 231, 341; temporalization and, 195, 266–67, 284, 294, 321–22, 336. *See also* Psychoanalytic movement
Psychoanalytic movement: as "circle," 17, 64, 139, 182; as a common culture, 6, 111, 139–42, 309; dissipation of, 38, 61, 191–208; and Freud-Jung relationship, 6, 30, 36, 61–65, 150; functions of, 79, 251, 256; functions of for Freud, 59, 73, 139, 288, 352 n. 1 (chap. 3); as group, 17–18, 59–67, 79, 101–3, 139–42, 280, 352 n. 2; institutionalization of, 193, 197, 198; Jones and, 178, 179, 190; parallel of Marxism to, 79, 363–66; Rank and, 163, 166; religious character of, 66, 68, 77–81, 101, 142, 209; sociological aspects of, 104, 113, 256, 320. *See also* Committee, The; Psychoanalysis
Psychoanalytic theory of culture. *See* Culture, psychoanalytic theory of
Psychological man, 45, 122, 265, 267, 301, 308
Psychological society: birth of, 265, 268, 297–306, 307; as heir to psycho-

Psychological society (*continued*)
    analytic movement, 2, 105, 262, 336.
    See also Psychological man
Psychological structure building: de-
    idealization and, 86, 133, 194, 300; in
    Freud's life and work, 43–44, 88, 104,
    193–94, 204; individuation and, 219,
    324; monuments and, 263, 276–78;
    as goal of psychoanalysis, 4, 104,
    124–25, 366; Rank's, 153, 166;
    Weber's, 242–44. *See also* Creativity;
    Structure building
Psychological thought, as marginal to
    common culture, 4, 92–93, 119, 126,
    284, 290. *See also* Analytic access
Rank, Otto: as example of analytic ac-
    cess, 152–71; Freud and, 112, 140,
    152–71; compared to Jung and Jones,
    140, 143, 152, 172, 185, 191; in psy-
    choanalytic movement, 143, 152–71,
    198, 223
Rationalization: as structure building,
    26–27, 110; Weber on, 76, 118, 244,
    246–48, 253
Reality principle: disillusionment and,
    27, 274; ego and, 186, 349 n. 1 (chap.
    1); transitional space and, 136, 274
Religion: as idealization of cultural ob-
    jects, 19, 80; as cultural symbol, 3,
    58, 276, 304; as component of com-
    mon culture, 118, 126; as group for-
    mation, 102, 201, 328; early analysts'
    too rapid de-idealizations of, 79–81,
    143, 149, 186; in Freud's life and
    work, 35–37, 51, 67–81, 88–95;
    Freud on, 51–52, 92, 100, 202–4, 321;
    Jones and, 37, 176–78, 188; psycho-
    analysis contrasted with, 32, 74–77,
    95, 101, 343; psychoanalysis as, 37,
    68, 77–81, 209; tension between sci-
    ence and, 10, 51–52, 71, 113, 211–14,
    246, 265, 268–69, 313–25; Weber
    and, 231–32, 239–41, 245–46, 250.
    See also Catholicism; Christianity;
    Judaism; Secularization
Repression: barrier, 118, 121, 123, 124;
    culture as, 165–66; Rivers on, 226
Revitalization movements, 363–66
Ricoeur, Paul, 2, 45, 263, 267, 298,
    301–6, 336

Riefenstahl, Leni, 338
Rieff, Philip, 2, 10, 45, 267, 297–300
Rivers, W. H. R., 226–28
Robert, Marthe, 68, 215
Role: differentiation, 118; hybridiza-
    tion, 251–56
Rolland, Romain, 35, 88–95, 192, 223,
    352
Rome: Freud, significance of for, 35,
    51–57, 91–92, 95; Freud in, 38–39,
    42, 135; Freud's Moses and, 46, 51,
    215; Weber in, 236, 242
Rorschach psychology, 49, 328–33
Rosenfeld, Otto. *See* Rank, Otto
Rozenblit, Marsha, 129–30

Sachs, Hans, 78, 208
Sartre, Jean-Paul, 266–67, 284, 291–93
Schachtel, Ernest, 49, 335
Schorske, Carl, 2, 23, 82–85, 307–8
Schutz, Alfred, 221, 264, 331, 340, 352
    n. 1 (chap. 3)
Science: de-idealization and, 4, 80,
    136–37, 323; Freud on psycho-
    analysis as, 34–35, 42, 77–81, 210–
    22, 253; Jones and, 171–91; Jung and,
    147; Lévi-Strauss on, 284–85, 291,
    295; psychoanalysis as, 77–81, 136,
    183–86, 189, 193, 253, 295; psycho-
    analysis compared to, 210–22, 231,
    302, 359–61; tension between re-
    ligion and, 10, 51–52, 71, 113, 211–
    14, 246, 265, 268–69, 313–25; social
    science and, 339–40; transitional
    space and, 274, 333, 343; Weber on,
    213, 218, 231–32, 246
Secularization: historical process of,
    313–25, 358–59, 362; mourning and,
    3, 4, 224, 229, 337; religion, science,
    and, 212, 217–18, 268. *See also*
    Industrialization; Social change
Self: category of, 354–56; split between
    ego and, 80, 245, 249, 257, 273, 334,
    352 n. 2; individuation and, 9, 151,
    257, 273, 278; Jung on, 145, 150–51;
    perception of movement and, 335;
    Rank on, 153, 160, 169; relationship
    of to society, 81, 109–28, 263, 298;
    Weber on, 245, 249, 257
Self-analysis. *See* Freud

Self-psychology, 58, 67, 125, 223
Self-understanding. *See* Analytic access
Shakespeare, William, 99, 344–48
Shamanic healing, 254–56
Social change: anomie and, 109, 112, 117–18, 229; origins of psycho-analysis, 79, 138, 338–39; time and, 287, 291. *See also* Industrialization; Secularization
Social objects: artistic objects and, 199; the ego and, 111, 119–20, 183, 325; psychoanalytic theory of, 223; typ-ification and, 331, 352 n. 1 (chap. 3). *See also* Cultural objects
Social science: psychoanalysis and, 115, 211, 231, 341; physical science and, 339–40
Social world: analytic access's rela-tionship to, 111, 123–25, 134, 138; ego's relationship to, 58, 110–28, 200–201, 207, 263–68, 326; Jones's disavowal of, 172, 183, 190; Jung on, 145–47, 151; science and religion and, 37, 114, 209, 249
Sociology of knowledge, 116, 353 n. 1
Stolorow, Robert, 16, 22, 54, 60, 150, 153
Structure building: fantasy and, 306, 333; individuation and, 306–7, 324; intermediate space as locus of, 293, 326; loss and, 27, 33, 271, 306, 317–18; psychoanalysis and, 80, 126, 285. *See also* Creation of meaning; Psy-chological structure building
Sulloway, Frank, 23, 78–79
Suttie, Ian, 226–28
Symbols: culture as shared, 119, 194, 264, 294, 304–5; creation of meaning and, 325, 327, 333; fantasy and, 302, 308–9, 325; Jung and, 150; transi-tional space and, 5, 120, 273, 293. *See also* Cultural objects; Social objects
Synchrony, 283–96, 336

Tavistock Clinic, 225–28
Television. *See* Mass communication
Tempest, The, 344–48
Thematic Apperception Test (TAT), 332, 352

Three blows, theory of (Freud): Acro-polis paper and, 94; *The Future of an Illusion* and, 202; history, religion and, 74–77, 103, 210, 313, 320–21
Time: Freud on, 194–95, 328; Ockham on, 316; problem of, 100, 266–67, 283–96, 321–22, 335–38; Ricoeur on, 302, 336
Totemism, 266, 283–87, 290
Transference: as focus of analytic situa-tion, 58, 221, 253–56, 296; Freud's to Fliess, 53, 135, 138; as illusion, 124–25, 135; Rank on, 153, 168; Ricoeur on, 304
Transference of creativity. *See* Creativity, transference of
Transience. *See* Time
Transition: Freud's, 120–21, 131, 207, 190–91; Freud's followers', 111–12, 301; Jones's, 172, 176, 185, 189–91; Marx's, 230; Rank's, 166; seculariza-tion as, 317; Weber's, 115, 186, 241, 249. *See also* De-idealization; Secularization
Transitional objects: disillusionment and, 25, 136, 273–75; Freud's, 53–54, 217; groups and, 7, 44, 60, 63, 73, 96; healing and, 255; monuments as, 278; as spatial, 284
Transitional space: as locus of creation of meaning, 121, 258, 334–35; be-tween ego and social world, 5, 73, 120, 124, 232; as social, 273–75, 333, 357 n. 4; social sciences and, 232, 343; in *The Tempest,* 344, 347. *See also* Intermediate space; Transitional objects
Trotter, Wilfred, 176, 179–82, 187, 189
True self, healing of, 66, 147, 243, 255
Turkle, Sherry, 280
Typification, 63, 272, 331, 352 n. 1 (chap. 3)

Unconscious: formation of concept of, 118–19; cultural locus of, 340–41; de-idealization, 27, 132–33; dreams and, 125, 211, 221; Jones on, 183–84, 188–89; Jung on, 145, 151; social/group, 4, 10, 297; Rank on, 162, 165;

Unconscious (*continued*)
  in *The Tempest*, 347; as timeless,
  283, 322

Value-free social science, 115, 210,
  231–32, 245–46, 339

Wallace, Anthony, 363–66
Weber, Helene, 232–35, 238–42
Weber, Marianne: as Weber's biog-
  rapher, 232–44, 250; Weber's relationship with, 232–36, 239, 241–42
Weber, Max: biographical details, 234–
  43, 263; compared to Freud, 114–15,
  186, 211, 231–34, 250–51, 256–58,
  338–39, 343; on disenchantment, 4,
  26–27, 118; on ideal-type, 122–23,
  357; on inner-worldly asceticism,
  213, 233, 244–45; on "internal relation," 71, 76; *The Protestant Ethic
  and the Spirit of Capitalism*, 233,
  237, 243, 249; on tension between
  religion and science, 113, 185–86,
  218; on value-free social science, 8,
  210, 245–46; works analyzed, 243–50
Weber, Max, Sr., 234–36
Weinstein, Fred, 80, 117, 224, 353 n. 1
Weintraub, Karl, 354–56
Winnicott, D. W.: on "the capacity to
  be alone," 244; conception of culture,
  25, 121, 273–76, 357 n. 4; on democracy, 66; on disillusionment, 4, 25,
  28, 100, 186; on "the manic defense," 229; on goal of psychoanalysis, 103, 243, 255; on
  transitional space and transitional objects, 5, 25, 44, 273–76, 357 n. 4
Wolf, Ernest, 21
World War I; effect of on Freud, 192,
  195–96, 288; metapsychology's collapse following, 114, 222–31; psychoanalytic movement and, 30, 87, 195,
  197